"THEY SHALL PURIFY THEMSELVES"

Society of Biblical Literature

Early Judaism and Its Literature

Judith Newman,
Series Editor

Number 24

"THEY SHALL PURIFY THEMSELVES"
ESSAYS ON PURITY IN EARLY JUDAISM

"THEY SHALL PURIFY THEMSELVES"

Essays on Purity in Early Judaism

Susan Haber
edited by Adele Reinhartz

Society of Biblical Literature
Atlanta

"THEY SHALL PURIFY THEMSELVES"
Essays on Purity in Early Judaism

Copyright © 2008 by the Society of Biblical Literature

All rights reserved. No part of this work may be reproduced or transmitted in any form or by any means, electronic or mechanical, including photocopying and recording, or by means of any information storage or retrieval system, except as may be expressly permitted by the 1976 Copyright Act or in writing from the publisher. Requests for permission should be addressed in writing to the Rights and Permissions Office, Society of Biblical Literature, 825 Houston Mill Road, Atlanta, GA 30333-0399, USA.

"Living and Dying for the Law: The Mother-Martyrs of 2 Maccabees," first published in *Women in Judaism: A Multidisciplinary Journal* Volume 4, Number 1. Reprinted with permission from the publisher.

Reproduced with permission from Susan Haber's estate, "A Woman's Touch: Feminist Encounters with the Hemorrhaging Woman in Mark 5.24–34," JSNT 26/2 (2003): 171–192, © JSNT 2003, by permission of Sage Publications Ltd.

Reproduced with permission from Susan Haber's estate, "From Priestly Torah to Christ Cultus: The Re-Vision of Cult in Hebrews," JSNT 28/1 (2005): 105–24, © JSNT 2005, by permission of Sage Publications Ltd.

"Common Judaism, Common Synagogue? Purity, Holiness and Sacred Space at the Turn of the Common Era," from *Common Judaism*, edited by Wayne McCready and Adele Reinhartz, copyright © 2008 Fortress Press. Used by permission of Augsburg Fortress.

Library of Congress Cataloging-in-Publication Data

Haber, Susan, 1957–2006.
  They shall purify themselves : essays on purity in early Judaism / essays by Susan Haber; edited by Adele Reinhartz.
    p. cm. — (Early Judaism and its literature ; v. 24)
  Includes bibliographical references and index.
  ISBN 978-1-58983-355-5 (paper binding : alk. paper)
    1. Purity, Ritual—Judaism—History of doctrines. I. Reinhartz, Adele, 1953– II. Title.
BM702.H33 2008
296.4´9—dc22   2008022474

15 14 13 12 11 10 09 08   5 4 3 2 1
Printed in the United States of America on acid-free, recycled paper conforming to ANSI/NISO Z39.48-1992 (R1997) and ISO 9706:1994 standards for paper permanence.

In memory of Susan Haber
August 7, 1957–July 3, 2006

Strength and dignity are her clothing . . .
She opens her mouth with wisdom, and the teaching of
kindness is on her tongue. (Proverbs 31:25–26)

Contents

Abbreviations ix

Introduction and Acknowledgments
   Adele Reinhartz 1

I. Bibliographic Studies

1. Ritual and Moral Purity and Impurity in the Hebrew Bible 9
2. Ritual and Moral Purity and Impurity in Second Temple Judaism 31
3. Ritual and Moral Purity and Impurity in the Dead Sea Scrolls 47

II. Literary Studies

4. Living and Dying for the Law:
   The Mother-Martyrs of 2 Maccabees 75
5. Metaphor and Meaning in the Dead Sea Scrolls 93
6. A Woman's Touch: Feminist Encounters with the
   Hemorrhaging Woman in Mark 5:24–34 125
7. From Priestly Torah to Christ Cultus:
   The Re-Vision of Cult in Hebrews 143

III. Historical Studies

8. Common Judaism, Common Synagogue? Purity, Holiness,
   and Sacred Space at the Turn of the Common Era 161
9. Going Up to Jerusalem: Purity, Pilgrimage, and the Historical Jesus . . . 181

Bibliography 207
Index of Ancient Sources 223
Index of Modern Authors 235
Subject Index 239

Abbreviations

AB	Anchor Bible
ABD	*Anchor Bible Dictionary*. Edited by D. N. Freedman. 6 vols. New York, 1992
AJSR	*Association for Jewish Studies Review*
ANRW	*Aufstieg und Niedergang der römischen Welt: Geschichte und Kultur Roms im Spiegel der neueren Forschung*. Edited by H. Temporini and W. Haase. Berlin, 1972–
ANYAS	Annals of the New York Academy of Sciences
BAG	Bauer, W., W. F. Arndt, and F. W. Gingrich. *Greek-English Lexicon of the New Testament and Other Early Literature*. Chicago: University of Chicago Press, 1979
BA	*Biblical Archaeologist*
BAR	*Biblical Archaeology Review*
BASORSup	Bulletin of the American Schools of Oriental Research: Supplement Series
BDB	Brown, F., S. R. Driver, and C. A. Briggs. *A Hebrew and English Lexicon of the Old Testament*. Oxford, 1907
BJS	Brown Judaic Studies
BR	*Biblical Research*
BRev	*Bible Review*
CBQMS	Catholic Biblical Quarterly Monograph Series
CIJ	*Corpus inscriptionum judaicarum*
ConBNT	Coniectanea Biblica: New Testament Series
CPJ	*Corpus papyrorum judaicorum*. Edited by V. Tcherikover. 3 vols. Cambridge, 1957–64
DSD	*Dead Sea Discoveries*
EvQ	*Evangelical Quarterly*
Hesperia	*Hesperia: Journal for the American School of Classical Studies at Athens*
HTR	Harvard Theological Review
IEJ	*Israel Exploration Journal*
IES	Israel Exploration Society
JBL	*Journal of Biblical Literature*
JIGRE	Horbury, William, and David Noy, eds. *Jewish Inscriptions of Graeco-Roman Egypt*. Cambridge: Cambridge University Press, 1992
JJS	*Journal of Jewish Studies*
JPS	Jewish Publication Society
JSJ	*Journal for the Study of Judaism in the Persian, Hellenistic, and Roman Periods*

JSNT	*Journal for the Study of the New Testament*
JSNTSup	Journal for the Study of the New Testament: Supplement Series
JSOTSup	Journal for the Study of the Old Testament: Supplement Series
JSPSup	Journal for the Study of Pseudepigrapha: Supplement Series
JTS	*Journal of Theological Studies*
KB	*Keilinschriftliche Bibliothek*. Edited by E. Schrader. 6 vols. Berlin, 1889–1915
LSJ	Liddell, H. G., R. Scott, and H. S. Jones. *A Greek-English Lexicon*. 9th ed. with revised supplement. Oxford, 1996
NJPS	*Tanakh: The Holy Scriptures. The New JPS Translation according to the Traditional Hebrew Text*. 2d ed. Philadelphia, 1999
NovTSup	Supplements to Novum Testamentum
NTL	New Testament Library
NTS	*New Testament Studies*
PEQ	*Palestinian Exploration Quarterly*
QDAP	*Quarterly of the Department of Antiquities in Palestine*
RelSRev	*Religious Studies Review*
SBL	Society of Biblical Literature
SBLDS	Society of Biblical Literature Dissertation Series
SBLMS	Society of Biblical Literature Monograph Series
SBLSymS	Society of Biblical Literature Symposium Series
SBT	Studies in Biblical Theology
SDSSRL	Studies in the Dead Sea Scrolls and Related Literature
SJLA	Studies in Judaism in Late Antiquity
SNTSMS	Society for New Testament Studies Monograph Series
STDJ	Studies in the Texts of the Desert of Judah
StPB	Studia post-biblica
TDNT	*Theological Dictionary of the New Testament*. Edited by G. Kittel and G. Friedrich. Translated by G. W. Bromiley. 10 vols. Grand Rapids, 1964–76
VT	*Vetus Testamentum*
WBC	World Biblical Commentary
WUNT	Wissenschaftliche Untersuchungen zum Neuen Testament

INTRODUCTION AND ACKNOWLEDGMENTS

The present volume collects the essays of the late Susan Haber on the topic of purity and impurity in early Judaism. Susan Haber was a doctoral student at the Department of Religious Studies at McMaster University who passed away in July 2006 after a brief illness. Although she had not yet begun her dissertation, she already had several publications to her name, and she was in the process of revising several more articles and chapters for publication when she fell ill.

At McMaster, Susan worked with several faculty members, but most closely with Eileen Schuller, who was the principal supervisor of her MA and doctoral work, as well as with Anders Runesson, and myself. Her interests were wide-ranging and included many topics from the role of covenant in the Hebrew Bible to spirituality in modern Judaism. The topic that was of greatest interest to her, however, was purity in early Judaism, and she had planned to write her dissertation on purity in the Dead Sea Scrolls. This book is a memorial to a talented individual who took scholarship very seriously. Its primary intention, however, is to contribute to the field by ensuring that the excellent work that Susan had already done will be accessible to others.

Purity is one issue that brings us face to face with the chronological and cultural distance between Judaism of antiquity and our modern sensibilities. Our secular culture has little place for the concept that one must attain a state of purity, unrelated to hygiene, in order to engage in certain activities. In the context of modern Judaism, the concept of purity pertains primarily to the so-called family purity laws, which regulate sexual relations in accordance with the women's menstrual cycle, and the dietary laws, which specify some foods such as pork and shellfish as "unclean" and hence forbidden. In the ancient world, however, the concepts of purity and impurity were frequently used to define the conditions that regulated access to the divine. Throughout the ancient Near East, Egypt, Mesopotamia as well as in classical Greece and Rome, acts that were defined as sinful and states defined as impure were obstacles to worship. Purity was required not only for the priests but also for the vessels they used and the temple in which they used them. As in ancient Israel, water was the most common means of purification, but other substances were also used.[1]

The notion of purity and its connection with holiness, the priesthood, and temples were well-established in the authoritative and foundational texts of Second Temple Judaism, that is, the Hebrew scriptures, as well as in the Mediter-

---

1. Gordon Wenham, "Purity," in *The Biblical World* (ed. John Barton; London: Routledge, 2002), 2:378-94. See also K. C. Hanson, *Ritual and Ceremony in the Graeco-Roman World. A Select Classified Bibliography (1970–1996)* (Minneapolis: Fortress, 1998).

ranean culture within which both the biblical and post-biblical perspectives were developed. Within Second Temple Judaism, purity—its legislation and its practice—was common to all groups. At the same time, purity laws and rituals were a means through which groups distinguished themselves from one another. More important, purity laws articulated particular ways of understanding holiness, the divine, and worship. In doing so, they were a major vehicle for Jewish views on the covenantal relationship between God and Israel, as well as between God and the individual Jew.

The various groups within Judaism, including the Dead Sea community and nascent Christianity, took the Hebrew Bible as their starting point when it came to understanding and applying notions of purity and impurity. But the Bible did not answer all questions, nor did it address all situations, especially as society continued to develop and change. To whom does purity apply—to the priests only or to non-priestly individuals and groups as well? Is purity a condition that is relevant only for access to the temple and its rituals, or are there other aspects of daily life that must be conducted in a state of purity? Do the states of purity or impurity affect only the status of the individual or do they have implications for the people as a whole, the state within which they live, and the land on which they dwell? Most elusive is the relationship between ritual purity and moral righteousness. Is purity primarily a ritual category that is morally neutral, or does purity also have ethical and moral dimensions? Related to this question is a literary consideration: is the biblical and post-biblical purity language always to be taken literally as a reference to the beliefs and practices around ritual purity or is it sometimes used metaphorically? And if so, does the metaphorical usage amplify or, alternatively, replace the ritual practice of purity?

The growing bibliography on purity and impurity in Second Temple Judaism testifies to the current fascination with the topic as well as to its breadth. The present volume does not claim to cover the field in a comprehensive manner, but rather to explore a number of aspects that are at the forefront of scholarly study of purity and impurity today. Its comments with regard to specific texts and questions bring to life the ways in which purity and impurity functioned in the construction of identity of specific Jewish groups and also help to flesh out one set of ideas and practices that were common to the Judaism in which these groups participated.

Given the nature of the present volume, the attempt has been made to maintain the author's distinct voice and viewpoint. The essays originated either as seminar papers for graduate courses at McMaster University, or as invited conference presentations. Those that have already been published in journals or edited volumes are reprinted here, with permission, in their original form except for such formatting changes as were necessary in order to conform to SBL style. The essays that have not been previously published have for the most part been edited to the same extent and in the same manner as is normally practiced by editors of anthologies. That is to say, the editing has focused on minor revisions to language, style, structure, and content, although, on occasion, more substantial changes have been introduced. These are clearly indicated in the summary below.

The essays are grouped into three sections. The first section contains three bibliographic essays that analyze the secondary literature on purity in the Hebrew Bible, in Second Temple Judaism in general, and, finally, in the Dead Sea Scrolls. These essays are drawn from the research project that Haber undertook for her MA degree. They focus specifically on the issue of ritual and moral purity—the ways in which scholars have characterized the relationship between the sorts of impurities that one acquired in the normal course of everyday life, for example, through sexual activity and contact with the dead, and those that came about as a result of major sin, that is, through idolatry, homicide or sexual transgression. The first chapter, on the Hebrew Bible, is the foundation for the second chapter, which concerns Second Temple Judaism in general, the third, which focuses on Qumran, and, indeed, the rest of the volume. The treatments of purity in the New Testament and in and rabbinic literature are not included in the survey, but arise as appropriate in the second and third sections of the book.

The second section includes four essays that relate to the theme of purity in a range of literature from the Second Temple period. These essays explore the theme of purity in a literary context. Their aim is to discern both the literary and theological dimensions of purity rather than to reconstruct the historical period or the historical practice of purity.

The first essay in this section, "Living and Dying for the Law: The Mother-Martyrs of 2 Maccabees," was originally published in the online journal *Women in Judaism: A Multidisciplinary Journal* 4, no. 1, in 2006.[2] The martyr texts of 2 Maccabees record the deaths of three mothers who sacrificed their lives, along with those of their sons, in order to uphold Jewish law under the persecution of Antiochus IV Epiphanes. Two of these anonymous women are briefly mentioned as having been sentenced to death for circumcising their sons, while a third is the subject of a lengthy account of martyrdom. This study examines the portrayal of all three women as both mothers and martyrs and demonstrates that these mother-martyrs lived for the Law in the same way as they died for the Law, taking on religious obligations that are traditionally attributed to men. In the background of this interesting story is the belief that the land of Israel has been profoundly polluted by the grievous sin of idolatry. The martyrdom of the three mothers helps to purify the land by atoning for the sin of the people. Their sacrificial act demonstrates the profound commitment to God and to the observance of the laws that express the covenant between God and Israel and thereby paves the way for forgiveness and the return of the land to the Jewish people.

The second essay, "Metaphor and Meaning in the Dead Sea Scrolls," looks at the metaphorical usage of the language of purity and temple in the Dead Sea Scrolls and tackles the question of the relationship between the metaphorical and literal levels of meaning in the scrolls. This essay combines two studies that were preparatory to a detailed examination of purity in Qumran. One of these studies, "When God Purifies the Sinner: Metaphor and Meaning in the *Hodayot* and *The Rule of the Community*," examined the metaphorical use of purity language in these two sets of texts. The second, "Community as Temple," considered the theory that the

---

2. Available online, http://jps.library.utoronto.ca/index.php/wjudaism/article/view/247.

Dead Sea community, as reflected in *The Community Rule* and *The Damascus Document*, viewed itself literally as the substitute for or replacement of the temple in Jerusalem. This latter paper was never completed and hence could not stand alone, but because it too concerned the relationships between metaphorical and literal language, it has been revised and included as a complement to the first study.

The final two papers in this section examine texts from the New Testament. "A Woman's Touch: Feminist Encounters with the Hemorrhaging Woman in Mark 5:24–34" was originally published in *the Journal for the Study of the New Testament* 26, no. 2 (2003): 171–92. This essay discusses the hemorrhaging woman of Mark 5:24–34 and asks two questions: (1) What is the significance of the woman's flow of blood? (2) How does Mark's representation of the hemorrhaging women serve his rhetorical agenda? These issues are addressed through an investigation of the pertinent biblical purity legislation, an analysis of the language in Mark 5:24–34, and an examination of Mark's portrayal of the woman in the context of his rhetorical agenda. This inquiry suggests that it is the woman's health, and not her ritual purity, that is the primary concern of the miracle story. The significance of her impurity cannot, however, be ignored. It remains an integral part of the narrative insofar as it is a consequence of her medical condition. But the point of the story, not least for feminist criticism, does *not* lie in any supposed critique of the purity laws. The Markan passages therefore should not be used to argue that Jesus abrogated Jewish purity legislation.

"From Priestly Torah to Christ Cultus: The Re-Vision of Cult in Hebrews" appeared in *the Journal for the Study of the New Testament* 28, no. 1 (2005): 105–24. This study of Hebrews focuses on the epistle's criticism of the Jewish covenant and cult and demonstrates that its persistent and systematic dismantling of the Levitical code, including the purity laws, is part of a larger polemic against Judaism.

The final section consists of two social-historical studies on the role of purity in first-century Jewish life. "Common Judaism, Common Synagogue? Purity, Holiness, and Sacred Space at the Turn of the Common Era" was prepared for a conference held at the University of Calgary in 2004 and appears in the volume from that conference, *Common Judaism Explored: Second Temple Judaism in Context*, edited by Wayne McCready and Adele Reinhartz (Minneapolis: Fortress, 2008). This essay takes E. P. Sanders's concept of "common Judaism" as its starting point and asks whether the synagogue was "commonly" thought of as a place of sanctity such that ritual ablution was required before entering. The evidence points to considerable diversity within the land of Israel with regard to the sanctity of the synagogue; by contrast, Diaspora synagogues were generally considered to be sacred space, and worshipers were required to immerse themselves before entering.

The concluding paper, "Going Up to Jerusalem: Purity, Pilgrimage, and the Historical Jesus," was prepared for the Travel and Religion in Antiquity Seminar of the Canadian Society for Biblical Studies in 2006 and will be reprinted in the volume of essays to be published from the seminar (edited by Philip Harland). This essay considers the question of whether Jesus would have purified himself before entering the temple when he went on pilgrimage to Jerusalem. It concludes that Jesus, like his co-religionists, would have participated in *all* the pilgrimage rites, including purification. That being the case, the synoptic traditions regarding Jesus' activities at the temple can be best explained by the practice of first-day ablutions. By immersing in the *mikveh* upon his arrival in Jerusalem, Jesus not only initiated the purificatory rite pertaining to corpse impurity, he also attained an intermittent level of purity that allowed him access to the outer court of the temple.

Hebrew quotations from the Dead Sea Scrolls are taken from Florentino García Martínez and Eibert J. C. Tigchelaar, *The Dead Sea Scrolls Study Edition* (2 vols.; Leiden and New York: Brill, 1997). The mode of citation of the Scrolls follows that of García Martínez and Tigchelaar. English translations of the Qumran material are original to Susan Haber, except as noted. The New Jewish Publication Society translation is used for most of the quotations from the Hebrew Bible. Exceptions are indicated in the footnotes. The New Revised Standard Version is used for the English translation of passages from the New Testament and Apocrypha. Occasional and very brief repetition of material is due to the fact that some of the chapters were originally published as separate articles.

I regret very much the sad circumstances that have given rise to this volume, which gives only a hint of the scholarly contribution that Susan Haber would have made. Nevertheless, it has been both comforting and pleasurable to work on these essays, from which I have also learned much. My profound thanks go to Susan's husband, Stephen Haber, for access to Susan's computer and academic papers and, even more, for his act of extraordinary kindness in giving me the opportunity to visit with Susan one last time. My thanks also to Susan's rabbi, David Seed, for his encouragement and his wisdom.

A number of colleagues and students were very helpful throughout the process of preparing these essays for publication. Eileen Schuller and Anders Runesson, of the Department of Religious Studies at McMaster University, provided editorial advice for a number of the essays. Ken Penner, professor at Acadia University, and a former graduate student colleague of Susan's at McMaster, provided invaluable assistance with the Greek and Hebrew fonts. Ruth Clements, head of English Publications for the Orion Center for the Study of the Dead Sea Scrolls, Hebrew University of Jerusalem, provided valuable bibliographic help. Eileen Morrison, doctoral candidate at the University of Toronto and one of Susan's many friends, provided encouragement in the early stages of the project, and Steven Scott, my research assistant and a doctoral candidate at the University of Ottawa, did the formatting and created the bibliography. Shoshana Walfish returned from Africa just in time to help with the indexing and final proofreading. Judith Newman, editor of the Early Judaism and Its Literatures series, as well as Leigh Andersen and Bob Buller of the Society of Biblical Literature ensured that this book appeared in an appropriate series and in a timely manner. Finally, I wish to express my appreciation to the University of Ottawa for research support, and to the National and University Library of the Hebrew University of Jerusalem, where I prepared the final manuscript in the fine company of the Library Ladies. Susan's full-time doctoral studies were supported by the most competitive and prestigious doctoral award available in Canada, the Canada Graduate Scholarship (through the Social Sciences and Humanities Research Council), as well as by McMaster University.

There is no doubt that Susan would have dedicated her dissertation and first book to her family: her husband, Stephen, and their children Gillian, Jeremy, and Joshua. Susan's family stood first in her life, and they in turn gave her all their love and support when she decided to continue her studies, complete a master's degree, and work full-time toward her doctorate. As editor, however, I dedicate this particular book to Susan's memory, as a token of our friendship.

ADELE REINHARTZ
UNIVERSITY OF OTTAWA

Part I

Bibliographic Studies

1

Ritual and Moral Purity and Impurity in the Hebrew Bible

Any approach to the topic of purity and impurity in Second Temple Judaism must begin with the biblical understanding of these concepts. One reason lies in the impact of the Bible on Jews in the Second Temple period; it was through the interpretation of the biblical concepts of purity and impurity that the various communities of the Second Temple period established their own distinct attitudes toward defilement. A second reason lies in the ongoing importance of the Bible to scholars of Second Temple–period Judaism, who, recognizing this fundamental continuity between pre- and post-exilic concepts of impurity, have relied heavily on biblical scholarship in analyzing ritual and impurity in post-biblical Judaism.

The Bible has numerous things to say about purity and impurity. One of the most interesting themes, however, is the relationship between ritual impurity and moral impurity. According to modern biblical scholarship, the Pentateuch articulates these two types of impurity in two separate literary constructs: ritual impurity, in the priestly source (P), and moral impurity or sin, in the holiness source (H).[1] Our review of the scholarship will focus on these two strata.[2]

David Zvi Hoffmann (1843–1921) has been credited as the first modern scholar

---

1. The priestly source (P) consists of Lev 1–16 as well as various verses in Genesis, Exodus, and Numbers. In addition to Lev 17–27, the holiness source (H) also contains verses from Genesis, Exodus, and Numbers. The last eleven chapters of Leviticus (Lev 17–27) are conventionally referred to as the Holiness Code. This study follows Milgrom in assuming that P and H are distinct sources originating in the pre-exilic period (Jacob Milgrom, *Leviticus 1–16: A New Translation with Introduction and Commentary* [AB 3; New York: Doubleday, 1991], 3–42); idem, *Leviticus 17–22: A New Translation with Introduction and Commentary* [AB 3A; New York: Doubleday, 2000], 1319–67. On the priority of P over H and the dates of P and H, see Israel Knohl, *The Sanctuary of Silence: The Priestly Torah and the Holiness School* (Minneapolis: Fortress, 1995),1–45, 199–244.

2. Scholars also make occasional reference to related purity texts in Deuteronomy and Ezekiel, the latter of which is considered a priestly writing. See, for example, the discussion of biblical purity in Tikvah Simone Frymer-Kensky, "Pollution, Purification, and Purgation in Biblical Israel," in *The Word of the Lord Shall Go Forth: Essays in Honor of David Noel Freedman in Celebration of His Sixtieth Birthday* (ed. C. L. Meyers and M. O'Connor; Winona Lake, IN: Eisenbrauns, 1983), 399–410. It should be noted that there are also references to impurity in such postexilic biblical texts as Ezra and Nehemiah.

clearly to identify two types of defilement in the priestly writings.³ Building on Hoffmann's work, Adolph Büchler (1867–1939) distinguished between natural "levitical" impurities and "religious" defilements that are caused by sin. More recent scholarship on ritual and moral impurity was initiated with the publication of Mary Douglas's comparative study *Purity and Danger* (1966). In the 1970s and 1980s, Jacob Neusner, Jacob Milgrom, and Tikva Frymer-Kensky presented their own formulations of the Israelite impurity system. As Milgrom continued his research into the 1990s, his former student, David P. Wright, added to the purity discussion by offering his own interpretation of the Israelite impurity system. Building on the work of these scholars, Jonathan Klawans refocused the impurity discussion by emphasizing the distinction between ritual and moral impurity.

Each of these scholars has made a significant contribution to the discussion on ritual and moral impurity. Interestingly, however, the scholarship in this area remains somewhat unbalanced. The survey below will show that while the impurity system associated with P has been well defined and debated, allowing for disagreements over details, the moral impurities associated with H have not received the attention they deserve. Although there have been attempts to describe and classify these laws, there has not, as yet, been a systematic approach that facilitates an understanding of the underlying theological structure that unites them.

I. Early-Twentieth-Century Biblical Scholarship

David Z. Hoffmann

In his seminal work on Leviticus, David Zvi Hoffmann conceptualizes an impurity system in which there are two distinct perceptions of defilement.⁴ The first is טומאת הגויות, a bodily defilement that stands in opposition to purity.⁵ Hoffmann classifies the sources of bodily impurity according to a threefold system.⁶ At the first level, impurity is contracted through contact with death, including human corpses (Num 19) and certain animal carcasses (Lev 11:24–40; 22:5). The second level is concerned with regular and irregular genital discharges of men and women (Lev 15), impurity from childbirth (Lev 12), and leprosy (Lev 14). The third is caused by contact with ritual objects that render the individual impure, including the scapegoat (Lev 16:26), the burnt חטאת or sin-offering (Lev 16: 27–28) and the ashes for the waters of lustration (Num 19:7–10). According to Hoffmann, these forms of bodily impurity are all transferable in the sense that impurity can be

---

3. Jonathan Klawans, *Impurity and Sin in Ancient Judaism* (New York: Oxford University Press, 2000), 13.

4. David Zvi Hoffmann, *Sefer va-Yikra Meforash* (trans. Z. Har Shefer and A. Liberman; 2 vols.; Jerusalem: Mossad HaRav Kook, 1952, 1953); trans. of *Das Buch Leviticus* (2 vols.; Berlin: M. Poppelauer, 1913, 1922). As Klawans notes, Hoffmann is not original in his perception of two forms of defilement. Rather, this dual concept of impurity can be traced to rabbinic sources (*b. Yoma* 80b) and is also found in the biblical interpretations of such medieval Jewish commentators as Ibn Ezra, Rashi, and Nachmanides. See Klawans, *Impurity and Sin*, 13 n. 59.

5. Hoffmann, *Sefer va-Yikra*, 1:212.

6. On Hoffmann's classification of bodily impurities, see ibid., 1:212–13.

passed to other individuals or objects upon contact. This state of impurity, however, is temporary, as it can be ameliorated by rituals of purification.[7]

The second form of impurity is טומאת הקדושות, a defilement that stands in opposition to holiness.[8] This form of impurity arises from sinful behavior, such as the eating of forbidden foods, acts of idolatry, and the violation of sexual prohibitions. According to Hoffmann, impurities of this sort do not affect the body of the individual in the same way as טומאת הגויות.[9] Rather, these impurities defile the inner being, or soul, of the individual (Lev 11:43; 19:31) and, by extension, cause defilement of the land and the exile of its inhabitants (Lev 18:24–25). Thus, suggests Hoffman, טומאת הקדושות is in fact טומאת הנפשות, a defilement of the soul.[10]

In contrasting these two forms of impurity, Hoffmann uses a concept of body-soul duality that would have been quite foreign to the priestly writer. Indeed, the term נפש in the priestly strata may refer to a "person" or to "a man or a woman," but never does it refer to the "soul." Hoffmann's equation of טומאת הקדושות with טומאת הנפשות may be appealing to the modern exegete, but the anachronistic use of the latter phrase does little to illuminate the biblical text in its contextual framework. By contrast, Hoffmann's original distinction between טומאת הגויות and טומאת הקדושות is much more reflective of the priestly understanding of the world—a place where the physical and the holy were related categories.

Hoffmann's distinction between two types of impurities—one standing in opposition to purity, and the other in opposition to holiness—is grounded in his syntactical analysis of the text. He suggests that occurrences of the expression טמא ל׳ refer to instances of טומאת הגויות, bodily defilement, whereas the usage of טמא ב׳ indicates טומאת הקדושות, defilement of the holy or sacred.[11] Whether this grammatical differentiation stands up to close scrutiny is unclear. Nevertheless, Hoffmann's analysis demonstrates his remarkable attention to detail and his sensitivity to the nuances in the biblical text. His insights would prove useful to future scholars, such as Jacob Milgrom, who relies heavily on Hoffman's scholarship.

Adolph Büchler

Adolph Büchler's *Studies in Sin and Atonement in the Rabbinic Literature of the First Century* posits a continuum between the biblical and post-biblical periods.[12] Most pertinent to the theme of purity and impurity is Büchler's chapter on the

---

7. Ibid., 1:212.

8. Ibid.

9. In his review of Hoffmann's scholarship, Klawans points out that Hoffmann can be easily misunderstood on this point. He states: "Although he [Hoffmann] does emphasize the defiling effect that sins have upon the soul, he believes that this defilement affects the body of the sinner as well. Yet the body of the sinner is not affected in the same way as the body of one who is ritually defiled" (Klawans, *Impurity and Sin*, 13–14).

10. Hoffmann, *Sefer va-Yikra*, 1:212. The term נפש is translated as "seele" in the German original (*Das Buch Leviticus*, 1:303).

11. Hoffmann, *Sefer va-Yikra*, 1:236.

12. Adolph Büchler, *Studies in Sin and Atonement in the Rabbinic Literature of the First Century* (London: Oxford University Press, 1928; repr., New York: Ktav, 1967).

defiling force of sin in the Bible. Here he argues that there are two categories of biblical defilement: a "levitical" defilement presumably associated with ritual law and a "religious" or "spiritual" defilement that is caused by sin.[13] Büchler does not elaborate on the concept of levitical impurity, but rather emphasizes religious impurity and its relationship to sin.[14] He asserts that the land of Israel is defiled by grave sins such as idolatry (Lev 18:1–28; Jer 2:4–28; 16:18; Ezek 36:17–18), bloodshed (Num 35:33; Ezra 9:11), and sexual sins (Lev 18:24–30; Deut 21:23; 24:4).[15] According to Büchler, these sins do not in any way pollute the land in a levitical sense. Rather, this form of defilement should be regarded as religious, spiritual, or moral. Accordingly, the use of purity language in these contexts should be read metaphorically rather than literally.

Büchler is among the few scholars who seriously consider the notion of the defiling force of sin. Lacking, however, is a clear classification of religious impurity.[16] Whereas Büchler indicates that religious impurity is not the same as levitical impurity, he does not define either form of defilement. Moreover, the defilement process itself remains ambiguous. In the case of idolatry, the sin appears to pollute the land directly. Yet, when referring to sexual sin, Büchler suggests that the sin "first defiles the person who commits it . . . and the persons in their turn defile the land."[17] It is not clear whether Büchler conceives of two separate mechanisms of defilement—one that pollutes the individual and a second that pollutes the land—or whether he is implying that all forms of impurity contain an element that defiles the individual.

As Klawans notes, Büchler's scholarship did not have a major impact on subsequent scholarship.[18] This may be due at least in part to his difficult prose and the absence of a fixed terminology to describe the phenomena related to impurity. Klawans rightly suggests that the use of multiple terms—"moral," "spiritual," and "religious"—to refer to a single form of defilement creates confusion for the reader.[19]

---

13. Büchler is here building on the distinction made earlier by David Z. Hoffman (*Sefer va-Yikra*, 1:212).

14. Harrington opposes "Büchler's effort to downplay the role of ritual impurity. . . . " I would suggest, however, that Büchler's omission of issues concerned with levitical impurity does not deny the importance of the phenomenon. It is just not relevant to the discussion on the defiling force of sin. See Hannah K. Harrington, *The Impurity Systems of Qumran and the Rabbis: Biblical Foundations* (SBLDS 143; Atlanta: Scholars Press, 1993), 2–3.

15. Büchler, *Studies*, 212–37.

16. Büchler's work is very much a product of its time, and its weaknesses may be partially attributed to his outdated methodology.

17. Büchler, *Studies*, 221.

18. Klawans, *Impurity and Sin*, 5–6.

19. Similarly, Klawans (ibid.) notes that Büchler continually shifts from "purity" to "cleanness" and from "purify" to "cleanse."

II. Recent Biblical Scholarship

Mary Douglas

Contemporary scholarship on impurity in the Hebrew Bible has been greatly influenced by the anthropological work of Mary Douglas. Of particular significance is Douglas's 1966 comparative study, *Purity and Danger*, in which she presents a sustained inquiry into the relationship between pollution behavior and social structure. In the field of biblical studies, this book has not only stimulated interest in the topic of pollution but also provided the theoretical framework for all subsequent scholarly discussions on biblical impurity.[20] Although some of Douglas's ideas have been refuted and sometimes even proven to be erroneous, many of her original assertions have endured.[21]

In *Purity and Danger*, Douglas contends that notions of impurity and taboo are frequently associated with anomalous people, objects, or situations. These notions are not exclusively associated with "primitive" peoples. Rather, all sorts of peoples, including those of so-called higher religions, have concepts of dirt and pollution that are structurally similar. For Douglas, "the difference between pollution behaviour in one part of the world and another is only a matter of detail."[22] In this way, Douglas removes the conceptual barrier between primitive and non-primitive religions that had been an essential feature of anthropological enquiry from the nineteenth century.

From a biblical studies perspective, one of Douglas's most prominent contributions is her systematization of cultural impurity practices. According to Douglas, dirt "is never a unique, isolated event. Where there is dirt there is system. Dirt is the by-product of a systematic ordering and classification of matter, insofar as ordering involves rejecting inappropriate elements."[23] Dirt is simply "matter out of place."[24] By analogy, polluted objects or people are those which fall outside designated categories, as defined by a given impurity system. Thus defilement is not

---

20. Klawans (ibid., 8) goes as far as to say that "virtually every academically oriented treatment of impurity in ancient Israel since 1966 has built on Douglas's work in some way."

21. Douglas's symbolic interpretation of the Israelite dietary laws has been largely discredited by Milgrom (*Leviticus 1–16*, 719–21, 726–28). In light of such criticism, Douglas has subsequently reevaluated her scholarly position in this area, and retracted much of what she initially wrote concerning "the Abominations of Leviticus." See the preface to the Routledge Classics edition (London: 2002) of *Purity and Danger: An Analysis of the Concepts of Pollution and Taboo*, xiii–xvi. For a fuller analysis of *Purity and Danger*, see Richard Fardon, *Mary Douglas: An Intellectual Biography* (London: Routledge, 1999), 75–101; Klawans, *Impurity and Sin*, 7–10. An analysis of Douglas's work in its historical context may be found in Howard Eilberg-Schwartz, *The Savage in Judaism: An Anthropology of Israelite Religion and Ancient Judaism* (Bloomington: Indiana University Press, 1990), 75–84.

22. Douglas, *Purity and Danger*, 43.

23. Ibid., 44.

24. Ibid.

an isolated element but, rather, a by-product of a greater organizational structure. She states:

> Defilement is never an isolated event. It cannot occur except in view of a systematic ordering of ideas. Hence any piecemeal interpretation of pollution rules of another culture is bound to fail. For the only way in which pollution ideas make sense is in reference to a total structure of thought whose key-stone, boundaries, margins and internal lines are held in relation by rituals of separation.[25]

Although some biblical scholars are not convinced by Douglas's definition of defilement-dirt as matter out of place, none has challenged the fundamental idea of cultural impurity *systems*.[26] Indeed, it was this premise that initiated the trend in biblical scholarship toward a holistic understanding of the Israelite impurity laws.

Douglas proposes a symbolic understanding of systems of defilement. In her view, ritual symbolism is "an attempt to create and maintain a particular culture [and] a particular set of assumptions."[27] Symbolic systems of impurity therefore have a social function: they influence and control human behavior and interaction. In a given culture, the transgression of impurity laws is perceived as the physical crossing of the social barrier and is treated as a dangerous pollution associated with severe consequences.[28]

Implicit in this formulation is an association between pollution and morality—the issue that is central to our inquiry. In this regard, Douglas is quite mistaken in her assessment that "a polluting person is always in the wrong."[29] This conclusion is simply not supported by the biblical text. Her analysis, however, is more nuanced than this summary statement would suggest. In fact she describes the relationship between impurity and sin in a highly complex way according to which purity regulations highlight only a small proportion of morally disapproved behaviors.[30]

---

25. Ibid., 51.
26. Milgrom, for example, is not entirely convinced that this definition is useful. He cites the work of Anna S. Meigs, who argues that although many phenomena may be out of place, only a few may be considered pollutants. It is only when such phenomena threaten to gain access to one's body that they are deemed polluting (Anna S. Meigs, "A Papuan Perspective on Pollution," *Man* 13 [1978]: 304–18). Milgrom suggests that Meigs's theory of pollution is "closer to the mark" than Douglas's theory of dirt (*Leviticus 1–16*, 721). In his view the latter premise has proved helpful but ultimately inadequate for explaining the animal classification of Lev 11. Commenting on this debate, Klawans (*Impurity and Sin*, 165 n. 30) suggests that Douglas's detractors have pushed her definition too far. In his view, Douglas had never intended to suggest that *all* matter out of place is defiling. Rather, in his view, she simply wished to convey the idea that impure objects and people fall outside the categories defined by the system in question.
27. Douglas, *Purity and Danger*, 158.
28. Ibid., 172.
29. Ibid., 140. Douglas is conflating the two categories of ritual and moral impurity and assuming that the pollution of the individual is the consequence of some misdeed.
30. Douglas, *Purity and Danger*, 160; see Klawans, *Impurity and Sin*, 9.

Douglas's systematization of cultural impurity practices offered a new and more comprehensive approach to the levitical purity laws.[31] Among them were Jacob Neusner and Jacob Milgrom, both of whom used Douglas's concept of an impurity system as the basis for their own studies of the biblical impurity laws.

Jacob Neusner

In his 1973 book, *The Idea of Purity*, Jacob Neusner presents a broad survey of sources on ancient Jewish impurity law, including literature from the biblical, Second Temple, and rabbinic periods. Of particular significance is the fact that he has collected and arranged the relevant sources according to particular stages in history. Neusner's principal interest was in the rabbinic ideas and laws pertaining to impurity.[32] Nevertheless, his treatment of impurity in the Second Temple period remains valuable in its own right and thus requires further examination.

For Neusner, ideas about impurity in the Second Temple period are based on the biblical legacy—that is, the biblical writings as they would have been known in the third century B.C.E.[33] Within this biblical corpus, Neusner identifies two distinct concepts relating to purity and impurity. He writes:

> Two important ideas about purity and impurity come down from ancient Israel: first, purity and impurity are cultic matters; second, they may serve as metaphors for moral and religious behaviour, primarily in regard to matters of sex, idolatry, and unethical action.[34]

The first idea of impurity is derived from the laws of ritual impurity articulated in the priestly law code. According to Neusner, these laws utilize the categories of purity and impurity primarily with reference to the cult.[35] Those who are pure may participate in the cult, whereas those who are impure are prohibited from any contact with the sacred. Thus the laws governing such primitive taboos as corpse

---

31. In the early 1990s, Douglas revisited much of what she wrote in *Purity in Danger*. Influenced by the work of Milgrom and other biblical scholars, Douglas furthered her knowledge of biblical Hebrew in order better to understand priestly law and its related narrative. The two books that resulted from this endeavour—one on Leviticus and the other on Numbers—were markedly different from her earlier work in both their scope and their basic understanding of the Israelite purity system. In her later work, she expresses the conviction that the Israelite purity system is distinctive. She writes: "[T]he more that we study and compare taboo systems around the world, the less the defilement laws of Judaism seem to have in common with them." See Mary Douglas, *In the Wilderness: The Doctrine of Defilement in the Book of Numbers* (Oxford: Oxford University Press, 1993), 153. For a more thorough analysis of Douglas's more recent work, see Fardon, *Mary Douglas*, 185–205; Klawans, *Impurity and Sin*, 18–19.

32. Jacob Neusner, *The Idea of Purity in Ancient Judaism* (Leiden: Brill, 1973), 3.

33. In discussing a "biblical legacy," Neusner expresses no interest in differentiating between biblical strata (e.g., P and H), but rather prefers to treat isolated passages in order to identify ideas about purity. This approach to the Hebrew Bible is much more reflective of rabbinic methods of interpretation than of biblical scholarship.

34. Neusner, *The Idea*, 108; cf. 11.

35. Ibid., 15.

contamination and bodily discharges all share a primary ideological motif: the maintenance of cultic purity.[36] This primary concern for the purity of the cult is extended to include the priesthood, the land, and the people.

The second idea of impurity derived from biblical literature is concerned with the usage of purity and impurity as metaphors for moral behavior.[37] According to Neusner, impurity often is used to symbolize a rejection of God and therefore by God, whereas its opposite, purity, is an indication of divine acceptance. Closely related to this dichotomy is the frequent biblical allusion to idolatry—the ultimate rejection of God—as a major source of impurity. Another metaphorical usage of impurity may be found in the biblical treatment of sexual transgressions. Whereas illicit sexual relationships cause impurity and are a sign of moral evil, marital fidelity is symbolic of moral blamelessness. Finally, the metaphor of impurity extends to the land, which may be made unclean by evil doings, especially those relating to idolatry.

For Neusner, the two ideas of impurity are related to Jewish law in two different ways.[38] Cultic impurity is by nature concerned with the details of the purity laws and the questions of how to restore and maintain purity. Metaphorical purity and impurity, on the other hand, are indifferent to the actual details of priestly law.[39] These distinctions are not entirely convincing. In her critique of Neusner's scholarship, which was published as an appendix to his book, Mary Douglas rejects the idea of metaphorical impurity. She argues that all the biblical texts related to impurity are part of a single symbolic system, which sustains "the whole moral and physical universe simultaneously in their systematic interrelatedness."[40] Klawans agrees, stating that "one cannot simply describe biblical uses of impurity language as either cultic or metaphorical."[41]

When Neusner goes beyond his dichotomy, he ultimately relates both ideas of impurity back to the temple. Just as ritual impurity is associated with the cult, so too does the metaphor of impurity originate in the association of purity with the temple:

> The Temple supplied to purity its importance in the religious life. As the Temple signified divine favour, and as the cult supplied the nexus between Israel and God, so purity, associated so closely with both, could readily serve as an image either of divine favor or of man's loyalty to god. From that fact followed the assignment of impurity to all that stood against the Temple, the cult, and God: idolatry first of all.[42]

---

36. Ibid., 24.
37. On the meanings of the biblical metaphors assigned to impurity, see ibid., 13–15.
38. Ibid., 25.
39. Ibid., 15.
40. Mary Douglas, "Critique and Commentary," in *The Idea of Purity in Ancient Judaism*, by Jacob Neusner (Leiden: Brill, 1973), 140. Klawans indicates that Neusner subsequently accepted Douglas' point. See his discussion in *Impurity and Sin*, 10–12, esp. n. 47.
41. Klawans, *Impurity and Sin*, 11.
42. Neusner, *The Idea*, 15.

This association between purity and the temple is fundamental to Neusner's understanding of purity issues in ancient Israel and provides the framework for his scholarship on purity in post-exilic Judaism, as we shall see in chapter 2.

Jacob Milgrom

No scholar has contributed more to our understanding of purity in the Bible than Jacob Milgrom. In his three-volume, 2,700-page commentary on Leviticus—perhaps the most thorough academic work of its kind—Milgrom provides comprehensive explanations of the various details of the purity laws.[43] In addition, he has published numerous articles on various aspects of the purity laws.

In his article "Israel's Sanctuary: The Priestly 'Picture of Dorian Gray,'" Milgrom argues that the חטאת, commonly referred to as a "sin-offering," is not a ritual of atonement, but a ritual of purification.[44] For this reason, he argues, the term חטאת is more accurately translated as "purification-offering."[45] According to Milgrom, what is purified is not the offerer but, rather, the altar and the sanctuary, both of which become defiled by major forms of ritual and moral impurity.

Milgrom identifies two sets of circumstances in which levitical law requires the offering of a חטאת. The first pertains to an individual who has suffered from a major form of impurity resulting from childbirth, leprosy, or an irregular genital discharge (Lev 12–15).[46] In each instance, the individual is required physically to purify him/herself through ritual ablutions and to bring an offering of a חטאת to the sanctuary. The second circumstance concerns the individual who has committed an inadvertent sin.[47] According to Milgrom, the inadvertence (בשגגה) of the violation, combined with the guilt (אשם) of the sinner, serves to "spiritually" purify the individual of the sin, in much the same way as ritual ablution removes physical impurity.[48] It is only after this inner purification is realized that the individual brings a חטאת offering to the sanctuary.

Milgrom demonstrates that in all cases in which a חטאת is required, the purification of the individual, be it external or internal, is attained *prior* to the offering of

---

43. Jacob Milgrom, *Leviticus: A New Translation with Introduction and Commentary* (AB 3, 3A, 3B; New York: Doubleday, 1991–2001). For a review of aspects of ritual and moral purity in Milgrom's commentary, see Jonathan Klawans, "Ritual Purity, Moral Purity, and Sacrifice in Jacob Milgrom's Leviticus," *RelSRev* 29, no. 1 (2003): 19–28.

44. Jacob Milgrom, "Israel's Sanctuary: The Priestly 'Picture of Dorian Gray,'" *Revue Biblique* 83 (1976): 390–99; cf. idem, *Leviticus 1–16: A New Translation with Introduction and Commentary* (AB 3; New York: Doubleday, 1991), 253–92.

45. Cf. Jacob Milgrom, "Sin-Offering, or Purification-Offering?" *VT* 21 (1971): 237–39.

46. A listing of the major physical impurities that require a חטאת can be found in Milgrom, *Leviticus 1–16*, 990. It should be noted that in this early article Milgrom translates צרעת as "leprosy." In his later work, however, he argues that the condition described in the levitical text is unrelated to the modern form of leprosy (Hansen's disease). Accordingly, he suggests that the term צרעת is more accurately translated as "scale disease." See ibid., 816–20.

47. See, e.g., Lev 4.

48. Milgrom, "Israel's Sanctuary," 390 (= *Leviticus 1–16*, 254).

the sacrifice. For this reason, it is clear that the object of purification of the חטאת is not the offerer, but the sanctuary. The blood of the offering is never applied to the individual, but is used to purge the sanctuary and its most sacred objects from impurity on behalf of the individual offering the sacrifice. Severe physical impurity and inadvertent sin not only affect the individual but also have a secondary consequence in that they indirectly defile the sanctuary. This defilement is conceived as a kind of aerial miasma that is attracted to the realm of the sacred.[49] The purpose of the חטאת, then, is to purge "the most sacred objects and areas of the sanctuary on behalf of the person who caused their contamination by his physical impurity or inadvertent offence."[50]

The process of defilement of the sanctuary occurs on three different levels.[51] On the first level, it is the individual's severe physical impurity or inadvertent sin that pollutes the outer altar. The priest purges this impurity by daubing the horns of the altar with the blood of the חטאת (Lev 4:25, 30; 9:9). A second and more serious level of impurity, caused by the inadvertent sin of the high priest or the entire community, defiles the shrine. The high priest eliminates this impurity by sprinkling the blood of the חטאת on the inner altar, in front of the veil (Lev 4:5-7, 16–18). The third and most severe form of impurity is caused by wanton, unrepented sin. This form of impurity not only pollutes the outer altar, it also penetrates the shrine, pierces the veil to the holy ark, and pollutes the adytum (Holy of Holies). Since the wanton sinner is not permitted to bring a חטאת (Num 15:27–31), this form of pollution can be eliminated only through the Day of Atonement rituals, which include purgation of both the inner and outer altar (Lev 16:16–19).

Milgrom's thesis suggests that the severity of an impurity or sin is directly proportional to the degree to which the impurity penetrates the sanctuary. In priestly theology the pollution of the sanctuary is considered very dangerous: if the impurity accumulates beyond a tolerable level, the God of Israel would leave the earthly abode and no longer dwell in the midst of the people.[52]

The importance of Milgrom's theory is twofold. First, he describes a process by which impurity can contaminate the sacred realm, even from afar. This contribution, alone, has greatly influenced our understanding of the priestly laws and their underlying theology in that it elucidates the relationship between sin and impurity. Second, he follows Hoffmann and Büchler in distinguishing between two types of impurity, one caused by severe physical defilement and the other caused by sin. This point, touched on in "Israel's Sanctuary," is further developed in his later article, "Rationale for Cultic Law: The Case of Impurity."[53] Here he argues that in the two uses of the חטאת, we find "the distinction between ... physically and

---

49. Ibid., 392 (= *Leviticus 1–16*, 256–57).

50. Ibid., 391 (= *Leviticus 1–16*, 256).

51. On the graded levels of sancta pollution and its amelioration, see ibid., 393 (= *Leviticus 1–16*, 257).

52. Ibid., 396–97 (= *Leviticus 1–16*, 258–59).

53. Jacob Milgrom, "Rationale for Cultic Law: The Case of Impurity," *Semeia* 45 (1989): 103–9.

morally generated impurity."[54] In the case of the physical or ritual impurity, the cause of the defilement is designated as טמאה, impurity, and the effect of the חטאת is summarized as follows: על־המטהר מטמאתו . . . וטהר וכפר, "And he [the priest] shall effect purgation on behalf of the one who is purifying himself for his impurity . . . and he shall be pure" (Lev 14:19). The ritually impure brings a sacrifice for the purpose of purification. The inadvertent sinner, however, does not merely seek purification but, rather, forgiveness on account of the חטא, or sin.[55] The text indicates that forgiveness is, indeed, achieved: "And the priest shall effect purgation on his behalf for his wrong that he may be forgiven" (Lev 4:26).

Further evidence to support the distinction between ritually and morally generated impurities can be found in the Day of Atonement ritual. During the ritual two goats are used. The first goat, selected for God, is sacrificed. It is the blood of this חטאת that purges the sanctuary of its טמאת, "impurities" (Lev 16:19–21). The second is the scapegoat, over which the high priest confesses all the עונת, "iniquities," of the people (Lev 16:21). In Milgrom's view, the use of the terms טמאת and עונת in connection with the two goats clearly shows a distinction between two kinds of impurity: the sacrificial blood of the חטאת purges the physical impurity of the sanctuary, while the scapegoat purges the moral impurity of the people.[56]

Milgrom further contributes to the discussion on ritual and moral impurity in his second volume of his commentary on Leviticus.[57] Of particular interest is the interpretation of Lev 18:24–30, which is concerned with the pollution of the land caused by sexual abominations.[58] Milgrom points out that the idea that human sin pollutes the land is found throughout scripture, but it is this text that most clearly presents exile as the prescribed punishment for such defilement. If the land becomes polluted by sexual sins, it will cleanse itself by regurgitating the Israelites, in much the same way as the Canaanites were previously expelled.

What does it mean to say that the land has become polluted by sin? For Milgrom, the answer can be found in the usage of the verb טמא, "to render impure." P uses the verb טמא in a cultic sense: pollution contaminates the sacred and is

---

54. On the causes of the sanctuary pollution and the corresponding effects of the חטאת, see ibid., 106–7; cf. Milgrom, "Israel's Sanctuary," 391–92.

55. In his earlier article, Milgrom explicitly states that the offender needs forgiveness not because of his actual act, but because of the consequence of his act—the pollution of the sanctuary. Whereas both types of חטאת result in purification of the sanctuary, only the חטאת for inadvertencies provides for forgiveness ("Israel's Sanctuary," 392).

56. Milgrom's argument is somewhat ambiguous at this point. His purpose is to differentiate between physically and morally generated impurities. In using the example of the Day of Atonement ritual, he rightly distinguishes between the "physical" impurity of the sanctuary and the "moral" impurity of the people. Yet, in doing so, he mistakenly equates the "physical" impurity of the sanctuary with the "physical" impurity of the individual. According to his own thesis, the physical impurity of the sanctuary is caused by sin, as well as by severe physical impurity of the individual. On the purgation of sin versus impurity on the Day of Atonement, see Milgrom, "Rationale," 106–7.

57. Jacob Milgrom, *Leviticus 17–22: A New Translation with Introduction and Commentary* (AB 3A; New York: Doubleday, 2000).

58. For Milgrom's interpretation of Lev 18:24–30, see ibid., 1571–84.

subject to ritual purification. H, however, uses the same verb in a non-cultic sense: H does not refer to the land as holy and provides no ritual remedy for the impurity of the land. The latter is a moral impurity that cannot be expunged.

Pollution of the land is caused by sexual sins and murder, which are considered capital crimes. The impurity they cause can be expunged only through capital punishment imposed by the community or the penalty of כרת (*karet*), divine extirpation of one's lineage. When, however, the entire community is guilty of such moral impurity, the inevitable outcome is pollution of the land (Lev 18:25; Num 34:35–37) and the exile of its inhabitants (Lev 18:28; 26:14–38).

Milgrom's analysis of the concepts of purity is for the most part persuasive and convincing. There is, however, an apparent contradiction that requires resolution. Milgrom claims that the defilement described in P is "concrete, cultic-ritual impurity," whereas in H it is "abstract, inexpungeable-moral impurity."[59] He cautions his readers, however, against concluding that H's concept of purity is metaphorical. Rather, "it is just as real and potent as P's impurity."[60] The claim that H's impurity is not metaphorical appears to contradict other statements made by Milgrom on this subject. For example, he states:

> H has taken the ubiquitous notion that homicide pollutes the land (e.g., Gen 4:10–12; Num 35:33–34; Deut 21:1–9 . . .) and applied it to other violations. The change is in keeping with H's terminological characteristic to metaphorize. Thus whereas homicide literally pollutes the area where the blood is spilled, in H, sexual violations metaphorically pollute the entire land.[61]

David P. Wright has attempted to reconcile the inconsistency by suggesting that while the expanded use of terminology—such as the use of the word טמא—may be seen as metaphoric in H, its conceptualization of impurity is very real.[62]

Other inconsistencies in Milgrom's analysis of the concepts of impurity in P and H are due largely to the development of his thinking over the course of three decades.[63] In his earlier writings, Milgrom had asserted that P was later than H. Yet, by the mid-1980s, Milgrom had reassessed his position, contending that H was not only later than P, but that H was P's redactor.[64] This reassessment occurred

---

59. Ibid., 1578.
60. Ibid.
61. Ibid., 1579.
62. David P. Wright, "Jacob Milgrom on Purity" (paper presented at the annual meeting of the Association for Jewish Studies, Boston, December 21, 2003). Perhaps some of the confusion may also be related to Milgrom's lack of precision in the use of terminology. Whereas Milgrom frequently uses the phrase "moral impurity," he sometimes substitutes "metaphoric impurity" or "non-cultic" impurity. See Jonathan Klawans, "Ritual Purity, Moral Purity, and Sacrifice in Jacob Milgrom's Leviticus," *RelSRev* 29, no. 1 (2003): 22
63. An informative discussion on the evolution of Milgrom's scholarship was offered by Wright, "Jacob Milgrom on Purity."
64. Milgrom was influenced, at least to some extent, by his discussions with Israel Knohl on the subject during the summers of 1984–87. Milgrom, *Leviticus 1–16*, 13.

precisely at the time that Milgrom was writing his first volume on Leviticus. Consequently, this volume offers only a limited treatment of the issue of P and H in its introduction. It is not until the publication of the second and third volumes that we find a comprehensive discussion of the issue that reflects Milgrom's revised opinion.[65] Throughout volumes 2 and 3, Milgrom includes, when appropriate, revised analyses of passages that were discussed in volume 1.

Milgrom's exhaustive treatment of the subject presents extensive evidence and well-thought-out conclusions. It also, however, raises a number of issues that are not thoroughly addressed. For example, Milgrom's thesis is predicated on differentiating between H and P with respect to their views on impurity. Yet his distinction between the two priestly conceptions of impurity is not as clearly articulated as one might expect given its importance in his own thought and in the scholarly literature as a whole.[66] More serious is the disparity in his treatment of the two major forms of impurity. Whereas he offers a highly systematized analysis of ritual defilement, the same cannot be said with regard to the category of moral defilement.[67] Although he discusses the main sources of moral impurity—idolatry, murder and sexual sin—on their own terms, he makes no significant attempt to show the relationships among them.[68]

In summary, Milgrom builds on Douglas's concept of a cultural impurity system to categorize and explain the impurity laws associated with P. The core of Milgrom's thesis is discussed in his "Dorian Gray" article in which he uses the sacrificial laws of Lev 4:27–35 to elucidate an entire theology of ritual impurity. Unfortunately, Milgrom offers no comparable analysis of the impurity laws found in H. The laws concerning moral impurity are not systematized, nor is there any clear explanation of the mechanism of defilement. Milgrom fails to articulate a theology of moral defilement, but he does succeed in opening the door wider to further inquiry and providing an important foundation for the work of others.

Tikva Frymer-Kensky

Building on Milgrom's earlier scholarship, Tikva Frymer-Kensky attempts to systematize the various types of biblical impurity, including those described in both P and H. In her article "Pollution, Purification, and Purgation in Biblical

---

65. Wright thus advises his students to begin studying Milgrom by reading his introduction to volume 2, rather than volume 1 ("Jacob Milgrom on Purity").

66. In his comparison of P and H, Knohl argues that P focuses on the priestly understanding of belief and ritual—the cult—and differentiates its view from those of the masses. In contrast, H attempts to integrate priestly elements of belief and ritual with popular traditions, thereby erasing the dividing line between cult and morality. This distinction—if it is correct—may very well account for differences between the two sources with respect to the concept of purity. See Knohl, *Sanctuary*, 1–7, 180–86.

67. Klawans, "Ritual Purity, Moral Purity, and Sacrifice in Jacob Milgrom's Leviticus," 22.

68. Although the first volume of the commentary contains several charts that map out ritual impurity, there are no comparable illustrations pertaining to moral impurity in the second volume. For a full critique of Milgrom's discussion on moral impurity, see ibid., 21–23.

Israel," Frymer-Kensky offers an analysis of the biblical purity system in which she identifies two categories of pollution: "contagious pollutions" and "danger beliefs."[69] She writes:

> Some forms of pollution could be eradicated by rituals; the performance of these purifications and expiations was a major function of the priesthood. The pollution caused by the performance of certain deeds, however, could not be eradicated by rituals; Israel believed that the person intentionally committing these acts would suffer catastrophic retribution. Wrongful acts could cause the pollution of the nation and of the land of Israel, which could also not be "cured" by ritual.[70]

Like Büchler and Hoffmann, Frymer-Kensky distinguishes between the ways in which these two forms of pollution are perceived to defile.[71] She argues that contagious pollutions can be categorized as either major or minor, depending on the duration of the impurity. Major pollution, which may be caused by either external or internal sources of defilement and results in the person becoming impure for seven or more days. The two external causes of such defilement are corpse-contamination (Num 19:11–21) and leprosy (Lev 13–14). Internal sources of major pollution result from bodily emission associated with childbirth (Lev 12), menstruation, and the irregular genital discharges of both males and females (Lev 15). Other bodily emissions, such as saliva, urine, or feces, or blood originating from a wound, are never mentioned as being polluting.[72] In general, minor pollutions are contracted from external sources, such as contact with an impure object or with an individual who has contracted a major impurity. The only internal source of minor pollution is a seminal discharge.

For Frymer-Kensky, the most important characteristic of major pollutions is their contagion. According to levitical law, an individual who has contracted a major pollution can defile objects. Moreover, anyone who comes in direct contact with either a defiled object or individual will contract a minor impurity which lasts the course of the day. Although major pollutions are contagious, they are not to be considered dangerous. No harm comes to the individual who becomes impure through contagious pollutions, nor is the impurity associated with forbidden or

---

69. For Frymer-Kensky's discussion on the biblical purity system, see "Pollution," 399–410. The use of this terminology is questionable. In his otherwise positive assessment of Frymer-Kensky's work, Klawans rejects the use of the term "belief" to describe one form of pollution but not the other. He correctly states that both forms of defilement require belief and suggests that the use of the term "belief" should be avoided. Klawans, *Impurity and Sin*, 15–16.

70. Frymer-Kensky, "Pollution," 399.

71. Neither Büchler nor Hoffmann is cited by Frymer-Kensky, suggesting that she arrived at her conclusions independently.

72. On this point, Frymer-Kensky correctly opposes Douglas's contention that, in Israelite law, all bodily emissions cause ritual defilement (Douglas, *Purity and Danger*, 64; Frymer-Kensky, "Pollution," 399–401). For a complete listing of the sources of major and minor pollutions, and their resolution, see also the chart on page 402.

improper actions.⁷³ On the contrary. Many of the actions that cause major pollution can be considered natural, inevitable, and even beneficial aspects of human existence. Contracting such impurity, according to levitical law, alienates one temporarily from the holy (Lev 15:31).⁷⁴ Thus an individual who has contracted impurity must wait the allotted period and perform the appropriate purification rituals before regaining full ritual participation. As long as the purity laws are obeyed, however, contagious pollution presents a danger neither to the individual nor to the community.⁷⁵

By contrast, impurities associated with wrongdoing, which Frymer-Kensky refers to as "danger beliefs," carry the threat of divinely sanctioned repercussions. Whereas ritual or contagious pollutions are temporary and last only for a designated period, the danger pollutions cannot be ameliorated through ritual purification or sacrifice. This form of pollution is not contagious and does not restrict the individual from contact with the sacred. Collective catastrophe, however, may strike if too many individuals become polluted in this way.

When a sin generates danger pollution, the punishment is often signalled by the phrase נשא את עונו, "he shall bear his penalty," though the nature of the punishment is not specified.⁷⁶ At other times the individual is condemned to be נכרת ("cut off"), a penalty that is best understood as the divine extirpation of one's lineage. According to Frymer-Kensky, the belief in these divine sanctions is an essential component of the biblical impurity system. The penalty of כרת "serves as a divine reinforcement of the boundaries between sacred and profane by providing a sanction for acts which violate these boundaries but which are not normally provided with legal sanctions."⁷⁷

Violation of the boundary between the sacred and profane may also result in serious consequences for the community. Following Milgrom, Frymer-Kensky suggests that some breaches of this boundary, such as the pollution of the temple caused by various types of sin, can be ameliorated by ritual means. But there is no ritual that can "cure" the danger pollution that is generated by apostasy (Lev 20:1–5, 27; Deut 13:7–12; 17:2–7), sexual misconduct (Lev 18), and murder (Deut 19:13; 21:8). These three classes of impurity pollute both the people and the land and create the risk of communal catastrophe.⁷⁸

---

73. The one exception is the biblical association of leprosy with divine punishment (Num 12:10–15; 2 Kgs 5:27; 2 Chr 26:19–21). Frymer-Kensky contends that the formal tradition of Israel attached no blame to lepers and that the tendency to suspect lepers of wrongdoing was simply a folk suspicion. Ibid., 403–4.

74. The separation of the impure from the holy is required of both Israelites (Lev 7:20–21) and priests (Lev 22:3–9). Moreover, the penalty for transgression of the purity laws is most severe: כרת, the extirpation of one's lineage. Ibid., 403.

75. Noncompliance with the purity laws does, however, present the threat that the pollution will spread, effectively alienating the entire community from God. Ibid., 403.

76. This phrase always refers to divine punishment (ibid., 404).

77. In her conception of boundaries that must be maintained, Frymer-Kensky is clearly drawing on the scholarship of Douglas (ibid., 405).

78. Ibid., 406–8.

Frymer-Kensky's major contribution to the study of biblical impurity is her categorization of the various forms of pollution. Particularly useful is her distinction between "contagious pollution" as an impermanent, natural, and communicable form of impurity and "danger belief" as a permanent pollution that is associated with wrongdoing and dangerous repercussions and affects both the people and the land. Frymer-Kensky goes beyond Milgrom in her classification of sin-related impurities, as well as in her identification of sexual sins, bloodshed, and idolatry as the cause of land defilement. She posits a theology of H according to which it is the pollution of the land caused by the sins of the people that necessitates both the destruction of Israel and the exile of the people.[79]

David P. Wright

An alternative system for the classification of the different kinds of impurity in the priestly legislation has been proposed by David P. Wright, in three recent studies.[80] Like Büchler and Milgrom, Wright differentiates between two major categories of impurity, but he also views them in the context of a coherent priestly purity system. He therefore posits a "spectrum" of impurity within which the different types of impurity remain connected to one another, both systematically and conceptually.[81]

In his *Koroth* and *Anchor Bible Dictionary* studies, Wright distinguishes between "permitted" and "prohibited" impurities.[82] However, in his subsequent paper, "The Spectrum," he redefines the "permitted" impurities as "tolerated" impurities.[83] The tolerated impurities are, for the most part, those impurities discussed in detail in Lev 11–15 and Num 19. These natural forms of defilement can be sub-classified according to origin or nature: death-related, sexual, disease-related, and cultic impurities;[84] they are linked together in the priestly legislation by one crucial element: the absence of a blanket prohibition.[85] One important exception is the legislation concerning eating or touching some impure animal carcasses (Lev 11:4–8,

---

79. Frymer-Kensky indicates that this paradigm of pollution existed alongside the legal paradigm found in the Deuteronomistic history, in which the people commit misdeeds and are subsequently punished by God with exile. The two paradigms are similar, but not identical. Ibid., 409.

80. David P. Wright, "The Spectrum of Priestly Impurity," in *Priesthood and Cult in Ancient Israel* (ed. Gary A. Anderson and Saul M. Olyan; Sheffield: JSOT Press, 1991), 150–81; cf. Wright, "Two Types of Impurity in the Priestly Writings of the Bible," *Koroth* 9 (1988): 180–93; Wright, "Unclean and Clean (OT)," *ABD* 6:729–41.

81. Wright, "The Spectrum," 180.

82. Wright's classification of the two forms of impurity is similar, but not identical, to those of Hoffmann, Büchler, and Frymer-Kensky. On Wright's categories of distinction, see "Two Types of Impurity," 181–82; "Unclean and Clean," 729–30.

83. Wright, "The Spectrum," 158.

84. On permitted/tolerated impurities, see Wright, "Two Types of Impurity," 182–84; "Unclean and Clean," 730–33; "The Spectrum," 152–58.

85. Wright, "Two Types of Impurity," 183.

10–12, 13–20, 23, 41–45; 22:8), which, though prohibited, are to be included in the tolerated category.[86]

According to Wright, the prohibited impurities may be divided into two sub-categories.[87] The first group consists of unintentional forms of defilement, such as those that arise from the mismanagement of tolerated impurities (Lev 5:2–3), the accidental corpse contamination of the Nazarite (Num 6:6–7), and other general inadvertencies (Lev 4:1–5; Num 15:22–29).[88] In each case, the unintentional sin causes defilement of the sanctuary (the outer altar or the outer shrine) and requires a חטאת sacrifice for purification.[89] The second category of prohibited impurities is derived from deliberate sin, which includes purposefully delaying the purification of defilement (Num 19:13, 20), deliberately polluting the sacred realm (Lev 7:19–21; 22:3–7), sexual misconduct (Lev 18:6–23; cf. 20:18), and sacrifices to Molech (Lev 20:2–5). These deliberate sins have two consequences: the perpetrator is punished by the penalty of *karet*, and the resultant pollution of the sanctuary penetrates to the innermost sanctum, requiring purification through the Day of Atonement sacrifices.

Wright places these categories on a scaled spectrum of impurity manifesting several grades of defilement.[90] At the lower end are impurities that require no sacrifice. Next come defilements that require individual sacrifice, followed by ad hoc communal sacrifice and the Day of Atonement sacrifices.[91] These four gradations of impurity correspond to progressions in the locus of pollution from least to most pervasive: the person; the outer altar and the person; the outer altar (and sometimes the shrine or the person); and finally the adytum or Holy of Holies (and sometimes the person). The increasing degrees of impurity also reflect increasing

---

86. Wright offers four reasons for including these impurities in the tolerated category: (1) Other than the fact that they are prohibited, they do not share the character of other prohibited impurities; (2) not all animal carcass impurities are prohibited; (3) the prohibitions against eating impure animals and touching their carcasses appear to refer to special cases concerning carcasses; (4) the priestly dietary laws appear to be derived from an independent pre-priestly source which was not originally part of the impurity "system." See Wright, "The Spectrum," 165–69.

87. On prohibited impurities, see Wright, "Two Types of Impurity," 184–87; "Unclean and Clean," 733–35; "The Spectrum," 158–64.

88. Wright includes the inadvertent corpse contamination of the priests and high priest, even though there are no explicit prescriptions against such accidental pollution, as in the case of the Nazarite ("Two Types of Impurity," 185).

89. Also included in this category are the impurities remaining from a deliberate sin from which the individual has repented. Here Wright follows Milgrom in his argument that intentional sins, when repented, are reduced to the level of inadvertencies. In such instances an אשם sacrifice is required (Lev 5:1–4; 16:21; 26:40; Num 5:6–7) and not a חטאת. See Wright, "Two Types of Impurities," 185–86; cf. Jacob Milgrom, *Cult and Conscience: The Asham and the Priestly Doctrine of Repentance* (SJLA 18; Leiden: Brill, 1976).

90. On the interrelatedness of the various grades of pollution, see Wright, "The Spectrum," 164–65; cf. fig. 1, 153.

91. In the third gradation, only some of the impurities require ad hoc communal sacrifices; most require individual sacrifices. See ibid., fig. 1, 153.

restrictions of the defilement. At the lower end of the spectrum, the individual is excluded from the sacred. With increasing levels of pollution, there is exclusion from both the sacred and profane habitation, followed by permanent exclusion from human society.

In Wright's view, this purity system, including tolerated impurities, has a moral basis and rationale; indeed, the system supports and sustains the moral order of society.[92] The suffering of a tolerated impurity, with its consequent purification and reintegration into the community, is symbolic of the more serious offense: contraction of a prohibited impurity for which there is no chance of communal reassimilation. It is through this symbolic interplay that the individual acts out the more detrimental side of human behavior and is thus inoculated against the higher evils.[93]

Wright's conception of a spectrum of impurity according to which the various forms of defilement are interrelated within the priestly impurity system is persuasive. The dichotomy that he posits between categories of impurity that are "permitted" or "tolerated" and those that are "prohibited," however, is problematic. As Klawans notes, many of the "tolerated" impurities inevitably arise from activities that may be more accurately described as obligatory, such as procreation and burial.[94] Second, the demonstrated overlap between the two categories, in which some so-called prohibited impurities are included in the tolerated grouping, calls into question the very system of classification that he has proposed.[95]

Another difficulty is the exclusion of any subcategory related to impurity caused by murder, a most significant form of defilement. Wright justifies this omission by claiming differences in the loci of pollution (the land), the treatment of the offender, the requirements for rectification, and the language used to describe the impurity.[96] Nevertheless, it is clear that the priestly writer viewed both unintentional and intentional homicide as sources of impurity (Num 35:33–34).

If Wright's attempt to define the relationship between defilement and sin seems forced and incomplete, it is because the applied schema does not accurately reflect the proposed conceptual framework of a so-called spectrum of impurity. A spectrum is a continuum in which individual components are arranged in order according to some varying factor. Such a continuum not only implies but necessitates a blurring of boundaries as one component blends into the other. Wright

---

92. Ibid., 170. For a compelling refutation of this idea, see Klawans, *Impurity and Sin*, 36–38.

93. Ibid., 174–75.

94. Klawans, *Impurity and Sin*, 17; cf. Wright, "Clean and Unclean," 731–32; Wright, "The Spectrum," 157; David P. Wright, *The Disposal of Impurity: Elimination Rites in the Bible and in Hittite and Mesopotamian Literature* (Atlanta: Scholars Press, 1987), 115–28.

95. This blurring of boundaries is found throughout Wright's schema, resulting in a significant number of overlapping categories and subcategories of impurity. Klawans comments that Wright's distinctions between major categories of impurities are not as sharp as Büchler's or Frymer-Kensky's, the latter of whom is never cited by Wright. Klawans, however, does not offer any further analysis of this problem (*Impurity and Sin*, 16).

96. Wright, "Two Types of Impurity," 187–88.

does not illustrate a true spectrum but, rather, groups together various kinds of impurities into categories, and then arranges these classes of impurity into what would more accurately be called a hierarchy of impurity. In effect, Wright's conception of a spectrum is undermined by the process of categorization, which impedes any inherent sense of continuity.

Jonathan Klawans

Like the scholars whose work we have already surveyed, Jonathan Klawans proposes two categories of impurity in the Hebrew Bible. He refers to these categories as "ritual" and "moral" impurity. Klawans himself acknowledges that this terminology is problematic.[97] These terms are not found in the biblical text, nor are they discernible categories in biblical or post-biblical Jewish literature.[98] Rather, these terms reflect a modern scholarly articulation of the meanings and messages of the ancient texts. Moreover, the term "ritual" is misleading, in that rituals are associated with both forms of impurity, albeit in different ways. Yet, the term is preferable to the alternatives, "cultic" or "levitical," each of which presents its own set of difficulties.[99] In Klawans's view, the use of the terms "ritual" and "moral" as two adjectives modifying the noun "impurity" enables us simultaneously to express "the difference and interrelatedness of the two types of defilements."[100]

Klawans classifies ritual impurity as those defilements arising from childbirth (Lev 12:1–8), scale disease (Lev 13:1–14:32), genital discharges (Lev 15:1–33), the carcasses of certain impure animals (Lev 11:1–47), and human corpses (Num 19:10–22), or as a by-product of purificatory procedures (e.g., Lev 16:28; Num 19:8).[101] The impurities in this category have three distinctive characteristics. First, the sources of ritual impurity are natural, usually unavoidable, and sometimes even desirable, reflecting the conditions of normal life. Second, these impurities are neither prohibited nor sinful. Third, ritual impurity conveys impermanent contagion upon contact with other individuals or objects. Both primary and

---

97. Klawans, *Impurity and Sin*, 22–23.
98. In a recent seminar paper critiquing Klawans's book, Martha Himmelfarb noted that the term "morality" is completely foreign to the Holiness Code. Consequently, she questioned whether it is really morality that is at stake in the sins of idolatry, forbidden sexual relations, and murder. Martha Himmelfarb, "Jonathan Klawans on Purity" (paper presented at the annual meeting of the Association for Jewish Studies, Boston, December 21, 2003).
99. The term "cultic" is misleading because the Israelite cult plays an equally important role in both forms of impurity. The introduction of the term "levitical" is equally problematic for two reasons. First, the discussion of both types of impurity extends beyond the parameters of the book of Leviticus. Second, the issue of impurity is not an exclusive concern of the Levites, but extends to all Israel (Klawans, *Impurity and Sin*, 23).
100. Klawans also points out that these terms present a certain pliability in that they have related adverbs ("ritually" and "morally"), the usage of which aids in the description of defiling substances and sins (ibid., 23).
101. On Klawans's understanding of ritual impurity, see ibid., 23–26.

secondary forms of this impurity are alleviated through purificatory procedures. Thus, even long-lasting impurities are considered impermanent.

Moral impurity, on the other hand, results from immoral acts, including sexual sins (e.g., Lev 18:24–30), idolatry (e.g., Lev 19:31; 20:1–3), and bloodshed (e.g., Num 35:33–34).[102] These sinful actions are often referred to as תועבות, or abominations. Moral defilement pollutes the sinner (Lev 18:24), the land of Israel (Lev 18:25; Ezek 36:17), and God's sanctuary (Lev 20:3; Ezek 5:11). Although this form of impurity is not contagious, it is considered permanent and therefore may not be ameliorated through rites of purification. The resolution of moral impurity may only be attained through repentance and punishment, the latter of which includes the execution of the sinner (כרת) and the expulsion of the people from the land.

At first glance, Klawans's classification of impurity does not appear to differ significantly from Frymer-Kensky's systematization. He does, however, make some significant contributions. In distinguishing between ritual and moral impurity, Klawans draws attention to the terminological differences that arise from the texts themselves. He notes that although the term טמא, "impure," is used in reference to both forms of impurity, the terms תועבה, "abomination," and טנף, "pollute," are used exclusively in connection with moral impurity.[103] This is an important observation, especially in light of the fact that most scholars use the term "pollution" as a synonym for "impurity," without regard for the nuances and subtleties in meaning that occur in the priestly literature.[104]

Also important is Klawans's insistence that moral impurity should not be understood as metaphorical or figurative. He argues that in the biblical context moral impurity is every bit as real as ritual impurity. Both forms of impurity— ritual and moral—are concerned with a physical process or event that has a perceived effect. Moreover, in both cases there are legal and social ramifications, ranging from exclusion from the sacred to exclusion from life itself. Although the sources and modes of transfer of these two types of impurities differ, they may be classified as "two analogous *perceptions of contagion*"[105] and therefore constitute "two purity systems [that] are articulated in two distinct literary constructs."[106]

III. Summary and Conclusion

The current discussion of ritual and moral impurity is indebted to such early-twentieth-century biblical scholars as David Zvi Hoffmann, who recognized two types of defilement, and Adolph Büchler, who placed considerable emphasis on moral impurity. In the mid-1960s, Mary Douglas's work provided the theoretical foundation upon which all subsequent scholarship on ritual purity in the Hebrew

---

102. On Klawans's understanding of moral impurity, see ibid., 26–31.

103. Ibid., 26.

104. Tikva Frymer-Kensky, for example, uses the term "pollution" in the title of her paper ("Pollution, Purification, and Purgation in Biblical Israel") and interchanges the terms "pollution" and "impurity" throughout.

105. Klawans, *Impurity and Sin*, 34.

106. Ibid., 42.

Bible has been based. Since that time, Jacob Neusner has offered a temple-centered perspective on impurity in ancient Israel, and Jacob Milgrom has developed an understanding of the power of sinfulness to defile the sanctuary from afar. Finally, scholars such as Frymer-Kensky, Wright, and Klawans have attempted to establish the relationship between ritual and moral impurity in the Hebrew Bible.

The biblical scholarship on impurity clearly demonstrates that the Torah presents two priestly concepts of defilement: one that originates in P and the other that is a product of H. These two sources were eventually integrated into the Torah and recognized by Jews as part of a unified work. Yet, even in its canonized form, the Torah articulated two recognizable concepts of impurity. The question is: "How did ancient Jews understand these biblical concepts of impurity?" Scholars of the Second Temple period suggest that ancient Jews debated the relationship between the two types of defilement. It is to their work we now turn.

2

Ritual and Moral Purity and Impurity in Second Temple Judaism

The most important studies of ritual and moral impurity in Second Temple Judaisms are Neusner's *The Idea of Purity in Ancient Judaism* (1973) and Klawans's *Impurity and Sin in Ancient Judaism* (2000). Written almost three decades apart, these books take very different approaches to the concept of defilement in the Second Temple period. For Neusner, the issue of impurity, whether ritual or moral, is inextricably connected to the temple. Klawans, by contrast, focuses on the relationship between ritual and moral impurity as such. This chapter will review the scholarship of Neusner and Klawans as it pertains to a variety of texts, including Ezra and Nehemiah, the Apocrypha and Pseudepigrapha, Josephus and Philo.[1]

I. Jacob Neusner

Neusner views purity as an essential element in the interpretation of Israel's religious system from the tenth century B.C.E. to well beyond the Second Temple period.[2] Its ongoing conceptual importance is evident in the fact that the relationships between purity and the temple, priesthood and cult continue beyond the physical destruction of the temple.[3] According to Neusner, some communities compare themselves to the Jerusalem temple; some claim to constitute the temple's surrogate or replacement, while others provide metaphors for social virtues and vices that achieve transcendent meaning simply because they originated with the sacrificial cult.

The various Jewish groups both in Judea and the diaspora used the purity laws as a means to define their relationship with the temple:

> Every important sect had to define its relationship to the Temple, and one predominant question concerned actually keeping or not keeping the purity laws,

---

1. Although Ezra and Nehemiah belong to the biblical canon, they are postexilic, and are therefore best considered in the context of the discussion on Second Temple Judaism.
2. On the importance of ideas associated with purity and impurity in the postbiblical literature, see the discussion in Neusner, *The Idea of Purity in Ancient Judaism* (Leiden: Brill, 1973), 27–31.
3. Ibid., 28.

making them into a metaphor for the ethical life, or otherwise reinterpreting them. The only thing no one could do was ignore them.[4]

The notion that there was an inextricable relationship between a community's interpretation of biblical purity law and its relationship with the temple is essential to Neusner's understanding of purity in the literature of Second Temple Judaism.

Apocrypha and Pseudepigrapha

Neusner treats the disparate writings of the Apocrypha and Pseudepigrapha together; in his view, these documents, with the exception of Jubilees, demonstrate an understanding of purity and impurity that is in accordance with the interpretive framework set forth in the biblical text.[5] In other words, these texts perceive impurity either as cultic (ritual) defilement or as a metaphor for moral and religious behaviour.[6] In his view, the most prominent idea of purity in the Apocryphal and Pseudepigraphic writings pertains to the pollution of the cult by idolatry. Examples of this idea can be found in 1 Esdras, which alludes to the defilement of the temple in the time of King Nebuchadnezzar (1:49), and in 1 Maccabees, which refers to both the pollution of the sanctuary under the rule of Antiochus and its subsequent cleansing and rededication by Judah Maccabee. Similar associations between impurity and the temple can be found in 2 Maccabees, in reference to Menelaus, who "took the holy vessels with his polluted hands" (2 Macc 5:16), and to the pagans, who polluted the temple when they "had intercourse with women within the sacred precincts" (2 Macc 6:4).

In Neusner's view, these texts testify to the close relationship between purity and the temple. He does not clearly assess, however, the ways in which these impurities fit into his classification system. Are they indeed cultic impurities, as Neusner implies, or are they metaphorical impurities? Closer examination of the sources in their original contexts sheds additional light on this issue. For example, 1 Esd 1:49 states:

> Even the leaders of the people and of the priests committed many acts of sacrilege and lawlessness beyond all the unclean deeds of all the nations, and polluted the temple of the Lord in Jerusalem—the temple that God had made holy.[7]

In the context of both 1 Esdras and its source (2 Chr 36:14), this impurity is related to unfaithfulness and sin. In taking the verse out of its original context, Neusner implies that this is a "cultic" impurity.

Neusner's interpretation of the pollution and purification of the temple in 1 Maccabees is equally problematic. Commenting that the source of the impurity is idolatry, Neusner states unequivocally that it is "concrete and this-worldly, not a

---

4. Ibid., 33.

5. For Neusner's discussion on purity in the Apocrypha and Pseudepigrapha, see ibid., 33–38. Neusner excludes Jubilees from this group and examines it in conjunction with the texts from the Dead Sea community.

6. See the discussion on Neusner's understanding of Israelite impurity in chapter 1.

7. Biblical translations are from the NRSV (1989) unless otherwise noted.

metaphor for some 'higher' meaning."[8] Neusner does not clearly elucidate why this particular impurity is concrete, while other occurrences of idolatry are deemed to produce a metaphorical impurity.[9] In his chapter on biblical purity and impurity, Neusner is careful to distinguish between the categories of cultic and metaphoric impurity. Yet in this attempt to relate impurity to the temple and its cult, the distinction between these categories is blurred.

Neusner's main interest, however, is not in the distinctions between cultic (ritual) and metaphoric (moral) impurity in early Judaism but in the relationship between purity and the temple cult. His twofold use of the term "cult" is ambiguous. In his treatment of the Psalms of Solomon, Neusner identifies several sources of what he terms *cultic* impurity, including the pollution of "the holy things of the Lord" (2:3) through moral transgression, and the defilement of "Jerusalem and the things that had been hallowed to the name of God" (8:26). Noting that the "holy things" were polluted by sexual transgression and other sins, Neusner contends that "the focus of impurity remains the cult, despite the sources of uncleanness."[10] His main concern is the relationship between purity and the temple *cult*, and not the relationship between his classifications of *cultic* (ritual) and metaphorical (moral) impurity.[11]

In addition to the pollution of the cult by idolatry Neusner discusses impurity (1) as a metaphor for illicit sexual behaviour, and (2) as a metaphor for other forms of sin or immorality. Sexual defilement is alluded to in Sarah's prayer in the book of Tobit: "I am pure from all uncleanness with man, and I never polluted my name or the name of my father" (3:15). This idea of purity is also found in the *Testaments of the Twelve Patriarchs*. For example, in the *Testament of Levi*, the rape of Dinah is considered defiling (7:4), as are illicit sexual relations (14:6–7). The *Testament of Joseph* refers to adultery as uncleanness (4:6–7).

In the *Testaments*, Neusner argues, the concept of purity extends beyond sexual conduct to include moral behavior in general. The practical effects of this impurity, however, remain linked to the cult. Thus the priest is admonished to take "a wife without blemish or pollution (*T. Levi* 9:10) so as to prevent the pollution of the holy place. Similarly, the priesthood must not be profaned, the sacrifices polluted, nor the holy places laid to waste (*T. Levi* 16:1–5).

Josephus

Neusner's introductory paragraph on purity in the writings of Josephus states:

---

8. Ibid., 34.

9. Ibid., 13–14. Neusner apparently considers the idolatry of 1 Maccabees to be concrete because there was an idol actually placed in the temple, and the object itself was considered contaminating. In the biblical description of idolatry, however, it is the act of idol worship outside the temple that pollutes the temple from afar.

10. Ibid., 35.

11. Neusner devotes more than half of his discussion on the Apocrypha and Pseudepigrapha to pollution of the cult by idolatry. He also identifies this theme in 4 Maccabees, the *Assumption of Moses*, the *Letter of Jeremiah*, and the book of Judith. See ibid., 35–36.

> [Josephus] interprets or explains the purity laws primarily in relationship to the Temple cult. He rarely treats purity in other than a cultic setting. This viewpoint was natural to him, for he was a priest and took for granted that the Mosaic legislation about purity applied primarily to the Temple.[12]

Several passages from Josephus's vast corpus are cited in support of this statement. Josephus alludes to the requirement for purification after a funeral, childbirth, or sexual intercourse as a procedure that protects the temple from impurity (*C. Ap.* 2.198). He also describes the burning of the red heifer and the use of its ashes in the purification rites for corpse contamination (*A.J.* 4.80).

According to Neusner, Josephus stresses three issues in his description of temple purity: the prohibition against foreigners entering the holy place (*B.J.* 5.194), the exclusion of those with gonorrhoea or leprosy (*B.J.* 5.227), and the rules concerning entrance to the temple for women, men, and priests (*B.J.* 5.227; 6.426–27; *C. Ap.* 2.103–4).[13] Of particular importance are the biblical laws concerning lepers, which constitute the basis of his polemic against the Egyptian writer Manetho. Manetho asserts that the Jews were forced to flee Egypt on account of leprosy or other forms of pollution. In his refutation of this claim (*C. Ap.* 1.279–86), Josephus cites the Mosaic laws concerning the exclusion of lepers, as well as those requiring purification and sacrifices upon recovery from the disease.

Josephus refers to purity outside the temple in two different contexts. The first refers to the establishment of the town of Tiberius. Josephus indicates that Herod forced the people to live there,

> For he knew that this settlement was contrary to the law and tradition of the Jews because Tiberias was built on the site of tombs that had been obliterated of which there were many there. And our law declares that such settlers are unclean for seven days. (*A.J.* 18.38)

Neusner contends that the "uncleanness should have been important only if the settlers later planned to visit the Temple, in which case they could purify themselves."[14]

The second context in which Josephus refers to purity outside the temple refers to the Essenes (*B.J.* 2.120–61; *A.J.* 18.18–22). Josephus describes the Essenes' purity practices, including their abstention from the use of oil because they consider it defiling (*B.J.* 2.123), their practice of eating in a state of ritual purity (*B.J.* 2.129–31), and their initiation processes. Candidates for the sect remain outside the fraternity for one year, after which they can "share the purer kind of holy water" (*B.J.* 2.138). Full initiation does not occur, however, until two years later, at which time the candidates swear tremendous oaths before being allowed to touch the common food (*B.J.* 2.139). Josephus claims that the Essenes "send votive offerings to

---

12. Ibid., 38. For Neusner's discussion of purity in Josephus, see *The Idea*, 38–44.

13. According to Josephus, only priests were admitted to the sanctuary, men to the inner court, and women to the women's court. Those who were in a state of impurity, however, were not allowed into the temple precincts at all.

14. Neusner, *The Idea*, 42.

the temple, but perform their sacrifices employing a different ritual of purification" (*A.J.* 18.19). For this reason, they are barred from the inner precincts of the temple and perform their rites by themselves.

According to Neusner, Josephus believes that the purity laws not only govern the temple, but are everywhere taken for granted. This belief is especially apparent in Josephus's characterization of the Zealots, who are portrayed as being impious and indifferent to the purity laws. In the civil war between the Zealots and the high priest Ananus, says Josephus, the Zealots defiled the sanctuary with their blood (*B.J.* 4.202). By contrast, Ananus attempted to protect the purity of the temple by deliberately avoiding the temple portals for fear of introducing crowds of unpurified individuals into the sacred precincts (*B.J.* 4.205). Time and again, Josephus criticizes the Zealots' indifference to the sanctity of the temple and praises their opponents' scrupulousness in preserving the temple's purity.

The importance of the temple in Josephus's writing cannot be denied.[15] But is the connection between purity and temple in Josephus as clearly elucidated as Neusner would have us believe? An examination of Josephus's usage of the word μίασμα (*miasma*, pollution) shows that Josephus's concept of defilement not only extends beyond the temple, but is also influenced by Greco-Roman ideas of purity.

In Josephus's writings there are seventy-five references to pollution, including forty occurrences of the verb μιαίνω, eleven of the noun μίασμα, and twenty-four of the adjective μιαρός. An analysis of these occurrences in their literary contexts reveals that 71 percent of these usages pertain to death and murder, including death pollution, death in the temple, the denial of burial, murder, and the stain of blood on the hands. The remaining 29 percent of the incidences may be classified as follows: three references to illicit sex as a cause of pollution (*A.J.* 2.55; 3.275; 7.168), two references to the rigidity of religious practice of the Essenes (*B.J.* 2.132, 149), nine references to idolatry (*A.J.* 5.42; 8.245; 9.262, 263, 273; 10.81; 12.286; 18.271; *B.J.* 2.289), and eight references attributed to Manetho suggesting that the Egyptians were polluted (*C. Ap.* 1.222, 236; 1.248, 251, 266, 271; 1.294, 296). Even a superficial glimpse at these categories suggests that Josephus's concern with purity was not necessarily associated with the temple.

Josephus's concern with death-pollution in the temple is particularly interesting. Neusner comments on the fact that Josephus does not describe the purification of the temple from corpse contamination after Jews are slaughtered at the altar during the siege by Pompey (*B.J.* 1.148–53). He explains Josephus's silence by

---

15. The organizational structure of *Antiquities* emphasizes the importance of the temple in Josephus's writing. The first ten volumes are concerned with the first temple, while the latter ten volumes record the establishment of the second temple and the events leading to its fall in 70 C.E. According to Steve Mason, who proposes a ring composition as the literary structure of *Antiquities*, the central panel and pivotal point in the narrative occurs in volume 10 and includes the fall of the first temple as well as an assertion of the Judean God's control over human affairs (Steve Mason, "Josephus and His Roman Audience: Reading between the Lines" [paper presented at the international conference "Flavius Josephus in Flavian Rome," Toronto, May 7, 2001]).

suggesting that the technical details of what surely would have been a considerable operation would have slowed down the plot and bored Josephus's audience. This explanation, however, fails to note the influence on Josephus of the Greco-Roman literary tradition, in which such divergences from the narrative are common, especially when they serve the rhetorical purposes of the author.[16]

Another problem with Neusner's analysis of the passage in *B.J.* 1.148–53 is that it overlooks the possibility that Josephus may have been influenced not only by the conventions of Greco-Roman literature but also by Greco-Roman ideas of purity. In ancient Greek literature, as in ancient Jewish literature, entering a temple after contact with a corpse was considered a sacrilege.[17] While the theme of death in the temple is highly prominent in Greek literature,[18] it does not constitute an important idea in either biblical or Second Temple Jewish literature.[19] Yet in Josephus's writings we encounter several instances of death and murder in the Jewish temple. Here Josephus does not rely on an exclusively Jewish concept of purity. Rather, he uses a distinctly Greek concept of *miasma* in order to further his rhetorical agenda. He depicts Pompey and others as committing sacrilege in the temple as a means of denigrating his literary characters in a way that would have been understood by his primary Roman audience.[20] If Josephus fails to mention any subsequent purification of the temple, it is not because he is afraid of boring his audience. Such rites, if they even existed, are simply not of any concern to him or his audience. Here, Josephus's focus is on the act of sacrilege and not on the relationship between temple and purity.

Philo

Neusner's overview of the idea of purity in Philo emphasizes Philo's allegorization of the purity laws.[21] His main interest is in the question "Which laws does

---

16. Per Bilde suggests that Josephus's writing combines elements of both religious Jewish historiographical tradition and Hellenistic literary culture and historiography (*Flavius Josephus between Jerusalem and Rome: His Life, His Works, and Their Importance* [JSPSup 2; Sheffield: JSOT, 1988], 200–206).

17. See for example, Eur. *Iph. taur.* 380–384.

18. See, for example, Plut. *Dem.* 29.5. Here Demosthenes, knowing that he will soon be captured, departs from the sanctuary of Poseidon in order to control the location of his death and ensure that his corpse does not pollute the temple of the deity. In addition to the theme of death in the temple, other Greek ideas concerning purity can be found in Josephus's writings, including the concept of blood on the hands and a concern with the denial of burial.

19. The theme of death in the temple, however, would have appealed to Josephus's secondary Jewish audience, who would have been familiar with the biblical story of Nadab and Abihu, who died in the tabernacle (Lev 10:1–20). It is important to note that in Lev 16:1 a connection is made between these deaths and the laws regarding the purgation of the sanctuary. However, this one incident hardly constitutes a prominent theme in the literature.

20. Another example of Josephus's use of *miasma* in character portrayals may be found in *B.J.* 6.124–28, where the Zealots are vociferously condemned for defiling their own temple with Roman and Jewish corpses.

21. For Neusner's discussion on purity in Philo, see *The Idea*, 44–49.

[Philo] choose, and in terms of what other issues or ideas does he attempt to interpret them?"[22] Neusner suggests that Philo takes into account a wide range of purity laws, but interprets them "in terms entirely divorced from the Scriptural sense."[23] Thus Philo's interpretations often make use of what Neusner terms the second-level metaphor. An example may found in Philo's contrast between purity and wickedness, in which he suggests that wickedness makes purity impure in the same way as it makes truth into falsehood: "Furthermore, they cleanse their bodies with lustrations and purifications, but they neither wish nor practise to wash off from their souls the passions by which life is defiled" (*Cher.* 94–95). According to Neusner, Philo is treating purity as a metaphor for moral cleanness in much the same way as does the biblical text. Purity becomes a second-level metaphor, however, when Philo further allegorizes the concept of moral cleanness as a metaphor for self-control. Without self-control, explains Philo, "A man may submit to sprinklings with holy water and to purifications, befouling his understanding while cleansing his body" (*Det.* 20).

Neusner identifies a second use of allegorization in Philo's interpretation of cultic and priestly purity laws, in which he emphasizes the spiritual or philosophical virtue symbolized by purity. The requirement that priests wash their hands and feet symbolizes the blameless life (*De vita Mosis* 2.138). Those who offer sacrifices must be pure in body and soul. According to Philo, the body is cleansed through sprinklings and ablutions, whereas the soul is purified through the contemplation of the perfection of the sacrificial victim. For this reason, the "careful scrutiny of the animal is a symbol representing in a figure the reformation of your own conduct" (*Spec.* 1.259–60). This emphasis on the cleanliness of body and soul is found in other contexts as well. For example, Philo states:

> Those who mean to resort to the Temple must needs have their bodies made clean and bright, and before their bodies, their souls.... The mind is cleansed by wisdom, and the truths of wisdom's teaching which guide its steps to the contemplation of the universe.... (*Spec.* 1.269–70)

Once again, Philo emphasizes the importance of cleanness in his appeal to lead a blameless life and maintain proper attitudes.

For Neusner, Philo's allegorization of the purity rules sometimes goes beyond his demand for the purification of body and soul. This is especially apparent in his varied interpretations of the laws pertaining to corpse contamination, menstruation, and leprosy. For example, Philo maintains that the vessels and furniture in the house of a corpse are unclean, suggesting that when the soul of a man departs, everything he leaves behind is in a state of defilement (*Spec.* 3.205). In considering the impurity of the menstrual woman, Philo suggests that she is deemed unclean so that a man will "remember the lesson that the generative seeds should not be wasted fruitlessly for the sake of a gross and untimely pleasure" (*Spec.* 3.32). Finally, he characterizes leprosy as a polymorphous disease that assumes many

---

22. Ibid., 45.
23. Ibid., 45–46.

forms. It symbolizes a "lack of firmness of judgment and an unstable, agitated life" (*Somn.* 1.202).

While he offers a glimpse of the purity laws that were most important to Philo, Neusner does not relate the Philonic material very closely to the main themes of his overall study. Thus he does not demonstrate how Philo's understanding of purity is linked to his interpretation of the temple, nor does he discuss the relationship between cultic and metaphorical impurity.

The Pharisees, Non-Priestly Purity, and the Temple

In *The Idea of Purity in Ancient Judaism*, as well as in other scholarly writings, Neusner contends that the laws pertaining to ritual purity were especially important to the Pharisees.[24] Accordingly, the Pharisaic sectarians formed *havurot*, or "fellowship groups," in which they ate their meals in a state of ritual purity, as if they themselves were temple priests.[25] They were also careful about giving the required tithes and offerings that were due to the priesthood.[26] Commenting on the purity practices of the Pharisees, Neusner states:

> The Pharisees, like the Dead Sea commune, believed that one must keep the purity laws outside of the Temple. Other Jews, following the plain sense of Leviticus, supposed that purity laws were to be kept only in the Temple. The priests also had to eat their Temple food in a state of purity, but lay people did not. To be sure, everyone who went to the Temple had to be pure, but outside of the Temple . . . it was not required that noncultic activities be conducted in a state of Levitical cleanness.[27]

---

24. See, for example, Neusner, *The Idea*, 64–71; Jacob Neusner, *From Politics to Piety: The Emergence of Pharisaic Judaism* (Englewood Cliffs, NJ: Prentice-Hall, 1973), 73–80, 83–85, 119–20; idem, *The Rabbinic Traditions about the Pharisees before 70* (3 vols.; Leiden: Brill, 1971), 3:286–304.

25. Neusner follows Gedalyahu Alon, who asserts that the Pharisees of the first century ate their ordinary food in a state of levitical purity. See Alon, "The Bounds of the Laws of Levitical Cleanness," in *Jews, Judaism, and the Classical World: Studies in Jewish History in the Times of the Second Temple and Talmud* (Jerusalem: Magnes Press, 1977), 190–234. The question of whether or not the Pharisees ate ordinary food in purity has become the subject of scholarly debate. E. P. Sanders, for example, argues that the Pharisees did not live like temple priests, nor did they handle all food in purity. See Sanders, "Did the Pharisees Eat Ordinary Food in Purity?" in *Jewish Law from Jesus to the Mishnah: Five Studies* (London: SCM Press, 1990), 248–50. Hannah Harrington contends that the Pharisees did not think of themselves as priests, nor did they adopt the total regimen required for a priestly way of life. They did think, however, that it was important to eat like priests and thus considered that their own food was holy to some degree. See Hannah K. Harrington, "Did the Pharisees Eat Ordinary Food in a State of Ritual Purity?" *JSJ* 26 (1995): 42–54, esp. 53–54.

26. Neusner's conception of the Pharisees is largely derived from two sources: the Gospels' portrayal of the Pharisees and the descriptions of the *havurah* found in the law codes of later rabbinic Judaism. See, for example, Neusner, *The Idea*, 65; idem, *From Politics*, 67–96, esp. 78–80, 87–90.

27. Neusner, *The Idea*, 65.

Once again, Neusner emphasizes the relationship between purity and temple. First he assumes that the ritual purity laws apply only to the priests and the temple; then he posits that the adoption of purity law outside the temple is an expression of the desire to live like a priest. In eating secular food in a state of purity, the Pharisees appropriated the status of priest for themselves and all Jews equally. The biblical commandment "You shall be a kingdom of priests and a holy people" was taken literally, as the table of every Jew attained the status of the altar of God.[28]

Neusner emphasizes that the table-fellowship of the Pharisees was not a special ritual but an ordinary daily routine. Like their neighbors, Pharisees ate most of their meals at home. The elements of Pharisaic law-observance that distinguished these meals from the ordinary were largely external to the meal itself. How and what one ate was circumscribed by the agricultural laws and purity rules. The field was the focal point for the observance of agricultural laws, whereas the kitchen was the locus for observance of the purity rules concerned with food preparation. Moreover, the act of washing before a meal was a purification rite performed prior to sitting at the table.[29]

Neusner's understanding of Pharisaic table fellowship has been challenged by E. P. Sanders.[30] Sanders argues that while the Pharisees were more meticulous than others in defining ritual impurity, they did not live like priests, nor did they keep their tables as pure as the altar.[31] Particularly pertinent to our discussion is Sanders' critique of Neusner's temple-oriented view of purity, which he claims is flawed by its inherent contradiction.[32] Sanders observes that in *The Idea of Purity in Ancient Judaism*, Neusner includes a detailed description of the biblical laws concerning defilement, clearly pointing out that there are non-priestly and non-temple purity laws. Yet, several pages later, Neusner asserts that in the Second Temple period the purity laws applied only to the priests and the temple.[33] It is only on the basis of this second assertion that he can make the claim that the Pharisees were expressing their desire to live like priests, when they accepted *any* of the purity laws.

The association of purity and temple is central to Neusner's conception of purity in early Judaism, as it relates to the Pharisees as well as to other groups. He views the language of purity as important in pre-70 C.E. Palestine "both as a

---

28. Ibid., 65–66.
29. Ibid., 66–67.
30. E. P. Sanders, "Did the Pharisees Eat Ordinary Food in Purity?" 131–254.
31. Ibid., 249.
32. Here I address one small issue in the long-standing debate between Neusner and Sanders, with respect to the Pharisees. The magnitude of this scholarly debate is evident from the number of articles and reviews that have been written on both sides. See, for example, Sanders, *Jewish Law from Jesus to the Mishnah*; Jacob Neusner, *Judaic Law from Jesus to the Mishnah: A Systematic Reply to Professor E. P. Sanders* (Atlanta: Scholars Press, 1993).
33. Sanders, "Did the Pharisees Eat Ordinary Food in Purity?" 176. Sanders states unequivocally: "[I]t is not the case, however, that the purity laws of the Bible affect *only* the temple and the priesthood. Some scholars . . . mistakenly think that 'settled *halakah*' of purity had to do only with these, but that is not so even in biblical law" (ibid., 147).

polemical theme for sectarian discourse, and as a means of defining a sectarian community's relationship to the Jerusalem Temple."[34] This "minimalist" view is contested by John C. Poirier, who argues that "in Second Temple times, there was no necessary connection between purity and the temple."[35] Poirier offers convincing and considerable evidence for a much wider application of the purity *halakhah* in early Judaism, finding evidence of Jews purifying themselves immediately after contact with the dead (Tob 2:9; *Spec.* 3.206) and before prayer (Jdt 12:6–10; *Sib. Or.* 3:591–93; 4:162–66; *Let. Aris.* 305–6).[36] This broad application of purity practices is supported by the archaeological evidence of *mikvaot* (ritual baths) or wash basins in proximity to synagogues and tombs of the period.[37] Stone jars, which prevented the spread of ritual impurity at mealtime, have been found in almost every known Jewish settlement in Palestine.[38] Poirier concludes: "The notion that the ritual purity laws of Second Temple Judaism existed solely for the sake of the temple is a scholarly construct with little basis in reality."

II. Jonathan Klawans

In his book *Impurity and Sin in Ancient Judaism*, Klawans investigates how various groups of ancient Jews interpreted the relationship between ritual and moral impurity. Did Jewish communities in the Second Temple period maintain the distinction between the two forms of impurity, or were these concepts of defilement restructured, conflated, or transformed in other ways?

Klawans begins his investigation of impurity in ancient Judaism with a discussion of passages from Ezra and Nehemiah, Jubilees, the Temple Scroll, the Damascus Document, and other texts.[39] This group of texts shows that "the biblical

---

34. Neusner, *The Idea*, 108.
35. John C. Poirier, "Purity beyond the Temple in the Second Temple Era," *JBL* 122 (2003): 247–65. Commenting specifically on Neusner, Poirier indicates that "Neusner sometimes asserts the temple orientation of the biblical purity laws, [but] he often properly qualifies this rubric (to the point of making it invalid)" (ibid., 254 n. 20).
36. Ibid., 256. A quick perusal of the indices at the end of *The Idea of Purity in Ancient Judaism* indicates that Neusner cites the same passages from Philo, Judith, and the *Letter of Aristeas*. Furthermore, he indicates in his introduction that "the Sibylline Oracles . . . testify to the requirement of washing hands before prayer" (*The Idea*, 3).
37. Poirier, "Purity beyond the Temple," 256–57.
38. Ibid., 257–58. According to rabbinic *halakhah* stone vessels can not be defiled, presumably because they are made from unworked material (*m. Ohal.* 5:5). Here, Poirier is relying on the scholarship of Eyal Regev, who suggests that "the spreading of the use of stone vessels from the time of Herod to the Bar Kokhba revolt indicates that in this period . . . non-priestly purity was widespread all across the Land of Israel" (Eyal Regev, "Pure Individualism: The Idea of Non-Priestly Purity in Ancient Judaism," *JSJ* 31 [2000]: 183; cf. idem, "Non-Priestly Purity and Its Religious Aspects according to Historical Sources and Archaeological Findings," in *Purity and Holiness: The Heritage of Leviticus* [ed. M. J. H. M. Poorthuis and J. Schwartz; Leiden: Brill, 2000], 233).
39. Klawans, "Moral Impurity in the Second Temple Period," in *Impurity and Sin*, 43–60. Also included in this chapter are discussions on Jubilees, the Temple Scroll, and the Damas-

idea of moral defilement persists into the Second Temple period."[40] In Klawans's view, scholars have not recognized adequately the conception of sin as a defiling force. For this reason, commentators often misconstrue references to moral impurity as being concerned with ritual impurity. In order to shed light on this problem, Klawans identifies passages from the literature that have routinely been associated with ritual impurity and demonstrates how they are best understood as representations of moral impurity. In the remainder of our review of ritual and moral impurity in ancient Judaism, we will examine Klawans's analysis of these texts concerning moral defilement. In addition, we will also consider Klawans's examination of impurity and sin in Philo, which appears in the section of his book pertaining to ritual and moral impurity in Ancient Jewish literature.

Ezra and Nehemiah and the Expulsion of the Foreign Wives

Klawans's discussion of Ezra and Nehemiah focuses on the issue of the Jews taking foreign wives.[41] Both leaders were opposed to exogamy and urged the dissolution of all marriages between Jews and Gentiles. The book of Ezra uses the language of defilement in reference to the problem (Ezra 6:21; 9:1, 11-14), and the book of Nehemiah describes the proposed solution of divorce as a purification (Neh 13:30). This latter point has led many scholars to conclude that the foreign wives were ritually impure, presumably because of their status as Gentiles. Klawans argues, however, that Ezra-Nehemiah is not concerned with ritual impurity. He notes that the two books address only the status of foreign women and not the impurity of *all* Gentiles. More to the point, he contends that the passages are not echoing the priestly traditions of ritual impurity found in P but rather the Holiness Code's traditions related to moral impurity.[42]

The book of Ezra's concern with moral impurity is evident in its use of the word תועבות to describe the abhorrent practices of the peoples of the land, whose daughters were marrying the priests, Levites, and people of Israel (Ezra 9:1-3). In Leviticus, the term תועבות is used exclusively in connection with moral impurity, and not ritual impurity.[43] Ezra's concern is as follows:

> Now, what can we say in the face of this, O our God, for we have forsaken Your commandments, which You gave us through Your servants the prophets when You said, "The land that you are about to possess is a land unclean [ארץ נדה היא] through the uncleanness of the peoples of the land through their abhorrent practices [בנדת עמי הארצות בתועבתיהם] with which they, in their impurity [בטמאתם], have filled it from one end to the other. Now then, do not give your daughters in

---

cus Document. These sections will not be reviewed at this point but will be included in the review of the literature from Qumran in chapter 3.

40. Klawans, *Impurity and Sin*, 43.

41. For Klawans's discussion on moral impurity in Ezra and Nehemiah, see ibid., 43-46.

42. Ibid., 44. According to Klawans, "no biblical text considers Gentiles to be ritually impure" (Jonathan Klawans, "Notions of Gentile Impurity in Ancient Judaism," *AJSR* 20 [1995]: 291).

43. Klawans, *Impurity and Sin*, 26.

marriage to their sons or let their daughters marry your sons; do nothing for their well-being or advantage, then you will be strong and enjoy the bounty of the land and bequeath it to your children forever." (Ezra 9:10–12)

The echoes of Lev 18 are clear: "The abominable acts (תועבות) of the women in question defile the land of Israel and threaten the chances that the people of Israel have of dwelling in their land for perpetuity (9:1, 12)."[44]

Even as Ezra echoes Lev 18, it also makes some modifications to the priestly text. An example is Ezra's use of the term נדה to articulate moral defilement (9:1). This term is commonly used in the Hebrew Bible to refer to menstruation, a ritual impurity that does not defile the land. Only on one occasion is the term used in the Holiness Code to articulate the moral defilement of sin (Lev 20:21). Klawans suggests that the passage in Ezra 9, like that of Lev 20:21, creates a simile between the moral impurity of the people and the ritual impurity of a menstrual woman. This usage is quite common in some of the Jewish literature from the Second Temple period, such that the term נדה (impure) becomes a synonym for תועבות (abominations). Thus the land defiled by abomination or sin is described as an ארץ נדה (impure land), as in Ezra 9:11.[45]

Ezra 9's most significant divergence from the Holiness Code is its association of moral impurity with intermarriage (9:11). While a small number of pentateuchal traditions ban marriages with certain foreigners, "there is no general prohibition of intermarriage articulated in the Torah."[46] Such a prohibition is absent even in the Holiness Code. In prohibiting intermarriage, Ezra 9 uses the language of the Holiness Code to express the ideology of Deut 7:1–4, which prohibits Israelites from marrying among the seven Canaanite nations. As in Deuteronomy, this issue is not one of ritual impurity but rather a concern that these nations are idolatrous and will lead the Israelites astray. The prohibition against intermarriage is also found in Neh 13:1, which builds on the ideology of Deuteronomy in a similar fashion (Deut 23:2–9).[47] Both Ezra and Nehemiah express the fear that intermarriage will lead to sin, as it did for Solomon (Neh 13:26).[48]

The idea of the Gentiles engaging in morally defiling behavior is not new to Ezra-Nehemiah. What is new, according to Klawans, is the idea that moral impurity is inherent to the Gentiles: the foreign women are unsuitable because they are sinful by their very nature.[49] For this reason, neither Ezra nor Nehemiah entertains

---

44. Ibid., 44.

45. Klawans comments that the use of the term נדה to describe the land that has been defiled through sin is particularly appropriate, since the word connotes an idea of separation. If Israel should defile the land with her moral sins, she will be exiled—that is, separated from the land (ibid., 45).

46. Ibid., 45. Klawans cites the biblical prohibitions against marrying from among the seven Canaanite nations (Deut 7:1–4), as well as the further prohibitions against the *mamzer*, the Ammonite, and the Moabite (Deut 23:2–9). See ibid, n. 9.

47. Ibid., n. 11.

48. In the deuteronomic traditions, Solomon was led astray by his foreign wife (1 Kgs 11:1–2). Ibid., 45.

49. Klawans correctly points out that this attitude toward Gentiles contradicts that of the

the possibility of conversion, but insists on expulsion as the only means by which to thwart their corrupt influence. Klawans views the necessity of expulsion as an extension of the notion of moral impurity.[50]

Sin and the Sanctuary in Other Texts

Klawans notes that while numerous biblical passages refer to idolatry as defiling the sanctuary (e.g., Lev 20:1–3), none suggests the same with regard to sexual sins.[51] Yet in the literature of the Second Temple period the idea that sexual sin defiles the sanctuary is quite common. By way of example, Klawans examines texts from *1 Enoch*, the *Testaments of the Twelve Patriarchs*, and the *Psalms of Solomon*.

The book of *1 Enoch* is based partly on Gen 6:1–4, in which the watchers or divine angels have illicit sexual relationships with the daughters of humankind who consequently give birth to giants (*1 En*. 7:1–2). In *1 Enoch*, the offspring of these relationships commit acts of evil, creating earthly chaos (7:2–6), and the angels are punished for wrongly initiating sexual relations with the women of the earth (chs. 9–10). Two aspects of this story are pertinent to the theme of purity. First, the sexual relations with human women defiles the watchers: "they went in unto the daughter of the people on earth; and they lay together with them—with those women—and defiled themselves, and revealed to them every (kind of) sin" (9:8; cf. 10:11; 12:4; 15:3). Significantly, this defilement does not bring about the impermanent state of contagion associated with ritual impurity but, rather, a state of permanent degradation (14:4–5). Second, the watchers are banished or exiled from heaven on account of their sexual defilement (14:5).

For Klawans, *1 Enoch* articulates an idea of moral impurity in which sexually defiling behavior leads to permanent exile. At the same time, however, its concept of moral defilement does not entirely conform to the biblical idea of moral impurity. In contrast to the Holiness Code, *1 Enoch* does not make any explicit reference

---

Holiness Code, which extends to the Gentiles of the land certain prohibitions that prevent moral impurity (e.g., Lev 18:26; Num 35:15). See ibid., 45.

50. Klawans states: "If ritual impurity were the concern, we would expect to see some possibility of ritual purification, but that is not the case. The only 'hope' (Ezra 10:2) for Israel, as far as the books of Ezra and Nehemiah are concerned, is the expulsion of the foreign wives" (ibid., 46). In her book *Gentile Impurities and Jewish Identities*, Christine Hayes supports Klawans's basic thesis that the foreign women in Ezra and Nehemiah were not considered ritually impure. She does question his claim that the use of purity terminology in Ezra-Nehemiah is an extension of the concept of moral impurity found in the Holiness Code. Noting that Klawans himself observes significant differences in the concepts of purity found in the two sources, she suggests that "he does not fully appreciate the implication of his own observation, namely, that this impurity is sufficiently different as to warrant a new designation." Building on the scholarship of Klawans, Hayes suggests that Ezra and Nehemiah were concerned not only for the foreign women's threat to the moral purity of the Israelites, but to the *genealogical* purity of Israel. See Christine E. Hayes, *Gentile Impurities and Jewish Identities: Intermarriage and Conversion from the Bible to the Talmud* (New York: Oxford University Press, 2002), 6–7.

51. For Klawans's discussion on impurity relating to other texts, see *Impurity and Sin*, 56–60.

to the defilement of the land. There is, however, God's command to "give life to the earth which the angels have corrupted" (*1 En.* 10:7), which implies that the sin of the watchers had an adverse effect on the land. Further, in *1 Enoch* the defiled sinners are banished from heaven and not the land. The angels' banishment from heaven, however, may be seen as analogous to the threat of human exile from the land in the Holiness Code. Finally, *1 Enoch* lacks any reference to the defilement of the sanctuary, not surprising given that the events it describes are deemed to have occurred long before the building of the temple.

Testaments of the Twelve Patriarchs is a second text in which sexual sin causes the defilement of the sanctuary.[52] In *T. Levi,* the use of purity language in relation to sin articulates an idea that moral impurity caused by sexual misdeeds leads to exile:

> You will rob the Lord's offerings; from the portions allotted to him you will steal; and before sacrificing to the Lord you will take for yourself the choicest pieces and share them like common food with whores.... You will pollute married women and defile the virgins of Jerusalem, and you will be united with prostitutes and adulteresses. You will take Gentile women as wives and purify them with a form of purification contrary to the law; and your unions will be like Sodom and Gomorrah in ungodliness.... And so the temple, which the Lord will choose, will be laid waste because of your uncleanness, and you will be carried off as captives by all the Gentiles. (14:5–15:1)

Moral impurity emerges clearly in other passages of the *Testaments*. For example, *T. Levi* 9:9 states: "Be on guard against the spirit of promiscuity, for it is constantly active and through your descendants it is about to defile the sanctuary." This text, like the Holiness Code, states that impurity causes pollution of the sanctuary and results in the exile of the people. Klawans, however, views an ambiguity in this *Testament* with respect to one crucial point: Do the sins defile the sanctuary directly, or do the sins defile in some other way, resulting in divine punishment that includes the desolation of the sanctuary by Israel's enemies? Although he cannot resolve this ambiguity, Klawans maintains that "the Testaments are, on the whole, aware of and concerned with the morally defiling force of sexual sins." In his view *T. Levi* is the clearest of all the *Testaments* in its articulation of the idea that sexual sins lead to the defilement of the sanctuary.[53]

---

52. Klawans indicates that the date of the *Testaments of the Twelve Patriarchs* is a subject of scholarly debate and that there is some question as to whether the texts are Jewish or Christian in origin. Having acknowledged these difficulties, he proceeds to analyze the passages that are concerned with purity. According to Klawans, the use of purity language can be found for example in *T. Reu.* 1:6; 4:8; 6:1; *T. Sim.* 2:13; 5:3–5; *T. Jud.* 14:3–5; *T. Iss.* 4:4; *T. Ash.* 4:3–5; 7:1–2; *T. Jos.* 4:6; *T. Benj.* 6:7; 8:2–3. Klawans indicates that although these passages all use the terminology of defilement in the context of sin, most do not go beyond this usage to articulate an idea of moral impurity (ibid., 57, and esp. n. 99).

53. Klawans quotes *T. Ash.* 7:1–2, which offers a clear example of defiling sin leading to the destruction of the sanctuary and exile brought about by Israel's enemies. Here there is no sense of an accumulation of sin leading to defilement of the sanctuary. This example is

Evidence that sexual sin defiles the sanctuary is also found in the *Psalms of Solomon*:

> Their sins were in secret, and even I did not know.
> Their lawless actions surpassed the gentiles before them;
> they completely profaned (ἐβεβήλωσαν) the sanctuary of the Lord. (1:7–8)

The *Psalms of Solomon* does not exclusively discuss sexual sin in this passage. According to Klawans, however, the phrase "gentiles before them" alludes to Lev 18:27, which states that the Canaanites were expelled from the land because of their sexual sins.[54] Klawans suggests that "secret" sins bring to mind sexual misdeeds, as in *Pss. Sol.* 4:5 and 8:9, both of which refer to sexual sins committed in secret. On the basis of these passages, Klawans suggests that the idea that sexual sin defiles the sanctuary may have been commonplace by the first century B.C.E.

Impurity and Sin in Philo's Thought

Klawans emphasizes the clarity with which Philo articulates the relationship between ritual and moral impurity.[55] He quotes:

> We have described to the best of our ability the regulations for sacrifices and will next proceed to speak of those who offer them. The Law would have such a person pure in body and soul, the soul purged of its passions and distempers and infirmities and every viciousness of word and deed, the body of the things which commonly defile it. For each it devised the purifications which befitted it. For the soul it used the animals which the worshiper is providing for sacrifice, for the body sprinklings and ablutions of which we will speak a little later. (*Spec.* 1.256–61)

Klawans suggests that Philo posits an analogical or allegorical relationship between ritual and moral impurity. Accordingly, the naturally occurring ritual impurity affects the body and thereby teaches individuals to direct their attention to the moral impurity caused by sin that afflicts their soul. For Philo, as in the Pentateuch, resolution of ritual impurity occurs through ritual purification, whereas the amelioration of moral impurity requires atonement and sacrifice. The difference here is that whereas the biblical concept of moral impurity specifies murder, idolatry, and sexual misconduct, Philo refers more generally to the defilement of the soul resulting from various forms of sin. Moreover, the Hebrew Bible emphasizes that moral sin defiles the land. In contrast, Philo is concerned with the effect of moral defilement on individuals and their souls.[56]

---

informative in that it offers an alternative way of interpreting the passage from the *Testament of Levi*, but it does not help to resolve the ambiguity (see ibid., 58).

54. Ibid., 59, and n. 107. Here Klawans also cites Büchler, who suggests a connection between the reference to the earth abhorring the sinners in *Pss. Sol.* 2:9 to the idea of the land spewing out the Canaanites in Lev 18:28 (Büchler, *Studies*, 274).

55. For Klawans's discussion on impurity and sin in Philo, see "Impurity and Sin," 64–66.

56. Ibid., 64–65. Klawans indicates, however, that Philo is aware of the notion that sin defiles the land (*Praem.* 68). See n. 8.

Philo diverges from the biblical text when he posits an explicit analogy between ritual and moral impurity, for the Hebrew Bible makes no correlation between the two forms of defilement. Just as the soul is more important than the body, so too is the purification of the soul more important than the purification of the body (*Mut.* 240; *Spec.* 1.269; 3.209). It is therefore the purification of the soul that is the prerequisite for immortality (*Her.* 276).

In Philo, as in the Hebrew Bible, ritual impurity is natural, unavoidable, and not at all related to sin (*Spec.* 1.117–19). To be sure, Philo's explanations of the ritual impurities sometimes involve moral lessons. Yet he never casts blame on the ritually impure (*Spec.* 1.118; 3.205–8), nor does he suggest that the ritually pure possess any inherent merit (*Det.* 20). According to Philo, sinners should be excluded from the sanctuary, not because their bodies are ritually impure, but because their souls are defiled, rendering them unworthy of approaching the sacred.

III. Summary and Conclusion

Jacob Neusner and Jonathan Klawans differ considerably in their understanding of the concept of purity in early Judaism. For Neusner, purity is inextricably linked to the temple in Jerusalem. As such, each community's relationship to the temple is essentially defined by its interpretation of the biblical purity laws. Klawans is also interested in how the various communities of ancient Jews interpreted the biblical legislation concerning purity. Yet he does not posit a necessary association between purity and temple. Instead, he traces the development of the biblical concepts of ritual and moral impurity in the Second Temple period. Klawans offers convincing evidence that ancient Jews were concerned with both ritual impurity and with the defiling force of sin. Moreover, he identifies an innovation in early Judaism's understanding of moral impurity in the idea that sexual sin leads to the defilement of the sanctuary.

3

RITUAL AND MORAL IMPURITY IN THE DEAD SEA SCROLLS

At the time that Neusner surveyed the purity texts from Qumran in his book *The Idea of Purity in Ancient Judaism*, Qumran scholarship was in its formative stage and most of the Dead Sea Scrolls were as yet unpublished. Neusner's discussion was among the first of its kind and influenced many subsequent scholars, such as Michael Newton and Florentino García Martínez. A noticeable shift in scholarship coincides with the publication of Hannah Harrington's book *The Impurity Systems of Qumran and the Rabbis*, as she seriously challenges the temple-centered perspective of Neusner and his followers. Her careful reading of the texts concerning ritual purity at Qumran offers an important contribution to the field. Harrington's subsequent paper, "The Nature of Impurity at Qumran,"[1] focuses on the relationship between sin and ritual purity at Qumran, arguing against Neusner and García Martínez. Most recently, the discussion of purity and impurity at Qumran has been shaped by the work of Jonathan Klawans and Martha Himmelfarb, neither of whom advocates a temple-centered view of purity at Qumran. While they agree on this point, they differ in their perspectives regarding the relationship between purity and sin at Qumran. Whereas Klawans argues that the independent concepts of ritual and moral impurity that are found in the Hebrew Bible become fully intertwined at Qumran, Himmelfarb maintains that there is no such conflation of these categories within the *yahad*. Three decades after Neusner, the full corpus of texts is now available. Texts pertinent to the study of purity include sectarian texts, such as the Rule of the Community (1QS), Habakkuk Pesher (1QpHab), 4Q *Miqṣat Ma'aseh ha-Torah* (4QMMT), and 4Q Ritual of Purification (4Q512) as well as the quasi-sectarian literature of *Jubilees*, the Temple Scroll (11QT), and the Damascus Document (CD). Nevertheless, the issue remains open for debate.

I. JACOB NEUSNER

The Yahad

Neusner's treatment of the ideas of purity at Qumran is grounded in his view that the community was founded by temple priests who viewed the Jerusalem temple as hopelessly defiled and its services as rejected and abandoned by God.

---

1. Hannah K. Harrington, "The Nature of Impurity at Qumran," in *The Dead Sea Scrolls: Fifty Years after Their Discovery, 1947–1997* (ed. L. H. Schiffman, E. Tov, and J. C. VanderKam; Jerusalem: Israel Exploration Society, 2000), 610–16.

As God's new dwelling place, the community constituted a new temple and their study and fulfillment of the laws a form of temple worship.[2]

Neusner surveys excerpts from the Damascus Document (CD), the Community Rule (1QS), and the Hodayot (1QH) to support his view that purity was central for the *yahad*.[3] The Damascus Document, for example, refers to purification with water (CD X, 12f) and is concerned with the purity of those offering sacrifices to God (CD XI, 19-21) and entering the house of meeting (בית השתחות) in order to pray (CD XI, 22).[4] Concern with impurity is also evident in the admonition against having sexual intercourse in Jerusalem (עיר המקדש), thereby conveying uncleanliness to the temple (CD XII, 1-2). According to the text, one must distinguish between the clean and unclean, as well as the holy and profane (CD XII, 19-20).

According to the Community Rule, purity is central to the process of initiation into the *yahad*. The individual who remains outside the community "shall not be reckoned among the perfect; he shall neither be purified by atonement, nor cleansed by purifying waters, nor sanctified by seas and rivers, nor washed clean with ablution" (1QS III, 3-6). In contrast, one who is initiated into the *yahad* "shall be cleansed from sins by the spirit of holiness.... And when his flesh is sprinkled with purifying water and sanctified by cleansing water, it shall be made clean by the humble submission of his soul to all the precepts of God" (1QS III, 8-9). The initiate is not allowed to touch the pure meal of the congregation until he has lived in the community for a full year and been examined with respect to his spirit and his deeds (1QS VI, 16). Transgressors of the law are prohibited from the pure meal of the congregation for various durations (1QS VI, 24-VII, 21).

The Hodayot include theological reflections on purity. God is said to "purify and cleanse them of their sin, for all their deeds are in thy truth" (1QH XIV [VI], 8-9). The strong link between purity and righteousness is also found in 1QH XVI, 10-11, which states: "I know thou hast marked the spirit of the just, and therefore I have chosen to keep my hands clean in accordance with [thy] will; the soul of Thy servant [has loathed] every work of inquiry." Conversely, impurity is associated with sin, and "wallowing in uncleanness" represents turning aside from God's truth—that is, the teachings of the *yahad*.

Neusner identifies two major innovations in the *yahad*'s ideas concerning pu-

---

2. Neusner follows Gärtner in his assertion that the community viewed itself as a temple (Bertil Gärtner, *The Temple and the Community in Qumran and the New Testament* [SNTSMS 1; Cambridge: Cambridge University Press, 1965], 1-15).

3. The passages from the Qumran documents are quoted directly from Neusner. For CD, Neusner uses Chaim Rabin, ed., *The Zadokite Documents* (Oxford: Clarendon Press, 1958); for other passages, Géza Vermès, ed., *The Dead Sea Scrolls in English* (Harmondsworth, England: Penguin, 1970), and André Dupont-Sommer, *The Essene Writings from Qumran* (trans. G. Vermés; Cleveland: Meridian, 1957). For Neusner's discussion on purity within the *yahad*, see *The Idea*, 50-54.

4. Neusner refers to בית השתחות as a local place of gathering for prayer. It is not clear whether this term refers to a house of meeting or the temple in Jerusalem.

rity. The first innovation is the requirement of purity outside the temple and for purposes other than the conduct of the sacrificial cult. Neusner remarks that

> the *yahad*'s obsessive concern for purity is matched by its claim to have a monopoly on it. Only the members are pure and control the means of purification, e.g. 1QS III, 4-6. In that sense alone do we find the purity-laws used as part of a much larger metaphor, comparing the Temple to the community; but within that metaphor, purity and impurity are understood in an entirely literal way.[5]

The notion of purity is therefore tied to the self-image of the community as a temple.[6]

The second innovation occurs in the community's understanding of the relationship between impurity and sin. According to Neusner, "the *yahad*'s laws treat committing a sin not as a metaphor for becoming unclean, but as an actual source of uncleanness."[7] By prohibiting transgressors from touching a pure meal, the community effectively excludes them from the purity of the sect. The uncleanness caused by sin is not merely a metaphor. Rather, the individual is actually rendered unclean by sin.

This point collapses the distinction between moral and ritual impurity, that is, the impurity caused by sin and that caused by contact with a corpse or a menstrual woman. Both types of impurity require separation and a rite of purification. In Neusner's view, the process that resulted in the conflation of these two categories was begun when the priests and prophets used purity as a metaphor for righteousness. Eventually, the biblical image of the sinner as being impure was transformed into a reality in which the one who sins actually becomes impure and requires purification. At Qumran, cultic and moral impurity are identical in both nature and consequence.

Jubilees

Another text relevant to the question of purity at Qumran is the book of *Jubilees*, multiple copies of which were discovered in the Qumran library.[8] For Neusner, Jubilee's interpretation of impurity is "standard"; in its application of

---

5. Neusner, *The Idea*, 53-54.

6. It is important to recognize the circularity in Neusner's argumentation, which assumes at the outset that the *yahad* viewed itself as a temple. First, Neusner demonstrates that purity was an important issue within this so-called temple. Then he goes on to suggest that the purity laws formed a basis for the larger metaphor of community as temple. Nowhere in this discussion does Neusner offer any comprehensive evidence to support the theory that the *yahad* did indeed regard itself as a temple. Rather, he relies entirely on the scholarly conclusions of Gärtner (*The Temple*, 1-15). While Gärtner's view that the *yahad* regarded itself as a temple has been cited and accepted by many scholars, I am not convinced that there is ample evidence to support this view. In 1QS, for example, there is significant emphasis on the idea of purity (as demonstrated by Neusner), but there is never any mention of either the Jerusalem temple or the community as temple.

7. Neusner, *The Idea*, 54.

8. For Neusner's discussion on the book of *Jubilees*, see ibid., 55-58.

defilement to such matters as sex, idolatry, food, and the cult, *Jubilees* does not significantly develop the biblical concept of impurity. Impurity language is associated with sexual sin and idolatry. Thus Noah commands his sons to "guard their souls from fornication and uncleanness and all iniquity, for owing to these three things the flood came upon the earth" (7:20–21). Similarly, Abraham admonishes his sons to refrain from "fornication and uncleanness" (20:3, 6), and to stay away from "idols and their uncleannesses" (20:7). Murder is a particularly potent source of "uncleanness": "for the earth will not be clean from the blood which has been shed upon it until it is purified" by the blood of the murderer (7:33).

Impurity is also imputed to the Gentiles. Thus Isaac warns Jacob, "Separate thyself from the nations, and eat not with them, and do not according to their works, and become not their associate, for their works are unclean, and all their ways are a pollution and an abomination and an uncleanness" (22:16). Isaac further cautions his son to remove himself "from their uncleanness and from all their error and beware . . . of taking a wife from any seed of the daughters of Canaan" (22:19–20). A similar warning against marrying Gentiles follows a reference to the Shechemites: "For this is unclean and abominable to Israel. And Israel will not be free from this uncleanness if it has a wife of the daughters of the Gentiles" (30:13–14).[9]

The discovery of *Jubilees* in the Qumran library suggests that the book's views on purity were consistent with those of the *yahad*. Neusner notes that both *Jubilees* and the *yahad* shared an "obsessive interest" in menstrual impurity.[10] The Scrolls, for example, accuse the Jerusalem priests of defiling themselves and the sanctuary by engaging in sexual relations with menstruating women (CD V, 6-7). Neusner relates this to the "taboo" against the woman after childbirth, as described in the creation story of *Jubilees* (3:8–14). The theme of cultic purity underlying *Jubilees*' association of the story of creation with the rules concerning the parturient would naturally appeal to the priestly circles at Qumran.

To sum up, Neusner makes two significant contributions to the scholarship on purity at Qumran. First, he finds significance in the concept of purity at Qumran as it relates to the self-image of the community as temple. Second, he contends that at Qumran there is no distinction between cultic and moral purity. These two premises establish the framework for much of the subsequent scholarship on the concept of purity at Qumran.

II. Michael Newton

In his book *The Concept of Purity at Qumran and in the Letters of Paul*,[11] Michael Newton contends that the ideas of purity held by both Paul and the Qumran sectarians reflected their perceptions of their respective communities as a new temple. With regard to Qumran, Newton writes:

---

9. Neusner does not recognize that these passages depart from the Holiness Code traditions in their prohibition of intermarriage.

10. Neusner, *The Idea*, 58.

11. Michael Newton, *The Concept of Purity at Qumran and in the Letters of Paul* (Cambridge: Cambridge University Press, 1985).

Qumran saw itself as a priestly community in its own right; and while it did not see itself as a surrogate Temple and carry out sacrifices it certainly conducted itself as a replacement for the defiled temple of Jerusalem and as a dwelling place for God. It becomes a "holy house for Israel and a foundation of the holy of holies for Aaron" (1QS VIII, 5, 6) and "a dwelling of the holy of holies for Aaron . . . and a house of perfection and truth for Israel."[12]

The Qumran community strived to maintain a pure precinct suitable for the indwelling of God and the performance of expiatory acts. Jerusalem became their model, and the biblical laws pertaining to purity were applied to the community and its members wherever possible. Newton states:

> Thus the novice may or may not have been familiar with the temple rules of purity; but what, in any case, would have been new to him was the application of these laws to a place outside the Jerusalem Temple, to men who were not in the traditional sense considered priests and to acts, which, while non-sacrificial, were considered expiatory.[13]

For Newton, there is a necessary association between concepts of purity and temple at Qumran,[14] and purity was a major focus of the Qumran community.[15] Purity regulations governed entry into the community, ongoing life within the community, and the disciplining of members. As a group, the Qumran sectarians regarded themselves as pure and outsiders as impure. Novices and penitents were also considered impure, at least to some extent, and were therefore excluded from the liquids and the common meal of the community.

Newton contends that the references to the "purity" of the community in the Scrolls refer to all things which belong to the community. In general, this includes all those solid objects susceptible to impurity, as well as the actual atoning life of the community. Everything related to the expiatory life of the community was required to be in a state of purity; only thus will God be able to dwell in their midst.

Newton views purity and morality as intertwined:[16]

> The Dead Sea Scrolls show without a doubt that an examination of the concept of purity cannot be carried out in the realm of the cult to the exclusion of a consideration of morality. The concern with purity that was manifested at Qumran

---

12. Ibid., 14. Here Newton relies heavily on the scholarship of Georg Klinzing, *Die Umdeutung des Kultus in der Qumrangemeinde und im Neuen Testament* (Göttingen: Vandenhoeck und Ruprecht, 1966), 41, 116ff. For further discussion of the notion of the *yahad* as temple, see chapter 5 of the present volume.

13. Newton, *The Concept of Purity*, 15.

14. Although Newton (ibid., 8) does not explicitly cite Neusner here, the influence of Neusner's scholarship is unmistakable. Indeed, Newton explicitly states in his introduction his intent to take up and expand on Neusner's contention that the role of purity must be understood in the context of the temple.

15. For Newton's treatment of *taharah* (purity), see ibid., 21–26.

16. See ibid., 40–49.

covered both the cultic and the moral life to the extent that the two areas were intermingled and at times indistinguishable.[17]

Indeed, it may be inappropriate to distinguish between ritual and moral impurity at Qumran at all, as sin is often described as engendering impurity. In CD X, 2-3, for example, sin makes an individual unclean and therefore unfit to act as a witness, whereas in 1QS VIII, 16-18 the individual's deliberate wrongdoing—sin—results in exclusion from the community and its purity. The punishment for sin at Qumran often involved exclusion from the purity. This exclusion functioned less as a punishment of the sinner than as a means of preserving the purity of the community by isolating and removing a potential source of pollution. Hence the deliberate sinner is permanently expelled from the community (1QS VIII, 21-24), while the unintentional sinner is excluded from the purity of the community until purified by perfect behavior (1QS VIII, 24, 26). The length of time that the sinner is isolated from the purity of the community is directly proportional to the severity of the sin.

Newton draws a parallel between the system of punishment at Qumran and the sacrificial system of the Jerusalem temple, both of which are designed to preserve the purity of the sacred. In Jerusalem, the inadvertent sinner brings a sacrifice in order to purge the sanctuary of the pollution that he had caused. At Qumran, inadvertent sin pollutes what the sectarians viewed as a temple—the community itself. The sinner cannot purge the pollution by offering a sacrifice. According to Newton,

> All that can be done under the present circumstances, until the real Temple is constituted, is to remove the offender, while the communal life of praise and perfection of way substitutes for the purification sacrifice whereby the sanctuary, for now represented by the community, is cleansed.[18]

In Newton's view, the *yahad* saw sin as communicable defilement which threatens both the purity of the sectarian community and the continued presence of God at Qumran. The sinner must be excluded from the community and is prohibited from having any part in its expiatory acts. In this sense, there is no distinction between moral and ritual impurity at Qumran.

III. Florentino García Martínez

In "The Problem of Purity: The Qumran Solution," Florentino García Martínez attempts to determine the development of thought and the theological system which distinguished the Qumran community from other Jewish groups of the period with regard to purity.[19] He begins with writings from the formative period of

---

17. Ibid., 40
18. Ibid., 46.
19. Florentino García Martínez, "The Problem of Purity: The Qumran Solution" in *The People of the Dead Sea Scrolls: Their Writings, Beliefs, and Practices* (ed. Florentino García Martínez and Julio Trebolle Barrera; Leiden: Brill, 1995), 139-57.

Qumran, the Temple Scroll, and 4QMMT, and then discusses texts from the later period, the Damascus Document, and the Rule of the Community.

The Temple Scroll

García Martínez identifies three apparent tendencies in the Temple Scroll.[20] The first is the extension of the level of purity required in the temple to the entire "city of the temple."[21] Thus, for example, the man who is rendered impure because of sexual relations (XL, 11-12) is excluded from the city for a period of three whole days. According to levitical law, however, the man would remain impure only until evening, after which he would be permitted to enter the "temple."

The second is the tendency to extend priestly regulations to the entire people. This feature can be found in the prohibition against a blind person entering the city of the temple. In the view of García Martínez, this prohibition is to be taken metaphorically as a reference to the imperfections cited in Lev 21:17-20 that preclude the exercise of priestly functions. He states: "The fact that the *Temple Scroll* forbids them entry into the city shows that it considers all the people as subject to the same requirements of purity in respect of the city as the priests are in respect of the Temple."[22]

The third tendency is to extend the field of defilement, as can be seen in the case of the pregnant woman with a dead foetus. According to *m. Hullin* 4:3, the woman is regarded as pure until the foetus is expelled from the uterus. The Temple Scroll, however, insists that "she shall be impure like a grave" (L, 10-11) from the moment the foetus dies.

4Q Miqṣat Maʿaseh ha-Torah

García Martínez does not undertake a full analysis of purity in 4QMMT because, at the time of his writing, the text had not been fully published. He observes, however, that the three trends concerning the purity laws in the Temple Scroll also occur in the legislation of 4QMMT. Further, the tendency in this text to extend the field of defilement is in agreement with Sadducee legislation, as in the ruling that flowing liquid transmits impurity (58-61), and in the practice of waiting until evening until ritual immersion. This differs from the Pharisaic practice of *tebul yom*, in which one who has bathed does not have to wait until sunset until purity status returns.

---

20. Cf. Florentino García Martínez, "Les limites de la communauté: Pureté et impureté à Qumrân et dans le Nouveau Testament," in *Text and Testimony: Essays on New Testament and Apocryphal Literature in Honour of A. F. J. Klijn* (ed. T. Baardia et al.; Kampen: J. H. Kok, 1988), 114-15.

21. Whereas García Martínez translates עיר המקדש as "city of the temple," other scholars often refer to the "city of the sanctuary." It is likely that עיר המקדש refers to the temple mount.

22. García Martínez, "The Problem of Purity," 146.

The Damascus Document

García Martínez bases his analysis of purity in CD on the copy from the Cairo Genizah, as well as on Milik's description of the then-unpublished manuscripts from Cave 4. In this text, he argues, purity rules are generally directed toward preserving the purity of the members of the community in their new situation of separation from the Jerusalem temple. The three trends identified with regard to earlier texts persist in CD alongside new elements that are characteristic of Qumran thought. CD posits a transfer of purity from the realm of the temple to the community itself. Thus the separation of sinners from purity (CD IX, 19–23) does not merely deny them the food of the *yahad*. Rather, the expression implies the impurity of the sinner and his or her expulsion from the community.

The Rule of the Community

It is in 1QS that the transfer of the requirements of purity from temple to community is most clearly developed. The penal code in VI, 24–VII, 25 presents a list of offenses along with a corresponding list of penalties. The concern with purity focuses not so much on the sins as on the punishments, which require the separation of the individual from the purity of the community for a duration that is commensurate with the severity of the wrongdoing.

The separation of the sinner from the community is best understood in connection with the sect's admission procedures. The would-be member must undergo a lengthy "process of progressive purification," in which the candidate attains a fuller share in the purity of the sect with each level.[23] Full membership is achieved when the candidate is allowed to share in the liquid food (1QS VI, 20–21). This process of gradual membership guarantees the purity of the community by ensuring that the candidate has attained the appropriate level of purity. Similarly, the imposed separation of the transgressor from the community ensures that the sinner will not spread his defilement; separation is an atoning act that substitutes for the atonement of the temple. These procedures create progressive levels of purity within the community that are parallel to the concentric levels of holiness and purity that surround the Holy of Holies.

García Martínez traces the idea of purity at Qumran to a formative period in which notions of purity were associated with the temple and its cult. In the texts from this period, however, there is a tendency to extend the requirement for temple purity to the whole city and to all of the people, rather than just the priests. Additionally, these early texts indicate an increase in the rigor of the purity requirements. Once the community breaks with the temple in Jerusalem, it accommodates the rules of purity to its new situation. The community becomes a substitute for the temple, and the requirements for purity are transferred to the *yahad*. Every transgression of a community precept is regarded as both a sin and a source of impurity within the *yahad*. The sinner is therefore required to undergo a process of purification.

The requirement for the purification of the sinner indicates a complete associa-

---

23. Ibid., 153.

tion of impurity and sin in the latter period of the Qumran community. Whereas sin defiles and results in separation from the community, atonement and purification enable the individual to reintegrate into the *yahad*.

IV. Hannah K. Harrington

Ritual purity is the focus of Hannah Harrington's *The Impurity Systems of Qumran and the Rabbis*.[24] Particularly relevant to this inquiry is Harrington's discussion of three areas: (1) the relationship of the sect to the temple in Jerusalem, (2) the sectarian interpretation of Scripture, and (3) the purity of the common meal.[25]

In contrast to Gärtner, Klinzing, and Newton, Harrington does not hold that the community at Qumran regarded themselves as a new temple. Rather, "the sectarians upheld the importance of the cult and its Jerusalem location albeit not in its present condition."[26] Discussions of purity matters in the Temple Scroll and the Cave 4 fragments testify to the sectarians' interest in the cult, not because they presently viewed themselves as participating in a temple cult, but because they would do so at a future time.[27] She states:

> Although they disagreed with the current Temple practice, the sectarians did not think that their communal meals conducted in ritual purity were equivalent to the sacrifices of the priests in the Temple. Their meals comprised merely a temporary and imperfect substitute.[28]

The Qumran sectarians believed the temple and its cult would be reestablished in Jerusalem in the eschaton. In the meantime, the sectarians regarded themselves as living in the pure status of ordinary Israelites.

The sectarian concept of purity was shaped through scriptural exegesis. Like other groups in the Second Temple period, the Qumran community regarded the biblical text as sacred. Their exegesis differed from that of other groups due to the exegetical technique of "homogenization" and the tendency toward stringency. Homogenization is an interpretive method by which biblical information about a given item is extended to other items which are similar to it.[29] This technique

---

24. Hannah K. Harrington, *The Impurity Systems of Qumran and the Rabbis: Biblical Foundations* (SBLDS 143; Atlanta: Scholars Press, 1993).
25. See ibid., 47–67.
26. Ibid., 51.
27. Harrington indicates that the most pertinent discussions on purity from the Cave 4 fragments are 4QThrA1 (4Q274), 4QTohoroth A1 (*4Q Purification Rules A*); 4QMMT, 4Q *Miqsat Ma'aseh ha-Torah*; 4QOrd^c (4Q514), *Ordonnances c*; and 4QFl (4Q174), *Florilegium*. Although these fragments reveal a striking affinity to 11QT, there are some significant discrepancies in the purity legislation. Harrington suggests that the Temple Scroll's divergence from the other sectarian scrolls is due to the fact that 11QT sets forth an eschatological ideal rather than a rule for the present community. Ibid., 48–50.
28. Ibid., 52.
29. Milgrom offers the following example: The priestly legislation requires that one who touches a carcass bathe (Lev 11:39), whereas one who eats of the carcass or carries it is

results in a more uniform interpretation of the legislation, usually in a more stringent direction.

The common meal was fundamental to the concept of purity. This meal, referred to as the "purity," is shared only by those who are clean (1QS V, 13-14; VI, 25; VII, 16, 19, 23). All persons who come in contact with impurity must bathe and launder their clothes before eating. Only after the required ablutions may they eat, and then only according to their status of purity (4QOrd^c 4-7). For example, the *zab* who contacts impurity is required to bathe and launder before eating. The ablution cleanses him of newly contracted defilement, but does not alter his status as a *zab*. Thus, he still remains excluded from the purity of the community.

In her subsequent paper, "The Nature of Impurity at Qumran," Harrington examines the relationship between ritual purity and sin.[30] In contrast to Neusner and García Martínez,[31] Harrington contends that the biblical distinctions between ritual impurities and those caused by sin are, indeed, discernible at Qumran: "[T]he fact that the community regarded sin as ritually (as well as morally) defiling (1QS III, 6-11; V, 13-14), does not prove the converse—that all impure individuals were considered sinners."[32]

Harrington argues her position on both logical and biblical grounds. Logic dictates that normal bodily functions such as menstruating or obligatory activities such as burying the dead are not to be categorized as sinful. These necessary activities may generate ritual impurity, but they cannot be construed as a rebellion against God. Harrington's argument from Scripture is based on the observation that the Qumran community was a bibliocentric group. The sectarians would have known that the scriptures did not view all acts requiring immersion as a violation of the commandments or a rebellion against God. For example, immersion is required after sexual intercourse and birth, but these normal activities are not sinful; to the contrary, intercourse was the sole activity through which to fulfill the divine commandment to "be fruitful and multiply" (Gen 1:28).

Harrington suggests that "impurities resulting from sin carried high penalties," while "those which were not sin-related were easily purified without moral stigma attached."[33] Two issues arise. The first pertains to the penitential tone in purification texts related to such impurities as menstruation and corpse contamination.

---

required to bathe and wash their clothing (Lev 11:40). The Temple Scroll homogenizes or equalizes the scriptural data when it requires even the one who has touched a carcass to both bathe and launder their clothes (51:1-2). See Jacob Milgrom, "The Qumran Cult: Its Exegetical Principles," in *Temple Scroll Studies* (ed. George J. Brooke; Sheffield: JSOT Press, 1989), 165-80.

30. Harrington, "The Nature of Impurity," 610-16.

31. Harrington also quotes from Klawans's preliminary article (1997) on the impurity of immorality: "At Qumran, sin was considered to be ritually defiling, and ritual defilement was assumed to come about because of sin.... The once independent concepts of ritual and moral impurity have become fully intertwined in the sectarian literature of Qumran." See Jonathan Klawans, "The Impurity of Immorality in Ancient Judaism," *JJS* 48 (1997): 10.

32. Harrington, "The Nature of Impurity," 613.

33. Ibid., 612.

In 4Q Ritual of Purification (4Q512), for example, the term נדה, "menstruant," is used in connection with various types of purification, including purification before festivals (cols. IV, IX–X) and purification of the corpse-contaminated individual (col. XII). According to Harrington, the use of the term נדה in 4Q512 is best translated not specifically as menstrual impurity but as a general term for ritual impurity.[34] In the context of 4Q512, this translation is not only more accurate, but it also eliminates the problematic association of the menstruant with sin.

A second issue concerns individuals who confess to sin while purifying themselves (4Q512). If the author of the Qumran authors did, indeed, distinguish between ritual impurity and sin, how can we account for such declarations of guilt? Harrington concludes that in each case, the Bible associates the impurity with sin. Column VII, for example, describes the purifying person as a Nazirite who has broken his vow. Similarly, column VIII most probably describes the purification of an individual who has contracted scale disease. While levitical law does not necessarily consider this individual sinful, several biblical texts do connect this form of skin ailment with sin (Lev 14:34; 26:21; Deut 28:27).[35]

Finally, the description of the corpse-contaminated individual in column XII uses the term כיפור, "expiation," in lines 3 and 14, thereby implying the association of sin with ritual impurity. But while the use of expiatory language contributes to the penitential tone of this text, other texts from Qumran use the term כיפור to express "a general and continual need for forgiveness felt by all members of the community, whether ritually impure or not."[36] It may be this persistent need to confess unconscious sin and acknowledge personal shortcomings that is reflected in 4Q512 rather than a declaration of human inadequacy associated with impurity.

V. Jonathan Klawans

Klawans examines ritual and moral impurity at Qumran in two chapters of his 2001 book. The chapter "Moral Impurity in the Second Temple Period" demonstrates that the concept of moral defilement persists into the Second Temple period in passages from *Jubilees*, the Temple Scroll, and the Damascus Document. The chapter "Impurity and Sin in the Literature of Qumran" examines the Habakkuk Pesher and 4Q *Miqṣat Maʿaseh ha-Torah* and addresses the identification of ritual and moral impurity at Qumran.

Jubilees

According to Klawans, the book of *Jubilees* is very much like the Holiness Code in its focus on moral impurity.[37] As in the Holiness Code, the primary causes of

---

34. As Harrington points out, there is precedent for this understanding of נדה in Scripture (e.g., Ezra 9:11; Ezek 7:19–20; Lam 1:8, 17; Zech 13:1). Ibid., 614.

35. Not only does God uses scale disease as a curse in Israel, but several individuals are also punished with this affliction because they have sinned, including Miriam (Num 12:10), Uzziah (2 Chr 26:23), and Gehazi (2 Kgs 5:27). See ibid., 613.

36. Harrington, "The Nature of Impurity," 616.

37. Klawans cites only two examples pertaining to ritual impurity in *Jubilees*: the purity

moral defilement are idolatry (1:9; 12:2; 20:7; 21:15; 22:17–18, 22), sexual misdeeds (4:22; 7:21–22; 20:3–6; 30:3; 33:7, 18–20), and bloodshed (7:33; 21:19). And as in the Holiness Code, the abominations are said to defile the land of Israel and the sanctuary of God. Sin does not cause ritual defilement, nor can the resultant impurity be rectified by ritual purification. In *Jubilees*, however, the punishment for sin is much worse than the exile predicted by the Holiness Code. People who defile themselves with sin will meet the same fate as the inhabitants of Sodom (21:21; 22:22; 23:18–21): obliteration from the face of the earth.

Another respect in which *Jubilees* diverges from the Holiness Code is the treatment of Gentile behavior. In *Jubilees*, as in Ezra and Nehemiah, the moral impurity is inherent in the Gentiles. For this reason, intermarriage is not only prohibited (30:7), but constitutes a source of moral defilement in its own right (30:8–9, 13–14), presumably because of the danger that intermarriage will lead to idolatry. *Jubilees* goes even further by prohibiting all forms of Jewish-Gentile interaction (22:16), including eating together. Here the concern is with the morally abominable behavior of the Gentiles, who are said to practice idolatry (22:17–22) and perform sexual transgressions (20:3–7).

The Temple Scroll

Klawans views the Temple Scroll as the mirror image of *Jubilees*.[38] The book of *Jubilees* is primarily concerned with moral defilement—the defiling force of idolatry and sexual misdeeds—and pays little attention to ritual impurity. By contrast, the Temple Scroll is greatly concerned with ritual impurity and has little interest in moral defilement.[39] Both, however, maintain a clear distinction between ritual and moral impurity.

Close to seven columns of the Temple Scroll are devoted to regulations pertaining to defilement (XLV, 7–LI, 10). Many of 11QT's laws agree with those found in the Torah; some strengthen older prohibitions, and others are innovations. Examples of the latter are the exclusion from the temple of males under twenty years of age (XXXIX, 7–9) and the description of the blind as ritually defiling and therefore excluded from the city of the sanctuary (XLV, 12–14). Here, as in other legislation, the "city of the sanctuary" provides a new locus for sanctity, which effectively "keeps more people at a greater distance from the sacred."[40] Other innovations in the Temple Scroll include stringencies related to purification procedures: the requirement to wait until sunset after immersion in order to be pure once again and the introduction of what Milgrom has termed "first day ablutions" (XLIX, 17–19).[41]

---

laws pertaining to the parturient in 3:8–14 and a reference to the second tithe in 32:13. For Klawans's discussion of purity in *Jubilees*, see *Impurity and Sin*, 46–48.

38. For Klawans's discussion of purity in the Temple Scroll, see *Impurity and Sin*, 48–52.

39. Nevertheless, Klawans includes his treatment of the Temple Scroll in "Moral Impurity in the Second Temple Period."

40. Klawans, *Impurity and Sin*, 49

41. The practice of *tebul yom*, the recognition of the purity of the individual who immersed on that day, was observed by the Pharisees. The tradition of waiting until the sunset

Many of these innovations agree with the sectarian literature from Qumran. With regard to moral impurity, however, 11QT is much closer in its ideology to the biblical text than to the sectarian literature. One example is 11QT LI, 11-15:

> You shall appoint judges and officers in all your towns, and they shall judge the people with righteous judgement. And they shall not show partiality in justice, and shall not take a bribe, and shall not pervert justice, the bribe perverts justice, and subverts the cause of the righteous, and blinds the eyes of the wise, and causes great guilt, and defiles the house because of the sin of iniquity.

Moral impurity is implied in the notion that bribery "defiles the house" (ומטמא הבית).[42] Although this source of moral impurity is not specified in the biblical text, Klawans suggests that this innovation is rooted in biblical exegesis. Particularly significant is an injunction in the Holiness Code against rendering an unfair decision: לא־תעשו עול במשפט. One must not favor the poor or show deference to the rich (Lev 19:15), nor may one falsify measure and weights (Lev 19:35). Related to this latter injunction is the prohibition of Deut 25:15-16, in which the use of honest weights and measures is associated with enduring long in the land. In contrast, those who deal dishonestly are viewed as "abhorrent" to God. The idea that bribery is morally defiling was derived through a creative process of exegesis that linked the concepts of deceit, abomination, and moral defilement. The Temple Scroll therefore expands, if slightly, the biblical notion of moral defilement.

The Damascus Document

Klawans does not attempt to characterize the Damascus Document's "eclectic" approach to defilement, in which some passages reflect a more general notion of moral defilement, and others indicate a sectarian approach that integrates the categories of impurity and sin.[43] Rather, he focuses on CD IV, 12-V, 11, which articulates the doctrine of moral defilement:

> But during all those years, Belial will run unbridled amidst Israel, as God spoke through the hand of the prophet Isaiah, son of Amoz, saying, "Fear and a pit and a snare are upon you, O inhabitant(s) of the land" [Isa 24:17]. This refers to the three nets of Belial, of which Levi, the son of Jacob, said that he [Belial] entrapped Israel with them, making them seem as if they were three types of righteousness. The first is unchastity [זנות], the second is arrogance, and the third defilement of

---

after immersion to be rendered pure is reported in rabbinic sources as being observed by the Sadducees. According to Milgrom, the first-day ablutions of the Temple Scroll enabled the reestablishment of contact with nonsacred persons and objects. Contact with the sacred, however, required a second immersion after a prescribed period of time. See Milgrom, *Leviticus 1-16*, 968-71.

42. Here Klawans opposes the view of Yadin that a person who takes a bribe ritually defiles the sanctuary only if he or she chooses to enter it. See Yigael Yadin, *The Temple Scroll* (3 vols.; Jerusalem: Israel Exploration Society, 1983), 2:227-28.

43. For Klawans's discussion of purity in the Damascus Document, see *Impurity and Sin*, 52-56.

the sanctuary [טמא המקדש]. He who escapes from this is caught by that and he who is saved from that is caught by this. (CD IV, 12–19)

The continuation of the text asserts that a group whom the sect opposes, the "builders of the barrier" (בוני החיץ), are caught up in two of these snares. The first is the snare of unchastity (זנות), "the taking of two wives in their lives" (IV, 20–21).[44] The second snare is defilement of the sanctuary:

> And they also continuously polluted the sanctuary by not separating according to the Torah, and they habitually lay with a woman who sees blood of flowing; and they marry each one his brother's daughter or sister's daughter. But Moses said, "To your mother's sister you may not draw near, for she is your mother's near relation." [Lev 18:13] (CD V, 6–9)

The juxtaposition of sanctuary defilement and sexual transgressions articulates a doctrine of moral defilement. The sin of cohabitation with a woman in a state of flux relates to the Holiness Code's prohibition against sexual intercourse with a menstruant (Lev 18:19), which is considered a source of defilement. Similarly, CD's reference to incest is a distinct allusion to the sexual sins of Lev 18. The prohibition in CD is expansive in its interpretation with respect to the inclusion of sexual relations between a man and his niece, as well as that of a man and his aunt.[45] Nevertheless, this expansion of the prohibition does not extend beyond the category of moral defilement.

CD IV, 12–V, 11 is based on an exegesis of Isa 24:17, which is concerned with the desolation of the land by the people's sin and uses terminology associated with the Holiness Code and the concept of moral defilement: "For the earth was defiled [והארץ חנפה] under its inhabitants" (Isa 24:5). Both the Holiness Code and Isaiah make reference to sin defiling the land, whereas CD is explicit in its concern for the defilement of the sanctuary. This divergence is insignificant, argues Klawans, because the idea that sexual sin morally defiles the sanctuary is quite common in the Second Temple period.

---

44. Klawans duly notes that, in the Holiness Code, polygamy and remarriage after divorce are not considered morally defiling sins. He indicates that one would be hard-pressed to find scriptural support for a prohibition of polygamy and remarriage after divorce. However, he suggests that the discussion of "unchastity" in CD does not allude to the sexual prohibitions of the Holiness Code, but to the verses in Genesis that purportedly praise monogamy (Gen 1:27 and 7:7–9) and to the deuteronomic law which prohibits the king from taking many wives (Deut 17:17). In the view of CD, the taking of two wives falls short of the monogamous ideal. See ibid., 55–56.

45. The expansion of CD's interpretation of Lev 18 is also found in its application of the laws of incest to women as well as men: "Now the precept of incest is written from the point of view of males, but the same [law] applies to women, so if a brother's daughter uncovers the nakedness of a brother of her father, she is a [forbidden] close relationship" (CD V, 9–11). See ibid., 54–55.

Sin and the Sanctuary in the Habakkuk Pesher

Habakkuk Pesher (1QpHab) includes the following passage:[46]

> "On account of the bloodshed of the town and violence [done to] the land" [Hab 2:17], the interpretation of it: the "town" is Jerusalem, where the Wicked Priest committed abominable deeds [מעשי תועבות] and defiled [ויטמא] God's sanctuary. And "violence [done to] the land" [refers to] the cities of Judah, where he stole the wealth of the poor ones. (1QpHab XII, 6-9)

According to Klawans's analysis, the "abominable deeds" are the Wicked Priest's thefts from the poor.[47] The avarice of the Wicked Priest is also discussed elsewhere in the Pesher:

> The interpretation of it concerns the Wicked Priest, who was called by the true name at the beginning of his course, but when he ruled in Israel, he became arrogant [רם לבו], abandoned God, and betrayed the statutes for the sake of wealth. He stole and amassed the wealth of the men of violence who had rebelled against God, and he took the wealth of peoples to add to himself guilty sin. And the abominable ways [ת[ו]עבות דרכי] he pursued with every sort of unclean impurity [בכול נדת טמאה]. (1QpHab VIII, 8-13)

Here too theft is described as an abomination. The use of the term נדה, along with תועבה, may allude to sexual abominations. The Pesher therefore implies that the wicked deeds of the priest included both theft and sexual misdeeds.

Klawans suggests that here the terms נדה and תועבה are not used exclusively in reference to sexual sin, as they are in Lev 18. Rather, these terms may refer to sinful behavior in general, as they do in the remainder of the Qumran corpus. It is also possible that the abominations are related to arrogance (1QpHab VIII, 10).[48] Proverbs 16:5 states: "Every haughty person is an abomination [תועבה] to the Lord."[49] On the basis of this and other passages, "it is possible that the author of 1QpHab has come to view arrogance—or more precisely, the greedy behaviour

---

46. For Klawans's discussion of purity in the Habakkuk Pesher, see *Impurity and Sin*, 69-72.

47. Since scholars have not been able to agree on the identity of the Wicked Priest(s), Klawans (ibid., 69) relies solely on what is in the text to interpret the passage. Klawans indicates that almost every high priest of the Hasmonean period has been identified as a possibility. Moreover, the Groningen Hypothesis suggests that this passage is concerned not with one priest, but with a series of so-called wicked priests.

48. Klawans (ibid., 71) also allows for the possibility that the abominations of the wicked priest were concerned with acts of bloodshed. Although this charge against the wicked priest is not found in the passages considered by Klawans, the accusation is made throughout the Pesher (1QpHab X, 9-10; XI, 4-6).

49. Here Klawans follows Brownlee in his suggestion that Prov 16:5 and Ezek 16:49-50 provide the biblical inspirations for the concept of arrogance as an abomination. See William H. Brownlee, *The Midrash Pesher of Habakkuk* (Missoula, MT: Scholars Press, 1979), 142.

that results from it—as an abomination."⁵⁰ If this is correct, then the connection between greed and abomination in both 1QpHab VIII, 8–13 and XII, 6–9 may reflect an expansion of scripture in which arrogance is viewed as a source of moral impurity.

Having examined the nature of the abominations committed by the wicked priest, Klawans discusses the mechanism by which the priest causes the defilement of the sanctuary. Although ritual defilement is a possibility, it is more likely that it is the morally defiling force of the priest's sins that causes the impurity.⁵¹ The most convincing textual evidence is the use of the term תועבה in connection with the charges against the priest. In scripture this term is primarily associated with sources of moral defilement such as murder, idolatry, and sexual misdeeds. Other sources of abomination are deceit (Deut 25:15–16) and arrogance (Prov 16:5), sins which the Habakkuk Pesher likely regarded as sources of moral impurity. If so, Klawans may well be correct in stating: "[It] is not that it is bad for the High Priest to sin, because he could then defile the sanctuary *ritually* by entering it, but . . . it is bad for the High Priest, of all people, to be responsible for the *moral* defilement of the sanctuary that results from the performance of grave sin."⁵²

Impurity and Sin in 4Q Miqṣat Ma'aseh ha-Torah

Like the Temple Scroll, 4Q *Miqṣat Ma'aseh ha-Torah* (4QMMT) is concerned primarily with ritual impurity rather than the defiling force of sin.⁵³ These two texts also agree with respect to some of the legal disputes concerning ritual impurity. Like the Temple Scroll, 4QMMT rejects the purity of the *tebul yom*, ruling that the priests who prepare the red heifer are ritually impure until sunset (4QMMTᵇ 13–17). 4QMMT is also concerned that the blind may defile the sacred (4QMMTᵇ 49–54), although it is not clear that they are considered inherently impure, as in 11QT.⁵⁴ Both texts advocate ritual legislation that is more stringent than both the Pentateuch and the Pharisaic-rabbinic tradition but that accords with the legal positions that the Pharisees attribute to the Sadducees. Finally, 4QMMT is similar to 11QT in its expansive approach to the realm of the sacred. Thus it ascribes the sanctity of the biblical war camp to the entire city of Jerusalem. Although 4QMMT is stringent with respect to ritual impurity, it does not focus on the defiling force of sin. Neither this document nor the Temple Scroll integrates the concepts of moral and ritual impurity.⁵⁵

---

50. Klawans, *Impurity and Sin*, 70.

51. Brownlee (*The Midrash Pesher*, 206) essentially advocates that the mechanism of defilement is ritual impurity when he suggests that the defilement of the sanctuary takes place when the priest subsequently enters the sanctuary.

52. Klawans, *Impurity and Sin*, 71–72.

53. For Klawans's discussion of impurity in 4QMMT, see ibid., 72–75.

54. Klawans notes that while 4QMMT excludes both the bind and the deaf, 11QT excludes only the blind. Other differences between the two texts are discussed briefly in ibid., 73 n. 33.

55. Klawans (ibid., 73–74) recognizes that this point remains tentative, as it is an argument from silence.

The Identification of Ritual and Moral Impurity at Qumran

In general, however, Qumran merges the once distinct concepts of ritual and moral impurity.⁵⁶ What we see at Qumran, he states, is "not merely an association between ritual and moral impurity, but a basically complete identification of ritual and moral impurity."⁵⁷

This identification of ritual and moral impurity manifests itself in Qumran's sectarian literature in five ways. The first is the use of impurity terminology in the context of sin. In 1QS, for example, the way of the Spirit of Deceit is described as the zeal for "abominable works in a spirit of fornication" (מעשי תועבה ברוח זנות) and "filthy ways in impure worship" (ודרכי נדה בעבודת טמאה; IV, 10–11). When the spirit is defeated, those under its power will be purified from "all the abominations of falsehood and from being polluted by a spirit of impurity" (מכול תועבות שקר והתגולל ברוח נדה; IV, 21–22). While such passages use language of ritual purity (נדה and טמאה), they are not concerned with violations of ritual purity law. Rather, this language is used to describe grave sinfulness in general, often referred to as "deceit" (עול; e.g., 1QS III, 19, 21; IV, 9). Similarly, the use of the term תועבה, "abomination," in connection with sin does not refer to a restricted set of immoral acts, but to general sinfulness, as indicated in the following passage:

> For your glory, you have purified man from sin, so that he can make himself holy for you from every impure abomination (נדה תועבות) and blameworthy iniquity. (1QH XIX[XI], 10–11)

The second way in which the identification of impurity and sin manifests itself at Qumran is in the description of sinful outsiders as ritually defiling:

> [The outsider] must not enter the water in order to touch the purity of the men of holiness. For they cannot be cleansed unless they turn away from the wickedness, for (he remains) impure among all those who transgress His words. (1QS V, 13–14)

The idea that the deeds and body of the outsider are impure is also found in 1QS III, 5–6, which states that an unrepentant outsider can never attain ritual purity.⁵⁸

The ritually defiling force of sin also applies to Klawans's third point of identification between ritual and moral impurity: those from within the community who commit moral sins are, like the outsiders, considered ritually defiled and excluded from the community's pure food (e.g., 1QS VII, 2–3, 15–16; VIII, 16–18, 24; CD IX, 16–23).

The fourth and fifth manifestations of the identification between moral and ritual purity pertain to the relationship between repentance and purification. On the one hand, the sectarians believed that moral repentance was not efficacious

---

56. For Klawans's discussion on the identification of ritual of moral impurity, see *Impurity and Sin*, 75–90; cf. also Klawans, "The Impurity of Immorality," 7–10.

57. Klawans, *Impurity and Sin*, 75.

58. In 1QS V, 18–20 the property of the outsider is also deemed impure (cf. CD VI, 14). Ibid., 80.

without ritual purification. Thus the repentance of the sinner is followed by purification and subsequent admission into the community (1QS III, 6-9).[59] On the other hand, the sectarians believed that the manifestations of ritual impurity resulted from sin. As such, rituals of purification required the recitation of penitential formulae. In 4Q512, for example, repentance is incorporated into a blessing that is presumably recited upon purification from menstrual impurity:

> And he will bless. He will start speaking and say: May you be blessed, [God of Israel, who] [forgave me all] my faults, and purified me from impure modesty /and atoned/ so that I can enter ... (4Q512 VII, 8-9)

Klawans acknowledges the inherent difficulties in interpreting a fragmentary document such as 4Q512. Nevertheless, he asserts that there is enough information in this well-preserved passage to confirm that the blessing was to be recited upon the performance of a purification ritual. In his opinion, this evidence also demonstrates that purification and atonement were conceptually intertwined at Qumran.

Klawans summarizes the relationship between ritual and moral impurity at Qumran as follows:

> At Qumran, sin was considered to be ritually defiling, and ritual defilement was assumed to come about because of sin. Sinners not only had to atone, but also had to cleanse themselves of the ritual impurity their sins produced. Insiders who sinned were assumed to be ritually impure, and insiders who were ritually impure had to atone. In short, what were, in the Hebrew Bible, the independent concepts of ritual and moral impurity have become, at Qumran, fully intertwined.[60]

The evolution of this sectarian approach to impurity can be traced through the literature. The proto-sectarian Temple Scroll and the early sectarian 4QMMT do not integrate the categories of ritual and moral impurity, nor do they use distinctively Qumranic purity terminology. The Damascus Document is more complex: some passages articulate a concept of impurity that is compatible with non-sectarian Jewish literature, whereas others take a distinctly sectarian approach. Finally, texts that are undoubtedly sectarian in origin, such as 1QS, 1QpHab, 1QH, and 4Q512, integrate the concepts of ritual and moral impurity into a single conception of defilement.

VI. Martha Himmelfarb

While Martha Himmelfarb agrees with much of Klawans's theory regarding purity and impurity at Qumran, she disagrees with his assessment of the relationship between impurity and sin at Qumran.

---

59. Although repentance is always prior to purification, Klawans (ibid., 86) contends that the former should not be viewed as a precondition for the latter. Rather, they are mutually dependent conditions that must be fulfilled.

60. Klawans, *Impurity and Sin*, 88 (= "The Impurity of Immorality," 10).

Sexual Relations and Purity in the Temple Scroll and Jubilees

In her paper "Sexual Relations and Purity in the Temple Scroll and the Book of Jubilees," Martha Himmelfarb concludes that there are significant differences between the Temple Scroll and *Jubilees* in their treatment of the laws of sexual relations and purity.[61] According to Himmelfarb, the Temple Scroll consistently intensifies the purity rules of the Torah.[62] This is evident in the Temple Scroll's adaptation of Num 5:2, in which three groups are excluded from the camp of Israel in the wilderness: those with skin eruptions, an abnormal genital flow, or corpse contamination. 11QT requires the establishment of three places of confinement to the east of the city of the sanctuary to be used by three categories of individuals. The Scroll's third category, however, does not consist of individuals with corpse contamination, but of men who have experienced a nocturnal emission (XLVI, 16-18). The Scroll is not entirely consistent in this regard, for in 11QT (XLVIII, 14-17), the third group consists of women who are either menstruating or post-childbirth.

For Himmelfarb, the legislation in 11QT XLVI, 16-18 and XLVIII, 14-17 demonstrates a more severe attitude toward impurities arising from genital flow than the priestly legislation in the Torah. Both the laws concerning the menstruant (Lev 15:19-24) and the first stage of post-partum impurity (Lev 12:1-5) assume that the women were living at home.[63] Yet while the Torah does not require isolation for women during these periods in their lives, the Temple Scroll requires confinement outside the city, thereby intensifying the biblical law.[64]

Stringency is also evident in the tendency of 11QT to elaborate on the purification rituals or extend the duration of the period of impurity. For example, in the Torah the impurity of seminal emission requires only that one bathe and wait for the sun to set.[65] In 11QT, however, a man who has experienced a nocturnal emission is excluded from the sanctuary for three days. During this period of exclu-

---

61. Martha Himmelfarb, "Sexual Relations and Purity in the Temple Scroll and the Book of Jubilees," *DSD* 6, no. 1 (1999): 11-36.

62. For Himmelfarb's discussion of purity in 1QH, see "Sexual Relations and Purity," 16-25.

63. The discussion in Lev 15:19-24 that details how impurity related to normal genital flow is spread through contact with the menstruant, her bedding, or other implements is predicated on the assumption that she is living at home with her family. Moreover, the comparison of the first stage of post-partum impurity with that of the menstruant suggests a similar situation for the parturient. Ibid., 17.

64. Himmelfarb (ibid., 17-18) finds another example of the intensification of the legislation in 11QT in her comparison of the legislation in Lev 15 to that of Num 5:2. Whereas the former assumes that the impure remain at home, the latter legislates exile from the camp of Israel. In accordance with its tendency toward stringency, the Temple Scroll chooses the stricter legislation.

65. Himmelfarb (ibid., 18) observes that Deut 23:10-15 requires exile from the camp but suggests that this is only because it is a war camp in which God himself is present (23:15). The period of impurity and procedures for purification outside the war camp are, however, the same as in Lev 15.

sion, he is required to undergo a process of purification that includes bathing and the washing of clothes on the first and third days. It is only after sunset on the third day that he is deemed pure (XLV, 7–10).[66]

It would seem, then, that the author(s) of the Temple Scroll found P's attitude toward impurity to be too lenient and therefore extended the realm affected by impurity beyond the temple to the land itself. By establishing places of confinement for those who were impure, pollution of the land could be prevented.

Its recounting of the stories from Genesis, *Jubilees* demonstrates particular concern with forbidden sexual relations and their consequence: the defilement of the sanctuary.[67] A good example is the story of Reuben, the firstborn son of Jacob who sleeps with his father's wife, Bilhah (33:1–20). In *Jubilees*, Reuben's sin is characterized as "impure, something detestable, a blemish, and something contaminated" (33:19). The narrator concludes the story with a general admonition against sexual sin in general, indicating that no such impurity is acceptable in Israel, since "it is a priestly nation" (33:20; cf. 16:18).

Similarly, *Jubilees* considers the rape of Dinah as defiling and praises her brothers' subsequent attack on Shechem as a noble defence of endogamy. This story illustrates the point that sexual misconduct causes defilement of the temple:

> If one does this [marries a foreigner] or shuts his eyes to those who do impure things and who defile the Lord's sanctuary and to those who profane his holy name, then the entire nation will be condemned together because of all this impurity and this contamination. There will be no favouritism nor partiality; there will be no receiving from him of fruit, sacrifices, offerings, fat, or the aroma of a pleasing fragrance so that he should accept it. (So) is any man or woman in Israel to be who defiles his sanctuary. (*Jub.* 30:15–16)

Himmelfarb relates the defilement of the temple caused by sexual misconduct to Jubilees' notion of Israel as a kingdom of priests (33:20).[68] She states: "Even the ordinary Jews are thus given a sort of priestly power. Only if they observe God's commandments regarding sexual relations will sacrifices, the priestly work *par excellence*, be acceptable."

Impurity and Sin in 4QD, 1QS, and 4Q512

Himmelfarb's essay "Impurity and Sin in 4QD, 1QS, and 4Q512" calls into ques-

---

66. A man with a seminal emission that results from intercourse is also excluded from the sanctuary for three days (1QH XLV, 11–12). Himmelfarb (ibid., 18–19) indicates that there is no place of confinement outside the city of the sanctuary for such men because the Temple Scroll does not envision sexual relations taking place there.

67. Throughout her analysis of impurity in *Jubilees*, Himmelfarb emphasizes the defilement of the sanctuary but makes no mention that sin also defiles the land. For Himmelfarb's discussion of impurity in *Jubilees*, see "Sexual Relations and Purity," 25–33.

68. Himmelfarb (ibid., 30) suggests that *Jubilees* goes even further than H in extending some of the status that P reserves for priests to all Israel.

tion the widespread view that the Qumran community conflated the categories of impurity and sin.[69] In her introduction she cites Joseph Baumgarten:

> Rabbinic tradition ... tended by and large to treat ritual impurity as a morally neutral phenomenon.... In this respect the penitential tone of the Qumran blessings after any kind of immersion seems to reflect another facet of the specifically sectarian view on uncleanliness. For if "impurity is inherent in all transgressor of divine law" (1QS V 4), might one not suppose conversely that all who are impure are in need of atonement for their trespasses? The dividing line between uncleanliness and sin at Qumran is thus not sharply drawn....[70]

Himmelfarb's disagreement with this view is based on her analysis of 4QD's laws concerning skin eruptions and genital impurity, as well as the relevant material in 1QS and 4Q512.[71]

Himmelfarb's analysis of purity in 4QD focuses on the laws concerning three conditions: the individual with skin eruptions (צרעת), the man with a flow (זב), and the woman with a flow (זבה).[72] The treatment of צרעת in 4QD attempts to clarify and systematize the somewhat confusing laws of Lev 13–14 (4Q266 6 i 1–13 and 4Q272 1 i 1–20) by regarding skin eruptions as a medical condition, as does the biblical source P. The condition of צרעת is not a punishment for sin as it is in the non-priestly sources of the Hebrew Bible and, hence, the impurity of skin eruptions has no moral component.

4QD's legislation concerning the זב (4Q266 6 i 14–16 and 4Q272 1 ii 3–7) reveals a distinct intensification of the related laws in Lev 15. The Torah differentiates between the man who has an abnormal genital discharge (זב; Lev 15:2–15) and the one who has a seminal emission either outside of sexual relations (Lev 15:16–17) or during intercourse (Lev 15:18). 4QD makes no such distinction and classifies the man who has had a seminal emission as a זב and therefore as marked by severe impurity.

In 4QD, "the rule of the זב" is immediately followed by "the rule of the זבה" (4Q272 1 ii 7). This category covers all women with a flow: the menstruant, the woman with an abnormal discharge, and the parturient. 4Q266 6 ii 10–11 provides a striking example of the intensification of levitical law with regard to the case of the parturient who is prohibited from nursing her newborn but must give her child to a woman who can nurse the child "in purity." According to Lev 12, the parturient's initial impurity is similar to menstrual impurity in that those who are in contact with her are impure until evening and must launder their clothes and bathe. Thus the infant would incur impurity by nursing or being touched by the

---

69. Martha Himmelfarb, "Impurity and Sin in 4QD, 1QS, and 4Q512," *DSD* 8, no. 1 (2001): 9–37.

70. Joseph M. Baumgarten, "The Purification Rituals in DJD 7," in *The Dead Sea Scrolls: Forty Years of Research* (ed. Devorah Dimant and Uriel Rappaport; Leiden: Brill, 1992), 199–209.

71. Himmelfarb specifically refers to Klawans's article "The Impurity of Immorality in Ancient Judaism."

72. For Himmelfarb's discussion of purity in 4QD, see "Impurity and Sin," 13–29.

mother. Himmelfarb notes that the consequences of this impurity are hardly relevant to the newborn, who would not be entering the sanctuary or touching holy things. The stringency of 4QD in this case suggests that purity is being valued for its own sake. While this attitude could very well lead to an association of impurity with immorality, 4QD provides no evidence for such a development.

Himmelfarb's discussion of 1QS, which delineates the special rules that govern the life of the community, focuses on three issues that may point to a conflation of impurity and sin: the use of purity terminology from P, exclusion from the pure food of the community, and the practice of "baptism."[73]

1QS draws on P's terminology with respect to impurity but employs it in a very different way. Whereas in P purity language is used to identify specific physical states, in 1QS it is used poetically or evocatively to refer to spiritual states and processes. One example is 1QS's description of the eschatological purification of humanity; God sprinkles upon man "the spirit of truth like waters for purification (מי נדה)" in order to remove "all the abominations (תועבות) of falsehood" (IV, 20–22). Another example is 1QS 3:4–9, which uses terms such as טהר "purify or become pure" (III, 4, 5, 7, 9), מי נדה "waters for purification" (III, 4, 9), מי רחץ "water for washing" (III, 5), and מי דוכי "waters for cleansing" (III, 9). Despite the physical nature of the imagery, physical purification is mentioned only at the very end of this passage. The greater part of the text is concerned with a concept entirely foreign to P: the purification of the soul.

A second element concerns the exclusion from the pure food of the community. Himmelfarb calls into question Klawans's claim that this denial of access to food constitutes a punishment.[74] She is unconvinced that 1QS views the food of the community as consecrated. Noting that sharing the community's food is closely associated with membership in the community (VIII, 16–19, 21–24), Himmelfarb suggests that exclusion from the food simply means exclusion from the community. If 1QS were concerned with applying the Torah's rules concerning consecrated food, members in good standing would also be excluded when in a state of physical impurity. 1QS does not legislate for this eventuality, and Himmelfarb offers an alternative perspective:

> Exclusion from the pure food and drink of the community is probably best understood not as a measure related to purity concerns but as a way of enforcing exclusion from the community. The punishment is thus independent of concepts of purity, although no doubt 1QS's view of outsiders as impure made it a particularly resonant punishment.[75]

The third example of the conflation of impurity and sin in 1QS concerns the theory and practice of "baptism," a ritual of purification that marks repentance.[76] 1QS V, 13–14, which gives instructions for new members of the community, indi-

---

73. For Himmelfarb's discussion of purity in 1QS, see "Impurity and Sin," 29–34.
74. Klawans, "Impurity and Immorality," 9.
75. Himmelfarb, "Impurity and Sin," 33.
76. Himmelfarb's use of the term "baptism" has theological implications that are misleading at best.

cates, in Himmelfarb's words, that "baptism does not purify people who have not repented."[77] Those who have not repented their sins cannot join the community and partake of its pure food.

1QS does not focus on the *physical* state of impurity that characterizes P. Rather, the categories of pure and impure are transformed into *spiritual* states. This suggests that the concept of impurity is central to the thought of 1QS in a metaphorical rather than a technical sense. It is therefore important to distinguish between language and legislation. The fact that P's technical terminology figures prominently in the hortatory passages of 1QS implies a conflation of impurity and sin in the language of the text, but not in the realm of *halakhah*.

Also relevant is 4Q512, a collection of purity liturgies.[78] The extremely fragmentary nature of the text precludes easy identification of the types of impurity that are associated with the blessings. Yet it is evident that 4Q512 purposefully blurs the categories of impurity found in the Torah. For example, the phrase נגע נדה, "the affliction of menstrual impurity" (V, 17; XII, 16), combines a term that refers to skin eruptions (נגע) with one that is used for menstrual impurity (נדה). 4Q512 is characterized by this blending of the various categories of impurity that P takes such care to separate.

The blessings in 4Q512 are concerned with the evocation of human imperfection, as evidenced in phrases such as ערות בשרנו "the shamefulness of your flesh" (III, 17) and ערות נדה "the shamefulness of (menstrual) impurity" (VII, 9). In Qumran, the terms ערות and בשר are often used in reference to the corporeal aspect of human nature, which is considered inferior to the spiritual.[79] For Himmelfarb, this use of language is an indication of the idea of purity in 4Q512. She states:

> For 4Q512, then, the significance of the various types of impurity carefully delineated by P is the same: all point to human frailty and failing. But impurity as an indication of human imperfection is not the same as impurity as a result of sin or impurity as in and of itself sinful.[80]

4Q512 includes two blessings in which the petitioner gives thanks for both purification from impurity and forgiveness from sin:

> [... to] ask mercy for all the hidden guilty acts ... you who are righteous in all your deeds ... from the affliction of impurity. (V, 15–17) Blessed are you [God of Israel, who saved me from all] my sins and purified me from the indecency of impurity. (VII, 9)

Here the references to purity and sin remain separate. There is no indication that sin causes impurity, nor is the impurity regarded as sinful. Rather, these passages

---

77. Himmelfarb, "Impurity and Sin," 34.
78. For Himmelfarb's discussion of purity in 4Q512, see "Impurity and Sin," 34–36.
79. Baumgarten, "Purification Rituals," 200–201, 208.
80. Himmelfarb, "Impurity and Sin," 36.

indicate that "sin and impurity are understood as two aspects of human finitude, corresponding to soul and body."[81]

In summary, Himmelfarb finds nothing distinctively sectarian about the purity laws of 4QD. Rather, the text follows P in its characterization of impurity as a ritual category. 1QS and 4Q512 are both sectarian documents that use the language of impurity. The significant differences between them, however, frustrate the attempt to identify a common and distinctive relationship between impurity and sin. The only common feature is their poetic or evocative use of purity language. For this reason, Himmelfarb argues that the association of sin and impurity in 1QS and 4Q512, and perhaps at Qumran in general, is primarily evocative and not *halakhic*.

VII. Summary and Conclusion

Jacob Neusner's initial survey of purity at Qumran emphasizes the significance of the concept for the theme of the community as temple and argues that the Qumran sectarians conflated the categories of ritual and moral impurity. These two points provide the foundation for subsequent discussion. Newton, for example, not only accepts the notion of the community as temple, but goes one step further by collapsing the distinction between purity and sin at Qumran. García Martínez sees an evolution of the purity concepts at Qumran that developed as a result of the historical situation of the community. Harrington's work challenges both of Neusner's premises concerning purity at Qumran. Finally, Klawans and Himmelfarb focus on the relationship between impurity and sin. Klawans offers a nuanced argument for a conflation of categories in the various texts, a point strongly disputed by Himmelfarb. At the root of this scholarly disagreement are two different approaches to the texts: Klawans insists on a literal interpretation of purity language, while Himmelfarb contends that there is a non-literal, evocative use of this terminology. Despite their disagreement, the contributions of these two scholars point to the fundamental ambiguities in the texts and provide the foundation for future research on impurity and sin at Qumran.

Undoubtedly, these scholarly discussions have opened the door to future investigation. Questions that require clarification abound: Is there, indeed, a conflation of the categories of impurity at Qumran, as Klawans and others suggest? If so, to what extent is sin regarded as defiling? And, to what extent is ritual impurity regarded as sinful? Finally, scholars may need to consider if the categories of ritual and moral impurity are, indeed, helpful, or whether we need to be thinking about new ways to approach the concepts of impurity at Qumran. Further studies need to consider these questions carefully in the context of the textual traditions associated with Qumran. The goal would not be to draw salient conclusions regarding a

---

81. Ibid., 36.

single concept of purity at Qumran, but rather to explore the variety of attitudes toward defilement represented in the literature.[82]

---

82. Editor's note: Haber's chapter originally concluded with the following: "To date, there has been no monograph-length study devoted specifically to the concepts of purity at Qumran. Such a study is long overdue." I believe that she saw the dissertation that she was planning to write as the work that would fill this gap. Since the completion of the bibliographic study, a book on purity on Qumran has indeed appeared: Hannah K. Harrington, *The Purity Texts* (New York: Continuum, 2004). This useful work is a handbook that includes the relevant texts as well as some discussion of each type of impurity. Haber's point likely remains true, however, in that the library of works on the Dead Sea Scrolls still has a place for the detailed scholarly analysis of the sort that Haber had proposed to conduct.

Part II

Literary Studies

4

Living and Dying for the Law:
The Mother-Martyrs of 2 Maccabees

The second book of the Maccabees (2 Maccabees) gives a historical account of the conflict between the Seleucid government and the Jewish people that took place in Judea during the period of 180–161 B.C.E.[1] Writing some half a century after the events, the anonymous author describes a period of Greek tyranny and persecution of the Jews and the successful war of Jewish liberation that followed.[2] Of particular interest is the interpretation of events offered by the martyrology of 2 Macc 6:7–7:42,[3] which gives details of the Hellenistic reform and the desperate resistance of the Jews at a time when it was forbidden for them to live in accordance with their ancestral law.[4] Those who refused to adopt the Greek way of life were subject to death.

The author of 2 Maccabees emphasizes the specific Jewish practices for which Jews are killed. There is mention of two women who circumcise their sons according to the Law and are subsequently tried and executed along with their babies (6:10). Likewise, a group of people who secretly gather to celebrate the Sabbath is sought out and massacred (6:11). Finally, there is a lengthy description of the mar-

---

1. Second Maccabees 2:19–15:39 is generally viewed as a historical work in its own right. The history begins with the reign of Seleucus IV (187–175 B.C.E.) and ends with the defeat of the Seleucid general Nicanor in 161 B.C.E. See, for example, Jan Willem van Henten, *The Maccabean Martyrs as Saviours of the Jewish People: A Study of 2 and 4 Maccabees* (Leiden: Brill, 1997), 17–19.

2. Second Maccabees was written in Judea sometime between 124–63 B.C.E., with the actual date of composition likely being toward the beginning of this period. In 2 Macc 2:23, the author claims that the work is not his own but rather an epitome of the five-volume account of one Jason of Cyrene. For the purposes of this essay I follow van Henten in considering the historical account in 2 Macc 2:19–15:39 as a unity and the epitomist as its author (ibid., 20). For discussion on the date and provenance of 2 Maccabees, see ibid., 50–56.

3. This is a distinct literary unit. See Robin Darling Young, "The 'Woman with the Soul of Abraham': Traditions about the Mother of the Maccabean Martyrs," in *"Women Like This": New Perspectives on Jewish Women in the Greco-Roman World* (ed. Amy-Jill Levine; Atlanta: Scholars Press, 1991), 69.

4. The transition to the martyrology occurs in v. 6: "No one was allowed to observe the Sabbath or to keep the traditional festivals or *even to confess he was a Jew.*" Commenting on this verse, Goldstein suggests that although Jews continued to practice Judaism in secret, it was suicidal for a practicing Jew to admit he was Jewish (Jonathan A. Goldstein, *II Maccabees* [AB 41A; Garden City, NY: Doubleday, 1983], 276).

tyrdom of the elderly sage Eleazar (6:18–31) and of a woman with her seven sons (7:1–42), all of whom refuse to transgress the Jewish dietary laws by eating pork. The account of the persecution is informative, for it gives insight into the practices that were perceived, by both author and audience, as separating Jews from the dominant culture: circumcision, the observance of the Sabbath, and the abstention from pork.[5] These three practices were central to Jewish self-definition, and their observance was a symbol of their loyalty to the Law. In 2 Maccabees, it was the pious Jews who were steadfast in these observances, living by and ultimately dying for the Law.[6]

Who are these pious Jews who chose to live and die for the Law? Remarkably, the heroes of this historical period are not found in the ranks of the priesthood or among the powerful leaders of Jewish society. They are primarily found among the ostensibly weak in society: the women, children, and the aged.[7] The role of women in the forefront of this movement is significant. They are not portrayed as wives, daughters, or daughters-in-law. Neither are they necessarily independent women, for there is no indication that they are widows or prostitutes.[8] These anonymous women are portrayed exclusively as *mothers* as they take on religious roles: they circumcise their sons, instruct their children in ancestral law, and ultimately give up the lives of both their children and themselves for the sake of the Law.[9] In death they become mother-martyrs.

---

5. In Greco-Roman literature, the distinctive character of the Jews is often associated with these three practices. See Peter Schäfer, *Judeophobia: Attitudes toward the Jews in the Ancient World* (Cambridge: Harvard University Press, 1997), 66–105.

6. [Editor's note: This essay does not focus directly on purity. But as noted in the introduction to the present volume, the failure to circumcise was seen as a pollution of the land, in punishment for which God wrested the land from the people Israel. The performance of circumcision and willingness to die for the Law were thus part of the people's repentance that, it was hoped, would eventuate in the restoration of the land, as indeed was the case in the aftermath of the Maccabean revolt.]

7. Rajak refers to the "heroic endurance by the ostensibly weak (women, children and the old)." See Tessa Rajak, "Dying for the Law: The Martyr's Portrait in Jewish-Greek Literature," in *Portraits: Biographical Representation in the Greek and Latin Literature of the Roman Empire* (ed. M. J. Edwards and Simon Swain; Oxford: Clarendon Press, 1997), 40.

8. Goldstein suggests the possibility that the text of 2 Macc 7 is a fulfillment of the prophecy in Jer 15:1–9, which explicitly refers to the plight of widows: "I have made her widows more numerous than the sand of the seas. I have brought against the mothers of young men a destroyer at noonday. . . . Forlorn is she who gave birth to seven; she has swooned away; her sun set while it was yet day; she has been put to shame and disappointed." If he is correct, then it is likely that the audience would have picked up on the allusion to the prophecy and assumed the widowhood of the mother in 2 Macc 7. However, the marital status of the two circumcising mothers in 2 Macc 6:10 still remains unexplained.

9. In her monograph on anonymity in the biblical narrative, Reinhartz argues convincingly that the "principal effect of the absence of a proper name is to focus the reader's attention on the role designations that flood into the gap that anonymity denotes" (Adele Reinhartz, *"Why Ask My Name?" Anonymity and Identity in Biblical Narrative* [New York and Oxford: Oxford University Press, 1998], 188). On a different level, Rajak interprets the

How does the author of 2 Maccabees portray these mother-martyrs? What does this depiction reveal about the role of women during this brief period of history? In this essay, I propose to examine the literary representation of the mother-martyrs in 2 Maccabees. Essential to this inquiry is the assumption that the author's portrayal of the mother-martyrs is fundamental to his rhetorical agenda. He was not writing as an impartial witness to the events that transpired, but rather he was offering a highly stylized version of the account that was intended to inspire his audience through the use of didactic historiography.[10] Within the framework of this recounting, we can consider what the author and his audience considered plausible and unremarkable in the lives of the mother-martyrs and speculate on how these representations may correspond to the social reality of the time.[11]

THE MOTHER-MARTYRS AS CIRCUMCISORS OF THEIR SONS

> For example, two women were brought in for having circumcised their children. They publicly paraded them around the city, with their babies hanging at their breasts, and then hurled them down headlong from the wall. (2 Macc 6:10 NRSV)

This brief description is all that the narrator tells his audience about the women who were executed for circumcising their sons. This single verse has rarely, if ever, been categorized as a martyrdom by modern scholars. Yet in its literary context it shares many characteristics with the longer accounts that have been established as part of the literary genre of martyrdom. According to van Henten, "A martyr is a person who in an extremely hostile situation prefers a violent death to compliance with a demand of the (usually pagan) authorities."[12] This definition is supplemented by a list of common narrative elements that often form a pattern in martyr texts, most of which can be found in the text of 2 Macc 6. First, there is the enactment of a law by the Greek authorities requiring Jews to adopt the Greek way of life. Those who chose not to comply with the law are subject to the death penalty (vv. 8–9). Second, the Jews are put into a position of conflict of loyalty, for in staying faithful to their God and his Law they are in contravention of the Greek law (v. 6). Third, placed in a position of complying with the decree or remaining

---

anonymity of these women in terms of their role as martyrs, suggesting that the omission of names depersonalizes the Jewish representation of the past and emphasizes religious heroism over identity. On this basis, she argues for anonymity as a "primary defining characteristic of Jewish-Greek martyrology in this period" ("Dying for the Law," 57–58).

10. van Henten, *The Maccabean Martyrs*, 25.

11. Kraemer points out that it is not necessary to argue for the historical accuracy of an ancient text when attempting to reconstruct the lives of women. She states: "Whether or not these specific incidents occurred, their recounting ... tells us much about what ancient authors and audiences took as plausible, unremarkable and the givens of ordinary social life...." See Ross S. Kraemer, "Jewish Women and Christian Origins: Some Caveats," in *Women and Christian Origins* (ed. Ross S. Kraemer and Mary Rose D'Angelo; New York: Oxford University Press, 1999), 42.

12. On the designation of a martyr text, see van Henten, *The Maccabean Martyrs*, 7–9.

faithful to their ancestral Law, the two women choose to circumcise their children and face the death penalty (v. 10). Fourth, there is a description of their execution (v. 10).

The difficulty in substantiating the account of the circumcising mothers as a martyr text arises from one apparent departure from the common pattern: the choice to remain faithful to the Law is made *before* their arrest, rather than during an examination by pagan authorities. The question arises as to whether or not the deaths of these women can be classified as voluntary. In other words, when they circumcised their children did they know for certain that they would be put to death on account of their actions? The parallel text in 4 Maccabees leaves no doubt in the minds of the audience when it indicates that the women circumcised their children even "though they had known beforehand that they would suffer this . . ." (v. 25). Our text is not nearly as explicit. Nevertheless, the vivid description of the decree and the persecution that precedes the account implies that the two women were aware that their actions would result in their deaths.[13] They are thus "brought in" for trial, examined, and then punished for their crime by being publicly paraded through the city and executed.[14] Presumably, the pagan authorities intended the public spectacle to act as a deterrent to others. From the perspective of other Jews, however, the women would have been regarded as heroes who gave their lives and those of their children for the Law. In death, they did indeed become mother-martyrs.

The brevity of the account of the martyrdom of the two mothers raises more questions than it answers. What does the representation of these women reveal about the role of the Jewish mother with respect to her newborn son? Why were the mothers executed, but not the fathers? Did women act as circumcisors? The significance of these questions becomes especially clear when considered against the background of ritual circumcision in its historical and sociological context.

From the emergence of Judaism, circumcision was considered a central ritual for Jewish culture as a whole—the quintessential male rite of passage transmitted

---

13. It is important to note that the nature of the law of circumcision presents a certain logistical difficulty for the author who would feature it as a basis of martyrdom. The requirement to circumcise is a positive command that is bound by time constraints: it must be performed on the eighth day after birth (Lev 12:3). As such, the observance or transgression of the law can only be ascertained *after* the designated time has passed. This precludes the possibility of pagan authorities using torture to induce voluntary transgression *prior* to the designated time. Such forms of coercion must be reserved for the transgression of negative non-timebound commands, such as the prohibition against eating pork.

14. Goldstein translates: "Two women were brought to trial . . . " (*II Maccabees*, 268). That there was a trial may be verified by the outcome: the women and children were executed. It is likely that the preferred method of executing women in the Greco-Roman world was hurling from a height. In the third century B.C.E., the Seleucid queen Laodice executed her ladies, Danaë, in this fashion (ibid., 279). Moreover, Epicurean philosophers who were condemned as effeminate were hurled from a wall dressed as women. On the parallels between the treatment of Jews who circumcised and effeminate Epicurean philosophers, see Jonathan A. Goldstein, *I Maccabees* (AB 41; Garden City, NY: Doubleday, 1976), 127 n. 143; 129 n. 153.

from father to son.[15] In Hellenistic Judaism, it became the mark that identified the Jew and distinguished him from his Greek counterpart. As such, it became the subject of a certain amount of controversy.[16] From a gender perspective, circumcision literally marked off the binary opposition between Jewish men and women and was seemingly confined to the ritual realm of men.[17] One notable exception in the literature is the biblical account of Zipporah circumcising her son (Exod 4:24-26). Yet even this image is subject to subsequent revision, as the rabbis attempt to erase any evidence that women were involved in the circumcision of their sons.[18] Accordingly, the rabbis instruct that instead of reading the biblical phrase "Zipporah took a flint" one should read "she caused it to be taken," indicating that she asked a man to do it for her. In the rabbinic version of the story, Zipporah did not remove her son's foreskin, since women were never qualified to perform circumcision.

For many a student of rabbinic literature, the apparent disqualification of women from the performance of circumcision affirms the exclusivity of the male-centered ritual from the post-exilic priesthood through to the rabbinic era.[19] Women simply did not circumcise their sons. Yet, if this were the case, why did the rabbis deem it necessary to state unequivocally that women were not qualified in this area? Could it be that, much to the chagrin of the rabbis, women were, in fact, taking an active role in the ritual of circumcision? The text of 2 Maccabees seemingly supports this theory, for it was two women—and not two men—who were put to death for circumcising their sons.[20] As such, 2 Macc 6:10 calls into question the

---

15. The post-exilic priestly author and redactor of the Bible emphasized circumcision and made it central to his agenda, writing back into the text the concept of circumcision as the external sign of the covenant between God and Israel. Consequently, in early Judaism the non-observance of the law of circumcision represented a break in the covenant (*Jub.* 15:1-4, 11-14) and dissociation from the Jewish community (*Jub.* 15:26; cf. Schäfer, *Judeophobia*, 93). On the priestly agenda regarding circumcision, see Lawrence A. Hoffman, *Covenant of Blood: Circumcision and Gender in Rabbinic Judaism* (Chicago: University of Chicago Press, 1996), 30-38.

16. In Greek culture, the body was revered in its perfection. In this light, circumcision was disapproved of as a form of mutilation (see, for example, Herodotus, 2.36f). In Hellenistic Judaism the practice became discredited among Jews who wanted to participate in the Greek culture around them (1 Macc 1:15; *Jub.* 15:33; *A.J.* 12.241). They underwent operations to disguise their circumcision (epispasm) and, according to Josephus, exercised naked in the gymnasium (*A.J.* 12.241). Although failure to circumcise is a clear transgression of the Law, it is not certain that disguising a circumcision is considered a sin (Jonathan Goldstein, "Jewish Acceptance and Rejection of Hellenism," in *Semites, Iranians, Greeks, and Romans: Studies in Their Interactions* [Atlanta: Scholars Press, 1990], 79 n. 92; cf. Robert G. Hall, "Epispasm: Circumcision in Reverse," *BR* [August 1992]: 52-57). It is clear, however, that from the point of view of both Jews and Greeks, circumcision was the mark that identified the Jewish man as a Jew.

17. Hoffman, *Covenant of Blood*, 22.
18. See b. 'Abod. Zar. 27a.
19. Ibid.
20. Goldstein points out that in the parallel texts in 1 Macc 1:60-61 and 4 Macc 4:24-25

accepted rabbinic perspective and substantiates the claim that there was a time in the Second Temple period when women participated in the ritual of circumcision. Women may have been excluded from the rite by virtue of their biology, but that did not mean that as Jewish mothers they did not have a role in the circumcision of their sons. The nature of that role requires further investigation.

The feminine participle ἀνήχθησαν is used to denote the mother's role in the act of circumcising her son in both 2 Macc 6:10 and the parallel text of 4 Macc 4:25. Without a doubt, the use of the word implies that it is the mothers who are held responsible for circumcising their sons, and it is they who suffer the consequences of their actions. It is important, however, to distinguish between taking responsibility for the performance of a ritual and actually performing the ritual oneself.[21] In this regard, the parallel text in 1 Macc 1:60–61 is informative:

> According to the decree, they put to death the women who had their children circumcised, and their families and those who circumcised them; and they hung the infants from their mothers' necks.

In this account, the women are mentioned first, indicating that they were the ones held responsible for the circumcision of their children. It is evident, however, that they did not perform the circumcisions themselves, as the text specifies that both the families and those who performed the ritual circumcisions were put to death along with the mothers. Here the use of the masculine participle περιτετμηκότας indicates that the procedure was likely performed by a man.[22] Curiously, the fathers are not mentioned. Perhaps they were included as part of the family or alluded to in the category of "those who circumcised."[23] It is more likely, however, that if the fathers were considered accountable they would have been ex-

---

there is no mention of the number of women. This specification adds a certain amount of authenticity to the account (*II Maccabees*, 279).

21. In modern Judaism, it is technically the obligation of the father to perform the circumcision himself. In many forms of the ceremony, the *mohel* asks the father if he wishes to perform the circumcision, to which he replies, "I want you to do it for me as my legal agent." See Hoffman, *Covenant of Blood*, 73.

22. Against Bar-Ilan, who suggests that in the same way that women traditionally tended to the needs of the newborn, cutting the umbilical cord, nursing, and clothing the child, they may have also removed the foreskin. He supports his claim that women circumcised their sons by citing *b. Yebam.* 64b in which there is a discussion concerning whether or not a women should circumcise her third son if the first and second had died as a result of the procedure. The text, however, does not indicate that the woman actually performed the ritual. Rather, it is concerned that the children of one family have a tendency to bleed profusely and die. In a time when a man could have more than one wife, the specification of the woman merely establishes that the sons were all from the same mother and had the same genetic predisposition. On the "circumcising women," see Meir Bar-Ilan, *Some Jewish Women in Antiquity* (BJS 317; Atlanta: Scholars Press, 1998), 16–19.

23. The word οἶκος, translated here as "family," literally means "houses." Goldstein acknowledges the literal translation in his commentary, but nevertheless translates οἶκους as "husbands." See Goldstein, *I Maccabees*, 227.

plicitly mentioned.²⁴ In 1 Maccabees, it is the mothers who assume responsibility for circumcising their sons.

Another text that gives some insight into the practice of circumcision in this period is the Aramaic re-working of the Books of Maccabees, "The Scroll of Antiochus":²⁵

> So drastic was the king's edict that when a man was discovered to have circumcised his son (מצאו איש אשר מל את בנו), he and his wife were hanged along with the child. A woman gave birth to a son after her husband's death and had him circumcised (ותמל אותו) when he was eight days old. With the child in her arms, she went up on top of the wall of Jerusalem and cried out: "We say to you, wicked Bagris, this covenant of our fathers which you intend to destroy shall never cease from us nor from our children's children." She cast her son down to the ground and flung herself after him so that they died together. Many Israelites of that period did the same, refusing to renounce the covenant of their fathers.²⁶

In this account there are two acts of circumcision. The first case involves a man who circumcises his son. Notably, both parents are held accountable for the circumcision, being put to death along with the child. In the second instance, a widow circumcises her son and then preempts her inevitable execution in what the author portrays as a heroic act of murder-suicide.²⁷ In the Hebrew, the use of the feminine imperfect *vav* consecutive ותמל indicates that it was the mother who took responsibility for the circumcision of her son. This text stands in opposition to the rabbinic view that, in the absence of a male relative, it is up to the religious court or the child himself, upon reaching adulthood, to arrange for his circumcision.²⁸ Here it is not entirely clear that the woman actually performed the circumcision, since the usage of ותמל can be understood either literally or figuratively. Nevertheless, it is clear that in the absence of a father, the mother acts, upholding the Law even in the face of death.²⁹

---

24. Josephus relies on 1 Maccabees as his source for this period in history. In his account, however, he indicates that the fathers were tortured and crucified for circumcising their sons, while the wives and children were strangled. It is notable that when the responsibility for circumcision is transferred to the father, the women's role becomes that of "wife" and not "mother."

25. According to Bar-Ilan (*Some Jewish Women*, 16–18, esp. n. 36), *The Scroll of Antiochus* may be dated to some time between the second century B.C.E. and the second century C.E.

26. Hebrew and English translations from *Daily Prayer Book: Ha-Siddur Ha-Shalem* (trans. Philip Birnbaum; New York: Hebrew Publishing Company, 1949), 717–20.

27. In circumcising her son, the mother not only upheld the ancestral law but she also saved her son from disaster by establishing his identity as a Jew and ensuring that he would not be barred from eternal life after death. Bar-Ilan, *Some Jewish Women*, 18.

28. *b. Kidd.* 29a–b.

29. Against Archer, who asserts that under the exceptional circumstances of the persecution of Antiochus Epiphanes, women performed circumcisions. See Léonie J. Archer, *Her Price Is Beyond Rubies: The Jewish Woman in Graeco-Roman Palestine* (JSOTSup 60; Sheffield: JSOT Press, 1990), 223 n. 3. I do not deny the possibility that women circumcised

Ultimately, the texts in 1 Maccabees and The Scroll of Antiochus can neither confirm nor rule out the possibility that the mothers in 2 Macc 6:20 actually performed the circumcisions. This literature does, however, lend credence to the contention that mothers did take responsibility for circumcising their sons, especially when the fathers were absent or in times of danger. It is therefore reasonable to conclude that, at the very least, the mother-martyrs of 2 Maccabees took sole responsibility for circumcising their sons, upholding the Law, and ensuring their sons' identities as Jews. They fulfilled this religious role in full knowledge of the consequences of their actions: certain death for both themselves and their children. The mother-martyrs lived for the Law, ensuring that their sons lived, albeit briefly, as members of the covenant between God and Israel.

The Mother-Martyr as Instructor of Her Sons

The portrayal of the mother-martyr in 2 Macc 7 is essential to the narrative. She watches as each of her sons, from the oldest to the youngest, bravely gives his life for the Law. Yet, in spite of the horror of seeing her seven sons perish in a single day, she bears her suffering with "good courage" (εὐψύχως) "because of her hope in the Lord" (διὰ τὰς ἐπὶ κύριον ἐλπίδας).[30] Here in v. 20, the mother is portrayed as a model of piety whose trust in God gives her the strength to heroically endure her anguish. Moreover, she is not a passive bystander, but rather she actively encourages them to choose death over transgression of the Law. Her extraordinary bravery is explained in Stoic terms: ". . . she reinforced her woman's reasoning" (τὸν θῆλυν λογισμὸν) "with a man's courage" (ἄρσενι θυμῷ, v. 21).[31] Thus the author presents the women's heroic actions in terms of a philosophical division between the emotional feminine element of the human constitution and the rational masculine element.[32] The mother-martyr is thus portrayed as a woman who possesses masculine virtues.[33]

The mother's words of encouragement are found in the form of two direct

---

their children in this period. However, given the rhetorical nature of the text, I do not think that one can assert with any degree of certainty the continuity between this literary representation of women circumcising their sons and real-life practice.

30. A similar expression of the mother's trust in God is found in 4 Macc 17:4.

31. Van Henten comments on the similar language used in Philo's portrayal of Julia Augusta in *Legat.* 320 and suggests that there is a *topos* of exceptional women who act like men in Jewish and Greco-Roman literature (*The Maccabean Martyrs*, 233–34 and nn. 236–37).

32. On the use of the Stoic division between masculine and feminine attributes in 2 Macc 7:21, see Young, "Woman with the Soul," 71, esp. n. 5. Philo assumes a similar contrast between masculine reasoning and female emotion. See, for example, *Leg.* 3.11; cf. 3.49–50.

33. In 4 Maccabees, the author glorifies the mother in masculine terms, asserting that she is "more noble than males in endurance, more manly than men in resistance" (15:30; cf. 16:14). Commenting on the author's insistence on the mother's superiority in the sphere of male virtue, Rajak ("Dying for the Law," 55–56) contends that "the identity of the heroic martyr is thus preserved as a masculine one." This tendency to masculinize the female martyr is especially apparent in later Christian martyrology, as is evident in, for example, *Acts of Thecla* 40 and the *Martyrdom of Saints Perpetua and Felicitas*. In 2 Maccabees, however, the

speeches, the first imparted to all of her sons (vv. 22–23) and the second to the youngest son after his brothers have already died (vv. 27–29). The speeches are intended to be didactic and persuasive. As such, they point to the mother's essential influence over her sons and her role in teaching them to live their lives in accordance with the Law.[34]

The first speech is an instruction to the brothers on the contemporary belief in the doctrines of *creatio ex nihilo* and resurrection to life. Here the pairing of creation and resurrection is essential to the mother's instruction: just as God gave life to them, in the same way that he created the universe and all of humankind, he will also restore them to life by a process of re-creation.[35] It is on the basis of this analogy between God's power to create and his ability to re-create that the mother encourages her sons to trust in the Lord and not to forsake his laws. They are to die as they have lived—for the sake of the Law—so that in God's mercy they will be resurrected to life.

That the mother's speech is intended as a private instruction and exhortation is indicated not only by its content but also by the manner in which it is communicated. Although others may be present, the mother does not speak publicly. Rather, she is portrayed as speaking privately to her sons "in the language of their ancestors" (v. 21).[36] The brothers are the only ones who can understand the content of the message. All others are excluded by the imposed language barrier.

In the context of 2 Macc 7, there are two other instances in which the author specifies that the speaker is communicating in the ancestral language: prior to the mother's second speech (v. 27) and before the second son's response to his torturer's demand that he eat pork (v. 8).[37] In the latter case, the brevity of the boy's reply—a single word, "no"—would have required no translation. It may be assumed that with the exception of this one instance, the seven brothers always spoke Greek when addressing the king and his men. Moreover, it is implied that the mother also understood and even spoke Greek, as indicated by her ability to respond when the king insisted that she convince her youngest son to save himself

---

male virtues of the mother are not developed, nor are they emphasized. Her role as mother is essential to her identity, as exemplified in her relationship with her youngest son (v. 27).

34. According to Young ("Woman with the Soul," 70), the mother's influence on the boys "must be seen as essential."

35. On the relationship between creation and resurrection in 2 Maccabees, see G. W. E. Nickelsburg, *Resurrection, Immortality, and Eternal Life in Intertestamental Judaism* (HTS 26; Cambridge, 1972), 107; cf. van Henten, *The Maccabean Martyrs*, 175–82.

36. The phrase τῇ πατρίῳ φωνῇ literally means "in the paternal language." The mother's use of the ancestral language gives a sense that the communication to her sons was of a private nature. See Young, "Woman with the Soul," 70. The identification of the language is subject to dispute. According to Young (ibid., 71), it is likely that she spoke Aramaic and not Hebrew. Van Henten, however, argues that, in 2 Maccabees, references to the ancestral language indicate Hebrew. See Jan Willem van Henten, "The Ancestral Language of the Jews," in *Hebrew Study from Ezra to Ben-Yehuda* (ed. William Horbury; Edinburgh: T & T Clark, 1999), 65–68.

37. Reference to the use of the ancestral language is also made in 2 Macc 12:37; 15:29.

by departing from the Law (7:25–26).[38] Here the use of the ancestral language is essential to the mother's deception of the king. It afforded her the opportunity to impart further instruction to the child and persuade him, contrary to the king's wishes, to accept martyrdom rather than transgress the Law.[39]

The choice to use her ancestral language in this specific circumstance is significant when considered in terms of the relationship between language and ethnicity, for the use of language can build or break down cultural barriers. In this case, the choice of language emphasizes the bond between the mother and her sons and the unanimity in their decision to live and die by the Law, while simultaneously distinguishing them from the king and his men and the larger Greek culture that they represent. Interestingly, however, the dichotomy between Jew and Greek with respect to language is not as sharp a distinction as one might expect, for the use of the ancestral language is clearly a matter of choice and not ability. These Jews were, indeed, proficient in their use of Greek.[40] They *chose* to use their ancestral language in the same way as they *chose* to obey their ancestral Law.

The mother's second speech is directed to her youngest son after his brothers have died and is composed of three parts: a plea, an instruction, and a command.[41] The instruction reiterates the mother's belief in the doctrine of *creatio ex nihilo*, thereby providing a basis for the belief in resurrection. The mother's plea and command heighten the sense of persuasion in a speech that is directed to a child who is perhaps too young to be convinced on the basis of rational argument alone.[42] These two elements appeal to the strength of the bond between mother and son, giving insight into the role of motherhood as perceived by the author and his audience.

When the woman speaks, it is as a mother speaking to her son. She begins

---

38. Van Henten (*The Maccabean Martyrs*, 196) asserts that the martyrs use Greek when speaking to the king and his people, but speak among themselves in the ancestral language.

39. The king did not understand the ancestral language, as indicated in v. 24: "Antiochus felt that he was being treated with contempt, and he was suspicious of her reproachful tone."

40. The process of Hellenization was not a matter of simple acceptance or rejection. It was a complex process in which a variety of cultural influences were selected, adopted, or adapted to varying degrees in different levels of society. On the one hand, the use of the ancestral language indicates the martyrs are part of a people with its own identity. See Jan Willem van Henten and Friedrich Avemarie, *Martyrdom and Noble Death: Selected Texts from Graeco-Roman, Jewish, and Christian Antiquity* (London: Routledge, 2002), 67 n. 92. On the other hand, their proficiency in Greek may indicate a degree of Hellenization that is not necessarily associated with the abandonment of religious identity. On the complexity of the Hellenization process see Lee I. Levine, *Judaism and Hellenism in Antiquity: Conflict or Confluence?* (Seattle: University of Washington Press, 1998), 17–28.

41. Young, "Woman with the Soul," 72.

42. From a literary perspective, the escalation of the mother's rhetoric balances the added incentive to transgress the Law that the king offers to the child (v. 24). Obeying the Law would bring about a painful death, but obeying the king would be rewarded with wealth and power.

with an opening plea: "My son, have pity on me." This utterance is laden with theatrical paradox as the author deliberately heightens the pathos in his portrayal of the mother pleading with her only surviving son to show compassion by allowing her to watch him die.[43] Included in her plea is a description of her role as mother: "I carried you (περιενέγκασαν) nine months in my womb, and nursed you (θηλάσασαν) for three years, and have reared you (ἐκθρέψασαν) and have brought you up (ἀγαγοῦσαν) to this point in your life, and have taken care of you (τροφοφορήσασαν)" (v. 27). A string of five verbs is used for emphasis in the quintessential maternal argument, which may be summarized as follows: "After all I have done for you, you must do as I say." Taken together, the five verbs not only underscore the identity of the woman as mother, as intended by the author, but also give valuable insight into what the author and his audience perceived as the role of the contemporary mother.[44]

The verb περιφέρω ("carried") refers to the carrying around of children and alludes to the pregnancy of the mother. The very mention of her pregnancy establishes the woman as the mother of the child and confirms her parental authority over him.[45] According to the Law, a child is required to honor his parents (Exod 20:12). This concept of honor is quite prominent in the Jewish literature of the second century B.C.E. and is most often equated with respect and obedience. A son is required to obey both his mother and his father.[46] Thus, by virtue of her maternity, the mother-martyr of 2 Macc 7 could expect and even demand the obedience of her son.

The second verb, θηλάζω ("nursed" or "suckled"), refers to the mother's care of the child during infancy. She nursed her son for a period of three years, nourishing the child with milk from her own breast. In a time when breast milk was the only source of nourishment available to an infant, it was essential to survival of children that they be nursed.[47] It is not certain to what extent Jewish women of

---

43. Goldstein, *II Maccabees*, 314.

44. Goldstein notes the sequence of five verbs and suggests that the text is an expansion on Lam 2:22 that also includes a rare word τροφοφορέω ("take care"), borrowed from Greek Deut 1:31. He argues (*II Maccabees*, 314–15) that the latter verb was not original and omits it from his own translation. Arguing against Goldstein, van Henten (*The Maccabean Martyrs*, 233 n. 233) asserts that there is no reason to change the text since the fifth verb, although somewhat redundant, fits the context.

45. Ben Sira establishes parental authority over children: "For the Lord honored the father above his children, and made firm the authority of the mother over her sons" (3:2). See Warren C. Trenchard, *Ben Sira's View of Women: A Literary Analysis* (BJS 38; Chico, CA: Scholars Press, 1982), 40–43.

46. Tobit 4:3–4 discusses the honor a son should give to his mother. In the book of *Jubilees* there are several examples of concern for honor: Rebecca exhorts Jacob to honor his father and brother (35:5), Jacob is portrayed as honoring both of his parents (35:12–13), whereas Esau shows them no honor when he treats them poorly (35:9–11).

47. Ilan notes that the artificial nipple and bottle were not used until modern times. See Tal Ilan, *Jewish Women in Greco-Roman Palestine: An Inquiry into Image and Status* (Peabody, MA: Hendrickson, 1996), 119. On the importance of breast milk in the ancient world,

this period nursed their own children or employed wet nurses for this purpose.[48] Neither is it possible to establish a standard length of time for nursing a child.[49] What is certain is that, in ancient society, breastfeeding was not only a means of providing physical nourishment to the child, it was also a metaphor for imparting knowledge. Most prominent in the Greco-Roman world was the image of the goddess Isis as divine mother, imparting life, protection, and saving knowledge to her son Horus through her maternal milk.[50] A similar metaphor is found in Jewish literature, with Philo's portrayal of God as nurse and source of Wisdom: "For he is the one who nourishes and nurses wise deeds, words, and thoughts" (*De migr. Abr.* 24:13).[51]

The metaphor of a divine being imparting knowledge through breast milk is continuous with the reality of women's lives, as indicated by literary evidence.[52] Gynecological manuals indicate concern for selecting the right nurse, "who will impart to the child the things necessary for his or her correct upbringing."[53] Similarly, a letter dated from the third to second century B.C.E. offers advice in choosing a temperate wet nurse who will put the child's welfare first, because nursing is "an important part, foremost and prefatory to the whole of the child's life."[54] It is evident that in the Greco-Roman world, as in Palestine, the nursing of a child was perceived as a necessary function that contributed to both the physical and moral nourishment of the child. Thus, for the mother in 2 Macc 7, the suckling of her son at her breast was both an act of sustaining and instructing the child. Along with his mother's milk, the boy imbibed his first lessons in the Law.

---

see Philo, who referred to it as "the happily timed ailment, which flows so gently fostering the tender growth of every creature" (*Virt.* 130; cf. *Spec.* 3.199–200).

48. Ilan, *Jewish Women*, 119–21. Ilan speculates that a wet-nurse was a luxury and was more apt to be employed by women of the aristocratic class. Similarly, Corrington indicates that "in the Hellenized and Roman upper classes, very few mothers actually nursed their own children...." See Gail Paterson Corrington, "The Milk of Salvation: Redemption by the Mother in Late Antiquity and Early Christianity," *HTR* 82, no. 4 (1989): 403.

49. In *Jub.* 17:1 there is a reference to the weaning of Isaac, but the age of the child is not mentioned. The Mishna indicates that two years is an appropriate length of time (*m. Git.* 7:6). The Tosefta establishes a minimum time of eighteen months to two years (*t. Nid.* 2:2–2:4). R. Eliezer, however, asserts that after twenty-four months, nursing was considered an abominable thing (*b. Ket.* 60a).

50. According to Corrington ("The Milk of Salvation," 398–404), the most widespread representation of Isis was as the goddess Isis *lactans*, seated on a throne nursing her son. Representations dating from the eighth century B.C.E. onward have been found throughout the Mediterranean world, where Isis presumably became associated with the Greek nursing deities, the *kourotrophoi*.

51. In Jewish literature, the personified Wisdom also shares many attributes with Isis, including "bestower of life" (e.g., Prov 8:35; Wis 8.3). See ibid., 405.

52. Corrington (ibid., 406) argues convincingly for the association between divine representation and social reality.

53. Ibid., 406.

54. Mary R. Lefkowitz and Maureen B. Fant, eds., *Women's Life in Greece and Rome* (Baltimore: John Hopkins University Press, 1982), no. 111.

A sense of instruction is inherent in each of the verbs ἐκτρέφω ("rear"), ἄγω ("bring up," "train" or "educate"), and τροφοφορέω ("take care," "nourish," or "sustain").[55] The use of these three verbs together emphasizes the mother-martyr's primary role in educating her son.[56] In early Judaism, both parents were responsible for the religious education of their children, but the chief responsibility rested upon the father as the head of the household.[57] In the Hebrew Bible the mother is often mentioned as a teacher, but in most instances her instruction is in conjunction with that of the father.[58] One exception is found in the maternal instruction of Lemuel, king of Massa, in Prov 31:1–9, a text that effectively lends credibility to the notion that both spouses shared the responsibility for teaching their children.[59] How this responsibility played out in reality, however, may have varied from one community to another or according to individual circumstances.[60] In the book of Tobit, for example, the duty to educate children in the Law is considered primarily a male duty (4:5–12), but because his father was dead, it was Tobit's grandmother who taught him the Law (1:8).[61] Not only did the woman know the Law, she was also quite capable, in the absence of a suitable male relative, of assuming the position of head of the household and taking full responsibility for the instruction of the child.

---

55. A note to the NRSV translation of 2 Maccabees indicates that "taken care of you" may be translated as "bore the burden of your education."

56. Van Henten suggests that the string of five verbs used in the mother's plea concerns five successive stages of growth for sons. To support this contention he cites Acts 22:3 with respect to Paul, indicating that the verse offers an example of three stages in a boy's life: birth, rearing, and education. See *The Maccabean Martyrs*, 233 n. 233. However, it should be noted that there is significant overlap between the last two categories. Similarly, in our passage the actions of rearing, training, and educating do not necessarily reflect successive stages of development but, rather, may be viewed as categories of responsibility of a parent toward a child, all of which involve some form of instruction.

57. Fletcher Harper Swift, *Education in Ancient Israel: From Earliest Times to 70 AD* (Chicago: Open Court, 1919), 52; cf. Carole Fontaine, *Smooth Words: Women, Proverbs, and Performance in Biblical Wisdom* (JSOTSup 356; New York: Sheffield, 2002), 30–35.

58. See, for example, Prov 1:8; 6:20. Corrington ("The Milk of Salvation," 405) suggests that "the role of the mother as the first instructor of children in Wisdom was one of authority in Israel."

59. James L. Crenshaw, *Education in Ancient Israel: Across the Deadening Silence* (New York: Doubleday, 1998), 189 n. 3.

60. Writing in first-century Alexandria, Philo asserts in general terms that it is the parents' responsibility to instruct their children from an early age (*Spec.* 2.228). Yet in other places he appears to perceive the father as the primary instructor of his child (*Spec.* 2.29) and the mother as a negative influence with regard to moral and intellectual development (*Spec.* 4.68). For a discussion on the responsibility of parents to instruct their children, see Adele Reinhartz, "Parents and Children: A Philonic Perspective," in *The Jewish Family in Antiquity* (ed. Shaye J. D. Cohen; Atlanta: Scholars Press, 1993), 73–74.

61. Beverly Bow and George W. E. Nickelsburg, "Patriarchy with a Twist: Men and Women in Tobit," in *"Women Like This": New Perspectives on Jewish Women in the Greco-Roman World* (ed. Amy-Jill Levine; Atlanta: Scholars Press, 1991), 133.

In 2 Macc 7 the father is noticeably absent and the mother-martyr assumes full responsibility for the instruction of her sons. Faced with this gap in the text, the author of 4 Maccabees offers additional information, portraying the mother as a widow (18:9) and the dead father as the educator of his sons (18:10–19).[62] Our text, however, does not give these explicit details. Thus, the marital status of the mother and the fate of the father remains the subject of speculation. More certain is the mother's role as instructor of her children. She teaches all of her sons to conduct themselves appropriately, living in the service of God and his Law, even in the face of death. Moreover, in the case of her youngest son, she is not only the woman who carried and nursed him, imparting his earliest instruction with the milk of her breast; she is also the individual solely responsible for his rearing, training, and education from the earliest years.

After offering a plea that establishes her maternity and role as teacher, the mother-martyr offers her final instruction to her youngest son and then issues a command: "Do not fear this butcher, but prove worthy of your brothers."[63] Here she relies on her established authority as parent and teacher to exact obedience from the child.[64] In accordance with the Law, he is required to honor his mother by obeying her wishes. The use of the imperative μὴ φοβηθῇς, "do not fear," evokes yet another dimension to the child's responsibility toward his mother, as fear is also an aspect of honor.[65] The child is instructed not to fear the king or the civil law that he represents. Instead, he must fulfill his obligation to fear his mother, in accordance with the ancestral law that she has taught him. And, in case the boy's choice is not clear, the mother throws in an added exhortation that he "prove worthy of his brothers" by following in their footsteps and accepting death as an alternative to transgression of the Law. Only if he acts virtuously will he be resurrected along with his brothers and ultimately be reunited with his mother.

The second speech of the mother is presented as an instruction that is enveloped in a complimentary plea and command. Its appeal to the youngest son is on a level that goes beyond rational instruction. The mother establishes her authority over her son as the woman who carried, nursed, and raised him to lead a life in the service of God and his Law. In accordance with this Law he must honor her with his obedience and fear. Thus, when she exhorts him to accept martyrdom she is

---

62. The description of the father's instruction includes the Law and the prophets, psalms, proverbs, and the lessons afforded by such biblical characters as Cain and Abel, Joseph, Phineas, and Daniel. The emphasis here is not on knowledge but on training in the proper conduct required to lead a life in the service of God and his Law. On the character of Jewish education in the Second Temple period and in Tannaitic literature, see Nathan Drazin, *History of Jewish Education from 515 BCE to 220 CE* (Baltimore: John Hopkins University Press, 1940), 11–15.

63. In the book of *Jubilees*, Rebecca is similarly portrayed as commanding her son, Jacob (26:9; 35:1, 25).

64. Crenshaw (*Education in Ancient Israel*, 189 n. 3) suggests that the command to honor one's father and mother is tied to their role in giving instruction to their children.

65. Philo indicates that honoring one's parents includes the following: respect, obedience, fear, courtesy, and nurture (*Spec.* 2.234–35).

supported by both her authority as parent and the full weight of the Law, in which she instructed him. Central to the narrative is the mother's role as instructor of her sons. In her lifetime, she trained her children to conduct themselves in accordance with God's law. In the hour of their death, she continued to instruct her sons on God's power and mercy, encouraging them to obey God's law even in the face of death. As they lived for the Law, they also died for the Law so that they would be resurrected to life. When the youngest son dies, the narrator offers a short statement regarding the mother's fate: "Last of all, the mother died, after her sons." Van Henten observes that compared to the mother's elaborate statements, the description of her death is very brief."[66] Indeed, her story is about how she lived for the Law. That she would also die for the Law was always a foregone conclusion.

The Mother-Martyrs in Rhetoric and History

In 2 Maccabees, the three mother-martyrs are portrayed in terms of their role as mothers. They ensure that their sons live their lives according to the Law by assuming the responsibility for circumcising their children and instructing them to conduct themselves in a fashion that is appropriate for a Jew. Ultimately, they choose to sacrifice their lives and those of their children in the service of God and his Law. In the absence of the fathers, these women are represented as heroes of the Jewish people and the guardians of Jewish Law and tradition for their generation. In the context of 2 Macc 6:7–7:42, the stories of the mother-martyrs and their sons, along with that of the elderly sage, Eleazar, clearly had a didactic function. They were ordinary members of society—mothers, children, and the elderly—who were held up to a subsequent generation of Jews as models of steadfast loyalty to God and his Law, even in the face of persecution.[67] No doubt, the portrayal of these martyrs is at least to some extent stylized in accordance with the author's rhetorical agenda, making it difficult to discern the line between rhetoric and reality in the portrayal of the mother-martyrs. Nevertheless, an examination of these portraits in their literary context may lend further insight into these representations and afford us a glimpse, albeit tentative, into the lives of real mothers in Judea in the second century B.C.E.

The author of 2 Maccabees has set up an opposition between two segments of society. On the one side are the powerful "Hellenizers," members of the priestly class and their associates who would bribe, steal, and even kill for personal power, as exemplified by Simon, Jason, and Menelaus. Their disloyalty to ancestral law is emphasized in their priestly neglect of temple duties (4:14), the contribution toward the sacrifice to Herakles (4:18–20), and the misappropriation of temple funds (4:32–34). On the other side are the pious individuals on the periphery of society who continue to live according to Jewish Law. In classic Greek rhetorical

---

66. Van Henten, *Martyrdom and Noble Death*, 70 n. 100. Compare the elaborate praise of the mother in 4 Macc 4:11–16:25.

67. On the didactic function of the martyr narratives, see van Henten, *The Maccabean Martyrs*, 122–24. Cf. Nickelsburg (*Resurrection*, 95), who suggests that some elements in 2 Macc 7 may, at some point, have been used to inculcate steadfastness in times of persecution.

tradition, he sets up a dichotomy between strong and weak, the sinner and the pious, Greek public ritual and the private and often secret observance of Jewish Law. While Jewish men publicly participated in Greek culture and religion, either through coercion or of their own volition, the women and children are associated with the elderly sage, Eleazar, and exemplified as the guardians of the ancestral tradition.

The use of comparison is fundamental to the author's rhetorical agenda. His perspective, however, is not necessarily anti-Hellenistic, for in terms of language and style 2 Maccabees is written in the tradition of contemporary Hellenistic literature.[68] Neither is his purpose in any way gender-related, for although he excludes the fathers from the accounts of the mother-martyrs, he does include other men among the pious: the Sabbath observers and the sage, Eleazar. It is in the characterization of this latter individual that we find clues to the author's agenda. The emphasis on Eleazar's advanced age throughout the martyr narrative places him, along with the women and children, as one of the weak in society.[69] In addition, he is described using the word γραμματέων, meaning scribe or teacher. Interestingly, the author of Syriac Maccabees clearly portrays Eleazar, not as a teacher, but as a priest (75). This discrepancy does not go unnoticed by the author of 4 Maccabees, who attempts to harmonize the other two accounts by portraying Eleazar as νομικός, a scribe or teacher, who came from a priestly family.[70] That the author of 2 Maccabees exemplifies a teacher and not a priest as the male model of piety fits well with his negative portrayal of the priestly aristocracy and their associates.[71]

In 2 Maccabees, power, corruption, and the pursuit of "Greek forms of prestige" (4:15) are associated with the aristocratic class to which the priesthood belongs, whereas the preservation of the ancestral law is attributed to ordinary people. The author portrays a world in which Israel's representatives to God are straying from the Law, and the priestly conception of the hierarchical structure of society does not apply. As such, women are not perceived as "other" by virtue of gender, but judged on their own merits. While the elite of Hellenistic Jewish society forsake the Law in their public pursuit of all things Greek, the perpetuation of Judaism falls on the shoulders of average individuals who continue to preserve Jewish tradition for the next generation. Among them are the elderly scribes and teachers, such as Eleazar, who lived his life dedicated to transmitting the Law to others and died in

---

68. Upon the examination of the syntax and style of 2 Maccabees, Doran concludes that the author was well trained in the schools of rhetoric. See Robert Doran, *Temple Propaganda: The Purpose and Character of 2 Maccabees* (CBQMS 12; Washington, DC: Catholic Biblical Association of America, 1981), 46.

69. 2 Macc 6:18, 23, 24, 25, 27.

70. I am grateful for the insights of Sigrid Peterson, who uses this example, among others, to demonstrate the harmonization of 2 Maccabees with Syriac Maccabees in the text of 4 Maccabees. Supporting her argument is the contention that, in the NT, νομικός and γραμματέων are equivalent terms. Sigrid Peterson, "Maccabean Martyrdoms: Versions and Varieties" (paper presented at the SBL Annual Meeting, Toronto, November 24, 2002).

71. Van Henten (*The Maccabean Martyrs*, 55) indicates that it is unlikely that the author belonged to a priestly group.

the hope that his loyalty to the Law would be an inspiration to the young. In much the same way, the mother-martyrs also represent an ordinary group within society who are essential to the propagation of Jewish law. They assume responsibility for the Jewish identity of their sons by ensuring that they are circumcised. Moreover, they speak to their children in the language of their ancestors as they nurse, rear, and educate them in accordance with Jewish tradition.[72]

The mother-martyrs of 2 Maccabees are not represented as exceptional women in terms of their roles as mothers. At a time when male family members are absent and the public male members of the priesthood have relinquished their role as the preservers of the tradition, it is only natural that the mothers take on the narrative role of circumcising and instructing their sons. To be sure, the author's use of rhetoric elevates these activities to heroic proportions. Yet it is in the very ordinary portrayal of the mothers that we can assert the continuity between literary representation and the reality of women's lives, for the portrayal of the mother-martyrs as heroes would only be convincing if it were based on an accurate depiction of their roles as mothers. It is therefore not unreasonable to speculate that Jewish mothers in the second century B.C.E. assumed active responsibility in raising their children to live according to the Law. As they lived for the Law, they taught those who came after them to do so as well. In this regard, the role of the Jewish mother remains unremarkable and unchanged.[73]

---

72. In portraying the mother-martyr of 2 Macc 7 as speaking the ancestral language and nursing her own child, the author indicates that she is not from among the aristocratic class.

73. I would like to express my gratitude to Dr. Eileen Schuller for our many fruitful discussions on women and martyrdom.

5

METAPHOR AND MEANING IN THE DEAD SEA SCROLLS

Metaphorical language contributes significantly to the beauty and meaning of texts from the Hebrew Bible onward, yet it also poses a serious challenge to the student of the Dead Sea Scrolls: How to distinguish between the literal and metaphorical usages of language? Interpreting a passage in one direction or another can have major implications not only for the understanding of that passage and the document in which it is found, but also for the theology, practice, and self-understanding of the Qumran community.

Literary theory is a useful starting point for addressing this question, as it can provide definitions and criteria that can then be applied to the literature found at Qumran. The literary critic I. A. Richards describes metaphor as follow: "When we use a metaphor we have two thoughts of different things active together, and supported by a single word, or phrase, whose meaning is a resultant of their interaction."[1] In other words, a metaphor is not a literal statement. The primary characteristic of metaphor is that it asserts a correspondence between two concepts or phenomena. For example, in the statement "man is a wolf,"[2] "man" is the principal subject or the topic, whereas "wolf" is the subsidiary subject or the vehicle. "Man" as the topic is being viewed through the lens or the filter of the vehicle, "wolf."[3]

If the primary characteristic of metaphor is its association between two concepts or phenomena, several secondary features follow.[4] First, metaphor draws

---

1. I. A. Richards, *The Philosophy of Rhetoric* (Oxford: Oxford University Press, 1936), 93. [Editor's note: Metaphor is discussed extensively in literary criticism and theory. Cf. Paul Ricoeur, *The Rule of Metaphor: The Creation of Meaning in Language*, trans. Robert Czerny with Kathleen McLaughlin and John Costello (London: Routledge, 2003). On metaphor in biblical literature, see David H. Aaron, *Biblical Ambiguities: Metaphor, Semantics, and Divine Imagery* (Leiden: Brill, 2001).]

2. Max Black, *Models and Metaphors: Studies in Language and Philosophy* (Ithaca, NY: Cornell University Press, 1962), 38-44.

3. Various terms are used to designate the two halves of a metaphor. For example, Richards suggests using the words "tenor" and "vehicle" (*Philosophy*, 96) whereas Black refers to "principal" and "subsidiary" subjects (*Models and Metaphors*, 39). For the purposes of this analysis, I follow Kittay in adopting the terminology "topic" (what the text is speaking about) and "vehicle" (the label and the content that label conveys literally). See Eva Feder Kittay, *Metaphor: Its Cognitive Force and Linguistic Structure* (Oxford: Clarendon Press, 1987), 25-26.

4. These features are explicated by Leland Ryken, "Metaphor in the Psalms," *Christianity and Literature* 31, no. 3 (1982): 11-13.

attention to the literal meaning of a word or phrase, and then it requires the interpreter to transfer that meaning to a figurative level. It is thus the role of the interpreter to ascertain the connection between the two systems of meaning through a process of comparison.

Second, metaphor works by means of indirection. On the literal level, a metaphorical statement is false. For example, the statement "man is a wolf" does not indicate that man [whether understood generically, or more literally as "the male of the human species"—*Ed.*] is literally a wolf, but it suggests that humans have wolf-like characteristics such as being fierce, hungry, and so on. Just because a metaphor is literally false, however, does not mean that it is illogical. The comparison between vehicle and topic can be validated on the basis of observation and rational analysis. Moreover, there are also occasions when metaphor goes beyond logic by pointing to the experience of the topic itself. This is evident in Ps 63:2, where the psalmist declares that his soul "thirsts" for God, thereby associating his spiritual longing with a physical and emotional state that can be experienced but not adequately articulated.

A third essential feature of metaphor is concreteness. As Ricoeur suggests, there is a "pictorial" dimension of metaphor, in which an image is evoked to account for the difference of level between topic and vehicle.[5] The use of such imagery enables a certain economy of expression. The metaphor becomes a kind of shorthand in which a whole set of associations can be brought to bear on a given topic, merely by naming another area of human experience.

It is not difficult to recognize "man is a wolf" or "the soul thirsts for God" as metaphorical rather than literal statements; we all know that men are men and not wolves, and that while our physical bodies can feel thirst literally, our souls can do so only figuratively. In the Dead Sea Scrolls, as in many other collections of religious texts, the distinctions are by no means as clear. This essay presents two case studies. The first section, "When God Purifies the Sinner," explores the language of purity and impurity in the Dead Sea Scrolls. The second section, "Community as Temple?" critically examines the frequent identification of the *yahad* as a temple. The essay concludes with some reflections on the implications of the metaphorical and literal reading of these terms for our understanding of the Scrolls and the community which they may describe.

I. When God Purifies the Sinner

In his book *Impurity and Sin in Ancient Judaism*, Jonathan Klawans distinguishes between two types of impurity: *ritual* impurity, a contagion that temporarily excludes the individual from participating in temple rituals, and *moral* impurity caused by sin, a form of defilement that is not related to temple worship.[6]

---

5. Paul Ricoeur, "The Metaphorical Process as Cognition, Imagination, and Feeling," in *On Metaphor* (ed. S. Sacks; Chicago: University of Chicago Press, 1979), 147.

6. Although Klawans is not the first to make this distinction, he may be credited with bringing the discussion on the relationship between ritual and moral impurity in Second

Ritual impurities include those that arise from common human experiences such as childbirth (Lev 12:1–8), scale disease (Lev 13:1–14:32), genital discharges (Lev 15:1–33), and death (Lev 11:1–47; Num 19:10–22) or certain cultic procedures (Lev 16:28; Num 19:8).[7] According to Klawans, there are three distinctive characteristics of ritual impurity. First, the sources of ritual impurity are natural, usually unavoidable, and sometimes even desirable. Second, these impurities are not prohibited, nor are they considered sinful. Third, ritual impurity conveys an impermanent contagion through contact with other individuals or objects, which may be alleviated through purificatory procedures.

Moral impurity, on the other hand, is perceived as the result of human sin and may cause defilement of the sinner (Lev 18:24), the land (Lev 18:25; Ezek 36:17), and God's sanctuary (Lev 20:3; Ezek 5:11). According to priestly law, moral impurity cannot be ameliorated through rites of purification. Rather, it can be eliminated only through a process of repentance, restitution and atoning sacrifice.[8] Failure to perform the appropriate cultic procedures results in the punishment of the transgressor.

Klawans makes two significant contributions to the study of purity and impurity. First, he asserts that these two types of impurity "are best understood as two *distinct but analogous perceptions of contagion*" (emphasis his).[9] Second, he contends that this distinction between ritual and moral impurity cannot be explained by the use of literal versus metaphorical language.[10] In his view, both ritual and moral impurity have legal and social consequences that result from actual physi-

---

Temple Judaism to the forefront of the scholarly debate on purity. See Jonathan Klawans, *Impurity and Sin in Ancient Judaism* (New York: Oxford University Press, 2000), 22–38.

7. On Klawans's understanding of ritual impurity, see *Impurity and Sin*, 23–26, and part I of the present volume.

8. Milgrom argues convincingly that the חטאת, commonly referred to as a "sin-offering," is not a ritual of atonement, but a ritual of purification. What is purified is not the offerer, but rather the altar and the sanctuary, both of which become defiled by moral impurity, as well as some major forms of ritual purity. See Jacob Milgrom, "Israel's Sanctuary: The Priestly 'Picture of Dorian Gray,'" *RB* 83 (1976): 390–99; idem, *Leviticus 1–16: A New Translation with Introduction and Commentary* (AB 3; New York: Doubleday, 1991), 253–92. It should be recognized, however, that the impurity caused by egregious sins (תועבות, or abominations) are considered permanent and cannot be removed by repentance or atonement. These include sexual sins (e.g., Lev 18:24–30), idolatry (e.g., Lev 19:31; 20:1–3), and bloodshed (e.g., Num 35:33–34). The only remedy for such sin is the punishment of the sinner. See Klawans, *Impurity and Sin*, 26–31.

9. Klawans, *Impurity and Sin*, 158.

10. Here Klawans argues primarily against Neusner, who suggests that ideas about purity and impurity serve as metaphors for moral and religious behavior. Jacob Neusner, *The Idea of Purity in Ancient Judaism* (Leiden: Brill, 1973), 108. Cf., for example, similar views expressed by H. Ringgren, "טהר," *TDOT* 5:288–96; H. Ringgren and G. André, "טמא," *TDOT* 5:330–42; Baruch A. Levine, *The JPS Torah Commentary: Leviticus* (Philadelphia: Jewish Publication Society, 1989), 134.

cal processes.[11] Thus, the impurity caused by sin is no less "real" than the impurity caused by corpse contamination.

Klawans does not deny that the language of purity is used figuratively or metaphorically in the Hebrew Bible. In some texts the image of a ritually impure person is used metaphorically to illustrate sinfulness. In Isa 1:16–17, for example, God, through the prophet, warns people: "Wash yourselves; make yourselves clean; remove the evil of your doings from before my eyes; cease to do evil, learn to do good; seek justice, rescue the oppressed, defend the orphan, plead for the widow." In Ezek 36:17, God says to the prophet: "Mortal, when the house of Israel lived on their own soil, they defiled it with their ways and their deeds; their conduct in my sight was like the uncleanness of a woman in her menstrual period."[12] On other occasions, the language of ritual purity is associated with righteousness, and the image of purification is used figuratively to express atonement. In Jer 33:8 God promises: "I will cleanse them from all the guilt of their sin against me, and I will forgive all the guilt of their sin and rebellion against me." In Prov 20:9 the narrator asks rhetorically: "Who can say, 'I have made my heart clean; I am pure from my sin'?"[13] In each of these passages the physical states of ritual impurity and purity are compared to moral categories of sinfulness and righteousness.[14] These examples indicate that purity language can be used both literally and metaphorically. How, then, can we know when a particular text is using purity language literally or metaphorically?[15]

We will approach this question by examining the usage of purity language in two texts from Qumran: the *Hodayot* (1QH^a and 4Q427–32) and the *Rule of the Community* (1QS).[16] The aim is to identify and interpret purity metaphors in these texts, to identify patterns of usage, and to consider their implications.

Identifying and Interpreting Purity Metaphors

The challenge of distinguishing between the metaphorical and literal usages of particular language involves interpreters in a rather circular process. In the first place, they must be attentive to terms or phrases which in their literary contexts are potentially metaphorical. This first step also requires a preliminary judgment call before the more rigorous investigation can even begin. Second, the literal meaning of the comparison must be established and, finally, the similarity between the vehicle and topic must be examined.[17] The use of purity language in

---

11. Klawans, *Impurity and Sin*, 34.
12. See also Isa 64:4–5 and Lam 1:8, 17.
13. See also Isa 1:15–17 and Job 4:17.
14. Klawans, *Impurity and Sin*, 34.
15. The connection between ritual impurity and sin is attested in, for example, 1QS V, 13–14, 19–20.
16. The metaphorical usage of purity language is absent from 11QT and 4QMMT (Klawans, *Impurity and Sin*, 85 n. 94).
17. Ryken suggests that the interpretation of a metaphor necessitates two tasks: iden-

Ps 51 provides a suitable example with which to demonstrate this threefold process as well as its necessary circularity:[18]

4. Wash me thoroughly of my iniquity,	הרבה כבסני מעוני
and purify me of my sin;	ומחטאתי טהרני:
5. for I know my transgressions,	כי־פשעי אני אדע
and my sin is always before me . . .	וחטאתי נגדי תמיד:
9. Purge me with hyssop and I shall be pure;	תחטאני באזוב ואטהר
wash me and I shall be whiter than snow.[19]	תכבסני ומשלג אלבין:

In verse 4, the psalmist's petitions to God to purify (טהר) him of sin (חטא) draw a direct line between ritual purification and atonement for sin.[20] The comparison between these two concepts is further emphasized as the poet acknowledges his sin (פשע, חטא) and asks God to purge (חטא) him with hyssop so that he will be pure (טהר).[21]

The first step in interpreting this passage is to assess this literal association between the concept of purification and sin in order to determine if it is true or false. In this example, there are two indications of literal falsehood. The first requires an understanding of ancient purity practices, according to which ritual purification cannot ameliorate the effects of moral impurity or sin. Only the informed reader will recognize this error.[22] The second indication concerns the role of God in purifying the individual: God does not and cannot literally or physically wash the individual. Such rituals are firmly situated in the realm of human practice, as indicated by priestly law (e.g., Lev 14:9; 15:5, 8, 11, 18). Both of these points point to the metaphorical rather than the literal use of purity language in this psalm.

Having established the use of metaphor in this preliminary way, it is necessary to identify the literal meaning of the comparison. What does it mean when the

---

tifying the literal meaning and discovering the similarities between the two halves of the metaphor ("Metaphor in the Psalms," 11–19).

18. It is especially significant that Klawans understands the use of purity language in this psalm to be metaphorical (*Impurity and Sin*, 35–36; cf. Neusner, *The Idea*, 13; William P. Brown, *Seeing the Psalms: A Theology of Metaphor* [Louisville: Westminster John Knox, 2002], 129–30).

19. Unless otherwise stated, all translations are by S. Haber.

20. [Editor's note: The use of the masculine pronoun reflects the Hebrew usage and also Haber's view that the biblical psalmist, as well as the Scrolls' authors, were more likely to be men than women. This is not to say, however, that women were absent from Qumran. On the role of women in Qumran, see Cecilia Wassen, *Women in the Damascus Document* (Leiden: Brill, 2005).]

21. The verb חטא in the *piel* is used to denote ritual purification of the altar (Lev 8:15; Ezek 43:20, 22, 23), the sanctuary (Ezek 45:18), the house of a leper (Lev 14:49, 52), and an individual who has touched a corpse (Num 19:19). See BDB 306–7.

22. The possibility always exists that the reader will fail to identify the literal level of the metaphor, especially if their experience of the phenomena is impoverished (Ryken, "Metaphor in the Psalms," 22–23). With respect to purity metaphors, the likelihood of misinterpretation is significantly high, since the concept of ritual purification is quite foreign to the modern reader.

poet speaks of God purifying him from sin? In this comparison, the verb טהר is the vehicle at the literal level of the metaphor. The word evokes images of physical purification such as ritual bathing or sprinkling with hyssop to remove corpse contamination. The metaphor articulates the experience of washing away ritual impurity as was the custom in ancient Israel and early Judaism. It is this literal meaning that is transferred from vehicle to topic in the process of interpreting the metaphor.

The third step in interpreting the metaphor is to evaluate the similarities between the vehicle, טהר, and the topic, חטא. According to Klawans, the concern of this passage is not with any supposed ritual impurity of the sinner, nor is there any indication that ritual purification effectively alleviates moral defilement.[23] Rather, the image of purification is being used metaphorically to illustrate that it is God himself who washes away (i.e., atones for) the sins of the individual. In his view, Ps 51:4–9 and other similar passages should be understood as follows:

> The hope expressed is that full atonement from sin could prove to be as easy a matter as purification from ritual impurity. Just as, say, a person who touches the carcass of an impure animal can purify himself or herself quickly and completely, so too does the sinner and prophet hope that God will effect atonement quickly and completely.[24]

Psalm 51:4–9 therefore illustrates how purity language is used metaphorically to equate an individual's physical purification from ritual impurity with God's atonement of the individual from sin.

It should be recognized, however, that not all purity metaphors offer such a vivid depiction of purification nor is the metaphorical level as easily perceived and analyzed. Yet in all cases there is at least one set of common and easily identified elements: the association among (1) ritual impurity and sin; (2) ritual purity and righteousness; and/or (3) purification and atonement.

Purity Metaphors in the Hodayot

The poetic compositions gathered in the *Hodayot* demonstrate considerable diversity in both form and content. Certain unifying themes, however, can be discerned.[25] First, these poems focus on God and his attributes as seen in relation to humankind. Emphasis is placed on God's eternal plan and final judgment. Second, the larger framework of the psalms is one of thanksgiving, as the psalmist expresses gratitude to God for deliverance from sin, distress, and evildoers. Finally, the poetry uses dichotomous language to discuss God/human beings, life/death, and salvation/damnation.

The intriguing use of purity language in the *Hodayot* can be understood within

---

23. See Klawans, *Impurity and Sin*, 22–31.
24. Ibid., 36.
25. For a summary of the central thrust of these psalms, see Bonnie Kittel, *The Hymns of Qumran: Translation and Commentary* (SBLDS 50; Chico, CA: Scholars Press, 1981), 12.

this larger thematic framework. The image of purification metaphorically describes God's power to effect atonement, and at the same time it emphasizes the impurity and sin of the individual. Purity language serves to express the psalmist's view of God as the source of purification/atonement for the impure/sinful human being.[26]

The verb טהר, *purify*

Seven passages in the *Hodayot* describe God as purifying the individual.[27] In our first example, God's ("your") holy spirit (רוח קודשך) is the agent of atonement:

ואחלה פניך ברוח אשר נתתה [בי] להשלים [הס]דיך עם עב[דך] ל[עד] <u>לטהרני</u> ברוח קודשך

I have appeased your face by the spirit which you have placed [in me] in order to complete your [kind]ness with [your] serv[ant] for[ever], <u>to purify me</u> with your holy spirit. . . . (1QH^a VIII, 19–20)

The metaphorical use of purity language in this text is similar to that found in Ps 51, in that both texts associate purification with atonement. This similarity has led some scholars to posit a direct connection between the psalm and this *Hodayot* passage. Holm-Nielsen speculates that the expression of purification found in 1QH^a VIII, 19–20 "may, though need not, be an expression which has arisen out of a combination of Ps. 51:4 and 51:13."[28] Klawans, on the other hand, argues that the purification imagery in the *Hodayot* is undoubtedly based in scripture and that 1QH^a VIII, in particular, takes much of its inspiration from Ps 51.[29] He does, however, concede that the image of God as purifying the sinner is much more frequent in the *Hodayot* than in the Psalms.[30]

A similar image occurs in 1QH^a XIX, 30–31:

שמח נפש עבדכה באמתכה <u>וטהרני</u> בצדקתכה כאשר יחלתי לטובכה ולהסדיכה אקוה

Gladden the soul of your servant with your truth <u>and purify me</u> with your justice, since I have trusted in your goodness and I have hoped in your kindness.

Whereas in column VIII the agent of God's purification is his holy spirit, here it is God's justice (צדקתכה) that effects atonement. In both cases the psalmist uses metaphorical language to describe God's redemptive action. Neither passage makes explicit reference to sin, yet it is clear from the context of each that the psalmist is referring to a form of inner purification or atonement.

---

26. Kittel indicates that there is a contrast between purity and sin that is characteristic of the *Hodayot* (*Hymns*, 12). I would suggest, however, that the relationship between these two phenomena is much more complex.

27. See also the restored 1QH^a IX, 32 and XII, 37.

28. Svend Holm-Nielsen, *Hodayot: Psalms from Qumran* (Acta theologica Danica 2; Århus, Denmark: Universitetsforlaget, 1960), 240.

29. Klawans, *Impurity and Sin*, 85.

30. This imagery only appears in Ps 51.

A third text, 1QH[a] XIV, 8, refers to the object of purification as opposed to the agent of purification:

ותזקקם <u>להטהר</u> מאשמה

You will refine them <u>to purify</u> them of guilt.

Here the connection between purification and sin is explicit.[31]
Similarly in 1QH[a] XI, 21–22:

ורוח נעוה <u>טהרתה</u> מפשע רב להתיצב במעמד עם צבא קודשים ולבוא ביחד עם עדת בני שמים

The twisted spirit <u>you have purified</u> from great transgression so that he can take a place with the host of the holy ones in order to enter together with the congregation of the sons of heaven.

A further example is found in 1QH[a] XV, 29–30:

וכול בני אמתכה תבי֯א בסליחות לפניכה ל֯[ט]<u>הרם</u> מפשעיהם ברוב טובכה ובהמון ר֯[ח]מיכה

All the sons of your truth /you bring/ to forgiveness before you, <u>you pu[ri]fy them</u> from their transgressions by the greatness of your goodness, and by the abundance of your com[pas]sion.

In these latter two examples, the use of the root פשע to denote sin may be especially significant in that it signifies "a willful, knowledgeable violation of a norm or standard."[32] The sins for which God effects atonement are not mere inadvertencies or mistakes, but deliberate violations of the law. It is only by virtue of God's goodness and compassion that the sinner receives purification from such flagrant sin. This point is emphasized in 1QH[a] XIX, 10–11, in which increasingly strong language is used to describe human transgression:

ולמען כבודכה <u>טהרתה</u> אנוש מפשע להתקדש לכה מכול תועבות נדה ואשמת מעל

For the sake of your glory, <u>you have purified</u> man from transgression, so that he can make himself holy for you from every abomination of impurity and guilt of sacrilege.

In the Hebrew Bible, the term תועבה is used in connection with the most egregious sins: sexual sin, idolatry, and bloodshed.[33] In the Qumran corpus, however,

---

31. In this verse, the vehicle is להטהר, while the topic is אשמה. The use of the feminine noun אשמה, rather than the masculine אשם, emphasizes the abstract nature of the topic, thereby emphasizing the metaphorical nature of the statement.

32. Robin C. Cover, "Sin," *ABD* on CD-ROM. Version 2.0c. 1995, 1996; cf. BDB, "פשע," 832–33.

33. Significantly, the term תועבה is never used in association with ritual impurity. See Klawans, *Impurity and Sin*, 26.

the terms תועבה and נדה are both used more generally to refer to grave sin.[34] The term מעל, sacrilege, indicates a serious sin perpetrated against God.[35] Taken together, these terms emphasize the gravity of human sin. In the worldview of the psalmist, God effects atonement for even the worst of sins, so that the sinner can make himself "holy" in the face of his "unholy" actions.

1QH[a] XIII, 15–16 offers a vivid description of the purification process:

ולמען הגבירכה ב' לנגד בני אדם הפלתה באביון ותביאהו במצר[ף כז]הב במעשי
אש וככסף מזוקק בכור נופחים לטהר שבעתים

> And in order to confirm your might /through me/ before the sons of Adam, you did wonders with the poor, you caused him to come into the cruci[ble like g]old to be worked by fire, and like refined silver in the furnace of the smiths <u>to be purified</u> seven times.

Here the psalmist compares God's purification of the individual to the seven-fold procedures by which silver is refined. In emphasizing the arduousness of the task, the psalmist not only points to the severity of human impurity/sin, but also draws attention to the nature of God as the divine source of purification/atonement.

The noun נדה, impurity

As shown, the passages that describe God's purification of the individual presume God's abundant goodness in effecting atonement in contrast to the impurity and sinfulness of the human condition. This comparison between God and human beings is further emphasized in passages in which the term נדה is used to highlight the impurity of the individual:[36]

כי בנדה התגוללתי ומסוד [אמת הלכ]תי

> Because I wallowed <u>in impurity</u> and I walked from the foundation [of truth] . . . (1QH[a] IV, 19)

In this verse, the psalmist portrays himself as straying from God's truth. The use of the reflexive verb wallowed (התגוללתי) emphasizes the individual's own responsibility for sinful acts. Such deeds have serious consequences:

מעשי נדה לתחלויים ומשפטי נגע וכלה [. . .]

> Deeds of <u>impurity</u> lead to illnesses and judgments of affliction and destruction [. . .]. (1QH[a] XXI bottom, 16)

---

34. Ibid., 70.

35. According to Milgrom, there are two subcategories of מעל in the priestly source: (1) an unintentional trespass, either real or suspected, against divine property—usually temple sancta (Lev 5:14–19), and (2) a deliberate transgression against the Name of the Deity, in the form of an oath violation (Lev 5:20–26). Jacob Milgrom, *Cult and Conscience: The Asham and the Priestly Doctrine of Repentance* (SJLA 18; Leiden: Brill, 1976), 16–21.

36. Cf. Lev 19:11, above; 4Q428 X, 4.

Sinfulness may therefore result in physical malady.³⁷

More extreme imagery is used in passages in which the psalmist imagines himself as a source of impurity:

הערוה ומקור הנדה כור העוון ומבנה החטאה רוח

> But, as for me, I am a creature of clay and a kneading of water, a foundation of shame and a source of impurity, a smelting pot of iniquity and a building of sin, a spirit of error that is twisted without understanding, which is terrified by righteous judgments. (1QHª IX, 22)

ואני מעפר לקח[תי ומחמר קו]רצתי למקור נדה וערות קלון מקוי עפר ומגבל [מים . . .]

> But, as for me, from dust I am tak[en] and from clay I am fo[rmed] to be a source of impurity and disgraceful shame, a pile of dust mixed with [water . . .]. (1QHª XX, 24–25)

The above passages are explicit in their description of the lowly state of the human condition. While the psalmist here portrays himself as a source of impurity, in other passages (e.g., IV, 19 above) he indicates that God is the source of truth.

The adjective טמא, defiled

Finally, we turn to 1QHª XIV, 20–21:³⁸

ואתה אל צויתם להועיל מדרכיהם בדרך קו[דשכה אשר ילכו] בה וערל וטמא ופריץ בל יעוברנה

> And you, God, commanded them to profit away from their ways, [walking] in the way of [your] hol[iness]. The uncircumcised, the impure, the violent, do not traverse it.

Here the participle טמא is used to describe those who do not follow God's path. In the context of this text, the defiled are associated with two other groups: the uncircumcised, who are thereby excluded from the covenant between God and Israel, and the violent, who are excluded from the community of Israel.³⁹ By association, we may suggest that the טמא are being excluded, not because of any physical

---

37. The relationship between impurity/sin and illness in the Dead Sea Scrolls is not entirely clear. Cecilia Wassen proposes a connection between evil spirits and impurity/sin in which (1) sin makes people vulnerable to evil forces and (2) evil forces cause people to sin. She also suggests that evil spirits were associated with illnesses and physical defects and could even intrude upon the body to spread disease. See Cecilia Wassen, "Common Demonology and Rules of Exclusion in the Dead Sea Scrolls," in *Common Judaism Explored: Second Temple Judaism in Context* (ed. W. McCready and A. Reinhartz; Minneapolis: Fortress, 2008).

38. Cf. 4Q429 IV, I, 9.

39. Those who commit violent acts such as murder are subject to the punishment of כרת, extirpation from the community.

impurity, but because they, like the uncircumcised and the violent, are sinners who do not walk in the way of God's holiness.

Summary

The use of purity metaphors in the *Hodayot* is fairly straightforward and consistent. Purification is associated with atonement, and God is seen as the agent of purification. Rhetorically, the passages contrast God—the foundation of truth and wondrous deeds —with human beings—a source of impurity/sin.

Purity Metaphors in 1QS

In 1QS the use of purity language is much more complex than in the *Hodayot*. Purity terminology is frequently used in a literal sense to denote the pure food of the community as טהרת רבים (e.g,. VI, 25; VII, 3) or טהרת אנשי הקודש (e.g., V, 13; VIII, 17). At other times, however, the usage is clearly metaphorical, as in the following passage:

ואז יברר אל באמתו כול מעשי גבר יזקק לו מבני איש להתם כול רוח עולה מתכמי בשרו ולטהרו ברוח קודש מכול עלילות רשעה ויז עליו רוח אמת כמי נדה מכול תועבות שקר והתגולל ברוח נדה

> Then God will cleanse with his truth all the deeds of man, and he will refine for himself from the sons of man, in order to destroy all spirit of deceit from the innermost part of his flesh, and <u>to purify him</u> with the spirit of holiness from all wicked deeds. He will sprinkle upon him the spirit of truth <u>like waters of purification</u> (to purify him) from all the abominations of deception and from wallowing in <u>a spirit of impurity</u>. (1QS IV, 20–22)

As in the *Hodayot*, here God effects atonement for the sinner by purifying him or her with his spirit of truth, so that he or she will no longer wallow in a spirit of impurity. We may observe, however, that there is a much less restrained and much more consistent use of purity language in this text than in the *Hodayot* passages. God is envisioned as sprinkling the spirit of truth on the individual in much the same way as the מי נדה, waters of purification, are sprinkled on the ritually impure.[40]

1QS XI provides another example in which God effects atonement for sin:

בצדקת אמתו שפטני וברוב טובו יכפר בעד כול עוונותי ובצדקתו יטהרני מנדת אנוש וחטאת בני אדם

> In the justice of his truth he will judge me, and in his abundant goodness he shall atone for all my iniquities, and in his justice he shall purify me from the impurity of man and from the sin of the sons of man. (XI, 14–15)

---

40. The technical term מי נדה is used in the Hebrew Bible to refer to the waters that are made from red heifer ashes and sprinkled on the individual who has contracted corpse impurity (Num 19:21).

Here the author uses the language of atonement and sin to describe God's action. God literally atones (כפר) for the sins (עוונות) of the individual. At the same time, he purifies (טהר) the individual from impurity of man (נדת אנוש) and from the sin of the sons of man (חטאת בני אדם). It is important to emphasize that there is no semantic error or literal falsehood in the notion that God effects atonement for human sin. Moreover, the idea that God "purifies" human impurity does not have the same figurative force as the imagery of divine purification from sin. In this passage God performs two separate but related actions: he atones for sin and purifies impurity. The parallel structure of the text points to the relationship between these two activities.

The most extensive use of purity language in 1QS may be found in 1QS III, 4–9, which describes sanctions against those who decline entrance into the community:

לוא יתחשב לוא יזכה בכפורים ולוא יטהר במי נדה ולוא יתקדש כימים ונהרות ולוא יטהר בכול מי רחץ טמא טמא יהיה כול יומי מואסו במשפטי אל לבלתי התיסר ביחד עצתו כיא ברוח עצת אמת אל דרכי איש יכופרו כול עוונותו להביט באור החיים וברות קדושה ליחד באמתו יטהר מכול עוונותו וברוח יושר וענו{ת}ה תכופר חטתו ובענות נפשו לכול חוקי אל יטהר בשרו להזות במי נדה ולהתקדש במי דוכי ויהכין פעמיו להלכת תמים

He shall not be cleansed with atonement, and <u>he shall not be purified with waters of purification</u>, and he shall not sanctify himself with seas and rivers, and <u>he shall not be purified</u> with all the waters of ablution. <u>Impure, impure</u> he shall be all the days of his rejection of the judgments of God, so as not to be disciplined in the community of his council, because it is with the spirit of the council of God's truth that are atoned the paths of man, all his iniquities, so that he may look upon the light of life. And by the holy spirit of the community, in its truth <u>he may be purified</u> from all his iniquities. And with an upright and humble spirit, his sin will be atoned. And by the humbling of his soul to all the statutes of God <u>his flesh shall be purified</u> by sprinkling with waters of purification and by sanctifying himself with waters of repentance.

This passage differs significantly from the previous texts in that the actions are not of divine origin, but are performed in the human realm. There are two issues of concern. First, the outsider may not be *physically* purified (טהר) with waters of purification (מי נדה) or ablution (מי רחץ), nor can he or she be sanctified by any natural sources of water.[41] Second, the text indicates that the individual remains *morally* impure (טמא טמא) as long as he or she rejects the judgments of God, since the human sins (עוונות) can be atoned (כפר) only through the council of God's truth. In the Hebrew Bible, the term טמא is used to refer to both ritual (e.g., Lev 12:2; 13:3, 8, 15; 15:4, 18, 25) and moral impurity (e.g., Lev 18:20, 23; 19:31). There is no metaphorical use of purity language here. Rather, the individual exists in a

---

41. As Himmelfarb points out, there are no biblical parallels for the terms מי נדה or מי רחץ. See Martha Himmelfarb, "Impurity and Sin in 4QD, 1QS, and 4Q512," *DSD* 8, no. 1 (2001): 30.

morally impure state as a consequence of sin. Such moral impurity can only be eliminated through repentance and atonement.

As shown, the text begins by drawing a clear distinction between physical purification on the one hand and repentance/atonement on the other hand. Yet as the passage continues, the boundaries between these two activities become blurry. The pivotal point is found in vv. 7–8. Here the holy spirit of the community is envisioned as purifying (טהר) the outsider from sin (עוונות). This is followed by a description of the two-step process by which the outsider may gain entrance into the community: by humbling his or her spirit and repenting, thereby atoning for the sin. Subsequently, the flesh can be purified with the waters of purification.

A similar relationship between repentance and physical purification is expressed in 1QS V, 13–14:

אל יבוא במים לגעת בטהרת אנשי הקודש כיא לוא יטהרו כי אם שבו מרעתם כיא טמא בכול עוברי דברו

> He should not go into the waters to touch the pure food of the men of holiness, for they are not <u>purified</u> unless they turn away from their wickedness, for he is <u>impure</u> among all the transgressors of his word.

For Klawans, "it is not enough to say that atonement is the precondition for purification, because that formulation obscures the fact that for the sectarians, both requirements are necessary and neither alone is sufficient."[42] He argues convincingly that both outsiders and backsliding insiders are required to atone and purify themselves before being (re-)admitted into the community. Atonement and purification are mutually dependent conditions.

In these passages, the association between atonement and ritual purity must be understood on a literal rather than a metaphorical level.[43] There are no semantic inconsistencies either in the notion of human repentance and physical purification, or in the idea that God atones for the sins of the repentant sinner. The close association of repentance/atonement and physical purification in 1QS does, however, represent an innovation not found in the biblical text. Underlying this relationship is the unique idea that the sinner is somehow ritually impure and vice-versa. One passage from 1QS clearly articulates this view:

וכול מנאצי דברו ישמיד מתבל וכול מעשיהם לנדה לפניו וטמא בכול הונ{י}ם

> And all those who scorn his word he shall annihilate from the world, and all their deeds are for <u>impurity</u> before him and their property is <u>impure</u>. (1QS V, 19–20)

The outsider is portrayed as a sinner whose deeds are morally impure. In addition, the outsider's belongings are viewed as being contaminated by what could only be a form of ritual impurity.

---

42. Klawans, *Impurity and Sin*, 86.
43. Contra Himmelfarb ("Impurity and Sin," 34), who suggests that "P's technical terminology figures prominently in the hortatory passages of 1QS, but it has been given new meaning in metaphors for sin and repentance."

1QS uses purity language both metaphorically and literally. On the metaphorical level, both God and the holy spirit of the community effect atonement for the sinner. On a literal level, purity and atonement are viewed as interdependent activities.

Conclusion

The *Hodayot* and 1QS exhibit different patterns with regard to their use of purity language. In the *Hodayot*, purity language is consistently metaphorical. The verb טהר is always used in connection with God's atonement/purification of the sinner, and the noun נדה as well as the participle טמא are used to emphasize the egregious nature of human sin. This usage implies that, for the psalmist, humanity is the quintessential source of impurity/sin, while God is an eternal source of truth.

In 1QS, purity language is used both metaphorically and literally. Metaphorically, the verb טהר indicates atonement of the individual by God or the holy spirit of the community. Yet, the same verb also expresses the act of physical purification required of the individual. Furthermore, the presence of purity language as well as terms related to atonement (כפר) and sin (עוון) within the same passage does not necessarily imply the presence of metaphor. 1QS posits an interdependence between moral and ritual impurity in 1QS. As a result, both repentance and ritual purification are required for entrance into the community.

II. Community as Temple?

As we have seen, 1QS—the *Rule of the Community*—uses purity language both metaphorically and literally and therefore describes not only the worldview but also the practice of the Qumran community. That is, entrance into the community required both repentance and ritual purification. If so, what are the implications for the community's self-understanding? Some scholars have provided an answer to this question by arguing that the *yahad* saw itself not only as a holy community but as the replacement for the temple in Jerusalem, which in its view had become hopelessly corrupt and therefore no longer pure. The question is whether this is the most convincing interpretation of 1QS itself.

The *Rule of the Community* contains regulations that pertain exclusively to the sectarian community and its members. It describes the laws and theological rationale governing contemporary community life in a time regarded by its members as eschatological, but pre-messianic.[44] For the most part, the rules are not based on biblical law,[45] and the historical connection to biblical Israel is absent.[46] If 1QS

---

44. J. H. Charlesworth, ed., *The Dead Sea Scrolls: Hebrew, Aramaic, and Greek Texts with English Translations* (6 vols.; Louisville: Westminster John Knox, 1994), 1:2.

45. J. M. Baumgarten, "Sacrifice and Worship among the Jewish Sectarians of the Dead Sea Scrolls," in *Studies in Qumran Law* (Leiden: Brill, 1977), 46.

46. E. J. Christiansen, *The Covenant in Judaism and Paul* (Leiden: Brill, 1995), 147–51.

does not describe the historical development of the community, neither does it explicitly mention the temple or suggest that it had been defiled.[47]

Yet the community's reverence for the cultic institution, and its critique of the temple cult as being corrupt, has led some scholars to argue that the *yahad*—as the community refers to itself in 1QS—regarded itself as a temple, and perhaps even as a permanent replacement for the Jerusalem temple. Based on texts such as 1QS V, 5-7; VIII, 4-11; IX, 3-6; and CD III, 18-IV, 12,[48] scholars point to the description of the community in terms of temple language, the references to the *yahad* as a "priestly" community, the importance of atonement, and the use of cultic language to describe the worship of the community.

Central to the community-as-temple argument is the observation that 1QS uses temple imagery metaphorically to refer to the community. This observation is correct, as this identification meets the criteria that we have already examined. After all, the community—a collectivity of people—is not literally a temple, that is, a building of stone and other materials. Second, the comparison between community and temple holds true with respect to purity requirements: purity is necessary for initiation into the community just as it is for physical entry into the temple, and it is a precondition for participation in the cultic activities that take place in the temple. Perhaps, then, Gärtner is correct in stating that the language of these texts expresses symbolism of the temple and "provides clear evidence of the idea of the community as a replacement for the official temple."[49]

As we shall see, however, a metaphorical reading of the temple imagery does not necessary lead to the conclusion that the community saw itself as a replacement for the Jerusalem temple.

We begin with a key text, 1QS VIII, 4-11:

4. וצרת מצרף ולהתהלך עם כול ב.{מדת האמת ובתכון העת בהיות אלה בישראל

5. נכונה {ה}עצת היחד באמת {.}   למ‍טעת עולם בית קודש לישראל וסוד קודש

6. קודשים לאהרון עדי אמת למשפט וב{י}ח'רי רצון לכפר בעד הארץ ולהשב

---

47. Baumgarten, "Sacrifice and Worship," 48.
48. Other secondary texts that are sometimes cited include 1QpHab XII, 3-4, 4QpIsa[d], and especially 4QFlor I, 1-7. The latter text is of particular interest because it makes reference to a *miqdaš* temple. However, even scholars who advocate the community-as-temple premise reject 4QFor I, 1-7 as a supporting text. See D. R. Schwartz, "The Three Temples of 4Q Florilegium," *RevQ* 10 (1979-81): 83-92. This discussion will be confined to the texts found in 1QS and CD.
49. B. Gärtner, *The Temple and the Community in Qumran and the New Testament* (SNTSMS 1; Cambridge: Cambridge University Press, 1965), 22. [Editor's note: Others who express a similar view include Joseph M. Baumgarten, "Sacrifice and Worship among the Jewish Sectarians of the Dead Sea (Qumran) Scrolls," *HTR* 46, no. 3 (1953): 141-59; Michael A. Knibb, *The Qumran Community* (Cambridge: Cambridge University Press, 1987), 130-31; Hannah K. Harrington, *The Purity Texts* (London: T & T Clark, 2004), 38. Jodi Magness states that the community saw itself as a substitute for the temple but that there is no evidence that animal sacrifices were performed (*The Archaeology of Qumran and the Dead Sea Scrolls* [Grand Rapids: Eerdmans, 2002], 119).]

7. לרשעים גמולם   היאה חומת הבחי פנת יקר בל

8. יזדעזעו יסודותיהי ובל יחישו ממקומם   מעון קודש קודשים

9. לאהרון בדעת כולם (עולם) לברית משפט ולקריב ר"ח ניתוח ובית תמים ואמת בישראל

10. להקם {...} ברית לח{.}קו̇ת עילם והיו לרצון לכפר בעד הארץ ולחרוץ משפט רשעה {בחמים דרך} ואין עולה בהכון אלה ביסוד היחד שנתים ימים בתמים דרך

11. יבדלו קודש בתוך עצת אנשי היחד וכול דבר הנסתר מישראל ונמצאו לאיש

(4b) ... When these exist in Israel, (5) the council of the community shall be established in truth as an eternal plant; a house of holiness for Israel and a most holy assembly (6) for Aaron, witnesses of truth for the judgment and chosen by the will (of God), to atone on behalf of the land and return to (7) the wicked their reward. It shall be the tested wall and the precious cornerstone, whose foundation shall neither (8) shake nor stir from their place. (They shall be) a most holy dwelling (9) for Aaron, with complete knowledge of the covenant of justice, and it shall offer a pleasing odor; and it shall be a house of perfection and truth in Israel (10) that they may establish the covenant according to the eternal statutes. And they shall be accepted to atone on behalf of the land and to determine the judgment of wickedness; and there shall be no more injustice. When these have been established in the fundamental principles of the community for two years in perfection of way, (11) they shall be set apart as holy within the council of the men of the community.[50]

According to Gärtner, the identification of the two distinct groups, Israel and Aaron, is commonly found in passages pertaining to the organization of the community and corresponds to the laity and the priests respectively.[51] Gärtner views these identifications also as references to the two most important rooms in the temple: a "holy place for Israel" and "the holy of holies" for Aaron.[52] Together, these two groups comprise a "new" temple, that is, a community in which resides the holiness that formerly inhered in the Jerusalem temple. In the context of this explanation, the architectural imagery, which describes the community as a "tested wall" and a "precious cornerstone," is also suggestive.

This reading of 1QS requires two interpretive moves: the identification of the community/temple language as metaphorical and the ascription of literal meaning to the metaphor. According to this view, the community is not literally a temple building, but it literally saw itself as a locus of purity and worship that replaced the

---

50. 1QS translations are by Susan Haber or adapted by Haber from M. A. Knibb, *The Qumran Community* (Cambridge: Cambridge University Press, 1987).

51. Gärtner, *The Temple*, 22–30.

52. Gärtner renders בית קודש as "holy place" and קודש קודשים as "holy of holies" (ibid., 29). It is not clear which area of the temple Gärtner is designating as the "holy place for Israel." The court of the (ordinary, male) Israelites was the area accessible to Israel and is the "room" that is most likely represented in Gärtner's interpretation of the passage. However, it was the court of the priests that ranked second in holiness to the holy of holies. See E. P. Sanders, *Judaism Practice and Belief: 63BCE–66CE* (London: SCM Press, 1992), 310–14.

temple in that regard. It must be noted, however, that 1QS nowhere explicitly refers to the Jerusalem temple nor does it discuss the relationship of the community to the temple. Implicit in Gärtner's theory about the community as replacement for the temple is a negative value judgment of the temple itself, as distinct from a critique of priestly conduct. This value judgment is then ascribed to the *yahad*.[53]

If we do not *a priori* assume that the community's rejection of the Jerusalem temple and cult underlies this passage, a different metaphorical reading emerges. In describing itself as a סוד קודש קודשים לאהרון "most holy assembly for Aaron" (VIII, 5-6) and a מעון קודש קודשים לאהרון ("most holy dwelling for Aaron," VIII, 8-9), the community may simply be affirming its priestly status, as chosen by God.[54] The language implies that the level of holiness usually reserved for the priesthood is transferred to this community as a whole.

Supporting this claim is the use of the noun קודש, *qôdeš*, and the adjective קדוש, *qādôš*, in the self-designation of the *yahad*.[55] It is regarded as עצת הקודש "council of holiness" (II, 25; VIII, 21), a יחד קודש "community of holiness" (IX, 2), and a עדת קודש "congregation of holiness" (V, 20). The division of the community into two distinct groups—"a holy house for Aaron" (IX, 6) and בית קודש לישראל "a house of holiness for Israel" (VIII, 5)—preserves the holiness of the community at large, while maintaining the superior status of the priesthood, whose holiness is determined both by descent and membership in the community.[56] In the hierarchy of the community, each and every member possesses a certain level of holiness.[57] This holiness extends to both the community and its individual members, indicating that it is essential to the self-definition of the community.

As a holy community, the main purpose of the *yahad* is to atone for sin:[58]

---

53. [Editor's note: Jonathan Klawans traces a trend in scholarship on ritual purity and the temple that is marked by evolutionism (*Purity, Sacrifice, and the Temple: Symbolism and Supersessionism in the Study of Ancient Judaism* [New York: Oxford, 2006], 22 and passim). He does not explicitly refer to Gärtner in this regard, but Gärtner's theory would fit into an evolutionist perspective.]

54. Robert A. Kugler, "Rewriting Rubrics: Sacrifice and the Religion of Qumran," in *Religion in the Dead Sea Scrolls* (ed. John J. Collins and Robert A. Kugler; Studies in the Dead Sea Scrolls and Related Literature; Grand Rapids: Eerdmans, 2000), 91.

55. J. Naude, "Holiness in the Dead Sea Scrolls," in *The Dead Sea Scrolls after Fifty Years* (ed. P. W. Flint and J. C Vanderkam; Leiden: Brill, 1999), 2:186-88.

56. D. R. Schwartz, "On Two Aspects of a Priestly View of Descent at Qumran," in *Archaeology and History in the Dead Sea Scrolls: The New York University Conference in memory of Yigael Yadin* (ed. Lawrence H. Schiffman; JSPSup 8; JSOT/ASOR Monographs 2; Sheffield: JSOT Press, 1990), 157-58.

57. Evidence that the hierarchy of the community extends to the level of the individual can be found in 1QS II, 19-23. Entrance into the covenant during the annual ceremony is according to rank, so that "each Israelite may know his standing in God's Community in conformity with an eternal plan." Cf. 1QS IX, 1-2.

58. See, for example, Kugler, "Rewriting Rubrics," 91; Christiansen, *The Covenant*, 158; Hermann Lichtenberger, "Atonement and Sacrifice in the Qumran Community," in *Approaches to Ancient Judaism* (ed. W. S. Green; Chico, CA: Scholars Press, 1980), 2:162.

5. ועינוהי ומחשבת יצרו (כ)יאאם ביחד למול עורלת יצר ועורף קשה ליסד מוסד אמת לישראל ליחד ברית

6. עולם לכפר לכול המתנדבים לקודש באהרון ולבית האמת בישראל והנלוים עליהם ליחד ולריב ולמשפט

7. להרשיע כול עוברי חוק ואלה תכון דרכיהם על כול החוקים האלה בהאספם ליחד כול הבא לעצת היחד

(5) . . . Rather they shall circumcise in the community the foreskin of their inclination and of their stiff neck to lay a foundation of truth for Israel, for the community of eternal covenant. (6) To grant atonement for all those who willingly offer themselves to holiness in Aaron and to the house of truth in Israel, and for those who join them for a community. In lawsuits and judgments (7) they shall condemn as guilty all those who transgress the statutes. These are the rules of conduct, in accordance with all these statutes, when they are admitted to the community. (1QS V, 5–7)[59]

The comparison between the community and the priesthood supports a metaphorical reading of temple imagery. Just as the priests in the temple atoned for the sins of the people through sacrificial rites, so too did the community make expiation through a life of holiness and obedience to the laws of Moses.[60]

This comparison, however, does not account for the nuances in meaning of the root כפר, as it is used in both cultic and noncultic contexts. The concept of atonement in the *Rule of the Community* can be best understood in light of the historical development of the term כפר, which is most often, but not always accurately, translated as "atone" or "expiate." In general, the direction of a word's development is from the concrete to the increasingly abstract. In its early stage, the term *kippēr* is associated with the Arabic *kafara* (cover) and the Akkadian *kuppuru* (wipe or purge).[61] The latter term, the Hebrew equivalent of which is *kippēr* (*pi'el*), has the literal sense of "rubbing off" or wiping away impurities.[62] In a later stage of development, however, there is no actual wiping and *kippēr* is rendered as an abstraction: purify, purge, or ransom. Impurities caused by sin must be purged in order to avert God's wrath, and it is the sinner who must bear the penalty or provide the prescribed ransom or substitute, in order to reconcile with the deity. In its final

---

59. The community makes atonement for its members (V, 6) and for the land (VIII, 6, 10), not metaphorically, but literally, as set out by the *Rule of the Community*.

60. So Gärtner (*The Temple*, 22–25, 44–45), who takes this association even further when he posits the necessity for a substitution for sacrifice as a means of atonement in light of the perceived desecration of the Jerusalem temple.

61. Superficially the two Semitic cognates suggest contradictory notions. However, common to both is an underlying action of rubbing. In a literal sense, substances may be rubbed on or rubbed off. For a thorough analysis of the verb כפר, see J. Milgrom, *Leviticus 1–16* (AB 3; New York: Doubleday, 1991), 1079–84; cf. B. Levine, *In the Presence of the Lord: A Study of Cult and Some Cultic Terms in Ancient Israel* (SJLA 5; Leiden: Brill, 1974), 56–77.

62. In the case of the *ḥaṭṭāt* offering, the blood of the sacrificial animal is literally sprinkled on the sancta in order to rub off the impurities. See Milgrom, *Leviticus 1–16*, 1081.

stage of development, the verb *kippēr* becomes even more abstract, connoting the figurative concept "atone" or "expiate."

It is in the most abstract sense that the *pi'el* form of כפר is used in the context of 1QS. In addition, it can be shown that the grammatical syntax reflects the unique noncultic setting of the sectarians. In the cultic setting, the subject of כפר is most often a priest, with the direct object being either a contaminated person or a sacred place. Outside the cult, however, God is generally the subject of expiation, and the direct object is usually a sin.[63]

This transfer of subject from priest to deity is not as radical as it may seem, since even in the cultic texts it is understood that while the priests perform the prerequisite rituals, only God has the power to grant expiation. In general, the Scrolls place a distinct emphasis on God as the source of atonement. However, in the *Rule of the Community*, only two of the six occurrences[64] of the *pi'el* form of the verb כפר (II, 8; XI, 14) conform to the norm cited for noncultic atonement. The remaining occurrences (V, 6; VIII, 6, 10; IX, 4) require further scrutiny.

In 1QS V, 6, the root כפר occurs in the context of a group of rules governing the internal life of the community. Here atonement is personal and concerns the "men of the community who willingly offer themselves to turn back from all evil" (1QS V, 1) and those "who have willingly offered themselves to return in the community to his covenant" (1QS V, 22). Seemingly, the community is both the subject and object of the *pi'el* infinitive, לכפר.[65] The community makes atonement for all who freely volunteer (לכול המתנדבים) to convert from the evil path and become part of the community. This personal atonement is achieved through a life of repentance and purity.

Of particular interest is the unusual use of the adjunct preposition ל in combination with a human subject,[66] for the construction כפר ל- usually means "grant

---

63. See Milgrom, *Leviticus 1–16*, 1083–84, for a discussion on the grammatical syntax of כפר in and outside of the cult.

64. The *pu'al* form of the verb is found in 1QS III, 6, 8. In both occurrences the object is the sins of the wayward member of the community. For a tabulation of the usage of כפר in the Bible and the Dead Sea Scrolls, see P. Garnet, *Salvation and Atonement in the Qumran Scrolls* (WUNT 2; Tübingen: J. C. B. Mohr [Paul Siebeck], 1977), 124–35.

65. Against Garnet (ibid., 60–64), who suggests that God is the most probable subject of כפר in V, 6. His argument is based on the support on an early suggestion of W. H. Brownlee that the controversial ואאם in line 5 is an abbreviation of the divine title אלוהי האלוהים ואדוני האדונים "God of gods and Lord of Lords." See Brownlee, *The Dead Sea Manual of Discipline: Translation and Notes* (BASORSup 10–12; New Haven, CT: ASOR, 1951), 19, 49–50. Alternatively, A. M. Habermann proposed that the first letter be read as a *yôd* and that a *kāp* be restored in order to render אם ביא. See *Megilot midbar Yehudah* (Tel-Aviv: Machbaroth Lesifrut, 1959), 64, 185. This latter recommendation has subsequently been substantiated by parallels in 4QS^b and 4QS^d, both of which read אם בי. See S. Metso, *The Textual Development of the Qumran Community Rule* (STDJ 21; Leiden: Brill, 1997), 27, 41.

66. The key to understanding the meaning of the *pi'el* form of the verb כפר may be found in its adjunct prepositions. See Milgrom, *Leviticus 1–16*, 707; cf. P. Garnet, who attests to the rarity of כפר ל- when it governs people who are to benefit from it. In the two passages

atonement to," a function reserved only for God.[67] As stated, "[I]t is by the spirit of the council of truth of God that the ways of man are atoned—all of his iniquities" (1QS III, 6–7). Those who are upright and humble and observe the Law are, by definition, granted atonement from God:

ויהכין פעמיו להלכת תמים בכול דרכי אל כאשר צוה למועדי תעודתיו ולוא לסור
ימין ושמאול ואין

לצעוד על אחד מכול דבריו אז ירצה בכפורי ניחוח לפני אל והיתה
לו לברית יחד עולמים

Let him make ready his steps that he may walk perfectly in all the ways of God as he commanded for the appointed times of his testimony, and not turn aside to right or left, and not transgress[68] any one of all his commandments. Then he will be accepted with pleasing atonement (בכפורי ניחוח) before God, and it will be for him a covenant of an eternal community (לברית יחד עולמים). (1QS III, 9–12)

It is not the community as such that grants atonement to its individual members. Rather, entrance into the community and the acceptance of a life of repentance and purity carry the promise of divine expiation, in accordance with the eternal covenant between God and the community.[69] In this context, then, the usage of כפר in V, 6 is not cultic but covenantal. There are no sacrificial rites, only an abstract form of personal atonement, rendered by God in the context of a covenantal agreement.

In addition to personal atonement, the community also aspired to eschatological expiation.[70] This too is found in the context of covenant. The theme of eschatological expiation is most apparent in the framework of the literary unit 1QS VIII, 1–IX, 11, in which the community and its boundaries are defined. VIII, 1–16 describes the character of the community; VIII, 16–IX, 2 discusses the rules pertaining to those who have either deliberately or inadvertently transgressed the covenant of the community; IX, 3–6 describes the mechanism for atonement within

---

that he cites (Deut 21:8; Isa 22:14), God is the subject. See Garnet, "Atonement Constructions in the Old Testament and the Qumran Scrolls," *EvQ* 46, no. 1 (1974): 155.

67. Levine, *In the Presence*, 65–66.
68. Lit. "step on."
69. Contra Leaney, who follows Mansoor in his suggestion that the root כפר (in 1QH IV, 37) has a double meaning. When man is the subject, כפר means "to offer repentance"; when God is the subject, it means "to forgive." However, the proposed categories are too simplistic and do not take into consideration the nuances of meaning resulting from the various forms of the verb in combination with different adjunct prepositions. See A. R. C. Leaney, *The Rule of Qumran and Its Meaning* (NTL; Philadelphia: Westminster Press, 1966), 132, 168; M. Mansoor, *The Thanksgiving Hymns* (Leiden: Brill, 1961), 131.
70. Similarly, B. Nitzan suggests that there are both personal and eschatological aspects of repentance (שוב) in the Qumran literature. See Nitzan, "Repentance in the Dead Sea Scrolls," in *The Dead Sea Scrolls after Fifty Years* (ed. P. W. Flint and J. C. VanderKam; 2 vols.; Leiden: Brill, 1998–99), 2:146–47.

the covenant; and IX, 7–11 the maintenance of boundaries between those inside and outside the community.

Inside the community, eschatological expiation is achieved by atoning for the land (VIII, 6, 10) and rendering judgment (VIII, 10) as well as retribution (VIII, 6–7) for the wicked. Here the juxtaposition of atonement of the land (כפר בעד הארץ) with the punishment of the wicked makes an important and innovative theological statement. The construction כפר בעד indicates that expiation is secured on behalf of the land.[71] The community takes on a priestly role in performing the prerequisite activities and hence creates the condition that will lead to divinely granted expiation. On one hand, the word כפר is used here in a cultic sense: it is the holy community that is taking on the priestly role with respect to atonement. On the other hand, there is a noncultic aspect to the expiation, in that it is directed toward an object contaminated by sin, not a person or sancta.[72]

The belief that the sins of the wicked pollute the land is reminiscent of the priestly theology of H, found in the Hebrew Bible.[73] The theological innovation of 1QS, however, is to associate the priestly category of atonement with that of punishment. The function of the community is not only to secure expiation on behalf of the land, but also to ensure the punishment of those who have sinned and caused its defilement. The word כפר is placed in its covenantal context with the emphasis on the word ברית, bĕrît. It is used three times in the literary framework of 8:1–9:11, with the final occurrence referring to the ברית היחד "covenant of the community."[74] Entrance into the community is synonymous with entrance into the covenant;[75] in accordance with the covenantal agreement, those accepted into the *yahad* are given the role of atoning for the land and judging the wicked.[76]

---

71. In accordance with the translation of כפר בעד suggested by Levine, *In the Presence*, 66.

72. When people or objects are dedicated to God, they are said to be holy as designated by the root קדש. In 1QS, the land is never referred to as being holy. Hence, it is not considered sancta and is in no danger of becoming profaned, although it may become defiled, that is, rendered impure. For a discussion of the relationship between holy/profane and pure/impure, see Milgrom, *Leviticus 1–16*, 729–32.

73. H is the priestly strata associated with most of the Holiness Code (Lev 17–27) and other insertions in Exodus, Lev 1–16, Numbers, and possibly Genesis. In accordance with the theology of H, the land is pure and in danger of being defiled by transgression of the commandments. In the case of non-observance of the laws concerning murder, with or without intent, it states: "You shall not defile the land in which you live, in which I Myself abide, for I the Lord abide among the Israelite people" (Num 35:34, njps). It is interesting to note that the danger to the land is defilement, and not desecration. In H, the land is never referred to as holy. On the purity of the land in H, see J. Joosten, *People and Land in the Holiness Code* (Leiden: Brill, 1996), 178–80. Although the precise content of H is disputed, it is most probable that Num 35 is attributed to this source. See I. Knohl, *The Sanctuary of Silence* (Minneapolis: Fortress, 1995), 59–110; J. Milgrom, *Leviticus 17–22* (AB 3A; New York: Doubleday, 2000), 1332–44.

74. 1QS VIII, 9, 10, 16–17.

75. Cf. 1QS V, 7–8.

76. The text does not give any indication of what it means to "atone for the land." Newton gives a literal interpretation suggesting that the community is atoning for the land on

From a theological perspective, acceptance into the covenant marks the boundary between the righteous and the wicked. Those who are members of the covenantal community live a life of study and obedience to the law (1QS VIII, 15) as a means to atonement, whereas those who remain outside the covenant are sinners who ultimately will be punished in the eschatological overthrow of the realm of darkness.[77]

The fourth and final incidence of the *pi'el* form of כפר is found in the third section of the literary unit 1QS VIII, 1–IX, 11 and is concerned with the form of atonement:

3. בהיות אלה בישראל בכול התכונים האלה ליסוד רוח קודש לאמת

4. עולם לכפר על אשמת פשע ומעל חטאת ולרצון לארץ מבשר עולות ומחלבי זבח ותרומת

5. שפתים למשפט כניחוח צדק ותמים דרך כנדבת מנחת רצון בעת ההיאה יבדילו אנשי

6. היחד בית קודש לאהרון להיחד קודש קודשים ובית יחד לישראל ההולכים בתמים

(3) When these exist in Israel, in accordance with these rules;
to establish a holy spirit of eternal truth,

(4) to atone with respect to guilt of transgression and sacrilege of sin on behalf of the land,
without the flesh of burnt offerings and without the fats of sacrifice.

So that the proper offering (5) of the lips is like a pleasing (odor of) righteousness
and the perfection of way is like an acceptable free-will offering.
At that time the men of the community shall separate themselves;

---

which it dwells. He compares the community to the Jerusalem temple, arguing that the purpose of atonement is to preserve the community from pollution in order to ensure the continued indwelling of the divine presence within the *yahad*. This interpretation, however, is problematic in that the text gives no indication of God's indwelling either within the community or the land. See Michael Newton, *The Concept of Purity at Qumran and in the Letters of Paul* (Cambridge: Cambridge University Press, 1985), 48. Christiansen (*The Covenant*, 157) opposes Newton's literal interpretation of the land and based on context insists that "land" is a reference to the community. This explanation, however, does not take into consideration the eschatological use of the verb כפר in 1QS IX, 4, as compared to the personal usage of 1QS V, 6. Sanders accurately places the atonement of the land in its eschatological framework when he states that "the Land, like the Temple, was at present being defiled by its occupation and use by non-sectarians." The purpose of the exilic community, therefore, is to atone for the land in preparation for their future return. See E. P. Sanders, *Paul and Palestinian Judaism* (Philadelphia: Fortress, 1977), 302–3. Although the land of Israel is not central to the theology of the community as it was to biblical Israel, the theology is not dissimilar to that of H (cf. Lev 26:43).

77. Christiansen (*The Covenant*, 156–58) notes that in the conceptual world of the community, the eschatological process had already commenced with the formation of the community.

(6) a holy house for Aaron for the community of the most holy
and a house of community for Israel for those who walk in perfection. (1QS IX, 3–6).

The phrase לכפר על אשמת פשע ומעל חטאת indicates that the atonement of the community is with respect to sin.[78] When the object of כפר is sin and the subject God, the context is usually noncultic. However, the expression of atonement is suggestive of a cultic context with respect to both the priestly role of the community and the cultic language used to describe the sin.[79] Of particular significance is the word מעל, which is commonly translated as "sacrilege." In a cultic context, מעל is strictly defined as a transgression against God in the form of a violation of sancta. In the later biblical priestly writings, however, the meaning of the word מעל is expanded to connote any transgression of the commandments.[80]

This expanded meaning is most explicit in the execration text (Lev 26:14–45) of the Holiness Code, where non-observance of the commandments is equated with breaking the covenant (v. 15) and is therefore called a מעל against God (v. 40).[81] Significantly, sin results in exile to the land of one's enemies (vv. 38–41), but atonement in exile results in God remembering the land (v. 41).[82]

Similarly, in 1QS IX, 4 the atonement of the exilic community, with respect to transgressions of the covenant, is credited toward the land. In keeping with the utilization of cultic terminology, the term רצון should be interpreted according to its priestly usage:[83] the act of atonement is "on behalf of" or "for" the land—not "of" the land. Hence, the usage of כפר in 1QS IX, 4 is similar to that of 1QS VIII, 6

---

78. For a thorough discussion of כפר על, see Levine, *In the Presence*, 63–67.

79. אשמה may refer to wrongdoing or guiltiness, whereas the אשם is the guilt offering that makes expiation for specific types of sin. Similarly the feminine noun חטאת refers to a sin or sin offering.

80. On the meaning of מעל, see J. Milgrom, *Cult and Conscience: The Asham and the Priestly Doctrine of Repentance* (SJLA 18; Leiden: Brill, 1976), 16–35; Knohl, *Sanctuary*, 184.

81. Knohl, in *Sanctuary*, asserts that in H "even a general violation of the commandments is called מעל as it contains an element of violation of the *bĕrît*." In addition, it is interesting to note other similarities between the covenant in 1QS and that of H: both have priestly content, cultic language, and references to the land. It is important to recognize that these elements are not unique to the *Rule of the Community* and may be rooted in the priestly strata of the Hebrew Bible, especially H and its final redactor H$_R$, the latter of which is dated to the end of the Babylonian exile. A full comparison of the covenantal theology of 1QS and H is beyond the scope of this essay but may be worthy of further research. On covenant in H, see Joosten, *People and Land*, 112–18; on H$_R$, see Milgrom, *Leviticus 17–22*, 1439–43.

82. Although the land is often personified in the biblical text, this is the only instance in which God is said to remember the land. B. Levine, *The JPS Torah Commentary: Leviticus* (Philadelphia: JPS, 1989), 191.

83. The priestly usage of the term רצון indicates God's acceptance of an offering, usually on behalf of the person who makes the sacrifice: "You shall not offer any that has a defect, for it will not be accepted in your favor (לרצון יהיה לכם)" (Lev 22:20, NJPS); cf. Lev 1:3; 19:5; 22:19, 21, 29; 23:11. See Levine, *Leviticus*, 6; Milgrom, *Leviticus 17–22*, 1619–20; BDB 953.

and 10 in that all three instances involve the community atoning on behalf of the land, in the context of covenant.

The interpretation of 1QS IX, 4–5 is decisive for our understanding of atonement within the community. The preposition "מ[ן]" in the phrase מבשר עולות ומחלבי זבח can be rendered in three different ways.[84] First, it can be interpreted as "by means of,"[85] indicating that atonement is achieved through animal sacrifice. This translation, however, is problematic in that it does not account for the parallelism of the two clauses that follow. Second, מן can be read as a comparative marker, implying that the atonement of the community is more effective than cultic sacrifice.[86] This rendering had led some to the conclusion that the community participated in a "spiritual"[87] form of sacrifice as implied by the use of cultic language in what follows: ותרומת שפתים למשפט כניחוח צדק ותמים דרך כנדבת מנחת רצון. The community's "offering of the lips" replaces the offering on the altar of God, and the sectarian lifestyle[88] is a replacement for acceptable sacrifice. The difficulty with this interpretation is twofold. First, it assumes the need for a replacement in a literary context that does not explicitly condemn cultic rites, either in principle or in polemic against the Jerusalem temple. Second, the introduction of the ambiguous term "spiritual" in reference to the community or its religious practice does nothing to clarify the meaning of the text.[89]

The third way is to understand the preposition מן as a privative marker,[90] sug-

---

84. For an analysis of 1QS 9:4–5, see Lichtenberger, "Atonement at Qumran," 161–62.

85. So P. Wernberg-Møller, *The Manual of Discipline: Translated and Annotated with an Introduction* (STDJ 1; Leiden: Brill, 1957), 35; cf. Gärtner, *The Temple,* 29.

86. So Brownlee, *Dead Sea Manual,* 34; Baumgarten, "Sacrifice and Worship," 47.

87. Gärtner (*The Temple,* 19, 29, 34, 44) contends that the sacrifices of the Jerusalem temple have been replaced by the "spiritual" sacrifices of the community. G. Klinzing, however, rejects the idea of spiritualization of either the temple or its sacrifices, insisting that the cultic language is used, but reinterpreted by the community. See Klinzing, *Die Umdeutung des Kultus in der Qumrangemeinde und im NT* (SUNT 7; Göttingen, 1966), 146.

88. The phrase used to connote the communal lifestyle is תמים דרך, literally the "complete way," is often translated as a perfection of way. In the priestly strata of the Hebrew Bible, the adjective תמים is used repeatedly to emphasize the requirement that a sacrificial animal be without blemish (e.g., Lev 1:3; 3:1, 6, 9; 22:17–25).

89. E. Schüssler Fiorenza points out that the term "spiritualization" is used in a variety of ways, such as to suggest opposition to the cult, the physical world, or even the secular. In the interest of clarity, she prefers to use the term "transference" ("Cultic Language in Qumran and in the NT," *CBQ* 38 [1976]: 159–61). J. Kampen, however, questions the adequacy of the concept of transference in explaining the use of temple imagery in the various Qumran documents. See Kampen, "The Significance of the Temple in the Manuscripts of the Damascus Document," in *The Dead Sea Scrolls at Fifty* (ed. R. A. Kugler and E. M. Schuller; Atlanta: Scholars Press, 1999), 185–87.

90. So Lichtenberger, "Atonement at Qumran," 162; Knibb, *The Qumran Community,* 138; Klinzing, *Die Umdeutung,* 40. Although Klinzing cites Hos 6:6 in support of his contextual understanding of מן, the example he uses may be substitutive rather than privative. See B. R. Waltke and M. O'Connor, *An Introduction to Biblical Hebrew Syntax* (Winona Lake, IN: Eisenbrauns, 1990), 214 n. 99.

gesting that expiation of sin on behalf of the land occurs "without" sacrificial rites. The implication is simply that the community has an alternative means by which to atone for sin. In this case, the parallelism of the two clauses that follow serves to emphasize the efficacy of the communal form of atonement. The community's prayers are like (כ) a pleasing (odor of) righteousness acceptable to God;[91] the communal life is like (כ) an acceptable offering. Communal observances are as valuable as sacrificial rites; *both* result in expiation from God. Prayer and communal lifestyle are an *alternative* form of atonement, not a *replacement* for cultic rites.[92] This reading does not assume that the community rejected the Jerusalem temple as such.[93] It implies only that the community has disassociated itself from a "cultic" self-image, while still maintaining a "priestly"[94] character. In other words, the community has emphasized the noncultic aspects of the priesthood over against the cultic ritual function. The cultic language is a metaphor for the communal form of atonement.[95]

These observations suggest that the *Rule of the Community* describes the *yahad* as a holy community, the main purpose of which is atonement. This atonement has both personal and eschatological aspects, both of which are connected to the concept of covenant. By definition, entrance into the community constitutes ac-

---

91. This may be an allusion to a somewhat rare cultic phrase ריח ניחוח, which indicates that a sacrifice is pleasing to God. The word ניחוח is also found in 1QS VIII, 9 in conjunction with a scribal insertion of ריח. For a detailed analysis of ריח ניחוח, see Milgrom, *Leviticus 1–16*, 162-63, 252.

92. Kugler ("Rewriting Rubrics," 92) correctly asserts that "the community's prayer, praise, study, and priestly-cultic self-definition *did not* replace the act of sacrifice."

93. Within the community, prayer and proper lifestyle are the primary means of atonement. These noncultic forms of atonement may characterize the exilic community of 1QS, but they do not preclude the possibility of occasional and/or future participation in the Jerusalem cult as a secondary means of atonement.

94. The function of the priesthood was never limited to the cult. In the biblical text there is evidence of the following priestly functions: oracular activity (Num 27:21), teaching (Ezek 44:23), blessing (Num 6:22-27), judging (Ezek 44:24), and the separation of sacred from profane and pure from impure (Lev 10:10). Although 1QS differentiates among priests, Levites, and Israelites on the basis of lineage, there is emphasis on all of these priestly tasks being performed, either by designated individuals or the community as a whole. Entrance to the community is determined by the casting of lots (VI, 16, 18-19, 21); teaching and interpretation of the law is assigned to the "priests of Zadok" (V, 8-9); the priests bless the lot of God and the Levites curse the lot of Belial (II, 1f); the judicial powers of the community are presumably held by the community council, comprised of twelve lay members and three priests (VIII, 1); and a distinct function of the community is to maintain a barrier between sacred and profane (VIII, 1–IX, 11). See F. García Martínez, "Priestly Functions in a Community without Temple," in *Gemeinde ohne Tempel: Community without Temple* (ed. B. Ego et al.; WUNT 118; Tübingen: Mohr Siebeck, 1999), 303-19.

95. The use of cultic language must be understood in the framework of the style and vocabulary of 1QS. In general, the use of biblical language, both cultic and noncultic, emphasized that the community viewed itself as a theological link to the biblical tradition and the "sole legitimate representative of biblical Israel." On the conceptual world of the *yahad* and the use of biblical language and style, see Talmon, *Community*, 133-35, 143-44.

ceptance into the *bĕrît*, but the content of the covenantal agreement is interpreted in priestly categories. In the context of 1QS, the priestly categories are noncultic, with prayer and communal life viewed as a viable alternative to sacrificial rites. Finally, the temple is never mentioned—not the one in Jerusalem, nor the one that the community allegedly imagined itself to be.

The Damascus Document

Certain sections of the *Damascus Document* have also been used to support the theory that the community took the temple metaphor literally by viewing itself as a replacement for the Jerusalem temple. A brief examination of the relevant passages will show that here too an alternative interpretation of this metaphor is not only possible but convincing.

The *Damascus Document* can be divided into two parts: the *Admonition* (I–VIII, XIX–XX) and the *Laws* (IX–XVI). Based on a model of a covenant formulary, the *Admonition* contains history (I, 1–IV, 12a), legal texts (IV, 12b–VII, 9), warnings (VII, 5–VIII, 19), and a supplement (IX, 33–XX, 34). In addition to being structured like a covenantal agreement, the *Admonition* is also about covenant. Furthermore, the text is permeated with direct biblical citations, biblical terminology, and allusions to biblical phraseology.[96] It is in this literary framework that we consider a text concerned with God's historical rejection of Israel and the covenant with a chosen remnant—the community:

18. ויאמרו כי לנו היא ואל ברזי פלאו כפר בעד עונם וישא לפשעם

19. ויבן להם בית נאמן בישראל אשר לא עמד כמהו למלפנים ועד

20. הנה המחזיקים בו לחיי נצח וכל כבוד אדם להם הוא כאשר

21. הקים אל להם ביד יחזקאל הנביא לאמר הכהנים והלוים ובני

1. צדוק אשר שמרו את משמרת מקדשי בתעות בני ישראל

2. מעליהם (מעלי הם) יגישו לי חלב ודם   הכהנים הם שבי ישראל

3. היוצאים מארץ יהודה והנלוים (והלוים הם הנלוים) עמהם   ובני צדוק הם בחירי

4. ישראל קריאי השם העמדים באחרית הימים הנה פרוש

5. שמותיהם לתולדותם וקץ מעמדם ומספר צרותיהם ושני

6. התגוררם ופירוש מעשיהם   הקודש (הם הרא)שונים אשר כפר

7. אל בעדם ויצדיקו צדיק וירשיעו רשע וכל הבאים אחריהם

8. לעשות כפרוש התורה אשר התוסרו בו הראשנים עד שלים

---

96. For an overview of the structure and plot of the *Admonition*, see P. R. Davies, *The Damascus Covenant: An Interpretation of the "Damascus Document"* (JSOTSSup 25; Sheffield: JSOT Press, 1983), 48–55.

9. הקץ השנים האלה כברית אשר הקים אל לראשנים לכפר

10. על עונותיהם כן יכפר אל בעדם ובשלום הקץ למספר השנים

11. האלה אין עוד להשתפח לבית יהודה כי אם לעמוד איש על

12. מצודו נבנתה הגדר רהק החוק ובכל השנים האלה יהיה

(18b) ... But God in his wonderful mysteries atoned for their iniquity and pardoned their sin (19) and built for them a sure house in Israel, such as there has not stood from ancient times until (20) now. Those who hold fast to it are to have eternal life and all glory of man is theirs. As (21) God swore to them by the hand of Ezekiel, the prophet, saying, "The priests and the Levites and the Sons of (1) Zadok, who maintained the service of my sanctuary when the people of Israel went astray (2) from me, they shall approach me (with) fat and blood." "The priests" are the penitents of Israel (3) who went out from the land of Judah, ("the Levites" are those) who joined them, and "the Sons of Zadok" are the chosen ones of (4) Israel, those called by name, who shall stand in the end of days. Here is a clear statement (5) of their names, according to their generations, and the time of their standing, and the number of their troubles and the years of (6) their sojourning and a clear statement of their deeds [. . . these are] the holy forefathers for whom God atoned; (7) and they declared the just man as just, and declared the wicked man as wicked. And all those who came (into the covenant) after them (8) to do according to the clear statement of the Law in which the forefathers were instructed, until the completion of (9) the time of these years. Like the covenant that God established with the forefathers, to atone (10) with respect to their iniquities, so, too, shall God atone for them. And in the completion of time according to the number of these years (11) there will be no more joining oneself to the house of Judah, but rather each man stands on (12a) his watchtower: "the wall is built, the statute extends far." (CD III, 18–IV, 12)[97]

CD III, 18–IV, 12 is a distinct literary unit.[98] The phrase בית נאמן, "sure house" (III, 19), has been interpreted as an allusion to the temple and hence a description of the community as a "spiritual" temple. According to Gärtner, the phrase בית נאמן alludes to 2 Sam 7,[99] where the term בית, house, connotes both the temple and the Davidic line.[100] The prophecy spoken through Nathan emphasizes the permanence of the "house" that God will establish:

---

97. Translation mine (Susan Haber).
98. D. R. Schwartz argues convincingly that CD III, 18b–IV, 12a is a distinct literary unit ("To Join Oneself to the House of Judah [Damascus Document IV, 11]," *RevQ* 10 [1981]: 435–46).
99. L. Gaston establishes a similar connection to 2 Sam 7. See Gaston, *No Stone on Another: Studies in the Significance of the Fall of Jerusalem in the Synoptic Gospels* (NovTSup 23; Leiden: Brill, 1970), 173.
100. Gärtner, *The Temple*, 82–83. In opposition, Joseph C. Coppens asserts that the concept of community as temple cannot be found in CD. See Coppens, "The Spiritual Temple in the Pauline Letters and Its Background," in *Studia Evangelica 6: Papers Presented to the Fourth International Congress on New Testament Studies Held at Oxford* (ed. E. A. Livingstone; Berlin: Akademie Verlag, 1973), 59–60.

ונאמן ביתך וממלכתך עד עולם לפניך כסאך יהיה נכון עד עולם

> Your house and your kingship shall ever be secure before you; your throne shall be established forever. (v. 16)[101]

Just as God once established the Davidic house, so God has now also founded the community as a permanent house. The term נאמן in CD III, 19 emphasizes both the eternal nature of God's established house and that it is a "true" house, as opposed to the defiled temple in Jerusalem.[102]

Gärtner links the house, as a metaphor for the community, to the concept of a temple by means of the midrash on Ezek 44:15 that follows.[103] A contextual analysis of this midrash is predicated on an understanding of the MT:

והכהנים הלוים בני צדוק אשר שמרו את משמרת מקדשי בתעות בני ישראל מעלי המה יקרבו אלי

לשרתני ועמדו לפני להקריב לי חלב ודם נאם אדני ה׳

> But the levitical priests descended from Zadok, who maintained the service of My Sanctuary when the people of Israel went astray from Me—they shall approach Me to minister to Me; they shall stand before Me to offer Me fat and blood—declares YHWH God.

In the biblical context of Ezek 44:10–14, the Levites have been excluded from priestly duties because they had ministered to the sinful. According to Ezek 44:15, they are to be replaced with the faithful priests, הכהנים הלוים בני צדוק, the levitical priests from Zadok, who have maintained the service of God's sanctuary.

Ezekiel 44:15 is quoted, in abbreviated form, in CD III, 21–IV, 1 with one significant change: the addition of "and" between the words "priests," "Levites," and "descendants of Zadok."

הכהנים והלוים ובני צדוק אשר שמרו את משמרת מקדשי בתעות בני ישראל מעליהם יגישו לי חלב ודם

> The priests *and* the Levites *and* the Sons of Zadok, who kept the watch of my sanctuary when the children of Israel strayed from me, they shall present me fat and blood. (italics mine)

The addition of the conjunctive "ו" alters the intended meaning: whereas in Ezekiel the terms "Levites" and "descendants of Zadok" modify the noun "priests," CD in effect treats all as independent nouns and thereby posits three categories of priests. The כהנים, priests, are the penitents who were the first to have left Israel;

---

101. All quotations from the Hebrew Bible are in accordance with the NJPS translation, unless otherwise stated. The tetragrammaton has been transliterated as YHWH, rather than translated as "the LORD."

102. Gärtner, *The Temple*, 73.

103. The intervening material, המחזיקים בו לחיי נצח וכל כבוד אדם להם הוא, forms a bridge between the biblical allusion and the midrash and is most likely redactional. See Davies, *The Damascus Covenant*, 90.

the לוים, Levites, who accompany them;[104] and the chosen of Israel the בני צדוק, the Sons of Zadok. According to Gärtner, this latter term refers to the entire community, whose members were identified in varying ways through the use of priestly terminology.[105] The combination of these priestly designations with the term "sure house" can be explained in light of the connection with the prophecy of the temple in Ezekiel. Just as the text in Ezekiel concerned itself with the temple and the true priesthood, the community saw itself as a temple run by priests and Levites.

Gärtner's argumentation is problematic in a number of ways. The phrase בית נאמן is not mentioned explicitly in 2 Sam 7:16; this casts some doubt on his analysis of the biblical background of this phrase. Furthermore, the transference of the wordplay on בית in 2 Sam 7 to the passage in CD is not convincing. In the former, בית means dynasty or temple whereas in the latter the dichotomy is between permanence and temple. Moreover, the key phrase in v. 16 is a clear reference to the Davidic dynasty and does not make any reference to the temple. Finally, the community's self-understanding as the "Sons of Zadok" is subject to scholarly dispute.[106] Any assumption that the group regarded itself as a community of "priests" contradicts other sectarian texts in which a clear distinction between priest and non-priest is maintained.[107]

The majority of scholars[108] associate the phrase בית נאמן in CD III, 19 not with 2 Sam 7, but with 1 Sam 2:35:

> והקימתי לי כהן נאמן כאשר בלבבי ובנפשי יעשה ובניתי לו בית נאמן והתהלך לפני משיחי

> And I will raise up for Myself a faithful priest, who will act in accordance with My wishes and My purposes. I will build for him an enduring house, and he shall walk before My anointed evermore.

This verse is set against a background of the sinful behavior of Eli's two sons. The unfaithful Eliad priesthood will be replaced with another priestly dynasty. The phrase בית נאמן makes no allusion to the temple but clearly refers to the "house" of the faithful priest as it is contrasted with Eli's "house." According to Schwartz,[109]

---

104. See Num 18:2–4 for the precedent of the Levites accompanying the priests.

105. Gärtner, *The Temple*, 4–5, 83–84; cf. R. Kugler, "Priesthood at Qumran," in *The Dead Sea Scrolls after Fifty Years* (ed. P. W. Flint and J. C. VanderKam; Leiden: Brill, 1999), 2:97.

106. The majority of scholars have assumed that the title בני צדוק was derived from the founding members of the community, who were priests from the Zadokite line. It is, however, not entirely clear that the title is exclusively used as a reference to priestly lineage. For a review of the scholarly discussion on this issue, see Kugler, "Priesthood at Qumran," 97–100.

107. García Martínez, "Priestly Functions," 303–5.

108. See, for example, C. Rabin, *The Zadokite Documents* (2d ed.; Oxford: Clarendon, 1958), 13; Schwartz, "To Join Oneself," 438; Davis, *The Damascus Covenant*, 90. J. Campbell contends that the other occurrences of בית נאמן in the Bible are not applicable because they refer to the Davidic dynasty. See Campbell, *The Use of Scripture in the Damascus Document 1–8, 19–20* (BZAW 228; Berlin: de Gruyter, 1995), 82 n. 52.

109. Schwartz, "To Join Oneself," 438.

the allusion to 1 Sam 2:35 found in CD may be interpreted as follows: Although the nation has sinned, there is a remnant of Israel that has continued to observe God's law. They represent the בית נאמן, the community of the faithful, whom God has established as the true inheritors.

In CD, the link between this allusion to 1 Sam 2:35 and the midrash on Ezek 44:15 is thematic.[110] Both biblical passages are concerned with God's replacement of an unfaithful priesthood with another priestly line. In 1 Sam 2:35, the unfaithful Eliad priesthood is replaced by a "house" of faithful priests; in Ezek 44:15, the unfaithful levitical priests are to be replaced by the Zadokite priests. The traditional interpretation of the passage in Ezekiel suggests that the Zadokites ministered only in the temple while their unfaithful contemporaries offered sacrifices in the high places. Yet the high places are never specifically mentioned in Ezek 44. Moreover, in the latter part of the Second Temple period, the source of dispute was not cultic practice outside the temple but the question of proper cultic procedure inside the temple. In CD, the passage in Ezekiel was reinterpreted in accordance with contemporary social issues. The Zadokites, like the faithful priests in 1 Sam 2:35, had remained faithful to the temple by not offering (improper) sacrifices during the sinful ministry of the Levites. In much the same way, the community regarded itself as the "sure house" in Israel—God's faithful who had separated themselves from the sinful Israel and awaited the end of the era of evil.

There is one final portion of this text that has been cited in support of the idea of community as temple. Klinzing[111] has suggested a restoration of CD IV, 6 to include another term from Ezek 44:15—מקדש, sanctuary: מקדש הם אנשי הקודש הראשונים, "they are a sanctuary, the first holy men." According to Klinzing, this continuation of the midrash on Ezek 44:15 interprets the term מקדש as a reference to the founders of the community and presumably establishes the community as a temple from its inception. It is important to understand this proposed restoration in the context of IV, 6, in which there is a lengthy lacuna. Directly preceding the lacuna are the words ופירוש מעשיהם, a list of names.[112] Presumably there is a missing genealogy, the omission of which has left the text immediately following in disarray.[113] It is this corrupted text, which reads הקודש שונים, that is the subject of Klinzing's restoration.

The corrupted text is part of the missing document that continues beyond the lacuna.[114] Rabin amends שונים to read הראשונים, noting a similar mistake in CD

---

110. Ibid., 438–39.

111. Klinzing's restoration is briefly reviewed by Schwartz, "To Join Oneself," 443–44.

112. On the content and specifications of this list, see Davies, *The Damascus Covenant*, 95–96.

113. M. Broshi, ed., *The Damascus Document Reconsidered* (Jerusalem: Israel Exploration Society, 1992), 16–17; cf. J. H. Charlesworth, who suggests that the list may have been deliberately omitted because of its dating or its length. See Charlesworth, *The Dead Sea Scrolls: Hebrew, Aramaic, and Greek Texts with English Translations* (Louisville: Westminster John Knox, 1995), 2:19.

114. The proof is in the phrase וכל הבאים אחריהם (IV, 7), which can only be explained in light of the preceding list. See Davies, *The Damascus Covenant*, 98.

XIV, 7.¹¹⁵ Based on this amendment, two proposed restorations have been endorsed by scholars. The first is אנשי הקודש הראשונים and the second is הראשונים הקודשים, with the latter being the preferred choice from a technical perspective.¹¹⁶ Here הראשונים refers to the founding members of the community, and the phrase itself likely refers back to the missing list.¹¹⁷ Speculative as any restoration may be, it is important to note that the word מקדש has not been included in this reconstruction, for to do so would call into question the structure of the text in CD. The interpretation of the various terms in Ezekiel was completed in 4:4 without any reference to מקדש.¹¹⁸ Clearly, the opportunity had passed, and the term מקדש was not essential to the interpretation of the passage. Hence there is no basis for using this text to support a self-image of the community as temple.

Conclusion

The metaphorical use of temple and purity language to describe the *yahad* permitted a rich and nuanced exploration of the fundamental concepts of God, sin, and atonement and described vividly the role that the community saw itself as playing vis-à-vis its members, the land, God, and the eschatological redemption of Israel. There is no evidence to suggest, however, that the community took the further step of concretizing the metaphor by viewing themselves quite literally as the new temple that replaced or superseded the Jerusalem temple. Had that been the intention of the metaphorical language, one might have expected a more explicit critique of the temple as such, and one might also have expected a direct role in the process of expiation, such as the administration of sacrifices, to be assigned to the priests within the *yahad* or to the *yahad* as a whole. Indeed, one might suggest that the concretizing of the imagery would have had the effect of limiting its descriptive possibilities and thereby, perhaps ironically, diminishing its efficacy as a metaphor in which the community as a whole could see its own reflection.

The two case studies demonstrate clearly the presence of metaphorical language in the Scrolls and also illustrate the complex relationship between the figurative and literal interpretations. With regard to purity language, our study suggests that the community understood moral and ritual purity to be interdependent and that both repentance—signaled by the metaphorical usage of the purity language—and ritual purification—signaled by a literal reading—were necessary for entrance into the community and for full participation in community life. With regard to temple language, our study suggests that the imagery was taken metaphorically and was very rich as a way of articulating the self-understanding of the community, but that it was not taken literally to mean that the community viewed itself as the replacement for the temple in Jerusalem or even as a place where the sacrificial cult would be carried out.

The metaphorical use of language provides a vehicle through which the *yahad*

---

115. Rabin, *The Zadokite Documents*, 14.
116. For an analysis of the two proposed restorations, see Davies, *The Damascus Covenant*, 98–100.
117. Ibid., 99–100.
118. See Schwartz, "To Join Oneself," 443–44.

could articulate its positive self-understanding as a community in covenantal relationship with God, devoted to following God, and living in a state of purity in which the lines of communication with God through prayer and other rituals would always remain open.

6

A WOMAN'S TOUCH:
FEMINIST ENCOUNTERS WITH THE HEMORRHAGING WOMAN
IN MARK 5:24–34

In what might be perceived as a covert and calculated move, the hemorrhaging woman in Mark 5:24–34 approaches Jesus from behind, touches his garment, and is instantly healed of her affliction. The text presents a tension between the healing touch of Jesus and the impure and therefore undesirable touch of the woman. Scholars agree that, in accordance with Levitical law, this woman is impure.[1] They also note the linguistic similarities between the description of the hemorrhaging woman within the narrative and the purity laws of Lev 15. However, there is no consensus of opinion regarding the significance of her impurity.

For a number of the earlier feminist scholars, the woman's impurity is fundamental to an interpretation of the narrative as a critique of Jewish purity laws.[2] Marla Selvidge, for example, argues that Jewish law marginalizes the hemorrhaging woman both because she is a woman and because she is impure. By allowing her to touch him, Jesus is viewed as a "liberal egalitarian" who abrogates the purity laws of Judaism in favor of a more compassionate view that eschews any form of social exclusion based on purity or gender. Selvidge's interpretation is predicated on two premises. The first is concerned with the purity legislation, which is portrayed as being oppressive to women. The second focuses on the narrative in Mark, which is presumed to highlight Jesus' rejection of the purity laws.

More recently, a second group of feminist scholars has opposed this view by

---

1. My thanks are due to Adele Reinhartz for her constructive comments on an earlier version of this essay.
See, e.g., Joel Marcus, *Mark 1–8: A New Translation with Introduction and Commentary* (AB 27; New York: Doubleday, 1999), 357–58; Marla J. Selvidge, *Woman, Cult, and Miracle Recital: A Redactional Critical Investigation on Mark 5:24–34* (London: Associated University Press, 1990), 47–70; Charlotte Fonrobert, "The Woman with a Blood-Flow (Mark 5:24–34) Revisited: Menstrual Laws and Jewish Culture in Christian Feminist Hermeneutics," in *Early Christian Interpretation of the Scriptures of Israel* (ed. Craig A. Evans and James A. Sanders; JSNTSup 148; Sheffield: Sheffield Academic Press, 1997), 121–40, esp. 122–26.

2. See, e.g., Selvidge, *Woman, Cult, and Miracle Recital,* 47–70, 83–91; Leonard Swidler, "Jesus Was a Feminist," *The Catholic World* (January 1971): 181; Karen A. Barta, "Paying the Price of Paternalism," in *Where Can We Find Her?* (ed. Marie-Eloise Rosenblatt; New York: Paulist Press, 1991), 31.

dismissing the issue of impurity entirely.³ Of particular interest is the work of Mary Rose D'Angelo, who interprets the narrative of the hemorrhaging woman in the context of Mark's Christology, an ideology of faith, healing, and miracles. In her view, the impurity of the woman is completely irrelevant to the story. The portrayal of Jesus as a liberator of women from oppressive Jewish law, she argues, is a misreading of the narrative in Mark and misunderstands the nature of Levitical law in general and its application to women in particular. Selvidge's "anti-Judaism" may make good feminist reading, but it is developed at the expense of the Jewish woman in her cultural context.⁴

Feminist interpretations of the narrative in Mark 5:24–34 thus seem to take one of two opposing positions with respect to the woman's impurity. The first position correctly identifies the woman's impurity but misinterprets the Markan text when it finds its focus of interest in the abrogation of supposedly oppressive purity laws. The second feminist position rightly rejects this polemic against Jewish law but goes too far in its critique when it dismisses any possibility that the impurity generated by the woman's physical condition contributes to the understanding of the narrative.⁵ We are still left with an unresolved question: "What is the significance of the woman's impurity in the narrative of Mark 5:24–34?"

In what follows I argue for a position in between the two opposing feminist readings, in which the woman's health is the central feature of the narrative and impurity is inextricably connected to her physical condition. Fundamental to my own reading of the text is the observation that the anonymous woman is described solely in terms of her physical affliction: a flow of blood that identifies her to the implied audience and marks her literary role in the narrative.⁶ She is the "hemorrhaging woman" and not the "impure woman." In emphasizing the woman's health, however, I cannot dismiss the significance of her impurity within the narrative. Her hemorrhage carries with it an impurity that could not have been ignored either by Mark's audience or the society in which she lived. Her illness is explicit; her impurity is implicit.

---

3. See, e.g., Fonrobert, "The Woman with a Blood-Flow," 122–26; Mary Rose D'Angelo, "Gender and Power in the Gospel of Mark: The Daughter of Jairus and the Woman with the Flow of Blood," in *Miracles in Jewish and Christian Antiquity* (ed. John C. Cavadini; Notre Dame, IN: University of Notre Dame Press, 1999), 83–109, esp. 83–85; Richard Horsley, *Hearing the Whole Story: The Politics of Plot in Mark's Gospel* (Louisville: Westminster John Knox, 2001), 209–10; cf. the similar argument pertaining to the parallel narrative in Matthew advocated by Amy-Jill Levine, "Discharging Responsibility: Matthean Jesus, Biblical Law, and Hemorrhaging Woman," in *Treasures New and Old: Recent Contribution to Matthean Studies* (ed. David R. Bauer and Mark Allen Powell; SBLSymS; Atlanta: Scholars Press, 1996), 379–97.

4. On anti-Judaism in Christian feminist interpretations of the New Testament, see Judith Plaskow, "Anti-Judaism in Christian Feminist Interpretation," in *Searching the Scriptures: A Feminist Introduction* (ed. Elisabeth Schüssler Fiorenza; 2 vols.; New York: Crossroad, 1993), 1:117–29.

5. D'Angelo ("Gender and Power," 91) states that "the gospel of Mark shows no interest in purity in the two miracles in 5.21–43."

6. On anonymity in biblical narrative, see Adele Reinhartz, *"Why Ask My Name?" Anonymity and Identity in Biblical Narrative* (Oxford: Oxford University Press, 1998), 188.

The present study will assess the extent to which purity issues are essential to the story of the hemorrhaging woman in Mark 5:24–34. This inquiry necessitates a survey of the relevant legislation and its interpretation in the Second Temple period, as well as an examination of the language used by Mark in the narrative. In addition, Mark's portrait of the hemorrhaging woman will be considered in the context of his rhetorical agenda.

Purity Legislation and Its Interpretation in the Second Temple Period

In Mark 5:24–34, there is an allusion to Israelite tradition evident in the use of language originating in the purity legislation of Leviticus.[7] In this use of language, Mark presumes that his intended audience was familiar with the legal aspects of purity legislation and would understand the narrative in light of those laws.[8] In order to understand the relevance of this allusion to purity in the narrative it is essential to investigate the relevant purity legislation and its interpretation in the Second Temple period.

The laws regulating purity that form the background for the narrative of the hemorrhaging woman can be found in Lev 15, which is concerned with normal and abnormal genital discharges and effluxes of both men and women.[9] According to this legislation, the hemorrhaging woman in Mark 5 is classified as a אִשָּׁה כִּי־תִהְיֶה זָבָה דָּם, a woman with an abnormal genital discharge.[10] Both the זבה (*zabah*) and her male counterpart, the זב (*zab*), are considered to have a severe form of

---

7. The most obvious use of Levitical language is in the identification of the woman as γυνὴ οὖσα ἐν ῥύσει αἵματος ("a woman being in a flow of blood"). See Lev 15:25–30.

8. Horsley (*Hearing the Whole Story*, 48–49) attests to the subtle allusions and explicit references to Israelite tradition that exist throughout Mark, suggesting that they could only have been intended for an audience with substantial knowledge of Judaism and its texts.

9. In Lev 15, the laws concerning men are listed first (vv. 2b–17) and are longer and more detailed than those concerning women (vv. 19–30). In the case of normal genital discharges, the length of impurity is designated according to biology. Thus impurity from a seminal emission lasts one day, whereas that caused by menstruation is appropriately seven days in length. In circumstances of abnormal discharges, men and woman are designated impure for the same amount of time, with both counting off seven days after the cessation before undergoing purification rites. Contra Selvidge (*Woman, Cult, and Miracle Recital*, 51–57), the text does not support the idea that the purity laws marginalized women more than men.

10. The law specifically distinguishes between a normal menstrual flow (vv. 19–24) and an abnormal discharge that occurs outside the boundaries of a normal menstrual cycle (vv. 25–30). Although many scholars recognize this distinction, there is still a tendency to conflate the two categories through generalization and the inappropriate application of menstrual law to the hemorrhaging woman of Mark. Selvidge (*Woman, Cult, and Miracle Recital*, 53–57, 86–91), for example, separates the two categories in her summary of Lev 15, only to use her synopsis to justify the "biological differences" of all women, and especially the woman in Mark. Fonrobert's ("The Woman with a Blood-Flow," 128–38) overlapping of categories is subtler as she clearly analyzes the law of the *zabah* but continues to refer to menstruation and menstrual regulation.

impurity that is contagious through contact with persons and objects. Anything that the *zab* or *zabah* sits on or lies upon is rendered impure, and those who come in direct contact with them or the contaminated objects around them will also be rendered impure, albeit only until the evening.[11] The cessation of the discharge is followed by a seven-day period of healing that culminates in a complex purification ritual, which includes both ritual immersion and sacrificial expiation.[12]

The implications of the purity legislation are crucial to the status of the *zab/zabah* in the community. In the Hebrew Bible, priestly law presents two separate traditions regarding their status. The first is found in Lev 15:11, where it states, "If one with a discharge, without having rinsed his hands in water, touches another person, that person shall wash his clothes, bathe in water, and remain unclean until evening." The phrase "without having rinsed his hands in water" is informative, for it suggests that if the *zab* takes the precaution of rinsing his hands before touching other persons, vessels, or utensils, he will not pass on his impurity.[13] The precaution of rinsing one's hands, found in the legislation regarding the *zab*, is not explicitly mentioned in the parallel law concerning the *zabah*. Since the more abbreviated law concerning the female is modeled on that of the male, this detail is assumed rather than repeated. Moreover, if one regards the purity laws as being part of a coherent theological system, then it makes sense that the touch of the *zabah*, like the touch of the *zab*, is contaminating and that the same leniency applies to both. The implications of this leniency are far-reaching, for it suggests that although the *zab/zabah* transmit their impurity by touch, they may still live at home and lead relatively normal lives during the duration of their illness.[14]

In contrast to the lenient attitude toward the *zab/zabah* found in Lev 15, the priestly law found in Num 5:1–4 requires that any individual who is classified as having a severe form of impurity be excluded from the Israelite camp. Thus, in ad-

---

11. In the Masoretic text it states, "whoever touches them (בָּם) shall be unclean," referring to the bedding or any object that has been sat upon. In contrast, two manuscripts and the Septuagint translation read, "whoever touches her (αὐτῆς) shall be unclean" (Lev 15.27), referring to the woman. Jacob Milgrom (*Leviticus 1–16: A New Translation with Introduction and Commentary* [AB 3; New York: Doubleday, 1991], 943) argues for the latter reading, which makes much more sense in a holistic reading of the legislation in Lev 15. Fonrobert ("The Woman with a Blood-Flow," 131), however, does not accept this reading. In the context of this discussion, I would point out that Mark's audience would have been familiar with the Septuagint and not the Masoretic text and would have understood the law to mean that touching the woman transmitted impurity (v. 27) as did touching her bedding (v. 26).

12. Ritual immersion is explicitly prescribed in the legislation concerning the *zab*, but it is not specifically mentioned in connection with the *zabah*. Nevertheless, the requirement to bathe is equally applicable in both cases, as it is evident in the chiastic structure of the laws set out in Lev 15. The details of the first law pertaining to the *zab* are assumed in the abbreviated version of the last law concerning the *zabah*, even though they are not repeated.

13. On the leniency of this law, see Milgrom, *Leviticus 1–16*, 920–21.

14. In contrast, the menstruant, who has a less severe form of impurity, does not contaminate through touch. For a detailed discussion of contact with the *zabah*, see Milgrom, *Leviticus 1–16*, 924–43.

dition to the *zab/zabah*, an individual with scale disease (צָרוּעַ)[15] and the one who is impure because of a corpse (לנפש) is isolated from the rest of the community.[16] The stringency of this priestly tradition has profound consequences with respect to the status of the individual who contracts a severe impurity. Whereas those with corpse contamination would be excluded only temporarily from the community, others with ongoing symptoms of scale disease or genital efflux could be separated from community and family indefinitely and forced to live out their lives in isolation on the edge of society.

The laws of Lev 15 and the legislation of Num 5:1–4 present two opposing priestly traditions concerning the treatment of the *zab/zabah* that have clear implications for the status of the hemorrhaging woman of Mark 5. Was she, like a *zabah*, isolated from her community in accordance with the stringency of the law in Numbers, or did the leniency of the Levitical legislation enable her to remain at home? Based on their own (mis)readings of the purity laws, Selvidge and other feminist scholars have speculated that the hemorrhaging woman was isolated and oppressed because of her impurity.[17] This interpretation is suspect because it does not take into consideration the opposing biblical traditions regarding impurity, nor does it consider how the legislation was interpreted in the first century C.E., several hundred years after it was formulated.

Unfortunately, the textual evidence pertaining to the status of the *zab/zabah* during the Second Temple period is contradictory and as such is not particularly useful in determining how the purity legislation would have affected the status of the hemorrhaging woman in Mark 5. Following the leniency of Lev 15, the rabbinic texts suggest that the *zab* was allowed to remain in the city but was barred from the temple and Temple Mount.[18] Josephus, however, indicates a stricter interpretation, claiming that both the *zab* and the individual with scale disease were banished from Jerusalem.[19] Even more stringent was the legislation from the Temple Scroll, which required the designation of three separate places to the east

---

15. The biblical terms צָרוּעַ and צרעת are often translated as "leper" and "leprosy" respectively, even though leprosy (Hansen's disease) was unknown in the Near East until the Hellenistic period. The condition has never been clearly identified, but it is more accurately translated as "scale disease." It is noteworthy that in the Septuagint and the New Testament the term use is *lepra*, and not the Greek term for leprosy, which is *elephas* or *elephantiasis*. For the most part, I will refer to individuals with scale disease, reverting to the term "leper" only for the convenience of distinguishing the individual whom Jesus heals in Mark 1:40–45. On the nature of scale disease, see Milgrom, *Leviticus 1–16*, 816–20.

16. In the priestly purity system, the most severe form of impurity is found in the זב/זבה, מצרע, and טמא לנפש. These impurities are considered more dangerous because they are contagious through contact with other persons and objects and thus require a lengthier and more complex process of purification than mild and moderate impurities. On the classification of impurity into major and minor categories, see the useful charts in Milgrom, *Leviticus 1–16*, 986–87.

17. See Selvidge, *Woman, Cult, and Miracle Recital*, 47–90, 83–91; Barta, "Paying the Price," 31; Swidler, "Jesus Was a Feminist," 181.

18. *M. Kel.* 1.8; *b. Ta'an* 21b.

19. *B.J.* 5.227; *A.J.* 3.261.

of the city for the individual with scale disease, the *zab* and the man who had an emission of semen.[20] Since the Temple Scroll prohibited women from dwelling in Jerusalem regardless of their state of purity, this law only concerns itself with the impurity of men.[21]

Although this literary evidence regarding the status of the *zab/zabah* is inconsistent, the existence of a variety of interpretations is in and of itself informative, for such rulings form part of a larger discussion on purity legislation that is prominent in Second Temple literature. These varied discussions indicate that issues of purity and impurity were central to Jewish life both in Judea and the Diaspora. As each sect and community of Jews defined their relationship with the temple in Jerusalem, there emerged a multiplicity of interpretations of the purity legislation. Some groups, like the pre-70 C.E. Pharisees, strictly observed the purity laws even outside the temple, whereas the other groups reinterpreted the purity laws as they applied to their daily lives.[22]

The centrality of purity practices to Jewish life in the Second Temple period is supported by archaeological evidence.[23] The discovery of *mikvaot* in such diverse places as Gamla, Sepphoris, Herodium, and Massada suggest that in Palestine the removal of impurity was not a rite reserved only for approaching the sacred precincts of the temple,[24] but was common practice for Jews of all walks of life. The use of these immersion pools was common to the priest and the Israelite, the rich

---

20. "You shall make three places, to the East of the city, separate from each other, to which shall come lepers and those afflicted with a discharge and the men who have an emission of semen" (11Q19 XLVI, 16-18).

21. Shaye Cohen regards the laws excluding women and men with impurities from dwelling in Jerusalem as utopian. In the Temple Scroll there is also legislation regarding the exclusion of impure individuals from cities other than Jerusalem, in which women are specifically mentioned (11Q19 XLVIII, 14-17). See Cohen, "Menstruants and the Sacred in Judaism and Christianity," in *Women's History and Ancient History* (ed. Sarah B. Pomeroy; Chapel Hill: University of North Carolina Press, 1991), 278.

22. Jacob Neusner, *The Idea of Purity in Ancient Judaism* (Leiden: Brill, 1973), 65. On the importance of the purity laws in the Second Temple period, see also E. P. Sanders, *Judaism: Practice and Belief: 63 BCE-66 CE* (3d ed.; London: SCM Press, 1998), 214-30; Paula Fredriksen, "Did Jesus Oppose the Purity Laws?" *Bible Review* 11, no. 3 (June 1995): 22-23.

23. On the relevant archaeological evidence, see Sanders, *Judaism: Practice and Belief*, 222-29.

24. Priestly law legislates against both inadvertent (Lev 5:1-13) and deliberate (Num 19:13) transgressions of the purity laws in which one who is impure delays their purification beyond the prescribed period of time. Since entering the temple is not mentioned in these laws, it may be assumed that the requirement to purify oneself applied regardless of participation in the cult. Significantly, Josephus's first-century interpretation of the purification laws upholds this view. He states unequivocally that any person who exceeds the appropriate number of days in a state of defilement has sinned against God and is required to make atonement (*A.J.* 3.262). Josephus's testimony supports the archaeological evidence from the period, indicating that at least some groups of Jews in the first century were observing purity laws outside the temple.

and the poor, the Pharisees and the Sadducees, and the sectarians from Qumran. Beyond Judea, however, there is little material evidence to support the widespread practice of ritual immersion. Nonetheless, the textual evidence suggests that the Jews of the Diaspora also purified themselves, if not through immersion, then by sprinkling, splashing, or hand-washing.[25]

The evidence pertaining to *mikvaot* and the removal of impurity during the Second Temple period is significant to the discussion of the hemorrhaging woman. It may not be possible to associate her with a particular sect of Judaism, nor can we ascertain how she may have interpreted the purity laws. Yet D'Angelo and other feminist scholars contend that, as long as she stayed away from the temple, her impurity was not a concern.[26] In light of the literary and material evidence, this claim cannot be substantiated with any degree of certainty. In fact, it would have been quite the opposite situation in communities that supported *mikvaot* for the very purpose of eliminating impurity outside the temple precincts. There, the woman's impurity would most certainly have been of significant concern.

When Selvidge argues that the purity laws are oppressive, she overlooks the possibility for leniency in the legislation. In viewing the legislation as specifically targeting women, Selvidge ignores the purity legislation that is directed equally toward men. Finally, when she argues that transmission of impurity has serious consequences, she fails to understand that in the case of the hemorrhaging woman, the transfer of impurity, though not desirable, was easily remedied. D'Angelo, on the other hand, deems the impurity of the woman to be irrelevant, disregarding the importance of Levitical law during the Second Temple period. Not only does she ignore the volume and variety of opinion pertaining to purity, she has difficulty explaining the existence of *mikvaot* in locations far removed from the temple in Jerusalem.

---

25. The *Letter of Aristeas* and the *Sibylline Oracles* mention hand-washing, but not immersion (*Let. Aris.* 304–6; *Sib. Or.* 3.591–93), whereas Philo refers to περιρρανάμενοι καὶ ἀπολουσάμενοι, which may be translated as "aspersion and ablutions" or "sprinkling and bathing" (*Spec.* 3.205–6). On purity in the Diaspora, see the detailed discussion in E. P. Sanders, *Jewish Law from Jesus to the* Mishnah (London: SCM Press, 1990), 258–71; cf. idem, *Judaism: Practice and Belief,* 223–24.

26. In support of his thesis that menstruants were not isolated in Judaism until the sixth century, Cohen ("Menstruants and the Sacred," 279) contends that during the Second Temple period "*most Jews*" were not concerned with impurity outside the Temple. He substantiates this statement by citing the stories of the hemorrhaging women found in Matthew, Mark, and Luke, claiming that there is not "any indication that the woman was impure or suffered any degree of isolation." Cohen's position is predicated on the erroneous assumptions that (1) the woman is portrayed equally in the three versions of the story and that (2) the literary representation of this one woman portrays an accurate historical reality. More to the point, Cohen can support his contention that impurity was not an issue outside the temple only by ignoring conflicting evidence, such as the very existence of *mikvaot* outside of Jerusalem. In spite of these uncertainties, D'Angelo ("Gender and Power," 84) and the others (e.g., Levine, "Discharging Responsibility," 388–89; Horsley, *Hearing the Whole Story,* 209) have unreservedly cited Cohen's scholarship in order to substantiate their contention that the impurity of the hemorrhaging woman is irrelevant.

Between the two extreme positions offered by feminist scholars is my view that the issue of impurity is essential to the narrative insofar as it relates to the health of the hemorrhaging woman. Supporting this view is the evidence from the Second Temple period, which suggests that purity issues were at the forefront of Jewish life and an important consideration in the various communities, including those of the early church. Undoubtedly, Mark and his intended audience were not only familiar with the purity legislation of Leviticus, they were also concerned with the relevance of impurity in their own community. It is with this in mind that we can assess the role of purity issues in the narrative of the hemorrhaging woman.

The Literary Representation of the Hemorrhaging Woman

The hemorrhaging woman of Mark 5:24–34 may or may not be a historical person, but she is certainly a literary figure whose identity and characteristics are molded to serve the rhetorical purposes of the author. It is important, therefore, to evaluate her literary role in the narrative relative to the intentions of the author and the effect of his word on his implied audience.

In Mark 5:25 the hemorrhaging woman is first introduced into the narrative. She is not given a name but is only identified in terms of her affliction: γυνὴ οὖσα ἐν ῥύσει αἵματος, literally "a woman being in a flow of blood." In the absence of a name or any other defining characteristics, it is only the woman's condition that marks her identity and distinguishes her from the other characters in the story.[27] For this primary audience, as for the modern scholar, she can only be referred to as "the hemorrhaging woman." Interestingly, Mark describes the woman's distress in some detail, but he does not specify the location of the hemorrhage. Most scholars assume that the woman's bleeding is vaginal.[28] Others note the omission, suggesting that Mark would have been less shy about relaying this information if the bleeding had been in a less modest location.[29] An opposing opinion is put forward by Amy-Jill Levine, who, in commenting on the Matthean version of the narrative, suggests that it is not clear that either Mark or Matthew had Levitical legislation in mind. In her view, the woman may have had a sore on her leg, breast, nose, and so on and was therefore ill, but not impure.[30] However, it is unlikely that in the narrative of Mark, at least, the bleeding refers to a mere sore, since such an interpretation is not consistent with the author's emphasis on the severity of the affliction nor his reliance on early Jewish tradition.[31] I concur with the majority

---

27. In literary characterizations, one of the functions of the proper name is to distinguish one character from another. On the function of the proper name, see Reinhartz, "*Why Ask My Name?*" 6–9.

28. See, e.g., D'Angelo, "Gender and Power," 83–85; Fonrobert, "The Woman with a Blood-Flow," 121–26.

29. Marcus, *Mark 1–8*, 357; cf. Hendrik van der Loos, *The Miracles of Jesus* (NovTSup 9; Leiden: Brill, 1965), 510 n. 1.

30. Levine, "Discharging Responsibility," 384.

31. It is also important to consider that in the other Markan miracle stories, Jesus heals people with very specific debilitating afflictions. These conditions include blindness (8:22–

of scholars who assume the hemorrhage is vaginal and that the description of the woman is intended to allude to Lev 15 and the laws concerning purity.

Mark's audience, being familiar with Israelite tradition, would have naturally interpreted this story against the backdrop of the Levitical purity laws. They would have imagined this woman not only as ill, but also as being in a state of impurity. This impurity is a direct consequence of her illness and is therefore an integral part of her identity as the "hemorrhaging woman." It must be emphasized, however, that it is the physical ailment, and not the ritual implications of her condition, that is of primary concern to the narrative. Like the paralytic and other characters in Mark's Gospel, the woman is in need of physical healing, but she will have to undergo ritual purification as well.

In describing the distress of the woman, Mark places considerable emphasis on the length and seriousness of the woman's illness. Having been ill for twelve years, she had sought out various physicians, but their attempts to cure her had only made her worse. Moreover, her pursuit of a cure had exhausted her financial resources and resulted in her destitution.[32] What is remarkable about this description is that it is the only time that Mark makes a reference to physicians in a healing story. Juxtaposed to this report on the ineptitude of the physicians is the assertion that the woman had heard about Jesus—that is, she had heard about his power to heal. Mark effectively sets up a contrast between the healing power of physicians, which in this case had been ineffective, and the supernatural healing power of Jesus to which the woman was now turning.

Having heard about Jesus, the hemorrhaging woman seeks out his healing power by coming up from behind him in the crowd and touching his garment. Her intent is clearly established: she believes that the act of touching his clothes will cure her affliction. The auditor recalls that other sick people wanted to touch Jesus because they expected to be healed.[33] Unlike the previous incidents, however,

---

26; 10:46–52), deafness (7:31–37), paralysis (2:3–12), and a withered hand (3:1–6). It is logical to assume that the hemorrhage of the woman was at least as debilitating as these other conditions and that the healing of her condition was equally life transforming.

32. The "length of distress" motif found in Mark 5:26 is quite common in miracle stories, especially those concerned with illness (Mark 9:21; Luke 13:11; Acts 3:2; 4:22; 9:33; 14:8; John 5:5; 9:1). According to Gerd Thiessen (*The Miracle Stories of the Early Christian Tradition* [trans. Francis McDonagh; Philadelphia: Fortress, 1983], 51–52), the counterpoint to this reference to the past is a projection into the future. If, after twelve years of illness, the woman has only become worse, the woman's prognosis for the future can only be deterioration of her condition, or what may be referred to as the "tendency to an unhappy ending."

33. In Mark 3:10, it states that "all who had diseases pressed upon him to touch him" (cf. Mark 6:56). In the Markan version the woman touches his garment (ἱματίου). Marcus comments that the passage presupposes that the power resident in Jesus' body can be stored, tapped, or transferred to other physical objects (*Mark 1–8*, 359). Both of the parallel accounts (Matt 9:20; Luke 8:44) indicate that the woman specifically touches the hem of his garment (τοῦ κρασπέδου τοῦ ἱματίου αὐτοῦ), thereby alluding to the fringe (צִיצִת) of Num 15:37–41. Since, in ancient Israel, the hem was considered an extension of the person and his authority (see 1 Sam 24:5–12), it is an appropriate and even likely conduit of Jesus' power. However, Mark seemingly misses the opportunity to refer to earlier tradition.

this woman is not forthright in her approach to Jesus. Rather, she comes up behind Jesus in a calculated move, which suggests a need for circumvention. This circuitous approach to Jesus is necessitated by her impurity, for, although her primary intent is to be healed, she realizes that her touch transmits impurity.[34] Lest she be prevented from touching Jesus, she approaches from behind, touching only his clothes, for she may have thought: "What the eye does not see the heart does not grieve over."[35]

As the narrative approaches a climax, Mark's attention to literary detail is crucial. The narrator's role in the story becomes explicit as he relays information, letting the audience know about the woman's intention and action before Jesus is aware of it. They are also aware that she is impure and that her touch transmits her impurity. The tension in the text is unmistakable. She needs healing by a touch, but that touch will transmit impurity to her healer. As the sense of drama builds, the audience cannot help but wonder: Will the woman's touch contaminate Jesus or effect a cure? The urgency of the silent question is met with the response of the narrator, who proclaims that "immediately ($\epsilon\vartheta\vartheta\varsigma$) her hemorrhage stopped" (v. 29). Here the narrator knows what only the woman can know: there has been a cessation of the blood-flow within her body. Jesus knows immediately ($\epsilon\vartheta\vartheta\varsigma$) that the power has gone forth from him, but he does not know where it has gone. At this point, the audience also knows more than Jesus does: they realize that the power of healing has been transmitted from Jesus to the woman and that Jesus has apparently not been affected by contact with her impurity. Seemingly, the transfer of impurity from the woman to Jesus has no consequences, perhaps because of his unique status. Anyone else would have surely been considered impure until the evening.

Among the literary devices that Mark uses, irony is most prominent in the physical interaction between the hemorrhaging woman and Jesus. The woman's touch transferred impurity to Jesus, but despite this fact there is a transfer of healing power in the other direction, from Jesus to the woman. At the heart of this irony is important information that Mark seeks to convey to his audience regarding the healing power of Jesus. First, the power of healing is so potent that it can be transferred from contact with Jesus' clothing. Second, the power goes forth from Jesus without him being aware of the woman or her affliction. His lack of either

---

I would speculate that Mark purposefully omitted any reference to Jesus' fringes in order to avoid any interpretation that they have "magical" power. See the discussion below on the supernatural power of Jesus.

34. A number of scholars suggest that the woman's circuitous approach is on account of her impurity. See, e.g., Marcus, *Mark 1–8*, 358–59; Vincent Taylor, *The Gospel according to St Mark* (London: Macmillan, 1952), 290; van der Loos, *The Miracles of Jesus*, 510.

35. Bas M. F. van Iersel, *Mark: A Reader-Response Commentary* (JSNTSup 164; Sheffield: Sheffield Academic Press, 1998), 205. Fonrobert ("The Woman with the Blood-Flow," 134) observes that the woman does not commit any transgression of the purity laws when she touches Jesus. The legislation does not proscribe passing on impurity, but rather provides a remedy in the event that an individual contracts a secondary impurity, requiring washing of the clothes and bathing. The individual remains impure only until evening.

knowledge or intent is emphasized when he abruptly turn around and asks, "Who touched my clothes" (v. 29).[36] By all indications, it was not Jesus' decision to bring about healing, but rather it was the will of God. Thus the healing power of Jesus is authenticated as the power of God. Finally, when the woman's touch results in the cessation of her blood-flow, the contrast set up earlier (v. 26) between the supernatural healing of God and the natural healing of physicians is clarified. God's power is indeed greater than the power of medicine.

The narrative of the hemorrhaging woman is concluded after the woman identifies herself to Jesus and tells him the truth regarding what she had done. He responds, "Daughter, your faith has made you well; go in peace, and be healed of your disease." In addressing the woman, Jesus refers to her as daughter, indicating that the change in her physical condition has also resulted in a change to her identity. She is no longer the "woman" with a flow of blood, but has been transformed into a "daughter" within the community. Moreover, this transformation has come about not by the will of Jesus, but by the profound faith of the woman. The Markan Jesus effectively confirms the change in the woman's physical status and emphasizes the indispensable role of faith in healing. The message to the audience is explicit: just as this woman believed (v. 28) and her faith made her well, you may also have access to the power of Jesus if only you too will believe. Hence, the woman is held up as a model of faith in the community.

Jesus' final words to the woman are grounded in the Jewish literary tradition. First, he uses a common expression of leave-taking, "go in peace" (ὕπαγε εἰς εἰρήνην), which corresponds to the Hebrew לכי לשלום.[37] The use of this phrase is juxtaposed with a second injunction, "be healed of your disease" (ἴσθι ὑγιὴς ἀπὸ τῆς μάστιγός σου). At first glance, these words seem oddly placed and redundant. After telling the woman that she has been made well because of her faith, Jesus immediately tells her to be healed. The statement is best understood against the background of Jewish purity law and its distinction, in the case of the *zabah*, between the cessation of the blood-flow, healing, and purification. In accordance with Lev 15:28–30, the cessation of the blood-flow is the first indication of a cure, but healing can be verified only after the counting of seven days.[38] It is only after this specified period of time that a woman is considered completely healed from her disease and thereby undergoes the purification procedure. Jesus' final words to the woman allude to the purity laws and present Jesus as advocating their observance. Now that her faith has effected a reversal of her condition, she should count her seven days, verify that she is healed, and undergo the appropriate purification

---

36. Further emphasis on Jesus' lack of knowledge is found in the response of the disciples: "You see the crowd pressing in on you; how can you say, 'Who touched me?'" (v. 31).

37. See, e.g., 1 Sam 1:17.

38. "When she becomes clean (טָהֲרָה) of her discharge, she shall count seven days, and after that she shall be clean (תִּטְהָר)" (Lev 15:28). Milgrom points out that the word טָהֵר indicates her physical state and not ritual purification. It is the usage of the word טָהֵר that here indicates ritual purification (Milgrom, *Leviticus 1–16*, 944). Obviously, if her blood-flow resumed during the seven-day period, her healing would not be verified and there could be no purification.

rites. The audience, being familiar with the purity laws, would pick up on the allusion to Lev 15. They would also recall that, earlier in Mark's narrative, the leper healed by Jesus was given similar, albeit more explicit, instruction to present himself to the priest for the appropriate cleansing and purifications rites (1:44).

In the narrative of the hemorrhaging woman, as in the story of the leper, Mark presents Jesus as operating within the framework of the purity legislation. Both individuals have conditions that induce a severe form of impurity, both are made well through physical contact with Jesus that is miraculous, and both are subsequently advised to undergo the appropriate purification rituals which are technical in nature. Each of these stories focuses on the health of the individual and the miraculous healing power of Jesus. Taken together, they demonstrate a consistency in the Markan Jesus' attitude toward the purity laws applicable to the ill and infirm, a stance that is particularly convincing for the very reason that it is incidental to both narratives.

There is no evidence to show that Jesus abrogates the purity laws, as Selvidge claims. The central story of Jesus in this narrative is about miracles, not about purity. The point of the story is not the abrogation of purity laws, but the miraculous healing powers of Jesus. Certainly if the abrogation of the Law were the main concern of the narrative, one would expect an explicit polemic against the purity legislation, similar to the one given in Mark 7:1–23 with respect to washing the hands before eating. Yet here the Markan Jesus is silent on the matter of the Law.[39] Feminist scholars advocating this position may argue that there is a polemic implicit in the narrative, since by allowing the hemorrhaging woman to touch him, Jesus seems to be abrogating the purity laws. Yet even this argument is weak, for it is evident that Jesus was not even aware of the woman's presence before that all-important touch, so how could he have made a conscious choice to allow it? Moreover, if the intention of the Markan Jesus were to "allow" the woman's touch, would his message not have been stronger if the touch had been directly to his person, and not indirectly to his clothing? Mark simply does not make purity an explicit concern of the narrative. This is especially obvious at the crucial moment in the narrative when the woman touches Jesus' clothing and the narrator focuses exclusively on the transfer of healing power and the cessation of the woman's bloodflow. The impurity that would have been presumably transferred to Jesus is never mentioned. Here, as in the rest of the narrative, it is the health of the woman and not her impurity that is the primary issue of concern.

The narrative of the hemorrhaging woman is, first and foremost, a miracle story concerning healing. A woman who is ill seeks and obtains a reversal of her condition because she has faith in Jesus. By definition, the woman's affliction has a secondary component: impurity. This impurity is alluded to in the story and is essential to the progression of the narrative. She approaches Jesus furtively *because* of her impurity and sets up a situation in which Jesus' power to heal is transmitted without his awareness. These circumstances are carefully constructed to authen-

---

39. So D'Angelo, "Gender and Power," 91.

ticate the power of Jesus as being supernatural—the power of God. This power is accessible to anyone, even the impure. The only requirement is faith.

THE HEMORRHAGING WOMAN, IMPURITY, AND MARK'S RHETORICAL AGENDA

In the narrative of the hemorrhaging woman, Mark uses rhetorical devices to convince his audience that (1) the healing power of Jesus is the supernatural power of God, (2) his power is superior to the human power of medicine, and (3) his power is accessible to anyone who has faith. Mark further emphasizes this threefold message through the use of intercalation, the insertion of this story into the middle of the narrative concerning Jairus's daughter. The purpose of such interpolation in the Markan narrative is always interpretive, enabling the framing story to be understood against the background of the inside narrative and vice versa.[40] Mark skillfully draws comparisons between the hemorrhaging woman and the dead girl as Jesus restores each of them to health.[41] It is through carefully crafted similarities and contrasts that the woman and girl are connected to one another and the narratives intertwine, enabling the auditor to derive the essential meaning of the evangelist's message.

As miracle stories the two narratives share some similar motifs, including the presence of the crowd, obstacles to healing, and the transfer of power through touch.[42] Both the woman and the girl are in desperate circumstances, the first in her blood-flow and the second by her impending death. The similarity between the two afflictions is readily apparent to the auditor of the ancient world who perceives the woman's condition in terms of the life force flowing out of her. Both woman and girl are physically and metaphorically crossing the line between life and death.[43] When the girl dies, the tie between the two shifts from a health issue to a purity issue, for in death the girl becomes a quintessential source of impurity.[44]

---

40. Elizabeth Struthers Malbon, "Narrative Criticism: How Does the Story Mean?" in *Mark and Method: New Approaches in Biblical Studies* (ed. Janice Capel Anderson and Stephen Moore; Minneapolis: Fortress, 1992), 39.

41. It is significant that the hemorrhaging woman is introduced just after Jairus, the synagogue leader, pleads with Jesus to heal his dying daughter. Both woman and girl remain nameless, but the contrast between the two is readily apparent. Unlike the girl who lives in an affluent family and has a father to act as her advocate, the hemorrhaging woman is apparently destitute and alone. This contrast not only places emphasis on the despair of the woman but also underscores the message that Jesus' power is accessible to all, regardless of social status.

42. Falling to the knees is also a motif found in both miracle stories. Just as Jairus falls to his knees to request a miracle (cf. Mark 1:40; 5:6; 7:26), so too does the hemorrhaging woman fall to her knees to confess after a miracle (cf. Matt 14:33; Luke 5:8; 17:16). See Thiessen, *Miracle Stories*, 53.

43. On the association of blood with life and its loss with death, see Milgrom, *Leviticus 1–16*, 766–68.

44. In accordance with the purity laws in Num 19:11–21, a corpse transfers the most virulent form of impurity. Anyone who touches a corpse or enters a dwelling in which there is a dead body is rendered impure for seven days, during which time their impurity may be

Both are in a state of impurity that is transmittable through touch, and yet both are restored to health through contact with Jesus. Significantly, the narrative of Jairus's daughter, like that of the hemorrhaging woman, is told against a background of illness, which generates impurity.

Two statements regarding faith frame the death of the girl, as Mark intertwines the two narratives so that the message of one is echoed and emphasized by the other. Jesus' claim that the woman's faith made her well (v. 34) is immediately followed by a message regarding the girl's death (v. 35) and Jesus' directive to Jairus: "Do not fear, only believe" (v. 36). The message is clear: as the faith of the hemorrhaging woman made her well, so, too, will Jairus's faith bring about his daughter's restoration to life.

Once again, the miraculous power of Jesus is affirmed as he revives the girl.[45] Touching her on the hand, he speaks to the girl in their native Aramaic, saying *talitha koum*, meaning "Little girl, get up" (v. 41).[46] As in the narrative of the hemorrhaging woman, it is through the touch of Jesus that healing is found.[47] Inevitably, the girl responds to Jesus' miraculous power by getting up and walking. It is only

---

transmitted to others. That these laws were widely observed in the Second Temple period is attested in Philo (*Spec.* 3.205–9), Josephus (*A.J.* 4.81), the Dead Sea Scrolls (11Q19 XLIX, 16–17; L, 10–14; 1QM XIV, 2–3), and the rabbinic texts (*t. Par.* 3.14; 10.2; 5.6; 7.4).

45. It is interesting to note that in both her impending death (v. 23) and death (v. 35) the child is referred to as "daughter," but in her sleep (v. 39) and her recovery (v. 41) she is a "girl." The transition from death to life transforms the "daughter" into a "girl" in much the same way as the hemorrhaging woman experiences a transition from "woman" to "daughter" through her interaction with Jesus. Both experience life-affirming changes in their identities.

46. This Aramaic phrase and its translation are omitted from the parallel stories in Matthew and Luke. Commenting on the narrative in Matthew, D'Angelo ("Gender and Power," 102) suggests that this omission may have been made "in order to avoid the impression that Jesus used magic words in the cure." Certainly, the use of foreign words was a common feature of magical incantations, and it is entirely possible that Mark's primary audience would have interpreted Jesus' healing of the girl as magic, rather than a miracle. We may speculate that Mark's inclusion of the Aramaic phrase was part of his rhetoric, his intention being to call attention to the magical possibilities and then to expose the secret and destroy the magic power of the work by offering a translation. He thus affirms that Jesus' power is miracle and not magic in the same way as he authenticates the power of miracle over medicine in the narrative of the hemorrhaging woman. On medicine, miracle, and magic as competing modes of healing in Judaism and the traditions of the late Hellenistic world, see Howard Clark Kee, *Medicine, Miracle, and Magic in New Testament Times* (SNTSMS 55; Cambridge: Cambridge University Press, 1986), 2–4. On the use of magic in Mark, see also John M. Hull, *Hellenistic Magic and the Synoptic Tradition* (SBT, 2d ser., 28; London: SCM Press, 1974), 85; Wendy Cotter, *Miracles in Greco-Roman Antiquity: A Sourcebook* (London: Routledge, 1999), 246.

47. At the point where Jesus touches the girl, the concern regarding impurity is incidental since Jesus was presumably exposed to corpse contamination upon entering the house. As in the narrative of the hemorrhaging woman, there appear to be no consequences to Jesus on account of his exposure to impurity. Two possibilities for interpretation present themselves: (1) Jesus is not affected because of his unique status or (2) the very presence of

then that the narrator imparts one last piece of information to his intended audience, adding parenthetically that the girl is twelve years old. On a literary level, the repetition of this symbolic number solidifies the connection between the girl and the hemorrhaging woman, who, it will be recalled, endured her condition for twelve years. In physical terms both the girl and the woman are associated with death, the former because she purportedly dies and the latter because her condition not only threatened her life, it also precluded the possibility that she would bring new life into the world by bearing children. Moreover, the woman's hemorrhage had profound theological implications, for in accordance with Levitical discourse the loss of vaginal blood was associated with the loss of seed. It signified "the diminution of life and, if unchecked, destruction and death."[48] Mark exploits this tension between life and death with rhetorical expertise, equating the duration of the woman's deathly condition with the life span of the girl and the moment of the woman's restoration to life with the girl's death. In the end, however, Jesus symbolically raises them both from death, restoring the woman's capacity to bear children and reviving the girl as she reaches the threshold of her child-bearing years. Life prevails over death, along with the distinctly feminine potential to bring forth new life.

The recovery of the girl and the healing of the woman are inextricably connected, as Mark's message to his audience becomes clear in the joint interpretation of the narratives. Taken together, these stories authenticate Jesus' power as divine and demonstrate that all who have faith have access to this power. This includes both the impure and the daughters of the community whose ailments represent the health concerns specific to women. Through his use of rhetoric, Mark does more than just report on two miracles. He also demonstrates how they fit into the larger framework of meaning in the mission of Jesus.[49]

Conclusion

Mark 5:24–34 presents a woman who is desperately ill. She has been hemorrhaging for twelve years. All medical treatments have failed her. Not only is she physically ill, but she is also ritually impure. Mark has carefully crafted the elements of his story, inviting us to share in this woman's desperation, her pain, and her hopelessness. The narrative generates a tension, which in its resolution presents the message that Mark wants to convey to his audience. I assert that this message is as follows: "Faith in Jesus brings healing, even when all else fails." This reflects Mark's Christology, and this is the main thrust of the story.

Jesus in the house negates the status of the girl. Supporting the latter interpretation is Jesus' claim upon arrival at the house: "The child is not dead, but sleeping" (v. 39).

48. Milgrom, *Leviticus 1–16*, 767.

49. In Mark, miracle is not an end in itself, but rather speaks to issues that are important to the primary audience. For example, the healing of the man with the withered hand (3:1–6) addresses the issue of work on the Sabbath in much the same way as the healing of the paralytic (2:1–12) authenticates Jesus' authority to pronounce forgiveness of sin. On the significance of the healing stories, see Kee, *Miracle in the Early Christian World*, 162–63.

The scholarly debate over this pericope is really about the resolution of the tension within the narrative, about the message that Mark wants to convey. According to Selvidge, Mark's message is that the purity laws are obsolete, and therefore they are now null and void. She argues that the very touch of the hemorrhaging woman nullifies the restrictions of her impurity. This touch becomes a symbol of the Christian woman's liberation from the allegedly oppressive purity laws. Selvidge's resolution of the pericope focuses primarily on the woman's impurity, an element that certainly adds tension to the story. For her, it is the abrogation of the purity laws that solves the woman's problems and brings the story to a satisfying conclusion. In focusing her argument exclusively on the purity issue, however, Selvidge deemphasizes and almost totally ignores another source of narrative tension: the physical affliction from which the hemorrhaging woman suffers. In her feminist interpretation, the woman's deteriorating physical condition remains secondary, her healing incidental, and the narrative tension pertaining to these issues unresolved.

D'Angelo resolves the narrative tension through a Christological approach to the narrative, and in doing so suggests that the purity laws were not abrogated, but rather they were irrelevant *ab initio*. In refusing to acknowledge the significance of the woman's impurity in the text, she effectively ignores an important source of narrative tension—a tension that would have been clearly understood by Mark's audience. As shown, impurity is a fundamental component of the woman's condition and therefore of her identity and role designation. Moreover, the issue of her impurity is vital to the progression of the plot. The woman's impurity not only explains why she approaches Jesus in a furtive manner rather than directly, it also sheds light upon Jesus' seemingly redundant command to the woman to be healed after the cessation of her blood-flow has already been established. These details concerning the woman's impurity make an essential contribution to the power of the narrative, which D'Angelo ignores. Consequently, she too leaves part of the narrative tension unresolved.

Levine, like D'Angelo, supports the contention that impurity is irrelevant to the narrative. She argues that the hemorrhaging woman's condition may not be vaginal bleeding at all and that the hemorrhage may, in fact, originate from some other part of the body. If Levine were correct, and the ailment is other than woman-specific, why then is this woman different from any other of the afflicted in Mark's Gospel: the blind, the deaf, or the man with the withered arm? In my view, the poignancy of the entire pericope is predicated on her being a woman and on her having an illness that affects her feminine role in bearing children. In other words, what makes a feminist reading of this story so significant is that the narrative specifically concerns Jesus' ministry to women with women's issues. When, however, the woman's vaginal hemorrhage is misinterpreted as a generic form of bleeding, the very issue of her being a woman becomes incidental to the narrative.

I have proposed a feminist reading of Mark 5:24–34 that emphasizes the woman's health as the central concern of the narrative. Significantly, the hemorrhaging woman's ailment is specific to women and has implications with respect to her ability to bear children. As a result of her condition, she is also ritually impure:

a metaphysical state that cannot be remedied until after her physical condition is healed. Just as there are implications resulting from her physical ailment, there are also implications arising from her metaphysical state. She cannot approach Jesus directly. Furtively, almost indirectly, she reaches out and touches Jesus' garment. Her touch is her affirmation of faith. It is through this faith that the woman is able to connect with the miraculous, and it is this faith that acts as the vehicle through which the various dimensions of narrative tension are resolved. The woman's faith brings her healing and restores her ability to bear children. Her healing enables her to undergo ritual purification so that she may, once again, take her full place in society. Mark's message is not about the abrogation of the purity laws. It is about a woman's faith: her affirmation that Jesus' power is the supernatural power of God. Undoubtedly, this power is superior to that of medicine, for Jesus succeeds even when the physicians have failed. In the end, faith in Jesus brings about a total reversal in the circumstance of the hemorrhaging woman and ultimately resolves all elements of the narrative tension.

The evangelist's message can be as powerful for the modern Christian woman as it was for the members of the Markan community. It asserts that there are no obstacles too great or ailments too inconsequential for the ministry of Jesus. All who are in need of healing may partake of his miraculous power: the sick, the childless, and those afflicted with ailments specific to women. Thus, the narrative of the hemorrhaging woman recalls Jesus' ministry to women and affirms that they, like their male counterparts, may gain access to his power. To do so, they need only recognize the significance of the woman's touch.

7

From Priestly Torah to Christ Cultus:
The Re-Vision of Covenant and Cult in Hebrews

The Epistle to the Hebrews offers a vision of a new covenant (7:22) mediated by Christ, a sinless and eternal high priest (7:26).[1] It is through Christ's perfect offering of his own blood (9:12) that he atoned for the sins of the people, once and for all time, rendering obsolete the Israelite cult and its ineffective sacrifices.[2] Fundamental to this theological vision is a comparative scheme, in which the concept of covenant is reinterpreted from a cultic perspective.[3] As the new covenant is contrasted with the old (Mosaic) covenant, the priesthood of Christ is compared with the Levitical priesthood, the heavenly sanctuary with the earthly tent and Christ's sacrifice with the bloody sacrifices of Leviticus. In each case the new order of Christ is affirmed as superior or more perfect, while its counterpart in the old order is denounced as flawed, weak, or inadequate.

Essential to the association of covenant and cult in Hebrews is the author's understanding of the Law. Here the Law does not represent Mosaic Law in its entirety but is confined almost exclusively to the priestly Torah, or cultic law of Leviticus.[4] The priestly Torah serves a dual but somewhat contradictory role in the argumentation of Hebrews. It provides the comparative categories through which the au-

---

1. A version of this essay was presented at the 2004 Annual Meeting of the Canadian Society of Biblical Studies in Winnipeg, Manitoba. I would like to thank Dr. Stephen Westerholm for reading and commenting on an earlier draft.

2. Chester suggests that this is the main argument of Hebrews. See A. N. Chester, "Hebrews: The Final Sacrifice," in *Sacrifice and Redemption* (ed. S. W. Sykes; Cambridge: Cambridge University Press, 1991), 57; cf. Lehne, who contends that the Christ event is "the perfect fulfillment of the cultic heritage of Israel." See Susanne Lehne, *The New Covenant in Hebrews* (JSNTSup 44; Sheffield: JSOT Press, 1990), 119.

3. Lehne, *The New Covenant*, 119.

4. Israelite cultic law is primarily found in Leviticus, with constituent parts of the priestly stratum also occurring in Genesis, Exodus, and Numbers. In the priestly stratum the word "Torah" is used to signify the content of instruction as it pertains to various cultic rituals. In the same sense the phrase "priestly Torah" is used here in reference to priestly instruction pertaining to the cult, including that which the priests have been taught and that which they in turn teach to the Israelites (Exod 12:49; Lev 6:2, 7, 18; 7:1, 7, 11, 37; 14:5-7; Num 15:29; 19:2, 14). See Baruch A. Levine, *The JPS Torah Commentary: Leviticus* (Philadelphia: Jewish Publication Society, 1989), 34.

thor validates the *continuity* of the Christ event with Israelite tradition: covenant, priesthood, and sacrifice.

At the same time, however, it becomes the quintessential foil against which the superiority of the new order is established, affirming the *discontinuity* of Israelite tradition. Inevitably, the new order is established with a new covenant, a superior high priest, and a better sacrifice, but there is no new Law. In Hebrews the Law belongs to the old order.[5] It is not salvageable.

Hebrews' denunciation of the Law is established indirectly through a sustained criticism of the Mosaic covenant and Israelite cult.[6] While the tone of the argument reflects a negative view of Judaism, the polemic is not typical of anti-Judaism in the ancient world, which is characterized by attacks on Sabbath, circumcision, and dietary laws.[7] These distinctly Jewish rites are rarely, if ever, mentioned in the epistle.[8] Instead, the author takes a unique stand against Judaism and its Law, by focusing on the Israelite cult as an obsolete order that has been replaced by the Christ cultus.

The present study will examine Hebrews' portrayal of Judaism as it pertains to the covenant and cult. First, it will demonstrate that the author's criticism is skillfully and deliberately formulated as part of a broader polemic against Judaism. Second, this study will establish that this systematic denigration of Jewish covenant and cult points to what Hebrews views as a fundamental flaw of the Law: its mechanism of atonement through the sacrificial cult is antithetical to the belief

---

5. According to Lehne (*The New Covenant*, 27), Hebrews indicates that the Law was spoken and mediated by angels (2:2), Although this aspect of the Law may be regarded in a positive light, this form of revelation is nevertheless considered inferior to the word directly given by the Lord (2:3) or the Son (1:1–2).

6. There are thirteen explicit references to *nomos* in Hebrews, all of which are associated with either covenant (7:19; 8:10; 9:19; 10:8, 16, 28), priesthood (7:5, 12, 16, 28; 8:4), or sacrifice (9:22; 10:1). The only usage of *nomos* that offers a more direct critique of the Law is found in the parenthetical comment of 7:19, where it states, "the law made nothing perfect."

7. The question of "anti-Judaism" in Hebrews is a subject of scholarly debate. Wall and Lane, for example, dismiss the anti-Judaism of Hebrews by justifying it as hermeneutical method. See Robert W. Wall and William L. Lane, "Polemic in Hebrews and the Catholic Epistles," in *Anti-Semitism and Early Christianity: Issues of Polemic and Faith* (ed. Craig A. Evans and Donald A. Hagner; Minneapolis: Fortress, 1993), 181. In opposition to this view, Wilson states, "The author of Hebrews knew enough about Judaism to know what he was doing, and the positive Christological case he makes could have been made, in principle, without the gratuitous denigration of things central to the Jewish tradition." See Stephen G. Wilson, *Related Strangers: Jews and Christians, 70–170 C.E.* (Minneapolis: Fortress, 1995), 122. Although I agree that a polemic against Judaism, its covenant, and cult is both explicit and implicit throughout the epistle, I do not find the application of the term "anti-Judaism" helpful here.

8. In Greco-Roman literature the distinctive character of the Jews and their religion is often associated with these three practices. See Peter Schäfer, *Judeophobia: Attitudes toward the Jews in the Ancient World* (Cambridge: Harvard University Press, 1997), 66–105.

in salvation through Christ. Finally, consideration will be given to the function of this theological argumentation in the socio-historical context of Hebrews.

Christ Covenant versus Mosaic Covenant

In Hebrews the term διαθήκη, "covenant," is used to refer to both the Mosaic covenant and the new covenant promised in Jer 31:31–34 and fulfilled in Christ. The "first" covenant (8:7, 13; 9:1, 15) was established by God after he brought the Israelites out of Egypt (8:9). It was inaugurated with the blood of a sacrifice offered by Moses:

> Hence not even the first covenant was inaugurated without blood. For when every commandment had been told to all the people by Moses in accordance with the law, he took the blood of calves and goats, with water and scarlet wool and hyssop and sprinkled both the scroll itself and all the people, saying, "This is the blood of the covenant that God has ordained for you." And in the same way he sprinkled with the blood both the tent and all the vessels used in worship. Indeed, under the law almost everything is purified with blood, and without the shedding of blood there is no forgiveness of sins. (Heb 9:18–22)[9]

The epistle offers a direct account of Moses' inauguration of the covenant in Exod 24:1–8, placing particular emphasis on cultic imagery, and especially blood. Here the author of Hebrews interprets the covenant ceremony from his own theological point of departure—the Christ event.

The use of blood in the inauguration of the Mosaic covenant foreshadows the new covenant that will be established with Christ's blood.[10] As such, Moses' reference to "the blood of the covenant" refers to both the animal sacrifice of the first covenant and the blood of Christ that establishes the second.

That Hebrews reinterprets the covenant ceremony in light of an unforeseen fulfillment is not particularly unusual. The biblical text lends itself to a multitude of interpretations, which are often augmented by minor additions, omissions, or changes in emphasis. Yet the author of Hebrews goes beyond interpretation, making deliberate revisions to the text, so that it conforms to his Christological vision of the new order.[11] The drastic nature of these revisions becomes apparent when Heb 9:18–22 is compared to its source in Exodus:

> And Moses wrote all the words of the Lord; and Moses rose up early in the morning, and built an altar under the mountain, and set up twelve stones for the twelve tribes of Israel. And he sent forth the young men of the children of Israel, and they offered whole burnt-offerings, and they sacrificed young calves as a peace-offering to God. And Moses took half the blood and poured it into bowls, and half the blood he poured out upon the altar. And he took the book of the covenant and read it in the ears of the people, and they said, "All things whatsoever the Lord has

---

9. Unless otherwise indicated, translations from the New Testament are from the NRSV.
10. Craig R. Koester, *Hebrews* (AB 36; New York: Doubleday, 2001), 426.
11. Mary Rose D'Angelo, *Moses in the Letter to the Hebrews* (SBLDS 42; Missoula, MT: Scholars Press, 1979), 243.

spoken we will do and hearken therein." And Moses took the blood and sprinkled it upon the people, and said, "Behold the blood of the covenant, which the Lord has made with you concerning all these words." (Exod 24:4–8, LXX)

When Heb 9:18–22 is read in conjunction with the Septuagint account of the covenant ceremony, it becomes apparent that the epistle has introduced two new elements in its revision. First, the author of Hebrews assumes a strong association between the covenant and the cult. He emphasizes this connection by merging the covenant ceremony with the consecration of the tent found in Num 7:1, so that the initiation of covenant and cult take place together on the altar. Accordingly, the sprinkling of the people during the covenant ceremony is followed by the sprinkling of the tent and cultic vessels. The association of covenant and cult is further emphasized with the use of the word ἐγκεκαίνισται, "was inaugurated."[12] In the LXX this verb is used in a cultic context with respect to the altar (Num 7:10, 88) and the temple (3 Kgdms 8:63; 2 Chr 7:5), but never in reference to the covenant.[13]

In incorporating cultic language into the covenant ceremony, the author of the epistle draws attention to the cultic aspect of the event. In Hebrews the Mosaic covenant is a cultic order. A second element in Hebrews' revision of the covenant ceremony is found in the association of the blood of the covenant with purification and atonement, a connection that is entirely absent from the Exodus account. This idea is established through a series of revisions pertaining to the covenantal sacrifice. For example, in the Exodus account young calves are offered in the form of whole burnt offerings and a peace offering to God. In the Hebrews account, however, neither of these sacrifices is mentioned, presumably because they do not usually serve an expiatory function.[14] Instead, the epistle indicates that goats and bulls were offered in sacrifice, alluding to the use of the animals required for the Yom Kippur ritual of communal atonement.[15]

In Hebrews, the atoning function of the covenant ceremony is further emphasized through the sprinkling of blood as a means of purification. The text envisions two separate sprinklings, the first over the scroll of the covenant and the people, and the second over the tent and the cultic vessels. In the Exodus account there is only one sprinkling of blood: half the blood is poured on the altar and half sprinkled on the people in a ritual act that cements the relationship between God

---

12. Cf. Heb 10:20.

13. D'Angelo, *Moses in the Letter*, 244–45.

14. The peace offering was only used on joyous occasions, whereas the burnt offering initially had a variety of functions corresponding to almost every conceivable psychological need including the need for expiation (Lev 1:4). Evidence suggests that in the early stages of the Israelite cult the burnt offering was the exclusive expiatory sacrifice, but with the introduction of the sin and guilt offerings (ninth to eighth centuries B.C.E.) there was a shift in emphasis from sinfulness to rejoicing. On the function of the burnt offering, see Jacob Milgrom, *Leviticus 1–16* (AB 3; New York: Doubleday, 1991), 172–77.

15. D'Angelo, *Moses in the Letter*, 245–46.

and Israel.[16] Hebrews, however, does not recognize the function of blood as binding the two parties in the covenant. Rather, it insists on the purifying and atoning function of sacrificial blood, as a precursor to Christ's sacrifice. In service to its Christological agenda, Hebrews omits all references to the dividing of the blood and the pouring of the blood onto the altar.[17] The image of covenant binding is then replaced by an allusion to purification, as the sacrificial blood is mixed with water, scarlet wool, and hyssop.[18]

The second sprinkling of blood in the Hebrews account is based not on the covenant ceremony but on the consecration of the tent in Num 7:1:

> And it came to pass in the day in which Moses finished the setting up of the tabernacle, that he anointed it, and consecrated it, and all its furniture, and the altar and all its furniture, he even anointed them, and consecrated them. (Num 7:1, LXX)

In the context of Numbers this text forms a literary bridge between the legal material that precedes it and the account of the chieftain's initiatory gifts that follow. More detailed accounts of the consecration of the tent are to be found in the command to consecrate the altar (Exod 40:9, 11) and its fulfillment (Lev 8:10–11). Why, then, does the author choose the abbreviated version in Numbers?[19] A superficial reading of the parallel passages reveals the answer. In both the Exodus and Levitical accounts it was oil, and not blood, that was sprinkled over the tabernacle, altar, and cultic utensils, for the purpose of consecration. In the Numbers passage, however, the act of sprinkling for the purpose of consecration is mentioned without reference to the oil. For the author of Hebrews it is blood that is the essential element of purification. The blood sprinkled by Moses during the inauguration of the covenant and cult anticipates the redemptive effects of Christ's sprinkled blood (12:24).[20]

The author's revision of the covenant ceremony in Exod 24:1–8 lends itself to a Christological interpretation of the text. Not only does the first covenant foresee the coming of Christ, but it also shares essential features with the second covenant

---

16. Nahum Sarna, *The JPS Torah Commentary: Exodus* (Philadelphia: Jewish Publication Society, 1991), 152.

17. D'Angelo (*Moses in the Letter*, 245) states that "this omission is not for the sake of brevity but is a deliberate revision."

18. The use of hyssop and scarlet wool is reminiscent of ingredients used for (1) preparation of red heifer ashes (Num 19:6) required for purification after corpse contamination and (2) rituals to cleanse those afflicted with scale disease (Lev 14:4, 6, 49, 51–52). In Num 19:6 hyssop is identified with the aromatic plant *Majoranan syriaca*, and "red dyed wool" refers to the dye extracted from a "crimson worm," the *Kermes bilious*. See Jacob Milgrom, *The JPS Torah Commentary: Numbers* (Philadelphia: Jewish Publication Society, 1990), 159.

19. D'Angelo (*Moses in the Letter*, 244) suggests that in the Hebrew Bible the covenant ceremony of Exod 24:1–8 culminates in the consecration of the tabernacle in Num 7:1. In combining the two, the author of Hebrews is suggesting that the consecration of the tent is an extension of the covenant ceremony.

20. The association of sprinkling and cleaning is also found in Heb 10:22.

that is mediated by him.²¹ Both covenants are initiated with the blood of sacrifice.²² Both covenantal orders are initiated by God (8:8–13), and both require the loyalty and obedience of the people.

Whereas the faithful receive the promise of an inheritance (9:15), those who are disobedient are subject to punishment (10:28–29). These corresponding features, however, are only superficial. Underlying the apparent similarities are comparative categories that are not inherently neutral: *second* versus *first,* and *new* versus *old.*²³ The polemical use of these adjectives is particularly evident in Heb 8:13, where "the new (καινὴν) covenant" is contrasted with "the first (πρώτην) covenant," the latter being described as obsolete, growing old, and soon to disappear.²⁴ Hebrews goes so far as to suggest that if the first covenant had been "blameless" (ἄμεμπτος), there would have been no reason to introduce a second and improved covenant, consisting of a more excellent ministry and a better promise (8:6–7). Thus, the superiority of the new covenant in Christ is affirmed over and against the Mosaic covenant that foreshadows it.

Hebrews is not unique in the New Testament in its portrayal of a new covenant, nor is it unique in its use of cultic language.²⁵ Its unique contribution is in envisioning both covenants as cultic orders. This Christological understanding necessitates a transformation of the covenant ceremony into an inauguration of the cult and the Israelites into a cultic assembly.

There is an accompanying shift in emphasis away from the binding of God and people toward the necessity of purification and atonement through blood.²⁶ These changes not only redefine the Mosaic covenant as a cultic covenant predicated almost exclusively on priestly Torah, they also foreshadow the new and better covenant that will be inaugurated with Christ's sacrifice and mediated by his priestly presence.

---

21. On the corresponding features of the old and new covenants, see Lehne, *The New Covenant,* 98.

22. According to Hebrews, "not even the first covenant was inaugurated without blood" (9:18).

23. Contra William Klassen, "To the Hebrews or Against the Hebrews? Anti-Judaism and the Epistle to the Hebrews," in *Anti-Judaism in Early Christianity* (ed. Stephen G. Wilson; Waterloo, Ontario: Wilfrid Laurier Press, 1986), 2:9.

24. Attridge suggests that the exegetical inference of this verse is straightforward: one of the two covenants is designated as "new" thereby implying that the other must be "old." See Harold W. Attridge, *The Epistle to the Hebrews* (Philadelphia: Fortress Press, 1989), 228.

25. On the new covenant in the New Testament, see, for example, Gal 3:15, 17; 4:21–31; 2 Cor 3; Rom 9:4; 11:27. For examples of cultic language in the New Testament, see 1 Cor 3:16; 2 Cor 6:16; and Eph 2:22, where the Christian community is portrayed as a temple. According to Schüssler Fiorenza, the use of cultic language in the New Testament "signifies not only a fundamental criticism of the Jerusalem cult but a redefinition and metamorphosis of both cultic language and cultic reality through Christology" (Elisabeth Schüssler Fiorenza, "Cultic Language in Qumran and in the New Testament," *CBQ* 38, no. 2 [1976]: 170–71).

26. So D'Angelo, *Moses in the Letter,* 246.

Christ Cultus versus Levitical Cult

Central to the theology of Hebrews is the portrayal of the Christ cultus, in which Christ is envisioned as a high priest (2:17–3:1; 4:14–5:10) who enters the heavenly sanctuary (8:2; 9:11–12, 24) and offers the one-time sacrifice of his own blood (7:27; 9:11, 26; 10:10), thereby obtaining eternal redemption (9:12, 27–28).[27] The continuity between the old order of Moses and the new order of Christ is established through the use of the cultic categories of priesthood, sanctuary, and sacrifice. In both orders the high priest acts as mediator between God and the people. In both orders he gains access to God's sanctuary. And in both orders he offers sacrifice to effect purification and bring atonement to all. For the author of Hebrews, however, these corresponding features are important only in that they provide a framework for discussing the second covenant and its cultic order in light of the first. It is through these categories of commonality that Hebrews compares the Levitical cult with the Christ cultus and ultimately affirms the superiority of the latter.

Priesthood

The portrayal of Christ as high priest is a fundamental feature of the Christ cultus. Christ's priestly function is alluded to in the exordium (1.3), with his title of high priest being introduced as early as 2:17.[28] He is described as being merciful (ἐλεήμων) and faithful (πιστός) in serving God through a sacrifice of expiation (ἱλάσκεσθαι).[29] These characteristics are essential to Christ's high priesthood, for it is through his mercy that he becomes a trustworthy intercessor for the people before God (2:18; 4:14–16; 7:25). Not only is he considered reliable in this capacity on account of his faithfulness to God in both life and death (3:1–2), but he is also held up as a model of fidelity for his followers to emulate (3:12–15, 19; 4:3).[30]

Hebrews' characterization of Christ as high priest is largely dependent on a

---

27. The word "cult" comes from the Latin *cultus,* meaning "care" or "adoration" and may be defined as a system of religious belief or ritual. For the sake of clarity, I use "cult" to refer to the ritual system associated with the temple in Jerusalem and the word "cultus" when referring to Hebrews' representation of the Christ event.

28. The abrupt introduction of Christ as high priest (ἀρχιερεύς) along with the frequent occurrence of the term throughout the epistle suggests the audience's prior familiarity with the priesthood. See John M. Scholer, *Proleptic Priests: Priesthood in the Epistle to the Hebrews* (JSNTSup 49; Sheffield: JSOT Press, 1991), 82. On the antecedents and development of high-priestly Christology, see Attridge, *Hebrews,* 97–103.

29. Although some scholars suggest that, based on etymology, the word ἱλάσκεσθαι should be understood in the sense of propitiating God, Attridge points out that in the LXX it is used for expiation as well as propitiation (Lev 4:20, 26, 31; 5:10; 16:16, 33–34). Moreover, in the context of Hebrews the purpose of Christ's sacrifice is atoning for sin and not the propitiating of God. See Attridge, *Hebrews,* 96 n. 192.

30. In Heb 3:1–6, Jesus' faithfulness is compared with that of Moses. On Christ as merciful and faithful, see Attridge, *Hebrews,* 95.

comparison between Christ's priesthood and that of the Levitical high priest. The author, however, does not offer an exhaustive comparison between the two, but rather selects characteristics of the Levitical high priest that are particularly relevant to the priestly image of Christ.[31] Three essential points of comparison emerge (5:1-4) and are subsequently elaborated upon.[32] First, every high priest from among human beings makes atonement for sin through the offering of sacrifices. Christ, like the Levitical high priest, has something to offer (5:1; 8:3). Yet his offering is inherently superior, for it is his very own blood that atones for the sins of the people. Using an *a fortiori* argument, the author argues that if the blood of animals could purify the flesh, then the blood of Christ must be that much more effective in purifying the conscience from sin (9:13).

Second, human high priests are sympathetic in their interactions with sinners. The Levitical high priest deals gently with the ignorant and the wayward (5:2). The use of the verb μετριοπαθεῖν, "to moderate emotion," is most commonly used in conjunction with anger. Its use here indicates that, by containing his anger, the mortal high priest is able to treat others with consideration. Similarly, Christ is able to sympathize (συμπαθέω) with the weakness of others (4:15), for even though he is sinless, he is likewise tempted and suffers (2:18; 5:7-8; 13:12).[33] Here the correlation between the mortal high priest's consideration (μετριοπαθεῖν) toward others and Christ's active sympathy (συμπαθῆσαι) is not exact.[34] Rather, Christ is viewed as superior to the Levitical high priest in his dealings with sinners and hence in his function of expiating sin.

The third point of comparison between the Levitical high priest and Christ as high priest is concerned with the authority of the office. Just as God called Aaron (5:4), so too did God appoint Christ as an eternal high priest (5:6).[35] The reference to Aaron is without further comment. Although scripture attests to the eternal nature of the Aaronic priesthood (Exod 40:12-15), Hebrews is conspicuously silent on the matter. Rather, emphasis is placed on the genealogy of the office and the inadequacy of a high priest who is subject to the limitations of the human condition. Death prevents him from continuing in office (7:23), and sin interferes with his function as God's intercessor, requiring him to make offerings of atonement for his own sins before he can expiate the sins of others (5:3; 7:27).[36] Inevitably, the Law appoints to the high priesthood those who are subject to weakness (7:28).

---

31. Attridge, *Hebrews*, 142.

32. Ibid., 142-45.

33. The word συμπαθεῖν, "sympathy," indicates a genuine bond which is expressed through mercy toward the suffering (Philo, *Spec.* 2:115; 4:202; cf. 4 Macc 6:13). See Koester, *Hebrews*, 283.

34. For a comparison between these two verbs see Attridge, *Hebrews*, 143-44; cf. Koester (*Hebrews*, 286), who states that "curbing emotions, while a virtue, is of lesser order than the active sympathy shown by Christ."

35. Koester (*Hebrews*, 287) notes that in Exod 29:29 Aaron and his immediate successors were called by God, but that subsequent generations inherited the priesthood from their fathers.

36. The Law takes into account the death of the high priest (Num 35:25) and records

In contrast to the shortcomings of the Levitical high priest, Christ is an eternal high priest (7.24) who is sinless, blameless, and exalted above the heavens (7:26; cf. 4:15).³⁷ The perpetuity of Christ's priesthood is established by the fact that he is appointed "according to the order of Melchizedek" (5:6). Hebrews explains this reference to Melchizedek in Ps 110(109):4 through an exegesis of Gen 17:20, in which he is also mentioned.³⁸ In the Genesis text Melchizedek is portrayed as both the king of Salem and a priest of God Most High. These twin themes of kingship and priesthood are crucial to Hebrews' association of Christ with Melchizedek.³⁹

The name Melchizedek provides a useful etymology for the author of Hebrews. According to his interpretation, Melchizedek means "king of righteousness." Furthermore, the kingdom over which he rules, Salem, is derived from the Hebrew *shalom,* meaning "peace."⁴⁰ As the king of righteousness and peace, Hebrews' Melchizedek evokes messianic imagery that foreshadows Christ's association with him.⁴¹ More important than the portrayal of Melchizedek as king, however, is his priestly identity. Capitalizing on the absence of a genealogy in the Genesis text, Hebrews portrays Melchizedek as being "without father, without mother, without genealogy, having neither beginning of days nor end of life, but resembling the Son of God, he remains a priest forever" (7:3).⁴² Unlike his Levitical counterpart, Melchizedek does not

---

the death of Aaron (Num 20:22–29). Josephus indicates that there were eighty-three high priests from Aaron to Phanasus (*A.J.* 20:227).

37. The word ἀπαράβατον, "inviolate," is used in 7:24 to indicate that either Christ's position as high priest is unbroken by death or that it is not transferable. There is no successor. See Koester, *Hebrews,* 365.

38. The exegetical technique of *gezera shawa,* in which a term from one verse of scripture is interpreted according to its use in a second verse, is often employed in rabbinic exegesis. Examples of this form of exegetical interpretation may also be found in Philo. See Attridge, *Hebrews,* 128–29 and n. 77.

39. The figure of Melchizedek appears twice in the Hebrew Bible (Gen 17:20; Ps 110[109]:4) and in the New Testament only in the Epistle to the Hebrews. It is not clear whether Hebrews' portrayal of Melchizedek relies exclusively on scriptural exegesis or if the author is also drawing on non-biblical Jewish interpretive traditions. There is considerable speculation regarding Melchizedek in early Jewish literature, and it is conceivable that the author of Hebrews was aware of these traditions. Most notable is the portrayal of Melchizedek in 11QMelch, in which he is represented as a heavenly warrior, judge, and high priest who appears in the final phase of history to redeem the elect of God. For a comparison of the figure of Melchizedek in 11QMelch and Hebrews, see, e.g., Anders Aschim, "Melchizedek and Jesus: 11QMelchizedek and the Epistle to the Hebrews," in *The Jewish Roots of Christological Monotheism* (ed. Carey C. Newman et al.; Leiden: Brill, 1999), 129–47.

40. Attridge, *Hebrews,* 189.

41. The term ἀγενεαλόγητος, "without genealogy," was probably coined by the author to indicate that Melchizedek's ancestry was unrecorded (Koester, *Hebrews,* 243). This lack of genealogy points to the uniqueness of Melchizedek's priesthood as contrasted with the Levitical priesthood that was sustained by a hereditary process. See William W. Lane, *Hebrews 1–8* (WBC 47A; Dallas: Word Books, 1991), 165–66.

42. The laws concerning tithes are significant in Hebrews' exegesis of Gen 14:17–20, in

have a priestly lineage. Yet he not only qualifies for the priesthood, he remains a priest in perpetuity.

Christ's priesthood, like that of Melchizedek, is eternal (7:24). It does not arise through a legal requirement pertaining to lineage, but rather it is a superior priesthood that is predicated on an indestructible life (7:16) and confirmed with God's oath: "The Lord has sworn and will not change his mind, 'You are a priest forever'" (7:21). Whereas Christ is appointed directly through God's oath, the Levitical high priests are appointed according to the Law (7:20-21)—a Law that is rendered obsolete by Christ's eternal priesthood (7:12, 18).

Implicit in Hebrews' denigration of the Levitical priesthood is an equally negative view of the Law, for in Hebrews the priesthood and the Law are interdependent. At times the priesthood is subject to the Law: tithe is according to the Law (7:5), and only priests offer gifts according to the Law (8:4). On other occasions, however, the Law is subordinated to the priesthood: a change of priesthood requires a change of Law (7:12).[43] This intimate connection between Law and priesthood is expressed in the author's contention that "the people received the law under the priesthood" (7:11). Here the phrase is perhaps best understood not as "under," but as "on the basis of."[44] The cultic conception of Mosaic Law places the priesthood at the foundation of the ancient legislation. Thus, when Hebrews insists that the Levitical priesthood is inherently defective because its priests are imperfect, it is simultaneously establishing that the Law, too, is flawed and obsolete.

Sacrifice

In Hebrews, Christ's sacrifice is the offering par excellence against which all other offerings are measured. This self-sacrifice is a singular act that makes atonement (ἱλάσκεσθαι, Heb 2:17) for the community once and for all time. It purifies (1:3; 9:13-14), removes sin (9:23), and delivers people from judgment (10:26-31; 12:29). Moreover, the benefits of Christ's sacrifice remain in perpetuity, so that those who approach God through Christ receive mercy and find grace

---

which Abraham gave one-tenth of the spoils from war to Melchizedek. This is interpreted as a tithe, which according to the Law was received by the Levites (Num 18:21-24), who divided it and gave a portion to the priests (Num 18:28). Melchizedek's acceptance of a tithe by Abraham affirms his unique status as a priest unconnected to the Levites. In an interpretive twist, Hebrews even suggests that Levi himself, who had not yet descended from Abraham, had indeed paid tithes to Melchizedek through the actions of the Jewish patriarch (7:4-10).

43. For a discussion on the interdependence of the Law and priesthood in Heb 7-8, see W. Horbury, "Aaronic Priesthood in Hebrews," *JSNT* 19 (1983): 52-59.

44. Attridge, *Hebrews*, 200.

on an ongoing basis (4:14-16; 7:25), ultimately attaining everlasting life in God's presence.[45]

Hebrews compares Christ's atoning sacrifice with the Day of Atonement ritual of Lev 16.[46] Just as the Levitical high priest makes his offering in the sanctuary, so too does the high priest, Christ, make an offering in a sanctuary, the spiritual archetype of the earthly tabernacle (8:2; 9:11). And, like his Levitical counterpart who enters the Holy of Holies once per year in order to offer the Yom Kippur sacrifice, Christ enters the Holy Place, once for all time (9:12). Finally, in both sacrifices blood is the agent of expiation, as each of the high priests enters the holy realm with the blood of his sacrifice. In comparing Christ's sacrifice with the Day of Atonement rite, Hebrews focuses on three elements: the locus, the frequency, and the nature of the sacrificial offering.

The locus of Christ's sacrifice is heaven itself, where he appears in the presence of God on behalf of the community (9:24). He enters this heavenly realm "through the greater and perfect tent (not made with hands, that is, not of this creation)"; he enters "once for all into the Holy Place . . ." (9:11-12). Christ, like the Levitical high priest, performs his atoning ritual in the "Holy Place" (εἰς τὰ ἅγια) or inner court of the "tent" (σκηνή).[47] The differentiation between inner and outer courts is an essential feature that the heavenly tabernacle shares with its earthly counterpart, the desert tabernacle.[48]

In the earthly sanctuary the daily sacrifices of the priests are offered in the outer court (9:6). Only once per year, on the Day of Atonement, does the high priest gain access to the inner court and the presence of God (9:7). This contrast between the use of outer and inner courts is significant as the very structure of the tabernacle becomes a metaphor for its inadequate function. Limited access to the interior is representative of the cult's lack of effect on the conscience of the worshiper (9:8-9), whereas the predominant use of the external court is an indication of the cult's concern with fleshy externals (9:10).[49]

The frequency of sacrifice is essential to the comparison between the offering of Christ and the Levitical high priest. Whereas the former offers a one-time sacrifice to achieve perpetual atonement for the people, his Levitical counterpart enters the Holy of Holies to expiate their sins once every year, on the Day of Atonement. The multiplicity of these atoning sacrifices is criticized by Hebrews, for surely if these sacrifices were truly effective, they would not need to be repeated on a yearly basis. Evidence of their inefficacy can therefore be found in the fact that there is no cessation of these yearly sacrifices (10:1-2). The Law makes no provision for a time when atonement will be achieved and sacrifice will be unnecessary.

This contrast between the efficacy of Christ's sacrifice and the inefficacy of Le-

---

45. Koester, *Hebrews*, 122.
46. Day of Atonement rites are referred to in 9:6, 7, 12, 21, 23, 25; 10:1-3.
47. This distinction between inner and outer courts is maintained with respect to both the heavenly and earthly tabernacles. See Attridge, *Hebrews*, 217-18.
48. The epistle never refers to the Jerusalem temple, but rather compares Christ's heavenly sanctuary to the desert tabernacle.
49. Attridge, *Hebrews*, 231.

vitical sacrifice becomes less convincing when the issue of frequency is extended beyond the Day of Atonement ritual to include daily sacrifices. Christ is portrayed as being unlike other high priests in that "he has no need to offer sacrifices day after day, first for his own sins, and then for those of the people . . ." (7:27). The claim that the high priest offers a double sacrifice of atonement on a daily basis is problematic, for this clearly occurred only on the Day of Atonement (Lev 16:11, 16).[50] Moreover, the daily sacrifices that were part of the public cult did not pertain to communal atonement.[51] Atonement through sin offerings and guilt offerings are mandated only in the event of individual transgression (Lev 4–5). Communal atonement remained the exclusive purview of the Yom Kippur rite. When Hebrews claims that the daily sacrifices are offered day after day but never take away sins (10:11), it fails to distinguish between the various forms of sacrifice and misrepresents the Levitical cult as a system exclusively concerned with communal atonement.[52] This revision of the sacrificial system, however, emphasizes Hebrews' argument: the multiplicity of both daily and yearly sacrifices proves its inefficacy. The final consideration in the comparison between Christ's sacrifice and the Day of Atonement sacrifice is the nature of the sacrificial offering.

Christ's blood is alternately compared to the blood of τράγων καὶ μόσχων, "goats and calves" (9:12, 19), or τράγων καὶ ταύρων, "goats and bulls" (9:13; 10:4). These are generalized but inaccurate references to the sacrificial offerings of the Yom Kippur ritual in which a bull, two goats, and a calf were used.[53] The imprecision with which the author of Hebrews refers to these sacrificial animals is an obvious expression of his disdain for what he considers antiquated offerings.[54] In his view, these sacrifices are superficial in that they purify only the skin. Since they are incapable of perfecting the conscience (συνείδησις) of the worshiper (9:9; 10:2), these sacrifices serve only as a yearly remembrance of sins (10:3–4).[55]

This emphasis on the Day of Atonement sacrifice as a rite of physical purification is emphasized through the author's introduction of a new element into the ritual: the sprinkling of the ashes of a heifer (9:13).[56] In the Levitical account of the

---

50. In an effort to emphasize the combined repetitiveness and inefficacy of Levitical sacrifice, Hebrews has conflated the daily sacrifices with the Day of Atonement rite. For this and other less tenable explanations of the verse, see Attridge, *Hebrews*, 213.

51. Regular sacrifices that were offered as part of the public cult were the burnt offering (Lev 1), the grain offering (Lev 2), and the sacred gifts of greeting (Lev 3).

52. Ironically, the author of Hebrews is accurate in his assertion that the daily sacrifices do not remove sin, not because they are inefficacious, as he claims, but rather because they were never intended for that purpose.

53. In the LXX the following sacrificial animals are mentioned: μόσχος (Lev 16:6, 11), χίμαρος (Lev 16:15), and κριός (Lev 16:5).

54. So Attridge, *Hebrews*, 248.

55. In the Hellenistic world the term συνείδησις, "conscience," was used in a moral sense to denote awareness of transgression. See Attridge, *Hebrews*, 242.

56. Numbers 19 describes the procedure for preparing the red heifer ashes (vv. 1–10) and the ritual for their use in purifying people and objects defiled by corpse contamination (vv. 14–20). The numerous references to this ritual in Second Temple literature attest to its significance in early Judaism. See, e.g., Philo, *Somn.* 1.209–12; Josephus, *A.J.* 4.81; 4Q394

rite the high priest sprinkles the blood of the sacrificial animals in order to make atonement for the sins of the people (Lev 16:14–16). There is no mention of red heifer ashes used for ritual impurity. That Hebrews refers to the red heifer ashes instead of sprinkled blood is a deliberate revision of the Yom Kippur rite that shifts its focus away from moral impurity and the atonement of sin to a notion of ritual impurity and the removal of physical but morally neutral barriers to worship.[57] Accordingly, the quintessential rite of communal atonement in the Levitical cult is transformed into a ceremony of ritual purification through animal blood and sprinkled ashes. Contrasted with this inefficacious ceremony of the Levitical cult is the sacrifice of the Christ cultus, in which Jesus' own blood purifies the conscience and atones for sin.

In comparing Christ's atoning sacrifice with the sacrificial rites of the Day of Atonement, Hebrews asserts that the Levitical cult and its sacrifices are defective. Whereas the repetitious nature of the sacrificial system indicates that there can never be a final purgation of sin, the use of animal blood affirms the inefficacy of the system. The blood of goats and bulls is limited to physical purification. It cannot cleanse the conscience of the sinner, nor can it effect atonement. The polemic against Levitical sacrifice is both forceful and deliberate, as reflected in the author's systematic revision of the Israelite cult. Levitical distinctions between different types of sacrifices are blurred or not recognized, daily and annual rites are conflated, and communal sin offerings are portrayed as an essential component of the daily rites. These are not random modifications of the priestly Torah resulting from ignorance of Levitical law on the part of the author. Rather, they are inten-

---

3–7, i, 16–20; 4Q276 1; 4Q277 1. In addition, both the Mishnah and the Tosefta devote the entire tractate *Parah* to the discussion of the regulations concerning the preparation of the ashes. Larger discussions in the Qumran and rabbinic literature are concerned with such issues as who may participate in preparing the ashes, who may perform the rite, and what level of purity is required for the individual performing the rite. The idea that the red heifer ashes were included in the Yom Kippur rite is not found in any of these discussions and is apparently unique to Hebrews.

57. Modern biblical scholars recognize that there are two types of impurity described in the Pentateuch and that they are articulated in separate literary constructs. The priestly source (P) is concerned with ritual impurity, a temporary contagion that results from unavoidable contact with natural impurities (corpses, genital discharges, etc.). The contraction of this form of impurity is not considered a sin. The holiness source (H) articulates a notion of moral impurity, a more permanent contagion that results from committing acts that are deemed defiling (sins). On the distinction between moral and ritual impurity, see Jonathan Klawans, *Impurity and Sin in Ancient Judaism* (Oxford: Oxford University Press, 2000), 21–31. It could be argued that Hebrews blurs the distinction between ritual and moral impurity in its account of the Day of Atonement rite. I contend, however, that the author deliberately misrepresents the ceremony as a ritual for removing ritual impurity when he substitutes the red heifer ashes (used to remove ritual impurity) for the sprinkled blood (used to remove moral impurity). In removing the sprinkled blood from the Day of Atonement rite, the author effectively reduces the efficacy of the ceremony and affirms that there is no removal of sin. For more detailed discussion of the relationship between ritual and moral impurity, as well as bibliography, see chapters 1 and 2 of the present volume.

tional revisions that reinvent the Israelite cult in the shadow of Christ's sacrifice, portraying it as a system dedicated exclusively to communal atonement, but failing to provide anything more than superficial purification.

From Priestly Torah to Christ Cultus: The Function of Theological Revision

This study of Hebrews' portrayal of Mosaic covenant and Levitical cult has revealed a persistent and systematic dismantling of the Levitical code. The covenant is inadequate because its laws are weak and ineffectual. The Levitical priesthood is inherently defective because its priests are sinful. Even the earthly structure of the tabernacle embodies a concern with fleshy purification rather than cleansing of the conscience. Moreover, it provides only limited access to God's presence and only for the high priest. Sacrifices are repeatedly offered, but they never achieve final purgation of sin.

Hebrews' polemic against Judaism is not concerned with the temple in Jerusalem or contemporary Jewish practice. Rather, it is grounded in a theological argument against the Israelite cultic order as legislated by the priestly Torah. The point of departure for this argumentation is the Christ event. The blood of Christ's sacrifice atones once and for all time for the sins of the community, rendering all other forms of atonement obsolete. The denial of the efficacy of the Levitical cult arises not out of practical concerns regarding Jewish ritual, but because the Levitical theology of atonement is antithetical to belief in Christ.[58] Thus, the negative portrayal of Judaism in Hebrews may be characterized as a polemic against a competing theology of atonement that threatens the Christological view of expiation from sin.

What is the function of this theological polemic against Judaism in the sociohistorical context of Hebrews? The answer to this question can only be speculative, since there has been little scholarly consensus regarding the situation of the addressees, let alone the date, authorship, and destination of the epistle.[59] Nevertheless, the author of the epistle does offer some hints regarding the specific circumstances of his addressees.[60] It is clear that this community of Christ-believers had suffered hostility and ill treatment from outsiders (10:32–34; 13:3). Additionally, there is evidence of internal disunity within the group manifested in reduced attendance at the communal assembly (10:25) and the threat of apostasy (6:4–6). It is against this background of social conflict that we may speculate on the function of the theological polemic of Hebrews.

Social conflict is not necessarily a negative force. Rather, it often serves as a

---

58. Chester ("Hebrews: The Final Sacrifice," 64) states that "there cannot be two rival modes of atoning for sin or providing mediation and access to God."

59. For an overview of the scholarly debates regarding the date and provenance of Hebrews, see, e.g., Attridge, *Hebrews*, 1–13; Iutisone Salevao, *Legitimation in the Letter to the Hebrews: The Construction and Maintenance of a Symbotic Universe* (JSNTSup 219; Sheffield: Sheffield Academic Press, 2002), 95–121.

60. Chester ("Hebrews: The Final Sacrifice," 58) stresses that Hebrews is dealing with "urgent and threatening issues" that concern the community it addresses.

catalyst for establishing and strengthening group identity, as groups under attack define themselves against real and perceived enemies.[61] For the author of Hebrews, the struggle to establish a distinct self-definition manifests itself on a variety of levels. First, the author responds to out-group conflict and testing (12:1–13) by using the language of belonging to emphasize the cohesiveness of the group and distinguish it from the larger society in which it exists.[62] The community is thus referred to as the "holy partners in the heavenly calling" (3:1), the sanctified (2:11), the believers (4:3), the people of God (4:9), the called (9:15), and the saints (13:24). These epithets serve to reinforce group identity by establishing clear boundary lines between the community and the hostile world.

Second, the author of Hebrews addresses in-group conflict by strengthening the internal cohesion of the community.[63] There are those within the community whose response to the danger from without is characterized by a waning of faith and lapse of attendance at communal functions. In the face of external attack, however, there could be no tolerance for disunity within the group. Thus, any form of withdrawal from the community is firmly suppressed through Hebrews' exhortations to faith and its insistence on "the impossibility of a second repentance" for apostates.[64] Inevitably, this emphasis on faith points to the main goal of Hebrews: to exhort the community to faithfulness and to encourage communal solidarity.[65] Throughout the epistle the doctrinal exposition is integrated with paraenesis in service of this objective.

Third, the self-definition of the community is clearly defined on an ideological level. It is not enough for the author of Hebrews to identify his community as "the believers"; he must define exactly what it is they believe and how they distinguish themselves from other groups of so-called believers. It is in this context that Hebrews offers its sustained polemic against Judaism. For the author of Hebrews, the struggle to establish a distinct communal self-definition is undermined by the reality that his community shares common scriptures and traditions with its parent, Judaism. The "threat" of Judaism, then, is that its very existence challenges any claim to distinctiveness on the part of the emerging Christian community. The author responds to this challenge by creating a clear ideological boundary between his community of Christ-believers and the Jewish community at large. His perva-

---

61. See Lewis Coser, *The Functions of Social Conflict* (New York: Free Press, 1956), 38, 87–95. Coser's work has previously been cited in a study on Jewish-Christian relations in the first century by John G. Gager. See Gager, *Kingdom and Community: The Social World of Early Christianity* (Englewood Cliffs, NJ: Prentice-Hall, 1975), 80–88; cf. idem, "Jews, Christians, and the Dangerous Ones in Between," in *Interpretation in Religion* (ed. Shlomo Biderman and Ben-Ami Scharfstein; Leiden: Brill, 1992), 251–52; Salevao, *Legitimation*, 149–59.

62. On the "language of belonging," see Wayne Meeks, *The First Urban Christians: The Social World of the Apostle Paul* (New Haven: Yale University Press, 1983), 85.

63. Social conflict often serves a group-binding function. See Coser, *Social Conflict*, 95–103.

64. Salevao, *Legitimation*, 155.

65. The faithful are to encourage (10:25) and love (13:1) one another and to remember the tortured and imprisoned (13:3).

sive scriptural revisions provide his community with a unique theological vision through which it may define itself, while his sustained polemic against Judaism effectively ensures the continued maintenance of newly formed boundaries.

That Hebrews presents the community of Christ-believers and its Christ cultus in opposition to Judaism and its Levitical cult, and not against the pagan society in which the community existed, is significant. Social groups inevitably define themselves against those with whom they are the closest, and the bond with Judaism was far stronger than any ties with pagan society.[66] Certainly, the out-group conflict described in Hebrews presented an ongoing physical threat to the community and provided the catalyst for strengthening group self-definition. But the more profound ideological threat to the group's identity came from the Jewish tradition from which the community of Christ-believers was emerging. It was, therefore, the threat of Judaism that offered the model against which the nascent Christian community forged its identity.[67] In this light Hebrews' revision of the priestly Torah and its theological polemic against the covenant and cult is representative of the process by which the fledgling community of Christ-believers struggled to establish its self-definition. It is a conscious attempt to separate and individuate from the parent religion by highlighting the superiority of the new order over the old and driving an irrevocable wedge between Judaism and the nascent Christian community. Within the larger framework of social conflict Hebrews' systematic revision of the Israelite covenant and cult affirms the self-definition of its emerging community over and against the closest and most threatening ideology—Judaism.

---

66. According to Coser (*Social Conflict*, 67–72), the closer the relationship between groups, the more intense the conflict. The intensity of this social conflict is manifest in the polemical tone of the epistle.

67. Wilson (*Related Strangers*, 122) suggests that the negative comments about Judaism that are explicit and implicit throughout the epistle give the impression that Judaism was an immediate threat.

Part III

Historical Studies

8

COMMON JUDAISM, COMMON SYNAGOGUE?
PURITY, HOLINESS, AND SACRED SPACE AT THE
TURN OF THE COMMON ERA

In his seminal work *Judaism: Practice and Belief*, E. P. Sanders looks beyond the factional disputes of Judaism at the turn of the Common Era to consider the theology and praxis of the majority of Jews in Palestine and the Diaspora.[1] While acknowledging the diversity of opinion regarding the interpretation of the law, he argues for a common Judaism: basic tenets and practices that were agreed upon by the various parties and the Jewish populace as a whole. According to Sanders, the synagogue was a major locus of Jewish life and worship in the first century.[2] It was the place where Jews assembled on the Sabbath to hear the recitation of Torah and the exposition of its law.[3]

Scholars agree that the first-century synagogue was a central institution in every Jewish community and that it accommodated a variety of liturgical and communal functions.[4] Within this broader position, however, there is no consensus regarding the status and role of the synagogue in Jewish life.[5] One area of dispute concerns the holiness of the synagogue.[6] Archaeological evidence indicates that synagogues were often located in coastal regions or had water facilities such as *mikvaot*, cisterns, or basins constructed adjacent to them. Scholars disagree, however, on whether this

---

1. E. P. Sanders, *Judaism: Practice and Belief, 63 BCE—66 CE* (London: SCM Press; Philadelphia: Trinity Press International, 1992).

2. Sanders, *Judaism*, 198.

3. I would like to acknowledge the gracious assistance of Anders Runesson who read and critiqued successive drafts of this essay.

4. Lee I. Levine, "The First Century CE Synagogue in Historical Perspective," in *The Ancient Synagogue from Its Origins until 200 CE: Papers Presented at an International Conference at Lund University, October 14–17, 2001* (ed. B. Olsson and M. Zetterholm; ConBNT 39; Stockholm: Almqvist & Wiksell, 2003), 3.

5. For an overview of synagogue research, see Anders Runesson, *The Origins of the Synagogue: A Socio-historical Study* (ConBNT 37; Stockholm: Almqvist & Wiksell, 2001), 67–168.

6. On the holiness of the synagogue, see especially Steven Fine, *This Holy Place: On the Sanctity of the Synagogue during the Greco-Roman Period* (Notre Dame, IN: University of Notre Dame Press, 1997); cf. idem, "From Meeting House to Sacred Realm: Holiness and the Ancient Synagogue," in *Sacred Realm: The Emergence of the Synagogue in the Ancient World* (ed. S. Fine; New York: Oxford University Press, 1996), 27–49.

close proximity to water indicates a connection between purity practices and the synagogue. Some believe that locating synagogues near water reflected a practice whereby Jews entering their places of worship performed some sort of ritual purification that was similar to those required at the entrances of Greco-Roman temples. Others argue that proximity was due to convenience; Jews made use of purification facilities regularly, and they attended synagogue regularly, but this does not mean that purification was required before entering the synagogue.

The present study examines the relationship between purity and the synagogue at the turn of the Common Era, as it relates to the sacred. Two questions lie at the heart of this investigation: first, did Jews perform ritual ablutions—immerse their bodies, wash their hands, or sprinkle themselves with water—in order to purify themselves before entering the synagogue? The answer to this question leads directly to the second question: did they regard the synagogue as a sacred realm?

Two methodological issues are pertinent to this investigation. The first is a matter of definition: what exactly do we mean when we use the term "synagogue"? Here I follow Anders Runesson, who describes four separate aspects of the synagogue: institutional, liturgical, non-liturgical, and spatial.[7] My concern is primarily with the liturgical aspects of the synagogue, that is, the activities that are usually categorized as "religious." In addition, consideration will be given to certain spatial aspects of the place in which these liturgical activities took place. A second methodological concern is the issue of unity and diversity. The ancient synagogue may have held a significant place in common Judaism, but the institution was not a monolithic entity, nor should it be treated as such. In order to account for geographic differences in practice, synagogues in the land of Israel will be considered separately from those existing in the Diaspora.

We begin by discussing the ancient concepts of purity and holiness and their perceived relationship to one another. It is against this background that the relationship between purity and the synagogue will be examined, first in the land of Israel and subsequently in the Diaspora. Consideration will then be given to the notion of the early synagogue as a sacred realm. It will be demonstrated that certain purity practices related to the synagogue point to its sanctity, but that the nature of this perceived holiness varies with location.

Purity and Holiness

Purity and holiness were prominent features of Jewish life in the late Second Temple period. Distinctions between pure and impure, holy and common applied to people, objects, space, and time. These categories were not only fundamental to the social structure of Jewish society, they also influenced a variety of interactions, as it was a basic tenet of the Law that impurity could not come in contact with the sacred.

Jonathan Klawans distinguishes between two types of impurity: ritual defilement, a contagion that temporarily excludes the individual from participating in

---

7. Runesson, *Origins*, 34–35.

temple rituals, and the more permanent moral defilement caused by sin, a form of impurity that is not related to temple worship.[8] Ritual impurities include those that arise from childbirth (Lev 12:1–8), scale disease (Lev 13:1–14:32), genital discharges (Lev 15:1–33), the carcasses of certain impure animals (Lev 11:1–47), and human corpses (Num 19:10–22). In addition, such impurity is encountered as a by-product of purificatory procedures (e.g., Lev 16:28; Num 19:8). According to Klawans, there are three distinctive characteristics of ritual impurity. First, the sources of ritual impurity are natural, usually unavoidable, and sometimes even desirable. They include birth, death, sex, disease, and other circumstances that reflect the conditions of normal life. Second, there are no prohibitions against contracting these impurities, nor are they considered sinful. The consequence of ritual impurity is relatively minor in that it precludes entrance to the sanctuary and other contact with the sacred. Third, ritual impurity conveys an impermanent contagion through contact with other individuals or objects. It should be emphasized, however, that both primary and secondary forms of this impurity may be alleviated through purificatory procedures. Thus, even long-lasting impurities are considered impermanent.

Unlike ritual impurity, moral impurity results from immoral acts, including sexual sins (e.g., Lev 18:24–30), idolatry (e.g., Lev 19:31; 20:1–3) and bloodshed (e.g., Num 35:33–34).[9] These sinful actions are often referred to as תועבות (to'evot), or abominations. The impurity that arises from such sin is a moral defilement that pollutes the sinner (Lev 18:24), the land (Lev 18:25; Ezek 36:17), and God's sanctuary (Lev 20:3; Ezek 5:11). Although this form of impurity is not contagious, it is considered permanent and therefore may not be ameliorated through rites of purification.[10] Sinners are thus forced to live out their lives in a degraded state or else to suffer capital punishment. The land upon which grave sin is committed is likewise subject to permanent degradation, which may result in the expulsion of its inhabitants.

Observance of the purity laws was widespread in both the land of Israel and the Diaspora.[11] In the land of Israel, purification required the "immersion" of the whole body in water from a natural source: the sea, a spring, a river, or a מקוה (mikveh), in which rainwater, spring water, or runoff was collected by a direct flow.[12] In the Diaspora, ritual ablutions took the form of sprinkling, splashing, or

---

8. Jonathan Klawans, *Impurity and Sin in Ancient Judaism* (New York: Oxford University Press, 2000), 23–31.

9. Klawans, *Impurity*.

10. One exception would be the Day of Atonement rites, which involve the purgation of the altar and shrine from the effects of sin (Lev 16:11–19), as well as atonement for the transgressions of the people (Lev 16:20–22).

11. Sanders, *Judaism*, 229; cf. Donald D. Binder, *Into the Temple Courts: The Place of the Synagogues in the Second Temple Period* (SBLDS 169; Atlanta: Society of Biblical Literature, 1999), 394.

12. Remains of *mikvaot* have been found throughout the land of Israel, attesting to widespread purity practices throughout the Second Temple period. These pools were cut into bedrock, had steps leading to the bottom, and were deep enough for full immersion of

hand-washing.[13] Jews everywhere performed these purificatory rites whether or not they approached the sacred precincts of the Jerusalem temple.[14]

Two factors help to explain this widespread practice. First, Jews of the first century believed that the biblical laws, including the purity laws, were divine in origin. For this reason, they viewed themselves as obligated to observe the laws to the best of their ability. Their concern was not whether to keep the law but how to do so within their own social and cultural context. Second, according to the Law only those who were in a state of purity could have contact with the sacred. Such holiness was not only associated with the temple but also with the biblical scrolls that were read on the Sabbath and perhaps, as we shall see, even with the synagogue in which the Torah was read and studied. Jews purified themselves so that they could draw near to that which was holy.

The concept of holiness implies separation—specifically, separation from the profane.[15] In the first century, ideas of holiness and separation were most apparent in the hierarchical structure of the Jerusalem temple, where access to the various levels of holy space was limited to various groups of individuals according to their level of sanctity.[16] Thus female Israelites were allowed only as far as the court of the women, while their male counterparts, who occupied a higher place on the

---

the body. Most often the pools were filled by channels that carried rain or springwater. Alternatively, the water from a nearby reservoir or *otsar* ("treasury") was released through a conduit that connected the two pools. See Ronny Reich, "The Synagogue and the Miqweh in Eretz-Israel in the Second-Temple, Mishnaic, and Talmudic Periods," in *Ancient Synagogues: Historical Analysis and Archaeological Discovery* (ed. Dan Urman and Paul V. M. Flesher; 2 vols.; StPB 47:1–2; Leiden: Brill, 1995), 1:289–97; Sanders, *Judaism*, 223; Binder, *Into the Temple Courts*, 393–94.

13. As of yet, there have been no *mikvaot* found in the Diaspora (Binder, *Into the Temple Courts*, 395). The only possible *mikveh* was at the Delos synagogue, but this has been ruled out in Trümper's thorough study of the edifice. See Monika Trümper, "The Oldest Original Synagogue Building in the Diaspora: The Delos Synagogue Reconsidered," *Hesperia* 73 (2004): 513–98. The *Letter of Aristeas* and the *Sibylline Oracles* mention hand-washing but not immersion (*Let. Aris.* 304–6; *Sib. Or.* 3:591–93), whereas Philo refers to περιρρανάμενοι καὶ ἀπολουσάμενοι, which may be translated as "aspersions and ablutions" or "sprinkling and bathing" (*Spec.* 3:205–6). On purity in the Diaspora, see the detailed discussion in E. P. Sanders, *Jewish Law from Jesus to the Mishnah* (London: SCM, 1990), 258–71; cf. idem, *Judaism*, 223–24.

14. Against Neusner, who emphasizes the association between purity and the temple in Second Temple–period Judaism. He contends that a community's interpretation of biblical purity law is inextricably linked to its relationship to the temple. See Jacob Neusner, *The Idea of Purity in Ancient Judaism* (Leiden: Brill, 1973), 33. This "minimalist" view of purity was recently contested by John C. Poirier, who views the temple-oriented view of purity as "a scholarly construct with little basis in reality." See John C. Poirier, "Purity beyond the Temple in the Second Temple Era," *JBL* 122 (2003): 247–65.

15. Jacob Milgrom, *Leviticus 1–16: A New Translation with Introduction and Commentary* (AB 3; New York: Doubleday, 1991), 730.

16. See Christine E. Hayes, *Gentile Impurities and Jewish Identities: Intermarriage and Conversion from the Bible to the Talmud* (New York: Oxford University Press, 2002), 34–37, 59–63.

continuum from profane to holy, enter the courtyard of the sacrificial altar.[17] The priests, being even holier, ministered in the adytum, where the incense altar was situated, and the high priest, the most holy of God's people, gained access to the innermost shrine, but only once a year on the Day of Atonement.

The relationship between holy/common and pure/impure is complex in that it concerns two separate but related continuums. What is certain is that, in the first century, Jews recognized that an individual or object was subject to four possible states: holy, common, pure, and impure. The dynamic between these states has been best illustrated by Jacob Milgrom.[18]

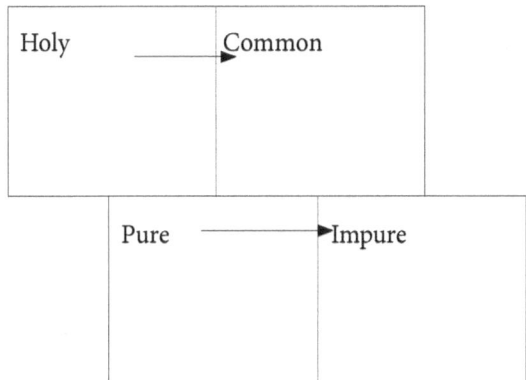

In this diagram the common is contiguous to the realms of both the pure and impure, but the holy is adjacent only to the pure. The categories of holy and impure are antagonistic; they never come in contact with one another.

The relationship between the concepts of holiness and purity is significant to the discussion of the synagogue as a sacred realm. If Jews in the first century regarded synagogues as sacred spaces, they would have been careful to separate them from all sources of impurity and therefore to locate them in "pure" locations and to provide facilities for ritual ablutions to ensure the ritual purity of all who entered.

PURITY AND THE SYNAGOGUE IN THE LAND OF ISRAEL

In the land of Israel, synagogues dated to the Second Temple period have been identified at Jericho, Gamla, Masada, Herodium, Qiryat Sefer, and Modi'in.[19]

---

17. It is commonly held that women had less access to the temple than men because of impurity. Yet the law makes no distinction between the level of purity of a pure Jewish female and a pure Jewish male. See Hayes, *Gentile Impurities*, 60–61.

18. Milgrom, *Leviticus 1–16*, 732.

19. On the dating of these and other ancient synagogues, see the helpful chart in Peter Richardson, "An Architectural Case for Synagogues and Associations," in Olsson and Zetterhoam, *The Ancient Synagogue*, 92–93. Commenting on this table, Binder suggests that the structures at Jericho, Qiryat Sefer, and Modi'in should be moved to the "uncertain" category, pending further investigation and argumentation. Levine, however, seems quite

While none of these buildings is located near natural bodies of water, the buildings at Jericho, Masada, and Herodium have *mikvaot* associated with them. Moreover, there have been *mikvaot* found at Qumran as well as in the villages of Modi'in and Qiryat Sefer, albeit in locations that do not suggest any spatial connection to a synagogue.[20] Finally, the Theodotus inscription attests to the existence of a first-century synagogue in Jerusalem that had water facilities associated with it.[21]

A brief survey of the archaeological evidence will help to discern whether the proximity of *mikvaot* to synagogues was intended to facilitate purification rites connected with synagogue attendance. The recently excavated synagogue in Jericho is located just outside the compound of the Hasmonean winter palace and is related to a row of houses to the east.[22] The hall, dated to the second phase of construction (70 B.C.E.), measured 16.2 x 11.1 meters and would have seated ap-

---

clear about the synagogues at Qiryat Sefer and Modi'in, although he does express some reservations about the building at Jericho. See Donald D. Binder, "The Origins of the Synagogue: An Evaluation," in Olsson and Zetterholm, *The Ancient Synagogue*, 124 n. 15; Lee I. Levine, "The First-Century Synagogue: Critical Reassessments and Assessment of the Critical," in *Religion and Society in Roman Palestine: Old Questions, New Approaches* (ed. Douglas R. Edwards; London: Routledge, 2004), 84–89. Also worthy of mention is a building in Khirbet Qana that may possibly be a synagogue dating to the first or second century C.E. According to Peter Richardson, there have, as yet, been no water installations discovered near the synagogue. One excavated house dating to the Byzantine period did, however, have a courtyard with a large cistern and a *mikveh* dating to the early Roman period. Moreover, there are two or three other installations that could be *mikvaot*, but further investigation is required to be sure. This information was conveyed in a private communication with Peter Richardson, April 28, 2005. For a preliminary description of some of the archaeological discoveries at Khirbet Qana, see Peter Richardson, *Building Jewish in the Roman East* (Waco, TX: Baylor University Press, 2004), 103–5.

20. For a description of the buildings in Qiryat Sefer and Modi'in, see Levine, "First-Century Synagogue," 84–87. Although Levine does not refer to the *mikvaot* found in Qiryat Sefer, they are mentioned in an online publication of the Israel Ministry of Foreign Affairs: "Kiryat Sefer: A Synagogue in a Jewish Village of the Second Temple Period," *Archaeological Sites in Israel* 8, http://www.israel-mfa.gov.il/MFA/History/Early+History+-+Archaeology/.

21. On the dating of the Theodotus inscription to the early first century, see John S. Kloppenborg, "Dating Theodotus (CIJ II 1404)," *JJS* 51 (2000): 243–80.

22. On the Jericho synagogue, see Ehud Netzer, "A Synagogue from the Hasmonean Period Recently Exposed in the Western Plain of Jericho," *IEJ* 49 (1999): 203–21. The identification of this building as a synagogue is not entirely certain. Levine, for example, is cautious in his assessment, suggesting that future excavations may enable Netzer to solidify his contention (*The Ancient Synagogue*, 69). See also the discussion between Ehud Netzer and David Stacey in the online journal *Bible and Interpretation*: Ehud Netzer, "A Synagogue from the Hasmonean Period Exposed at Jericho," http://www.bibleinterp.com/articles/Synagogue.htm; David Stacey, "Was There a Synagogue in Hasmonean Jericho?" http://www.bibleinterp.com/articles/Hasmonean_Jericho.htm. Commenting on the location of the synagogue, Netzer speculates that it was used by the king's employees, some of whom may have lived in the adjacent houses. Runesson also calls attention to the fact that the building is near the Hasmonean palace complex but disconnected from any formal village structure. He suggests that the organization of the people would be best described as a guild and that

proximately 125 people.²³ It was bisected by a water channel that originated at a conduit to the north of the hall and terminated at the *mikveh* to the south. A basin located in the northern aisle of the synagogue was also attached to the channel and was likely used for ritual washing of the hands.

The synagogue at Gamla was a public village assembly hall, centrally located near the city gate.²⁴ The interior of the building (20 x 16m) was lined with two to four rows of benches, which would have seated some 340 people.²⁵ Significantly, there is a water channel from an aqueduct outside the city that penetrates the northeast wall of the building and ends in a small basin in the northern corner of the synagogue. It is likely that this basin was used for hand-washing.²⁶ A *mikveh*, dating to the period of the first Jewish revolt (66–67 C.E.), is located about ten meters to the southwest of the building.²⁷ The presence of three other ritual baths in Gamla indicates a particular concern for purity in this town.²⁸

At Masada, the building identified as a synagogue is dated to the time of Herod (37-4 B.C.E.).²⁹ The building was converted into an assembly hall during the occupation by the Jewish rebels between 66 and 74 C.E. The large hall (12 x 15m) was lined with one to four rows of benches, which would have seated 250 people. Its identification as a synagogue is confirmed by the discovery of fragments from the books of Deuteronomy and Ezekiel in the adjoining room. There is also a *mikveh* located fifteen meters north of the synagogue that was apparently built by the rebels. In addition, three other *mikvaot* dating to the first Jewish rebellion are scattered throughout the complex.

Like the synagogue at Masada, the assembly hall at Herodium was also converted from a preexisting structure.³⁰ In the first phase of the building the hall

---

their synagogue was used for semi-public assemblies, both social and religious. See Netzer, "Synagogue," 217; Runesson, *Origins*, 357–59.

23. Netzer estimates fifty centimeters as the average space for one person ("Synagogue," 220 n. 29).

24. For a description of the synagogue at Gamla (Gamala), see, for example, Shmaryahu Gutman, "Gamala," in *The New Encyclopedia of Archaeological Excavations in the Holy Land* (ed. Ephraim Stern; 4 vols.; Jerusalem: Israel Exploration Society, 1993), 2:459–63; Binder, *Into the Temple Courts*, 162–72.

25. Netzer, "Synagogue," 220.

26. So Gutman, "Gamala," 461. Binder indicates that a separate bench was placed along the northeastern wall of the synagogue near the water basin. Commenting on the prominent location of this bench overlooking the rest of the hall, he speculates that the leaders of the assembly sat there and that they used the water basin before handling the sacred scrolls (Binder, *Into the Temple Courts*, 170–71).

27. Lee I. Levine, *The Ancient Synagogue: The First Thousand Years* (New Haven: Yale University Press, 2000), 52.

28. See Gutman, "Gamala," 462–63; Danny Syon, "Gamla: Portrait of a Rebellion," *BAR* 18, no. 1 (1992): 21–37.

29. Ehud Netzer, *Masada: The Yigael Yadin Excavations, 1963–1965. Final Reports* (6 vols.; Jerusalem: Israel Exploration Society, 1989), 3:402–13; Binder, *Into the Temple Courts*, 172–79.

30. Gideon Foerster, "The Synagogues at Masada and Herodium," in *Ancient Synagogues*

served as a triclinium in Herod's fortress palace. It was only during the occupation of the rebels during the first Jewish revolt that the hall was converted into a synagogue. The Herodium synagogue (10.5 x 15m) was similar in size to the synagogue at Masada, seating approximately 250 people.[31] Just outside the hall was a *mikveh*, which abutted the eastern wall of the synagogue.[32] In addition there was a storage pool and adjacent bathtub nearby, from the same phase.

The discovery of several *mikvaot* at Qumran also warrants our consideration, especially since the purificatory rites of the Qumran community were related to liturgical activities that were often associated with a synagogue. According to Jodi Magness, *mikvaot* are found in areas in which purity was required, as well as those areas in which impurity was incurred. It is therefore not surprising to find a large *mikveh* (loci 56–58) near the entrance to the communal assembly hall (locus 77), which was used for dining. While there are no archaeological remains from Qumran to establish the presence of a synagogue, it is likely that locus 77 was also used for this purpose.[33] Runesson contends that the activities that took place in this room were likely those described in 1QS VI, 2–5; these activities included eating, praying, and deliberating together in a fashion that is reminiscent of Hellenistic associations. Moreover, the *yahad* referred to in 1QS may well have been a religious association that was organized much like the synagogue communities of the Diaspora.[34]

The association of water facilities with a synagogue is also attested in the Theodotus inscription:

> Theodotus, the son of Vettenos, priest and archisynagogos, son of an archisynagogos and grandson of an archisynagogos, built the assembly hall (Synagogue: ΣΨΝΑΓΩΓ[Η]Ν) for the reading of the Law and for the teaching of the commandments, and the guest room, the chambers, and the water fittings, as an inn for those in need from foreign parts, (the synagogue) which his fathers founded with the elders and Simonides.[35]

Kloppenborg argues that while the first portion of the inscription describes

---

Revealed (ed. Lee I. Levine; Jerusalem: Israel Exploration Society, 1981), 24–29; Binder, *Into the Temple Courts*, 180–85.

31. Binder, *Into the Temple Courts*, 184–85.

32. Foerster, *Masada and Herodium*, 26.

33. Jodi Magness, *The Archaeology of Qumran and the Dead Sea Scrolls* (Grand Rapids: Eerdmans, 2002), 127. Magness (*Archaeology*, 127) suggests that a second dining room in the secondary building of the complex also had two *mikvaot* (loci 117–18) in proximity.

34. So Matthias Klinghardt, "The Manual of Discipline in the Light of Statutes of Hellenistic Associations," in *Methods of Investigation of the Dead Sea Scrolls and the Khirbet Qumran Site: Present Realities and Future Prospects* (ed. J. J. Collins et al.; Annals of the New York Academy of Sciences 722; New York: The New York Academy of Sciences, 1994); cf. Moshe Weinfeld, *The Organizational Pattern and the Penal Code of the Qumran Sect* (Göttingen: Vandenhoeck & Ruprecht, 1986). Klinghardt's comparison of 1QS to a statute of an association offers some insight, but I think that he goes too far when he suggests that the Qumran community should not be characterized as a sect.

35. As translated by Kloppenborg, "Dating Theodotus," 244.

various portions of the building, the final relative clause treats all of these components collectively, as being part of the synagogue.[36] Thus, in addition to an assembly hall, this synagogue had several rooms for lodgers as well as some sort of water facilities. It is unclear whether these water facilities were used for ritual purposes or to meet other needs of the visitors. Given that the synagogue was founded by a priestly family, however, we might speculate that these facilities included a *mikveh* along with other facilities for drinking and washing.

The archaeological and epigraphic evidence points to two types of ritual ablution associated with synagogues in the land of Israel, namely, ritual hand-washing and full immersion. The water basins found inside the assembly halls at Jericho and Gamla suggest that the rituals performed within the synagogue, such as the handling of Torah scrolls, required ritual hand-washing.[37] It is less certain that full immersion was also associated with synagogue rituals. Binder argues that the presence of *mikvaot* in proximity to Second Temple–period synagogues is an indication that purity requirements were connected with the synagogue in much the same way as they were associated with the temple. Such a view, however, is problematic. First, priestly law attests to the fact that an individual could not enter the temple in a state of ritual impurity (Lev 15:31). This biblical prohibition is alluded to throughout the Second Temple literature, yet none of the sources describe a similar ruling pertaining to the synagogue.[38] Second, it is difficult from a logistical perspective to envision how one synagogue *mikveh* could accommodate a large group of people all intending to immerse prior to an assembly in the synagogue. At their maximum capacity, the synagogues under consideration could seat hundreds of people. Yet the *mikvaot* associated with them were relatively small and therefore clearly intended only for individual immersion.[39] If we estimate that it would take one minute for an individual to enter the *mikveh*, immerse, and emerge, a crowd of 120 people would require some two hours to complete their purification. Given

---

36. The final relative clause is "having been founded." See Kloppenborg, "Dating Theodotus," 244 n. 5.

37. On the sanctity of the Torah, see Martin Goodman, "Sacred Scripture and 'Defiling the Hands,'" *JTS* 41 (1990): 103–4; cf. Shamma Friedman, "The Holy Scriptures Defile the Hands—The Transformation of a Biblical Concept in Rabbinic Theology," in *Minhah le-Nahum: Biblical and Other Studies Presented to Nahum M. Sarna in Honour of His Seventieth Birthday* (ed. M. Brettler and M. Fishbane; JSOTSup 154; Sheffield: JSOT Press, 1993), 117–32; Chaim Milikowsky, "Reflections on Hand-Washing, Hand Purity, and Holy Scripture in Rabbinic Literature," in *Purity and Holiness: The Heritage of Leviticus* (ed. M. Porthuis and J. Schwartz; Leiden: Brill, 2000), 149–62; Fine, *This Holy Place*, 30.

38. See, for example, *B.J.* 5.194, 227; 6.426–27; *Cher.* 94–95; *Det.* 20; CD XI, 19–21; XII, 1–2; 1QM XLV, 11–12.

39. One exception would be the large Qumran *mikvaot*, which resemble the "Jerusalem type" *mikveh* identified by Reich. This type of *mikveh* can be used by several people simultaneously and is characterized by (1) its relatively large entrance on the broad side of the structure, (2) steps that alternate with wider and narrower treads, and (3) a double entrance and/or a small partition built down the center of the stairway. See Ronny Reich, "They Are Ritual Baths: Immerse Yourself in the Ongoing Sepphoris *Mikveh* Debate," *BAR* 28, no. 2 (March/April 2002): 50–55.

that synagogue worship was a communal rather than an individual act, this scenario is hardly feasible.

More likely, the association of water facilities with the central Jewish institution was a matter of practicality. The public *mikveh* would have been built at the communal center in order to facilitate the observance of Jewish purity practices within the community, in the same way as the synagogues were built to facilitate the communal reading and study of the Torah. Thus members of the community would have used the *mikveh* at the appropriate times in order to maintain their ritual purity on a regular basis. They would have also assembled in the synagogue on the Sabbath, as well as on other occasions, but they probably would not have routinely used the *mikveh* before entering. It is likely that only those who had direct contact with the Torah scrolls would have been required to perform ritual ablutions in connection with synagogue rituals. These individuals would have utilized water basins for the washing of their hands.

Purity and the Synagogue in the Diaspora

The archaeological remains of two Diaspora buildings have been securely identified as synagogues dated to the Second Temple period: the Ostia synagogue and the synagogue on the island of Delos.[40] Both synagogues are located on the seashore, and both have man-made water facilities adjacent to the building. It is often assumed that the proximity of these synagogues to water is associated with purity practices. Yet the existence of both natural and man-made water facilities is somewhat perplexing, since either one or the other would have sufficed to meet any purity requirements associated with the synagogue.

Purity and the Location of the Synagogue

The synagogue on Delos, dated to the second century B.C.E., is the earliest known structure of its kind in either the Diaspora or the land of Israel. It is situated directly on the shore of what was the eastern side of the city, at some distance from the city center and its residential buildings, sanctuaries, and public places.[41] Similarly, the synagogue at Ostia, dated to the first century C.E., stood outside the city walls near the ancient seashore.[42] The epigraphic and literary evidence suggests that synagogues were often to be found in proximity to water (the sea or a river) and at a distance from the city center. A second-century B.C.E. land survey from Arsinoe in Egypt, written on papyrus, indicates that a synagogue was located on the outskirts of the town and was situated by a canal.[43] Josephus mentions a

---

40. Richardson, "An Architectural Case," 92–93.

41. Trümper, "The Oldest Original Synagogue," 513–14.

42. Anders Runesson, "The Synagogue at Ancient Ostia: The Building and Its History," in *The Synagogue of Ancient Ostia and the Jews of Rome: Interdisciplinary Studies* (ed. B. Olsson, O. Brandt, and D. Mitternacht; ActaRom-4o 57; Stockholm: Paul Åströms, 2001), 31, 37.

43. *CPJ* 1, no. 134. It should be noted that the original editors of the text indicate that the synagogue was outside the town. See B. P. Grenfell, A. S. Hunt, and J. G. Smyly, eds., *The Tebtunis Papyri* (4 vols.; London: Oxford University Press, 1902), 4, no. 86.

decree of the citizens of Halicarnassus that permitted the Jews to build synagogues or houses of prayer near the sea in accordance with their ancestral customs:

> [T]o the effect that their sacred services to God and their customary festivals and religious gatherings shall be carried on, we have decreed that the those Jewish men and women who so wish may observe their Sabbaths and perform their sacred rites in accordance with the Jewish laws, and may build places of prayer near the sea in accordance with their native custom. (*A.J.* 14.258 [Marcus, LCL])

Finally, Acts 16:13 indicates that Paul and his companions went outside the gates of Philippi to the riverside to look for the synagogue: "On the Sabbath day we went outside the gates by the river, where we supposed there was a place of prayer; and we sat down and spoke to the women who had gathered there." It is quite evident from this passage that Paul expected to find the synagogue outside the city, by the river. Although these sources mention only proximity to water, such locations would often perforce be at the periphery of the city.

Ismar Elbogen points out, however, that synagogues in the Diaspora were not always located beside a source of water. Moreover, there are no halakhic rulings pertaining to building synagogues near water, either in the land of Israel or in the Diaspora. For Elbogen the significance of the passage in Acts is not that Paul expects to find the synagogue by the riverside, but that he presumes that it is outside the city gate. He writes: "The Jews avoided worshipping inside cities that contained pagan sanctuaries; only if special Jewish quarters existed, as in Alexandria, were synagogues established in them."[44]

If Elbogen is correct, the location of Diaspora synagogues outside the city gate does not reflect a concern with ritual impurity that requires ablutions, but with a moral impurity that cannot be washed away. Synagogues—devoted to the worship of the one God—could not be built on land that was considered polluted by idolatry. Philo's description of the events that occurred after the Jews of Alexandria heard about the arrest of their enemy supports this conclusion:

> All night long they continued to sing hymns and songs of praise and at dawn pouring out through the gates, they made their way to the parts of the beach near at hand, since their meeting-houses (προσευχάς) had been taken from them, κἀν τῷ καθαρωτάτῳ στάντες they cried out with one accord "Most Mighty King of mortals and immortals..." (*Flacc.* 122–123)

F. H. Colson translates the phrase κἀν τῷ καθαρωτάτῳ στάντες as "and standing in the most open place" (*Flacc.* 122 [Colson and Whitaker, LCL]). An alternative translation is offered by Runesson, who suggests that in the Jewish context of this passage it would be more accurate to retain the basic meaning of the term καθαρός, which is "clean" or "pure." One might suggest, however, an even more nuanced reading of the text, in which the term καθαρός is understood in a

---

44. Ismar Elbogen, *Jewish Liturgy: A Comprehensive History* (trans. R. P. Scheindlin; Philadelphia: Jewish Publication Society, 1993), 340; translation of *Der jüdische Gottesdienst in seiner geschichtlichen Entwicklung* (Leipzig: G. Fock, 1913).

moral sense as being free from pollution.⁴⁵ In the context of Philo's narrative, the Jews of Alexandria sought a "pure" place to worship God, because their city had been polluted by immorality. Not only had their synagogues been taken from them, and the Jewish quarters destroyed, many of the Jews had been tortured and murdered. The blood of innocent people polluted Alexandria, both literally and morally.

According to Philo, the Jews go to a place outside the city—a place that replaces their destroyed synagogues. It is there that they pray in a location that is not defiled by moral pollution. The issue of concern is the status of the land as it pertains to the two continuums of holy/profane and pure/impure. In contrast to the land of Israel, which is considered holy, Gentile lands are regarded as profane but not necessarily impure. The purity or impurity of a Gentile land depends upon the activities of the inhabitants. Thus the Alexandrian Jews could gather on the beach outside of Alexandria to pray, on land that was considered profane but pure.

In summary, the location of the Diaspora synagogue in proximity to natural sources of water coincides with its position at the periphery of the non-Jewish city. It is probable that Jews built their synagogues outside the city because they considered the land "pure"—that is, unpolluted by the moral impurity associated with idolatrous practices and other sin. That these locations are often near natural sources of water has no implication with respect to moral impurity.⁴⁶ It is possible, however, that the water was used for ritual ablutions prior to prayer or the handling of the Torah.

Purity and the Association of Water Facilities with the Synagogue

From as early as the second century B.C.E. until late antiquity, Diaspora synagogues shared one common feature: the presence of a cistern, water basin, or fountain at the entrance area.⁴⁷ Most frequently, there was a water basin placed in the center of the atrium, just outside the main entrance of the building, in the hall, or in the narthex that led from the street to the sanctuary.⁴⁸ Installations of this type were found in a number of synagogues in the Diaspora, including the synagogues of Delos and Ostia.⁴⁹

The water installations associated with the synagogue on Delos include three

---

45. Cf. LSJ, καθαρός, 850-51.

46. Contra A. Runesson, who contends that the purity of the location is at least partially defined by its proximity to the water. See Runesson, "Water and Worship: Ostia and the Ritual Bath in the Diaspora Synagogue," in Olsson, Mitternacht, and Brandt, *Synagogue of Ancient Ostia*, 119-23.

47. Leonard Victor Rutgers, "Diaspora Synagogues: Synagogue Archaeology in the Greco-Roman World," in Fine, *Sacred Realm*, 74-75.

48. Levine, *The Ancient Synagogue*, 308.

49. Levine also cites En Gedi, Dura Europos, Sardis, Philadelphia in Lydia, Priene, and Gerasa, thereby covering a time period from the second century B.C.E to the fifth century C.E. (*The Ancient Synagogue*, 308-9).

water basins and a cistern.⁵⁰ Fragments from one of the basins are presently located between two benches near what was purportedly the main entrance of the building. A second was found in a room inside the building and a third in the cistern. It is most probable that these marble basins held water for ritual ablutions.⁵¹ There has been some speculation that the cistern inside the synagogue may have been used for ritual bathing, especially since it allowed for human access.⁵² If this were the case, it would be among the earliest known *mikvaot* in the world, the earliest associated with a synagogue, and the only ancient *mikveh* discovered outside the land of Israel. Yet the architecture of the Delian water reservoir does not conform to that of contemporaneous *mikvaot* found in the land of Israel. Moreover, its proximity to the sea, which could have served the same purpose as a *mikveh*, makes this identification questionable. In all likelihood, the water from the cistern was used for daily activities such as drinking, cooking, washing, and cleaning.⁵³

The earliest plan of the synagogue at Ostia included a well and a shallow cistern that stood to the right of the main entrance.⁵⁴ It also had other features that were shared by the guilds of Ostia, including an assembly room and a triclinium.⁵⁵ It is likely that the well and the cistern served a similar function in the synagogue as they did in other Ostian guilds, including both ritual and non-ritual purposes. During the first renovation of the synagogue a basin was constructed in the area to the right, just inside the entrance to the eastern main door.⁵⁶ The basin holds a large amount of water, some four times the amount that would be required for a *mikveh* constructed according to rabbinic requirements. Yet the form of the basin differs significantly from a traditional *mikveh* in that it is very large and shallow, rather than narrow and deep. Moreover, it was probably filled with water that had been drawn from the well, rather than by direct access. Runesson concludes that the basin was used for ritual washing and suggests that its shallowness may imply washing of the hands and feet.

---

50. Binder, *Into the Temple Courts*, 297–317; Trümper, "The Oldest Original Synagogue," 513–98. Cf. White, whose analyses are, however, disputed by Binder and Trümper. See L. Michael White, "The Delos Synagogue Revisited: Recent Fieldwork in the Graeco-Roman Diaspora," *HTR* 80 (1987): 133–60.

51. Trümper, *The Oldest Original Synagogue*, 577.

52. Levine, *The Ancient Synagogue*, 101; Runesson, "Water and Worship," 124 n. 84. On human access to the cistern, see Binder, *Into the Temple Courts*, 306–7 n. 153.

53. Trümper, *The Oldest Original Synagogue*, 575–77.

54. L. Michael White, "Synagogue and Society in Imperial Ostia: Archaeological and Epigraphic Evidence," *HTR* 90 (1997): 23–58; Anders Runesson, "The Oldest Synagogue Building in the Diaspora: A Response to L. Michael White," *HTR* 92 (1999): 409–33. White responded to Runesson in "Reading the Ostia Synagogue: A Reply to A. Runesson," *HTR* 92 (1999): 435–64, and Runesson offered a subsequent response in "A Monumental Synagogue from the First Century: The Case of Ostia," *JSJ* 33 (2002): 171–220; cf. Runesson, "The Synagogue of Ancient Ostia," 29–99. An important contribution is also made by Binder, *Into the Temple Courts*, 322–36.

55. Richardson, "An Architectural Case," 97–105.

56. Runesson, "The Synagogue of Ancient Ostia," 69–71; cf. idem, "Water and Worship," 125.

The archaeological evidence suggests that ritual ablutions were associated with synagogues in the Diaspora and that these purification procedures did not involve immersion in a *mikveh*.[57] It is not clear, however, how this ritual ablution was performed. The literary sources attest to the relationship between hand-washing and synagogue activities. For example, the *Sibylline Oracles* indicate that Jews washed their hands before praying (3.591–93). Similarly, Josephus indicates that the elders who translated the Law from the Hebrew into Greek washed their hands before handling the sacred scripture (*A.J.* 12.106). A parallel account in the *Letter of Aristeas* is particularly informative:

> Following the custom of all the Jews, they washed their hands in the sea in the course of their prayers to God, and then proceeded to the reading and explication of each point. I asked this question: "What is their purpose in washing their hands while saying their prayers?" They explained that it is evidence that they have done no evil, for all activity takes place by means of the hands. (305–6)

In this passage, hand-washing is associated with both prayer and the handling of scripture. The purported reason for hand-washing, however, is not ritual purification, but moral purity. In this passage, there is an overlap between the two categories of ritual and moral impurity. Because sin is regarded as being ritually defiling, it may be removed by washing one's hands.

It is also possible that Jews purified themselves by sprinkling with water. Philo attests to the practice of splashing or sprinkling oneself after sexual relations (*Spec.* 3.63) and a combination of sprinkling and bathing in order to remove corpse impurity (*Spec.* 3.205; cf. 1.261). The practice of purification by sprinkling with water is widely attested in the Greco-Roman world.[58] At the entrances to Greek temples there were vessels containing water (περιππαντήρια, or "sprinkling basins"). Prior to entering, the worshiper would dip his hand into the vessel and sprinkle himself with water.[59] Since only the pure could be admitted to the sanctuary, everyone was required to make use of the water basin in order to achieve a state of purity necessary for approaching the gods. This all-purpose purification rite ensured that no one would defile the temple with *miasma*, a pollution that came from natural sources such as sexual intercourse, birth, and death as well as from guilt or sin.

Whether Jews washed their hands or sprinkled themselves with water, it is probable that the water facilities located at the entrance to the Diaspora synagogue were intended for the use of all who entered. Like their Greek neighbors, Jews in

---

57. The notion that ritual ablutions were associated with synagogues in the Diaspora may be substantiated by epigraphic evidence. A papyrus from Egypt, dated to 113 B.C.E., records the expenses incurred to supply two synagogues with water. The sums of money reflect the usage of considerable quantities of water, which may have been used for both ritual and non-ritual activities. See *CPJ* 2, no. 432; cf. Rutgers, "Diaspora Synagogues," 74–75.

58. Walter Burkert, *Greek Religion* (trans. J. Raffan; Cambridge: Harvard University Press, 1985), 75–84.

59. Roman sanctuaries also provided basins for ritual ablutions. When the worshiper entered the shrine, he would wash his hands in the basin and pray facing the image (John E. Stambaugh, "The Functions of Roman Temples," *ANRW* 16.1:579).

the Diaspora would have purified themselves prior to entering the buildings in which they worshiped. In so doing, they would not have necessarily differentiated between the categories of ritual and moral impurity. Rather, it is likely that within the larger cultural context in which Jews of the Diaspora lived such distinctions became blurred.

Purity, Holiness, and the Synagogue

At the turn of the Common Era, as we have seen, the relationship between purity and the synagogue varied with geographic location and cultural context. These regional variances in practice are significant to the discussion of the synagogue as a sacred realm. In the Diaspora, there was a close association between purity and the synagogue. Living among other peoples, Jews made every attempt to isolate their synagogues from the pollution caused by idolatry and other egregious sins. In addition, they adopted the practice of performing ritual ablutions involving hand-washing or sprinkling prior to entering the synagogue. This concern with impurity indicates that Jews living in the Diaspora at the turn of the Common Era probably regarded the synagogue building as sacred.

The terminology used to refer to synagogues in the Diaspora attests to the apparent sanctity of the institution. The most common term, προσευχή (*proseuche*), is used in inscriptions from Egypt dated as early as the third century B.C.E. to refer to Jewish institutions that had "temple-status," as indicated by their honorific dedications to rulers and the right of asylum.[60] The reference to a προσευχή is also used in conjunction with other terms to denote a sacred precinct.[61] Additionally, a second-century papyrus describes a plot of land associated with a προσευχή in Arsinoe-Crocodilopolis as a sacred grove.[62] All of these usages seem to imply the synagogue building was regarded as sacred from an early period.

The textual evidence indicates that in the first century C.E. the Diaspora synagogue was still considered to be a sacred edifice. Philo, for example, almost always uses the term προσευχή to refer to the synagogue and employs terms such as τέμενος, ἱερός, and ἱεροί περίβολοι to indicate the sanctity of the institution (for example, *Legat.* 137; *Flacc.* 48; *Spec.* 3.171). Similarly, Josephus uses the term ἱερόν in reference to a synagogue on at least five occasions. Most interesting is his description of the synagogue in Antioch, to which the successors of Antiochus IV restored the votive offerings previously plundered from the Jerusalem temple (*B.J.* 7.44-45). What is significant here is that the synagogue was considered a suitable place to house these brass ornaments and gifts. Clearly, Josephus's use of the term τὸ ἱερόν indicates that the Antiochian synagogue was regarded as a consecrated edifice.[63]

---

60. William Horbury and David Noy, eds., *Jewish Inscriptions of Graeco-Roman Egypt* (*JIGRE*) (Cambridge: Cambridge University Press, 1992), nos. 22, 24, 25, 27, 28, 125.

61. *JIGRE*, nos. 9, 129. For a full discussion on epigraphical and papyrological evidence in relation to the Egyptian synagogue, see Levine, *The Ancient Synagogue*, 75-84.

62. *CPJ* 1, no. 134.

63. Binder, *Into the Temple Courts*, 123.

The sanctity of the Diaspora synagogue is derived from its liturgical and spatial aspects. In this respect, the synagogue is similar to the Greco-Roman temple and the association building. For our purposes, it is noteworthy that all three types of buildings are places in which worship takes place, and all have water basins located at their entrances. The significance of these water facilities is explained by the Greek scholar Pollux (second century C.E.): "The area inside of the περιπραντήρια is possessed by the gods, sacred, consecrated, and inviolable while that outside is open to ordinary use."[64] In the Greco-Roman world, access to sacred space required purification. Just as the Gentile approaching the shrine of a deity was required to sprinkle him- or herself with water, so too did the Jew entering the Diaspora synagogue perform ritual ablutions.

This direct correlation between ritual ablutions and entrance to the synagogue has no parallel in the land of Israel. The proximity of the *mikveh* to the synagogue cannot be taken as conclusive evidence that the synagogue was considered sacred, since Jews probably maintained a certain level of ritual purity regardless of their intention to participate in communal gatherings. One possible exception may be found at Qumran, where there are *mikvaot* in proximity to locus 77, the room most likely to have been used as a synagogue. Yet even here it is difficult to determine the extent to which purity practices were specifically related to worship. Finally, we must consider that water basins associated with the synagogue were not located at the entrance to the building, but inside the assembly hall. Thus these basins could not have been used for purification purposes prior to entering the building.

If material remains are inconclusive, there is some literary evidence to support this claim to holiness. In Philo's detailed account of the Essene community, it is in the sacred spots that they called synagogues that the Essenes gathered on the Sabbath for the reading and expounding of the Torah (*Prob.* 81–82). It could be argued that Philo is evaluating the Essene synagogues on the basis of his experience with Egyptian synagogues, imposing the holiness from one context on the other. Philo's use of terminology, however, suggests that he is differentiating between the προσευχή of Egypt and the συναγωγή of this community. Additionally, his extensive description of the Essenes points to the likelihood that he had genuine knowledge of the sanctity of the Essene synagogues.

Philo's reference to the holiness of the Essene synagogues is also supported by evidence from the Qumran literature. Liturgical texts, such as the *Songs of the Sabbath Sacrifice*, 4QBerakhot, and 4QDaily Prayers, indicate that the worshipers regarded themselves as a sacred assembly and that the angels were envisioned as joining with the community in prayer.[65] This evidence is local-specific, however, and relates to a non-public synagogue.

While there is uncertainty pertaining to the sanctity of the early synagogue,

---

64. Pollux 1.8 as cited by Robert A. Wild, *Water in the Cultic Worship of Isis and Sarapis* (Leiden: Brill, 1981), 130.

65. For a discussion of the communion of angels, see, for example, Carol Newsom, *Songs of the Sabbath Sacrifice: A Critical Edition* (HSS 27; Atlanta: Scholars Press, 1985) 17–19; Esther Chazon, "Prayers from Qumran and Their Historical Implications," *DSD* 1 (1994): 265–84; idem, "The Function of the Qumran Prayer Texts: An Analysis of the Daily Prayers

it is generally assumed that by late antiquity Jews living in the land of Israel regarded their synagogues as sacred. According to Steven Fine, after the destruction of the Jerusalem temple in 70 C.E. the importance of the synagogue was expressed "through an ever-increasing attribution of sanctity."[66] In his view, one of the sources of this holiness was the Torah scrolls. Fine is undoubtedly correct in suggesting that the sanctity of the synagogue was at least partially derived from the presence of the Torah. What is problematic, however, is his insistence that the transfer of this holiness is triggered by a single historical event, even one as traumatic as the destruction of the temple.

More fruitful, in my view, is evidence concerning the relationship between the Torah and the synagogue. Scholars agree that the public reading and studying of the Torah was the central liturgical function of the synagogue from its origins.[67] At some point during the liturgical development of the synagogue the Torah became more than sacred scripture, and the scrolls themselves were perceived to be sacred objects in their own right. Evidence for the beginning of the ritualization of the Torah scroll can be traced to the Persian period, when the Torah reading took place at the city gate. This rite, described in Neh 8:1-12, was characterized by a distinct reverence for the Torah. As the Torah scroll was opened in the sight of the people, they changed their posture to a standing position (v. 5). The priest then offered a blessing, to which the people responded in agreement with uplifted hands. Finally, the people prostrated themselves, praying before the Lord (v. 6). Only after the completion of these rituals was the Torah scroll read (vv. 7-8).

The rituals that preceded the reading of Torah served to ritualize the scroll itself by lending sanctity to the very act of unfurling it. Eventually, it was no longer just the text that was considered holy, but also the physical scrolls that contained the scripture. The Jews came to perceive the Torah scrolls as sacred ritual objects in much the same way as Gentiles viewed their idols.[68] By the late Second Temple period, these scrolls were protected by laws governing ritual purity. This attribution of holiness to the scrolls is substantiated by the presence of water basins inside synagogues in the land of Israel. As previously indicated, these basins were likely associated with the handling of the Torah scrolls by the leader of the assembly. This evidence strongly suggests that it is the growing sanctity of the Torah scroll and not the destruction of the temple in 70 C.E. that caused the sacralization of the synagogue.

Within the context of a worldview in which space was divided into categories of sacred and profane, the sanctity of the synagogue would not have had the sa-

---

(4Q503)," in *The Dead Sea Scrolls Fifty Years after Their Discovery* (ed. L. H. Schiffman, E. Tov, and J. C. VanderKam; Jerusalem: Israel Exploration Society, 2000), 217-25.

66. Fine, "From Meeting House to Sacred Realm," 24.

67. See Lee I. Levine, "The Nature and Origin of the Palestinian Synagogue Reconsidered," *JBL* 115, no. 3 (1996): 425-48. For a discussion on the public reading of the Torah during the Persian Period, see Runesson, *Origins*, 278-99; James W. Watts, ed., *Persia and Torah: The Theory of Imperial Authorization of the Pentateuch* (Atlanta: Society of Biblical Literature, 2001).

68. See Goodman, "Sacred Scripture," 103-4.

cred status of the Holy of Holies, the perceived dwelling place of God. Yet neither would it have been regarded as entirely common, for it was within the synagogue that the sacred scripture was read and studied. It is likely that for some groups, such as Philo's Essenes and the sacred assemblies described in the Qumran literature, there was a highly developed perception of sanctity associated with the synagogue. For other groups, however, any sanctity associated with the synagogue would probably have been less palpable. As a sacred object, the Torah scroll may have been perceived as importing sanctity to either the building or the assembly that gathered together on the Sabbath to participate in sacred ritual. It is likely that Jews who gathered in sacred assembly on the Sabbath to read their holy texts perceived that they were entering a sacred realm. The nature of this sanctity may not have been permanent in the sense that it was associated with a sacred space per se. Rather, it was the holiness of the Torah that lent its sanctity to the "synagogue," not as a physical building, but as an assembly of the people. Thus, on the continuum between the common and the holy, the early synagogue in the land of Israel may have possessed an emerging sanctity.

In summary, it seems probable that the early synagogue in the Diaspora and the land of Israel was regarded, at least to some extent, as a sacred realm, but the nature of this sanctity varied according to geographic location. Jews in the Diaspora were more likely to have regarded their synagogues as being inherently sacred. That is, they may have perceived a permanent holiness associated with both the liturgical and spatial aspects of the synagogue. In the land of Israel, however, the idea of the sanctity of the early synagogue was not as highly developed and may have been a temporary quality associated with the performance of Torah rituals. Finally, it is apparent that in both the Diaspora and the land of Israel the sanctity of the synagogue developed under the influence of a variety of social and cultural factors. Its holiness must therefore be considered independently of historical events such as the destruction of the Jerusalem temple.

Conclusion

In his book *Judaism: Practice and Belief*, Sanders convincingly establishes that there was a generalized concern with purity issues among Jews during the period under consideration. At the same time, he distinguishes between the purity practices of Jews living in the land of Israel and those who resided in the Diaspora. Our analysis takes this distinction one step further by considering the purity practices associated with the synagogue. As has been shown, the local-specific evidence pointing to the association of *mikvaot* with synagogues appears to be spatial rather than functional. While it is likely that Jews in the land of Israel immersed themselves in order to maintain a level of ritual purity on a regular basis, it is doubtful that they routinely purified themselves for the specific purpose of entering the synagogue. In contrast, Jews living in the Diaspora seemed to have been much more concerned with both ritual and moral impurity as it pertained to the synagogue. They likely performed ritual ablutions prior to entering the synagogue, utilizing water basins for the hand-washing or sprinkling that removed ritual and moral impurity. Moreover, it would appear that they took care to locate their synagogues on "pure" land untainted by the moral pollution of Gentile idolatry and sin.

Within the context of common Judaism, Sanders also considers the function of the synagogue in first-century Judaism. He contends, as do other scholars, that the synagogue was important to Jewish life and worship throughout Israel and the Diaspora. Most significantly, it was the place where Jews assembled on the Sabbath to hear the reading of the Torah and the exposition of the Law. Sanders does not, however, address the issue of the sanctity of the synagogue during this period. The investigation of this question has offered some insight into perceptions of the holiness of the synagogue in both the Diaspora and the land of Israel. It has shown that the terminology used to describe synagogues in the Diaspora often alluded to their sacred status. In addition, the Diaspora synagogue had architectural features similar to other structures, such as the Greco-Roman temple and the association building. In the latter two cases, access to sacred space required purification. Since similar purity practices were also connected to the synagogue, it is quite probable that Jews in the Diaspora considered their synagogues to be holy from both a spatial and liturgical perspective.

Within the land of Israel the situation was much more diverse. There is evidence to suggest that the synagogues of the Essenes were regarded as sacred in both their spatial and ritual aspects. For the most part, however, the synagogue sanctity in the land of Israel was not inherent but derived from the Torah scrolls that were read and stored within its confines. On a local level, the presence of water basins inside the synagogue supports this position. While we cannot determine the extent to which the synagogue would have been considered sacred in the first century, we can speculate that there was an impermanent sanctity associated with the liturgical function of the institution.

These observations remind us not to lose sight of the local context in our attempt to demonstrate the existence of a "common Judaism" and encourage us to see the synagogue as a locus that will allow us to elucidate both similarities and differences within and between Jewish practice in the Diaspora and in the land of Israel.

9

GOING UP TO JERUSALEM:
PURITY, PILGRIMAGE, AND THE HISTORICAL JESUS

It has become common in recent years to divide the modern "quest" for the historical Jesus into three stages: (1) the first quest, initiated in the eighteenth century by Reimarus, in which Jesus was represented as a teacher of eternal ethics whose message conformed with the liberal and rational ideals of contemporary Europe;[1] (2) the Post-Bultmannian "new quest" of the mid-twentieth century with its focus on reconstructing the authentic sayings of Jesus using various criteria;[2] and (3) the current "third" phase that is characterized primarily by its placement of Jesus in his Jewish context.[3] This latter approach paves the way for interdisciplinary studies

---

1. The first quest could be characterized as a backlash against (Catholic) church authority during the Enlightenment. Its proponents were mostly Protestant Christians, including Hermann Samuel Reimarus, David Fredrich Strauss, Albrecht Ritschl, Johannes Weiss, and Albert Schweitzer. This phase of the historical Jesus debate ended in the first half of the twentieth century when Rudolf Bultmann argued that historical research on Jesus was theologically insignificant. For a convenient anthology of the first quest, see Gregory W. Dawes, ed., *The Historical Jesus Quest: Landmarks in the Search for the Jesus of History* (Louisville: Westminster John Knox, 1999).

2. It was Rudolf Bultmann's student Ernst Käsemann who reopened the question in 1953 with a speech delivered to former theological students in Marburg. He insisted that scholars should look for "the distinctive elements in the earthly Jesus" and proceeded to outline the principle that would become known as the criterion of dissimilarity. This second phase of the historical Jesus debate ended gradually as the direction of research began to change course, sometime in the 1970s or 1980s. See Ernst Käsemann, "The Problem of the Historical Jesus," in *Essays on New Testament Themes* (trans. W. J. Montague; SBT 41; London: SCM Press, 1964), 15–47; repr. in Dawes, *The Historical Jesus Quest*, 279–313. On the criterion of authenticity, see Donald L. Denton, *Historiography and Hermeneutics in Jesus Studies: An Examination of the Work of John Dominic Crossan and Ben F. Meyer* (London: T & T Clark, 2004), 193–209; John P. Meier, *A Marginal Jew: Rethinking the Historical Jesus* (3 vols.; New York: Doubleday, 1991), 1:167–95.

3. Depending on the approach, the Jewish Jesus has been portrayed in a variety of roles, including that of wisdom sage (e.g., John Dominic Crossan, Robert Funk, Burton Mack), savior (e.g., N. T. Wright), social prophet (e.g., Richard Horsley, Gerd Theissen, Marcus Borg), and eschatological prophet (e.g., E. P. Sanders, John P. Meier, Paula Fredriksen). Telford identifies four major trends in the study of Jesus during the 1980s and the early years of the following decade: (1) the tendency to ask broader questions, (2) the attempt to set Jesus within the wider context of the Jewish and Hellenistic world, (3) the emphasis on the

in which historical Jesus research can be conducted within the larger framework of Second Temple Jewish studies.

It is extremely difficult to construct the life of the historical Jesus with any accuracy. It is likely, however, that Jesus, like other Galilean Jews, maintained some level of observance of the laws of Israel.[4] The Gospels ascribe to Jesus considerable concern with regard to the law. In Q 11:42 (Matt 23:23 || Luke 11:42),[5] for example, Jesus is portrayed as criticizing the Pharisees for tithing mint, dill, and cumin, but neglecting the weightier matters of the law. It is not suggested that the Pharisees should have dispensed with the "lighter" laws in order to devote more attention to those laws that were presumed to be more important, but, rather, that they should have attended to all legal obligations. The underlying assumption is that observance of the law is not negotiable.[6] Similarly, Luke indicates that the women at Jesus' tomb observed the Sabbath, resting "according to the commandment" (Luke 23:56). Acts assumes that the temple cult was valid for apostolic Jews

---

Jewishness of Jesus, and (4) the adoption of a sociological perspective. Drawing attention to the lack of uniformity of methodologies and the diversity in the results, he also questions whether the scholarly activity that began in the 1980s should be regarded as a third quest. In his view, the recent developments in historical Jesus research might be viewed as being broadly in continuity with the New Quest. See William R. Telford, "Major Trends and Interpretive Issues in the Study of Jesus," in *Studying the Historical Jesus: Evaluations of Current Research* (ed. B. Chilton and C. A. Evans; Leiden: Brill, 1997), 33–74; cf. James Carleton Paget, "Quests for the Historical Jesus," in T*he Cambridge Companion to Jesus* (ed. M. Bockmuehl; Cambridge: Cambridge University Press, 2001), 138–55.

4. On Jesus and the law, see, for example,William R. G. Loader, *Jesus' Attitude towards the Law: A Study of the Gospels* (WUNT 97; Tübingen: Mohr Siebeck, 1997); James D. G. Dunn, *Jesus, Paul, and the Law: Studies in Mark and Galatians* (Louisville: Westminster John Knox, 1990); Robert Banks, *Jesus and the Law in the Synoptic Tradition* (Cambridge: Cambridge University Press, 1975).

5. I follow the reconstruction of Q in James M. Robinson, Paul Hoffmann, and John S. Kloppenborg, eds., *The Critical Edition of Q: Synopsis Including the Gospels of Matthew and Luke, Mark, and Thomas with English, German, and French Translations of Q and Thomas* (Minneapolis: Fortress, 2000). My position on the synoptic problem is that I accept the two-source theory, recognizing Markan priority and Q as an explanation for the double tradition. There is some scholarly discussion on whether the special material of Matthew reflects a single source, but for the purposes of this paper this issue is of little consequence. On the likelihood of M as a single source for Matthew, see Robert E. Van Voorst, *Jesus Outside the New Testament: An Introduction to the Ancient Evidence* (Grand Rapids: Eerdmans, 2000), 143–48.

6. Regarding the Jesus movement as it developed after Jesus' death, Saldarini insists that the Matthean community operated well within the framework of first-century Judaism, and that the Matthean Jesus and his disciples were fully observant of the Jewish law. See Anthony J. Saldarini, *Matthew's Christian Jewish Community* (Chicago: University of Chicago Press, 1994), 124–64: cf. Alan Segal, "Matthew's Jewish Voice," in *Social History of the Matthean Community: Cross-Disciplinary Approaches* (ed. David Balch; Minneapolis: Fortress, 1991), 3–37. In a similar vein, Loader contends that there is underlying assumption in both Luke and Acts that Jesus, those who surround him, and those who later follow him are faithful to Torah (Loader, *Jesus' Attitude*, 379–82).

(e.g., Acts 3:1-10).[7] These latter two examples point to a continuity between the practices ascribed to Jesus and those attributed to the movement that continued to develop after his death.

If there is reason to believe that Jesus may have observed Jewish law to some extent, would this observance have extended to the purity laws? In recent years, several studies have considered this question but without reaching a consensus. Paula Fredriksen argues that Jesus was "truly a Jew of his own time"; he observed the purity laws and, indeed, took them for granted "as fundamental to the worship of God."[8] Roger P. Booth, by contrast, interprets Mark 7:15 as evidence that Jesus believed that "there is nothing outside a person that by going in can defile, but the things that come out are what defile."[9] Booth's analysis of this logion leads him to the conclusion that Jesus viewed the moral impurity caused by sin as a much more serious condition than ritual impurity.[10] Thomas Kazen suggests that Jesus was part of a moral trajectory that placed relative importance on social justice and morality and did not allow the purity law to take precedence over issues of table fellowship and community.[11] Kazen contends that Jesus remained within the framework of the purity paradigm even as he disregarded impurity in a way that the Jewish religious establishment may have perceived as a threat.

For the most part, the debate over Jesus' attitude toward impurity has not focused on the purity laws as they pertain to the festivals.[12] According to the Gospel accounts, Jesus' travels to Jerusalem coincided with the Jewish festivals, when Jewish men were required to make pilgrimage to the temple. Whereas the Synoptic Gospels mention only one journey to Jerusalem prior to Passover (Mark 11:1-11 [Matt 21:1-11 || Luke 19:28-40]), the Gospel of John indicates that Jesus made four such pilgrimages: twice at Passover (John 2:13; 11:55), once for the celebra-

---

7. Mark Nanos and Anders Runesson recently coined the term "apostolic Judaism" to designate Christ-belief within the context of first-century Judaism. Anders Runesson, "Rethinking the Parting(s) of the Ways" (paper presented at the Annual Meeting of the Society of Biblical Literature, Philadelphia, November 19, 2005).

8. Paula Fredriksen, *Jesus of Nazareth, King of the Jews* (New York: Random House, 1999), 203; cf. idem, "Did Jesus Oppose the Purity Laws?" *Bible Review* 11, no. 3 (1995): 20-25, 42-47.

9. Roger P. Booth, *Jesus and the Laws of Purity: Tradition History and Legal History in Mark 7* (JSNTSup 13; Sheffield: JSOT Press, 1986), 219.

10. Klawans distinguishes between two types of impurity: ritual defilement, a contagion that temporarily excludes the individual from participating in temple rituals, and the more permanent moral defilement caused by sin, a form of impurity that is not related to temple worship. See Jonathan Klawans, *Impurity and Sin in Ancient Judaism* (New York: Oxford University Press, 2000), 22-38, and part I of the present volume.

11. Thomas Kazen, *Jesus and Purity Halakhah: Was Jesus Indifferent to Impurity?* (ConBNT 38; Stockholm: Almqvist & Wiksell, 2002), 347; cf. James D. G. Dunn, "Jesus and Purity: An Ongoing Debate," *NTS* 48 (2002): 465. [Editor's note: See also Susan Haber's review of Kazen in the *Bryn Mawr Classical Review* (March 28, 2006). Online: http://ccat.sas.upenn.edu/bmcr/2006/2006-03-28.html.]

12. See, however, Fredriksen, *Jesus of Nazareth*, 205-7; cf. Kazen, *Jesus and Purity Halakhah*, 249-50.

tion of an unspecified feast (5:1), and once for Tabernacles (7:10).[13] While the historicity of these specific references cannot be substantiated, they do suggest that the author(s) and readers/hearers of the Fourth Gospel believed that Jesus made pilgrimage to Jerusalem as prescribed by the Torah.

If we consider the testimony of the Gospels with respect to Jesus' travels to Jerusalem within the socio-historical context of the late Second Temple period, we can be reasonably certain of two things. First, Jesus probably made pilgrimage to the temple in Jerusalem on at least some of the festivals. Second, Jews entering the temple on the festivals or on any other occasion were required to be ritually pure.[14] Between these two poles of certainty, however, there is a question that remains unanswered by the texts: When Jesus made pilgrimage to the temple, did he purify himself prior to entering?

The present study attempts to shed light on the practices of Jesus with respect to purity and pilgrimage by using textual and archaeological evidence to reconstruct pilgrimage patterns and purification rituals in the late Second Temple period. The intent is to cast as wide a net as possible, relying on a variety of textual sources including the Hebrew Bible, Pseudepigrapha, New Testament, Philo, Josephus, and the Tannaitic traditions. In considering direct evidence about Jesus, I reject the minimalist approach advocated by those who would adopt the criterion of dissimilarity to determine the authentic traditions. Rather, I follow Gerd Theissen in employing the criterion of historical plausibility to demonstrate a positive connection between the Jesus traditions and the Jewish milieu of first-century Galilee and Judea.[15] Essential to the task of placing Jesus in his Jewish context is the interpretation of literary sources in conjunction with an evaluation of material remains.[16] The identification of Jewish ethnic markers such as stone vessels and *mikvaot* is not only essential to establishing a Jewish context in the regions under consideration, it also constitutes indisputable evidence for the observance of purity prac-

---

13. [Editor's note: According to the Fourth Gospel, Jesus remained in Jerusalem from the autumn feast until the winter celebration of the Feast of Dedication (John 10:22), which commemorates the Maccabees' purification of the temple. This extrabiblical feast is not to be confused with the three biblical festivals for which Jewish men were required to make pilgrimage to the temple (Deut 16:16). Note, however, that he did not go up for the intermediate Passover festival (John 6:1-4) but remained in Galilee, where many other Galileans are said to have joined him for a supper of loaves and fishes. For discussion of the literary and theological reasons for Jesus' Galilean Passover, see Adele Reinhartz, "The Gospel of John: Jews and Judaism," in *The Cambridge Dictionary of Christianity* (Cambridge: Cambridge University Press), forthcoming.]

14. According to Levitical law, those who are in a state of ritual impurity are prohibited from entering the sancta or coming in direct contact with holy foods (Lev 7:20-21; 15:31; 22:3-7).

15. Gerd Theissen and Annette Merz, *The Historical Jesus: A Comprehensive Guide* (trans. J. Bowden; London: SCM Press, 1998), 115-18.

16. Cf. Freyne, who adopts the criterion of historical plausibility to determine Jesus' social context while simultaneously using archaeological evidence to reconstruct first-century Galilee (Sean Freyne, *Jesus, a Jewish Galilean: A New Reading of the Jesus-Story* [London: T & T Clark, 2004], 1-23).

tices in specific locations.¹⁷ Also pertinent are geographic surveys and remains of ancient highways, which provide clues to various aspects of ancient pilgrimage, including travel routes, length of journeys, and road conditions. The synthesis of this material evidence with information gleaned from the textual sources will provide a contextual framework for a discussion of Jesus, the Jewish pilgrim.¹⁸

Jewish Pilgrimage in the First Century C.E.

The origin of Jewish pilgrimage can be traced to the biblical injunction found in the book of Deuteronomy: "Three times a year all your males shall appear before the Lord your God in the place that He will choose" (Deut 16:16).¹⁹ The Israelite male was thus required to bring a sacrifice on the three specified feasts of Passover, Pentecost, and Tabernacles. The purpose of these festivals was to commemorate the exodus and to express gratitude for the harvest.²⁰ In this sense, the pilgrimage was very much a communal experience, one that enhanced group identity and affirmed the relationship between Israel and her God.

Although there is no record of when pilgrimages to Jerusalem began, it is evident that the practice increased significantly in the Second Temple period.²¹ By the first century, there were a large number of pilgrims arriving in Jerusalem on the festivals, especially the festival of Passover, which was considered the most important.²² Josephus estimates that on one Passover the pilgrims numbered 2.7 million (*B.J.* 6.425) and on another no less than three million (*B.J.* 2.280). One rabbinic source calculates the number to be as high as twelve million (*t. Pesahim* 4:15). Scholars have recognized that these numbers are inflated and have used various methods to calculate more realistic figures. Joachim Jeremias, for example, bases

---

17. Reed identifies four archaeological indicators of Jewish religious identity: (1) stone vessels, (2) *mikvaot*, (3) secondary burial with ossuaries in loculi tombs, and (4) bone profiles that lack pork. See Jonathan L. Reed, *Archaeology and the Galilean Jesus: A Re-examination of the Evidence* (Harrisburg, PA: Trinity Press International, 2000), 42–49.

18. Here I follow the example of Crossan and Reed, who do not prioritize one kind of evidence over the other, but insist upon an integration of textual sources and material remains. See John Dominic Crossan and Jonathan L. Reed, *Excavating Jesus: Beneath the Stones, behind the Texts* (rev. ed.; San Francisco: HarperCollins, 2001), xvii–xxi.

19. This law, dated to the seventh century B.C.E., is part of the deuteronomistic reform that marks Israel's transition from a tribal confederation to a centralized monarchy. On the dating of this reform, see, for example, Moshe Weinfeld, *Deuteronomy 1–11* (AB 5; New York: Doubleday, 1991), 69–74.

20. Jeffrey H. Tigay, *The JPS Torah Commentary: Deuteronomy* (Philadelphia: JPS, 1996), 152.

21. F. E. Peters, "The Holy Places," in *City of the Great King: Jerusalem from David to the Present* (ed. Nitza Rosovsky; Cambridge: Harvard University Press, 1996), 41 n. 8; cf. Hunt Janin, *Four Paths to Jerusalem: Jewish, Christian, Muslim, and Secular Pilgrimages, 1000 BCE to 2001 CE* (Jefferson, NC: McFarland, 2002), 46.

22. For a recent discussion on the numbers of pilgrimages in Jerusalem, see Lee I. Levine, *Jerusalem: Portrait of the City in the Second Temple Period (538 B.C.E.–70 C.E.)* (Philadelphia: JPS, 2002), 250–51.

his estimate on a Mishnaic tradition that the people who brought the Passover sacrifice filled the Court of the Israelites three times over.[23] After determining the court's area, estimating its capacity, and taking into account that there were at least ten people per sacrifice, Jeremias comes up with a figure of about 125,000 people. A slightly higher number of 300,000 to 500,000 is suggested by E. P. Sanders, who uses an estimate of the Jewish population in the land of Israel as his point of departure.[24] Yet another approach is taken by Lee Levine, who begins with an estimate of the permanent population of Jerusalem and suggests that it is reasonable to suggest that this number was doubled, tripled, or perhaps quadrupled during the pilgrimage festivals.[25] He specifies a range of 125,000 to 300,000 people, which varied with the specific festival as well as with the political-religious climate at the time.

The Pilgrims

Pilgrims came to Jerusalem not only from within the land of Israel, but also from the farther reaches of the Diaspora.[26] According to Philo, "countless multitudes from countless cities come, some over land, others over sea" (*Spec.* 1.69). Luke also claims that Pentecost was a time when Jews from every nation gathered in Jerusalem, including

> Parthians and Medes and Elamites, and residents of Mesopotamia, Judea and Cappadocia, Pontus and Asia, Phrygia and Pamphylia, Egypt and the parts of Libya belonging to Cyrene, and visitors from Rome, both Jews and proselytes, Cretans and Arabians. (Acts 2:9–11)

Although only the men were required by the law to make the pilgrimage to Jerusalem, the textual evidence indicates that it was common for the whole family to make the journey. At Passover, "all the people streamed from their villages to the city and celebrated the festival in a state of purity with their wives and children" (*A.J.* 1:109). Counted among those travelers were the parents of Jesus who, according to Luke 2:41–42, "went to Jerusalem every year" at this time. Presumably, Jesus routinely accompanied them on this journey.[27]

---

23. *m. Pesahim* 5:5–7. See Joachim Jeremias, *Jerusalem in the Time of Jesus: An Investigation into Economic and Social Conditions during the New Testament Period* (London: SCM Press, 1969), 77–84.

24. E. P. Sanders, *Judaism: Practice and Belief, 63 BCE–66 CE* (London: SCM Press; Philadelphia: Trinity Press International, 1992), 125–28.

25. Levine, *Jerusalem*, 251.

26. Philo, for example, comments in passing on his pilgrimage from Alexandria to the "ancestral temple" in order to "offer up prayers and sacrifices" (*Prov.* 2.64).

27. The Greek text is somewhat ambiguous: Καὶ ὅτε ἐγένετο ἐτῶν δώδεκα, ἀναβαινόντων αὐτῶν κατὰ τὸ ἔθος τῆς ἑορτῆς. Commenting on the awkwardness of the Greek, Marshall indicates that "the story does not necessarily imply that this was Jesus' first visit to Jerusalem." See I. Howard Marshall, *The Gospel of Luke: A Commentary on the Greek Text* (Grand Rapids: Eerdmans, 1978), 126–27. The opposite view is held by Safrai, who interprets this passage as indicating that Jesus made his first pilgrimage at the age of twelve. See Shemuel Safrai, "Pilgrimage to Jerusalem at the End of the Second Temple Period," in *Studies on*

If Luke's reference to Jesus' parents' annual pilgrimage signifies their absence from Jerusalem during the other two pilgrimage periods of Tabernacles and Weeks, then it implies that the commandment to "appear before the Lord" three times a year was not being strictly observed. Laxity with regard to observance of the biblical commandment to make three pilgrimages per annum may be attested in various other sources. The book of Tobit recounts how the God-fearing Tobit, who always walked in the ways of truth and righteousness, made pilgrimage from Assyria "often" or "several times" (Tob 1:6). It does not indicate that he attended every pilgrimage feast.[28] Philo of Alexandria apparently made pilgrimage only once in his life (*Prov.* 2.64). Philo places significant emphasis on the temple and Jerusalem in his writings. Yet his explication of Deut 16:16 focuses much more on the allegorical meaning of "appearing before the Lord" than on the obligation to make pilgrimage. These observations indicate that, with regard to ritual practice, pilgrimage was not a priority for Philo and that he did not travel to the temple on a regular basis.[29]

It is likely that only a small percentage of Jews living in the land of Israel, and an even smaller percentage of Diaspora Jews, went up to Jerusalem for every pilgrimage feast.[30] This modified observance probably emerged as a response to practical issues of feasibility with respect to time, economic resources, and physical capability.[31] The

---

the Jewish Background of the New Testament (ed. O. Michel et al.; Assen, Netherlands: Van Gorcum, 1969), 18.

28. Safrai, "Pilgrimage to Jerusalem," 17–18.

29. Kerkeslager suggests that neither Philo nor the Therapeutae believed that it was absolutely necessary to make pilgrimage to the temple in Jerusalem. See Allen Kerkeslager, "Jewish Pilgrimage and Jewish Identity," in *Pilgrimage and Holy Space in Late Antique Egypt* (ed. David Frankfurter; Leiden: Brill, 1998), 107.

30. So Safrai, "Pilgrimage to Jerusalem," 19. Elsewhere, Safrai notes that our literary sources make no reference to pilgrimage from the Diaspora to Jerusalem in the period before Herod. See Shemuel Safrai, *Pilgrimage at the Time of the Second Temple Period* [in Hebrew] (Tel Aviv: Am Hassefer, 1965), 55. Goodman suggests that this silence is not accidental. He indicates that prior to Herod's time pilgrimage feasts only involved Jews from the land of Israel, and that their contemporaries from the Diaspora only began making the journey after Herod's massive expansion of the temple. Citing economic reasons, Goodman further contends that Herod probably made a concerted effort to attract these pilgrims from beyond the Land of Israel. See Martin Goodman, "The Pilgrimage Economy of Jerusalem in the Second Temple Period," in *Jerusalem: Its Sanctity and Centrality to Judaism, Christianity, and Islam* (ed. Lee. I. Levine; New York: Continuum, 1999), 69–76, esp. 71–75.

31. As Sanders (*Judaism*, 130) points out, it would have been a significant hardship for Jews living far from the temple to make frequent journeys to Jerusalem. According to his calculations, a person living one hundred miles (169 kilometers) from Jerusalem, walking at a pace of fifteen miles (twenty-four kilometers) a day, would require seven or eight days to travel to their destination. Assuming that he stayed a week in Jerusalem before embarking on the return trip, the total time commitment would be three weeks. If he attended all three festivals, he would spend nine weeks per year away from home.

commandment to make pilgrimage was thus observed by individuals according to their piety, their strength, and their means.[32]

The Journey

Prior to the festivals, there would have been thousands of pilgrims traveling on the roads to Jerusalem. It is likely that most of the travelers made the journey on foot, although there is some evidence for travel by donkey or ass.[33] In normal terrain, a traveler can cover some fifteen to twenty miles (twenty-four to thirty-two kilometers) per day on foot.[34] The pace would be somewhat slower on toilsome slopes. Since the choice of possible routes to Jerusalem was limited by the topography of the region, it is possible to reconstruct the paths that the pilgrims would have taken, using both literary and archaeological evidence.[35]

The ancient city of Jerusalem was located near the main mountain road junction, where routes from the four points of the compass meet.[36] Josephus indicates that the quickest route from Galilee to Jerusalem is a three-day journey through

---

32. Safrai indicates that the Tannaitic literature does not mention any obligation to make a temple pilgrimage three times a year. Rather, the commandment fell into the category of "a command which has no limit," that is, a positive commandment which was encouraged but not demanded. It can be risky to apply halakhic constructs from rabbinic law to ritual observances of the Second Temple period. Safrai's observations are useful, however, in offering insight into later developments in the interpretation of Deut 16:16. We can assume that sometime between the codification of the law in the seventh century B.C.E. and the closing of the Mishnah at the beginning of the third century C.E., a nonliteral interpretation of Deut 16:16 emerged. Given the textual evidence cited above, it is likely that such an interpretation was well in place by the end of the Second Temple period. See Shemuel Safrai, "Temple," in *The Jewish People in the First Century* (ed. S. Safrai and M. Stern; 2 vols.; Assen, Netherlands: Van Gorcum, 1974–76), 899–900.

33. For a brief discussion on the use of animals for pilgrimage, see Safrai, *Pilgrimage*, 113–14.

34. See Lionel Casson, *Travel in the Ancient World* (London: George Allen & Unwin, 1974), 189.

35. Fischer contends that there was an extensive road system in place during the First and Second Temple periods. It was not until the First Revolt, however, that the construction of a paved network of Roman roads began in Judea. Because of the limitations of the topography, these Roman highways were constructed on pre-existing roads leading to Jerusalem. An archaeological investigation of the regional road system around Sepphoris confirms a similar situation in Galilee. According to Strange, the second-century Legio-Sepphoris road was founded on a known but unpaved route. In addition, there was an alternate (pre-Roman) road that by-passed Sepphoris and led to villages and hamlets to the west. This latter route may very well have been part of a larger infrastructure of local roads/paths that connected one village to another. See Moshe Fischer, Benjamin Isaac, and Israel Roll, *Roman Roads in Judaea II: The Jaffa-Jerusalem Roads* (BAR International Series 628; Oxford: B.A.R., 1996), 2; James F. Strange, "First-Century Galilee from Archaeology and from the Texts," in *SBL Seminar Papers, 1994* (SBLSP 33; Chico, CA: Scholars Press, 1994), 84–85.

36. On the convergence of roads at Jerusalem, see Menashe Har-El, "Jerusalem and Judea: Roads and Fortifications," *BA* 44 (winter 1981): 8–19.

Samaria (*Vita* 269).³⁷ The distance from Xaloth, the southernmost point of Galilee (*B.J.* 3.39), to Jerusalem is approximately sixty-three miles (one hundred kilometers) measured aerially, further by ground. This would require a very brisk pace of twenty-two miles (thirty-five kilometers) or more per day.³⁸ The more popular route for pilgrims, however, was via the rift valley alongside the Jordan River.³⁹ This longer journey may have taken a week or more, since it required an initial detour to the east and then, once past Jericho, there was an arduous ascent westward through the Judean hills to Jerusalem.⁴⁰ A third route was through the foothills of Mount Ephraim, from Kefar Othnai to Antipatris and then to Jerusalem.⁴¹

Approaching from the south, pilgrims from Beersheba would have traveled to Jerusalem along a main road through the rough terrain of the Hebron Mountains. The fifty-two-mile (eighty-four-kilometer) route would have taken them through Hebron and Bethlehem. Those who traveled to Jerusalem from the west may have taken one of two major routes leading from the port city of Jaffa on the coastal plain, through the Shephelah into the Judean Mountains.⁴² The first road would have been a thirty-seven-mile (sixty-kilometer) journey through Lydda, Modi'in, the Ayyalon valley, Lower Beit Horon, Elyon, and Gibeon. This road has only one steep section, which is located between Lower and Upper Beit Horon and is a little over 1.86 miles (three kilometers) in length.⁴³ After this point, the road to Jerusa-

---

37. This route would have passed through Ginaea on the border between Galilee and Samaria (*B.J.* 2.232; *A.J.* 20.118). From there, the road would have continued south and then veered eastward through the mountain pass between Mount Ebal and Mount Gerizim to the Samarian city of Sychar (John 4:5), situated some sixty-five kilometers north of Jerusalem. Turning southward again, the mountain road twisted through the valley of Levona and continued through Gophna and Gibeah (*B.J.* 5.50–51) to Jerusalem.

38. Steve Mason, *Life of Josephus: Translation and Commentary* (vol. 9 of *Flavius Josephus: Translation and Commentary*; ed. Steve Mason; Leiden: Brill, 2001), 120.

39. It is likely that pilgrims took the longer route to avoid traveling through Samaria. Josephus relates an incident in which Jewish pilgrims from Galilee were attacked by Samaritans while travelling near Ginaea (*A.J.* 20.118). A memory of Samaritan animosity toward the Jews is also preserved in Luke. According to this tradition, Jesus was not received in a Samaritan town because "his face was set toward Jerusalem" (Luke 9:53).

40. Mason, *Life*, 120. Although the distance between the two ancient cities is only about twenty kilometers, there is a significant change in elevation from 250 meters below sea level to 750 meters above. Wilkinson reports that it took seven hours and forty-nine minutes for his group to travel on foot from Jericho to Jerusalem and estimates that it would take about six hours for the return trip (John Wilkinson, "The Way from Jerusalem to Jericho," *BA* 38 [March 1975]: 10–24, esp. 11, 24).

41. Safrai, "Temple," 901.

42. Har-El lists a total of eight roads that run from Jaffa to Jerusalem, five of which followed the Ayyalon valley. Two of these routes are identified by Fischer as being the most practical: (1) the Beit Horon road, which was used by Cestius Gallus on his march to Jerusalem in 66 and for his disastrous withdrawal (*B.J.* 2.513–555), and (2) the alternative southern road from Lydda to Jerusalem through Abu Ghosh. See Har-El, "Jerusalem," 14; Fischer, *Roman Roads*, 6–21.

43. A passage in the Babylonian Talmud attests to the difficulty of the Beit Horon ascent:

lem follows an easily negotiated plateau formation. The second route that pilgrims followed was forty-one miles (sixty-six kilometers) long and was by way of Lydda, Gezer, the Ayyalon valley, Emmaus, Mazad, Abu Ghosh, and Givat Shaul. This road crosses difficult terrain and is the most arduous of the routes between Jaffa and Jerusalem.[44] Pilgrims who arrived by ship at Caesarea Maritima would have followed the coastal road to Lydda and then turned eastward to Jerusalem on either the Beit Horon or Abu Ghosh road.

Travel along these ancient roads was both difficult and dangerous. While the terrain was not easily negotiated at the best of times, it was often more precarious during the Passover pilgrimage when roads and bridges could be damaged after the winter rains.[45] In addition, pilgrims had to guard against the perils of ancient travel, including attacks from wild animals and bandits. The concern for banditry, in particular, is addressed frequently in the ancient literature.[46] Josephus, for example, indicates that a long convoy of pilgrims from Babylonia helped to protect the delivery of the temple tax to Jerusalem from raids of the Parthians (*A.J.* 18.313). In another place, he relates the story of how Herod established Zamaris and his Babylonian settlers in Batanaea in order to protect both the local population and the pilgrims from Babylonia against the banditry from Trachonitis (*A.J.* 17.26). There is no evidence, however, that Herod took similar measures to protect pilgrims in the land of Israel.

Pilgrims on route to the temple in Jerusalem often traveled together in large groups. We might imagine that when whole cities of Jews made a festival pilgrimage, such as the city of Lydda in 66 C.E. (*B.J.* 2.515), the journey became a communal endeavor. More direct evidence comes from Josephus, who reports an incident in which a Galilean from among a large company of pilgrims is murdered on the road to Jerusalem (*B.J.* 2.233). Similarly, Luke indicates that Jesus and his parents traveled in a "caravan" or large group (ἐν τῇ συνοδίᾳ) when they made their Pass-

---

"Two camels which ascend the ma'alot [steps] of Beit Horon and meet each other; if they both ascend [at the same time], both will fall off; [but if they go up] one after another, both can ascend" (*b. Sanhedrin* 32b). According to Har-El, steps were actually hewn out of this ascent sometime during the Second Temple period ("Jerusalem," 16). For a detailed description of the Beit Horon road, see Fischer, *Roman Roads*, 70-83.

44. For a description of this route, see Fischer, *Roman Roads*, 87-98.

45. The Tosefta makes reference to the damaged roads: "On the fifteenth day of [Adar] agents of the court go out and repair the paths and roads which were ruined in the rainy season, a month before the festival [of Passover], toward the time [in which] the festival pilgrims come up, so that they should be prepared for the three festivals" (*t. Sheqalim* 1:1; cf. *m. Sheqalim* 1:1).

46. In his discussion of banditry in the Roman Empire, Blumell indicates that bandits usually engaged in theft as a part of a group, sometimes using violence against the owner of the property. Moreover, banditry was predominantly associated with rural areas, most often occurring along the roads and highways outside of city of walls. See Lincoln H. Blumell, "'Beware of the Bandits!' The Perils of Land Travel in the Roman Empire" (paper presented at the Canadian Society of Biblical Studies, London, Ontario, May 31, 2005), 5. For references to banditry in Josephus, see, for example, *Vita* 126-27; *B.J.* 2.125, 228-30; cf. *A.J.* 20.113-117.

over pilgrimage to Jerusalem (Luke 2:44). Indeed, he offers us a rare glimpse into the turmoil that must have been associated with mass travel when he relates that the parents traveled a full day's journey toward home before they realized that Jesus was not among their band of travelers.

Sustaining themselves on the road was another challenge for large groups of pilgrims. In the absence of direct evidence, travelers may have taken refuge in cities and towns along the road to Jerusalem, stocking up on provisions and making use of local facilities such as cisterns and wells to provide them with water for washing and drinking.[47] An analysis of the distribution of cities, towns, and villages in the land of Israel using "central place theory" lends support to this supposition.[48] According to Ian Hopkins, major urban centers such as Jerusalem, Jaffa, Caearea, and Scythopolis were surrounded by towns that served a smaller territory and population.[49] Within the area served by these towns, but at some distance from a city, were rural centers consisting of large villages with marketing and administrative functions. This ancient settlement pattern spaced urban and rural centers within a reasonable walking distance from one another, presumably to facilitate local marketing functions as well as other types of commerce. A prime example of this pattern may be found in the area surrounding Jaffa. Moving away from this major urban center, there is a clear sequence of urban settlements spaced at ten- to twelve-mile (sixteen- to nineteen-kilometer) intervals. Each ring of cities is a similar distance to the next, approximately half a day's journey. A similar pattern can be discerned in the area of Jerusalem. The urban centers of Jericho to the east and Bethel to the north were each half a day's journey away, while Hebron to the South and Gezer to the east were a full day's walk. Depending on what route the pilgrims were taking, they may have stopped at one of these minor urban centres, or at any one of the satellite towns along their way.

The Destination

Pilgrims began arriving in Jerusalem several days before the feast, and most remained for the full duration of the festival.[50] Many of the worshipers slept in tents on the outskirts of the city (*A.J.* 17.213–17). It is likely that they were concentrated near the three sources of water in the city: the Pool of Siloam to the south,

---

47. An early rabbinic text makes reference to the repair of cisterns and wells prior to the Passover pilgrimage (*t. Sheqalim* 1:2).

48. Central place theory conceives that "a region has a major urban centre surrounded by a hierarchy of lesser centres with a smaller population, but each ranking of settlement is seen as consisting of places of similar size and importance." See Ian W. J. Hopkins, "The City Region in Roman Palestine," *PEQ* 112 (1980): 19; Agnes Choy, "The Traveling Peasant and Urban-Rural Relations in Roman Galilee" (paper presented at the Canadian Society of Biblical Studies, London, Ontario, May 31, 2005), 11–12.

49. For a complete discussion on settlement distribution in the land of Israel in the Roman period, see Hopkins, "The City Region," 19–32.

50. On pilgrims in Jerusalem, see Goodman, "The Pilgrimage Economy," 70; Levine, *Jerusalem*, 250–53; Safrai, "Temple," 903–4.

the Pools of Bethesda to the north, and the two aqueducts to the west.[51] Other pilgrims found accommodation in hostels, inns, and homes in the city or in nearby villages (Mark 11:11 [Matt 21:17 || Luke 21:37]), for which they paid in cash or in kind.[52] Pilgrims also stayed in synagogues established to serve members of particular Diaspora communities (Acts 6:9).[53] In addition to lodgings, visitors to the city required food, drink, and other personal provisions, which they purchased in Jerusalem.[54] The numerous shops along the street also provided facilities for changing money and purchasing animals for the required sacrifices.[55]

The highlight of the pilgrimage was undoubtedly the visit to the temple.[56] The main approach to the Temple Mount was from the south, where there were two main gates.[57] The eastern Huldah Gate was used for entering the temple precincts, while the western gate, with its monumental staircase, served as an exit. According to the Mishnah, these gates were used to facilitate the circulation of pilgrims (*m. Middot* 1:3).[58] Once inside the temple precincts, pilgrims could congregate in the outer court, a huge trapezoid-shaped *temenos* (sanctified location), which was built to accommodate a large number of people.[59] On three sides of this so-called Court of the Gentiles there were porticoes, about nine meters high, and on the fourth there was an immense basilica hall. Toward the center was a raised mound upon which the temple and its sacred courts stood.[60] It was within these sacred precincts that pilgrims offered their sacrifices.

---

51. Yoram Tsafrir, "Jewish Pilgrimage in the Roman and Byzantine Periods," in *Akten des XII internationalen Kongresses für christliche Archäologie* (2 vols.; Munster, Germany: Aschendorff, 1995), 1:371. The inspiration for this suggestion comes from Josephus, who describes three camps of pilgrims who converged on Jerusalem for the festival of Shavuot (Pentecost) in 4 B.C.E. (*B.J.* 2.44).

52. One rabbinic tradition insists that it was forbidden to charge rent in the city of Jerusalem, since the houses belonged to all the tribes (*t. Ma'aser Sheni* 1:12). In lieu of money, pilgrims would make a gift of the skins from the sacrifice.

53. The Theodotus inscription describes a synagogue that had several rooms for lodgers as well as water facilities. See the discussion below.

54. Sanders indicates that, according to Deut 14:26, there was an obligation to spend "second tithe" money (the value of 10 percent of the year's crop) in Jerusalem (*Judaism*, 113, 128–29).

55. Pilgrims converted their own currencies into the half-shekel coin in order to pay the required temple tax.

56. By all accounts, the expansion of the temple during Herod's reign resulted in a structure unparalleled in size and magnificence. On the physical structure of the temple, see Levine, *Jerusalem*, 219–43.

57. There were also four gates on the west side of the temple.

58. According to Levine, evidence for the direction of the flow of traffic can be found in the monumental staircase outside the western Huldah Gate. The larger staircase was required for a large number of people who would all exit at the same time when the ceremonies came to an end (*Jerusalem*, 230 n. 53).

59 Tsafrir, "Jewish Pilgrimage," 1:372.

60. According to Josephus, the stone balustrade that surrounded these sacred precincts had signs posted in Greek and Latin, warning Gentiles not to enter the temple area (*B.J.*

The offering of individual sacrifices took place on all the festivals. Passover was the only time, however, that the pilgrims actually participated in the ritual slaughter. Groups of ten or more individuals shared in the slaughter of a paschal lamb (B.J. 6.423). As was customary, the sacrificial meal that followed was consumed in households and courtyards within the boundaries of Jerusalem.[61]

Ritual purity was an essential requirement for the performance of these rites. One could not enter the temple or participate in the sacrificial meal in a state of defilement. Pilgrims were therefore required to purify themselves prior to the festival. What were the appropriate ritual ablutions? When and how were they performed? A discussion of purity practices in the first century will shed light on these issues and provide a framework for understanding the relationship between purity and pilgrimage.

Purity Practices in the First Century c.e.

The laws pertaining to impurity find their origin in the priestly strata of the Pentateuch.

Ritual impurities include those defilements that arise from certain situations such as childbirth (Lev 12:1–8), scale disease (Lev 13:1–14:32), genital discharges (Lev 15:1–33), and death (Lev 11:1–47; Num 19:10-22). There are no prohibitions against contracting these impurities, nor are they considered sinful. They do, however, convey an impermanent contagion through contact with other individuals or objects, which may be alleviated through purificatory procedures.[62] On most occasions, purification involves waiting a prescribed period followed by ritual immersion in a natural body of water or a *mikveh*.[63] In the case of corpse impurity, the most virulent of the contagions, the purification process is more complex. According to the law, those who contract this form of impurity are rendered impure for a period of seven days, during which time a two-part purification process takes place. The afflicted are sprinkled with a combination of red heifer ashes and water

---

5.194; A.J. 15.417). This is confirmed by the discovery of at least two Greek inscriptions which preserve the warning. The first was published by C. Clermont-Ganneau, "Une stele du temple de Jérusalem," *RA*, new ser., 23 (1872): 214–34, 290–96 + Pl. X (= CIJ II 1400 + photo). A second fragmentary inscription found in 1935 was published by J. H. Iliffe, "The Thanatos Inscription from Herod's Temple: Fragment of a Second Copy," *Quarterly of the Department of Antiquities in Palestine* 6, no. 1 (1936): 1–3, plus two plates. For a description of the temple, see Levine, *Jerusalem*, 238–39.

61. Deuteronomy 16:1–8 legislates that the celebration of Passover take place in Jerusalem. Safrai indicates that it was the practice for pilgrims in this period to remain in Jerusalem to eat the sacrificial meal ("Temple," 892).

62. On the characteristics of ritual impurity, see Klawans, *Impurity and Sin*, 23–26.

63. The prescribed amount of waiting time depended on the nature of the impurity. For major impurities such as genital discharge or scale disease the duration is seven days, whereas for minor impurities, including those contracted secondarily through touching an impure individual or object, the individual is required to wait only until sunset.

on the third and seventh day. After the final sprinkling, they wash their clothes and ritually immerse in order to complete the purification process (Num 19:14–20).[64]

It is a basic tenet of the biblical purity laws that those who are in a state of ritual impurity are prohibited from approaching the sacred precincts or partaking of holy foods, such as sacrificial meat (Lev 7:20–21; 15:31; 22:3–7). In particular, the law prohibits individuals with corpse impurity from participating in the all-important paschal meal at the same time as other Israelites. Rather, they are required to make their offering a month later during the second Passover (Num 9:10–12).

The biblical legislation concerning impurity was subject to a variety of interpretations among Jews in the late Second Temple period. Underlying these diverse opinions, however, was a fundamental accord pertaining to the essential nature of the purity practices. This is confirmed by the archaeological record from first-century Galilee and Judea, which indicates the widespread use of *mikvaot* for ritual immersion, as well as the utilization of stone vessels for eating and drinking in order to prevent the transmission of impurity.

Stone Vessels

Stone vessels or Herodian stoneware are ubiquitous in Jewish sites throughout the land of Israel, including Jerusalem, the Judean hill country, the Judean Desert, Galilee, the Jordan Valley, Golan, and the coastal plain.[65] They are dated to the first century C.E. and fade out of use after the Bar Kokhba revolt of the early second century. Most of these vessels are small domestic mugs, pitchers, and bowls which were used for holding liquids and foods for daily meals. The presence of these stone vessels in domestic space is related to the observance of purity laws. According to the halakhah of rabbinic sources, these vessels are impervious to ritual impurity (*m. Kelim* 10:1).[66] The use of Herodian stoneware therefore has important

---

64. For a discussion on corpse impurity, see Jacob Milgrom, *JPS Torah Commentary: Numbers* (Philadelphia: Jewish Publication Society, 1990), 158–63, 438–47.

65. Yitzhak Magen, *The Stone Vessel Industry in the Second Temple Period: Excavations at Hizma and the Jerusalem Temple Mount* (ed. Levana Tsfania; Jerusalem: Israel Exploration Society, 2002), 148–64; idem, "Jerusalem as a Center of the Stone Vessel Industry during the Second Temple Period," in *Ancient Judaism Revealed* (ed. Hillel Geva; Jerusalem: Israel Exploration Society, 1994), 244–56; Eyal Regev "Non-Priestly Purity and Its Religious Aspects according to Historical Sources and Archaeological Findings," in *Purity and Holiness: The Heritage of Leviticus* (ed. M. J. H. M. Poorthuis and J. Schwartz; Leiden: Brill, 2000), 229–34.

66. Cf. *m. Ohalot* 5:5 *m. Parah* 5:5; *m. Yadayim* 1:2. These rabbinic texts indicate that in addition to stone vessels, cattle-dung vessels and earthen vessels were also considered to be insusceptible to ritual impurity, probably because they were made from materials originating in the earth. It is significant that the material remains pertaining to stone vessels are consistent with the rabbinic traditions pertaining to purity. This convergence of evidence implies a continuity between rabbinic Judaism and late Second Temple Judaism. Although we cannot assume that rabbinic observances were normative or that rabbinic law was authoritative across different groups, we can, in certain instances, use rabbinic texts to shed light on common Jewish practices of that earlier period. Indeed, it is likely that, in the

social and ritual implications, as it enabled both pure and impure people to share the same vessels without neglecting the observance of the purity laws.

The abundance of stone vessels throughout the land of Israel in the first century points to a heightened interest in ritual purity among Jews of this period. Recent excavations have confirmed that this concern was not limited to the priestly class but was associated with all social and economic levels of society.[67] While the use of stone vessels crossed geographic, social, and economic boundaries, it is not surprising that the center of both manufacture and consumption remained in Jerusalem, where there were increased purity demands associated with the temple.[68] A large quantity of these vessels was discovered in proximity to the Temple Mount, especially in the vicinity of Robinson's Arch, along the southern wall and on the eastern slope of the western hill. A typological analysis of these vessels indicates a significant quantity of mugs, bowls, cups, goblets, lids, jars, and stoppers—utensils that were used for eating and drinking.[69] It may not be possible to determine whether these stone vessels were used by priests, levites, or lay people. Yet, given the location and quantity of these stone vessels, we might speculate that they were left behind by the large number of pilgrims who congregated in Jerusalem for the festivals.[70]

Mikvaot

The process of purification requires immersion of the whole body in water from a natural source such as the sea, a spring, or a river. Alternatively one could use a *mikveh*—a specially designed ritual bath in which there is a direct flow of water from a natural source.[71] Remains of hundreds of *mikvaot* have been discovered throughout the land of Israel, the majority of which are dated to the Second Temple period.[72] That these ritual baths were a central component in Jewish life is

---

course of developing their *halakhah*, the rabbis acknowledged as valid many of the laws and customs that were already in existence among the majority of the population.

67. Yitzhak Magen, "Ancient Israel's Stone Age: Purity in Second Temple Time," *BAR* 24, no. 5 (1998): 46–52, esp. 48.

68. Magen, *Stone Vessel Industry*, 163.

69. A stone stopper securely fitted to the rim of a jug or jar made of pottery prevented the vessel from contracting impurity (*m. Ohalot* 5:5). For a typological analysis of stone vessels discovered near the Temple Mount, see Magen, *Stone Vessel Industry*, 63–115.

70. Along the same lines, Regev suggests that the large quantity of stone "measuring cups" discovered near the Temple Mount may have been used by pilgrims, as well as priests and levites ("Non-Priestly Purity," 231).

71. According to the Mishnah, the water of a *mikveh* cannot be "drawn water" but must come from a natural source (*m. Mikwa'ot* 2:4).

72. In his study of ancient *mikvaot*, Reich evaluates 306 installations that were excavated by the late 1980s. He dates 280 of the installations to the Second Temple period and twenty-six to a later period. See Ronny Reich, "Miqwa'ot (Jewish Ritual Immersion Baths) in Eretz-Israel in the Second Temple and the Mishna and Talmud Periods" (in Hebrew) (PhD. diss., Hebrew University, 1990), 62–81. In the years following Reich's study, David Amit has compiled data on thirty-five additional *mikvaot* in the Hebron Hills as well as sixty-four ritual baths located in other parts of the country. See Amit, "Ritual Baths [Mikva'ot] from

evidenced by their presence in every type of Jewish dwelling from urban palaces to rural farmhouses.[73] In addition, they were associated with many public facilities, including wine and oil presses, synagogues, bath-houses, and cemeteries. Regardless of whether they were intended for public or private use, these *mikvaot* all shared several common characteristics.[74] They were cut into bedrock, had steps leading to the bottom, and were plastered to prevent linkage.

Moreover, they had sufficient capacity to hold a minimum amount of forty *se'ah* of water (*m. Mikwa'ot* 1:7) and were deep enough to allow for full immersion of the body.[75]

The most common type of *mikveh* found in the hill country of Galilee and Judea were gravity-fed pools, which were filled by channels that carried rainwater, spring water, or runoff from a roof or courtyard. Less frequently, a *mikveh* was built with a secondary pool adjacent to it, called an *otsar* ("treasury").[76] At times when the water levels were low, hand-drawn water would be added to the larger pool, and a conduit between the two pools would be opened. The pure water in the smaller

---

the Second Temple Period in the Hebron Mountains" (in Hebrew) (M.A. thesis, Hebrew University, 1996). Another study conducted by Boaz Zissu resulted in the discovery of several more *mikvaot* that had mistakenly been identified as graves, cisterns, silos, or other structures. See Boaz Zissu, "Rural Settlement in the Judaean Hills and Foothills from the Late Second Temple Period to the Bar-Kokhba Revolt" (in Hebrew) (Ph.D. diss., Hebrew University, 2001).

73. I am grateful to Boaz Zissu for pointing this out to me (private communication, May 2005).

74. On the architectural characteristics of a *mikveh*, see Reich, "Miqwa'ot," 5; Ronny Reich, "The Synagogue and the Miqweh in Eretz-Israel in the Second-Temple, Mishnaic, and Talmudic Periods," in *Ancient Synagogues: Historical Analysis and Archaeological Discovery* (ed. Dan Urman and Paul V. M. Flesher; Leiden: Brill, 1995), 1:289–97; Sanders, *Judaism*, 223. There has been considerable scholarly debate on the criteria for identifying a *mikveh*. Wright, for example, challenges Reich's methodology when he suggests that similarity of form does not necessarily lead to identity of function. See Benjamin G. Wright III, "Jewish Ritual Baths—Interpreting the Digs and the Texts: Some Issues in the Social History of Second Temple Judaism," in *The Archaeology of Israel: Constructing the Past, Interpreting the Present* (ed. N. A. Silberman and D. Small; JSOTSup 237; Sheffield: Sheffield Academic Press, 1997), 204. See also the controversy over the ritual use of the baths discovered in Sepphoris in Hanan Eshel, "The Pools of Sepphoris: Ritual Baths or Bathtubs? They're Not Ritual Baths," *BAR* 26, no. 4 (2000): 42–45; Eric M. Meyers, "Yes, They Are," *BAR* 26, no. 4 (2000): 46–48; Hanan Eshel, "We Need More Data," *BAR* 26, no. 4 (2000): 49; Ronny Reich, "They Are Ritual Baths: Immerse Yourself in the Ongoing Sepphoris *Mikveh* Debate," *BAR* 28, no. 2 (2002): 50–55.

75. The minimal volume of forty *se'ah* of water is in accordance with rabbinic standards and is estimated as being in the range of 0.5–1 cubic meters (Reich, "Miqwa'ot," English abstract, 13). All *mikvaot* discovered in the land of Israel to date comply with this minimum requirement. The consistency of this evidence may indicate that, in formulating their laws, the rabbis accepted the common Jewish practice of the time.

76. This type of *mikveh* has been found at Masada, Herodium, Jericho, Sepphoris, and Jerusalem. See Reich, "Miqwa'ot," English abstract, 4; idem, "They Are Ritual Baths," 53.

pool would effectively purify the water in the larger pool upon contact.[77] This is in accordance with the rabbinic provision that any body of water which is connected to the waters of a *mikveh* has equal status with those waters (*m. Mikwaʾot* 6:1). Another type of *mikveh* consisted of a single pool built near a cistern, such as those found in Sepphoris and in private houses in Jerusalem. As long as a minimum of forty *seʾah* of pure water was maintained in the *mikveh*, drawn water from the cistern could be added.[78] The underlying premise is that the water of the *mikveh* has the power to purify. Just as it purifies people or utensils, it can also render pure the small quantities of drawn water that are added (*m. Mikwaʾot* 2:3).[79]

Mikvaot dating to the first century have been found in a variety of locations throughout Judea and Galilee, with the highest concentration being in Jerusalem. Although many *mikvaot* in Jerusalem are associated with domestic space, the vast majority have been found in the area of the Temple Mount.[80] Excavations of this important site have revealed dozens of *mikvaot* dating to the Herodian period. Most of these *mikvaot* have a single entrance on the broad side of the structure, with stairs that are divided by a low parapet in the center. Others have a double entrance as well as the partition on the stairs.[81] These double staircases facilitated the use of the ritual bath by several individuals at a time. One side of the stairs would have been used by the impure to descend into the water, while the other side was utilized for ascending the stairs after immersion. The divided staircase was thus helpful in preventing transmission of impurity through physical contact.[82]

Two *mikvaot* from the Temple Mount excavations are especially pertinent to this enquiry. First, there is the discovery of a *mikveh* under the eastern Huldah Gate. The location of the *mikveh* and its original alignment on a northwest-southeast axis suggest that it was originally associated with a Second Temple–period dwelling. The residence was destroyed during Herod's expansion of the temple. The *mikveh*, however, was left intact beneath the staircase leading to the Hulda

---

77. The use of such a conduit is described in *t. Mikwaʾot* 5:5.
78. "Every immersion-pool which contains forty *seʾah* of water is suitable for receiving further [drawn] water [if need be]" (*t. Sheqalim* 1:2).
79. So Reich, "They Are Ritual Baths," 53–54.
80. An excavation on the eastern slopes of the Upper City conducted by Meir Ben-Dov revealed a residential area in which almost every house on the slopes of the western hill had a *mikveh*, otsar, and cistern. At the time of publication he had excavated a total of forty-eight *mikvaot* of various types. This is roughly one-third of the 150 *mikvaot* discovered in Jerusalem. See Meir Ben-Dov, *In the Shadow of the Temple: The Discovery of Ancient Jerusalem* (trans. Ina Friedman; Jerusalem: Keter, 1985), 150–53; Reich, "Miqwaʾot," English abstract, 6.
81. Eilat Mazar, *The Complete Guide to the Temple Mount Excavations* (trans. D. Glick and N. Panitz-Cohen; Jerusalem: Old City Press, 2002), 61.
82. Reich identifies a "Jerusalem type" *mikveh* (also found at Qumran), which can be identified by (1) its relatively large entrance on the broad side of the structure, (2) steps that alternate with wider and narrower treads, and (3) a double entrance and/or a small partition built down the center of the stairway. See Reich, "They Are Ritual Baths," 54–55; cf. idem, "Miqwaʾot," 34–39.

Gate and may have been used later by pilgrims entering the temple.[83] Second, a large rectangular *mikveh* was found near the Ophel road in the southeastern area of the excavations. This bath is unique in its configuration both because of its size and because of the fact that it is surrounded on all four sides by steps leading down to the pool. Moreover, there are no partitions dividing the stairs. It is likely that this *mikveh* was built to serve the large number of pilgrims who visited the temple during festivals.[84]

Another related find from the Temple Mount excavations is the famous Theodotus inscription, which attests to the existence of a first-century synagogue in Jerusalem that had guest rooms and water facilities associated with it:[85]

> Theodotus, the son of Vettenos, priest and archisynagogos, son of an archisynagogos and grandson of an archisynagogos, built the assembly hall (THN ΣΥΝΑΓΩΓ[H]N) for the reading of the Law and for the teaching of the commandments, and the guest room, the chambers, and the water fittings, as an inn for those in need from foreign parts, (the synagogue) which his fathers founded with the elders and Simonides.[86]

In addition to its assembly hall, this synagogue had several rooms for lodgers as well as some sort of water facilities. It is not evident from the inscription whether these water facilities were used for ritual purposes or to meet other needs of the visitors. Given that the synagogue was founded by a priestly family, however, we might speculate that these facilities included a *mikveh* along with other facilities for drinking and washing.

The large number of *mikvaot* in Galilee and Judea point to widespread purity practices in the late Second Temple period. Within this larger context of this ritual observance, it is significant that the greatest concentration of these pools is found in Jerusalem, and especially near the Temple Mount. Presumably, these *mikvaot* were used for ritual purification prior to entering the temple. On the pilgrimage festivals, in particular, numerous facilities for purification would have been required to accommodate the thousands of people converging on Jerusalem.

We might imagine that a large number of pilgrims who were living in tents on the outskirts of the city would have made use of the dozens of "pilgrimage" *mikvaot* to the west and south of the Temple Mount, which were built with partitions on the stairs to accommodate a steady stream of people entering and exiting the pool. Others may have preferred to use the large *mikveh* at the southeast corner of the Temple Mount, with its easy access from all four sides. Not every pilgrim, however, would have made use of these public *mikvaot*. Those who had

---

83. Ronny Reich, Gideon Avni, and Tamar Winter, *The Jerusalem Archaeological Park* (Jerusalem: Israel Antiquities Authority, 1999), 37.

84. Mazar, *The Complete Guide*, 61. In addition to being used by pilgrims, this *mikveh* may have also facilitated the purification of large household objects. See Reich, *Jerusalem Archaeological Park*, 21.

85. On the dating of the Theodotus inscription to the early first century, see John S. Kloppenborg, "Dating Theodotus (*CIJ* II 1404)," *JJS* 51 (2000): 243–80.

86. As translated in ibid., 244.

found accommodation in synagogues, hostels, or inns may have used ritual bathing facilities provided by these establishments. Similarly, those who lodged with residents of Jerusalem or in nearby villages may have had access to private *mikvaot* associated with these households.

Pilgrims living in Jerusalem or the surrounding area would probably have performed their ritual ablutions in their own homes or communities prior to their departure. It is likely that even those living farther away may have stopped during their journey to immerse in a river, stream, or roadside *mikveh*. The discovery of a *mikveh* complex near Alon Shevut on the main road leading from Hebron through the Judean Hills to Jerusalem is particularly significant, especially since there is no evidence of a settlement in the vicinity.[87] The complex consists of two exceptionally large installations that are separated by a distance of ten meters. The western *mikveh*, which is the smaller of the two, has two arched openings with parallel staircases divided by a massive stone partition.[88] The larger *mikveh* to the southeast has a similar entrance. Taking into consideration the size and location of the *mikvaot*, as well as the similar typology to the ritual baths found in the immediate vicinity of the Temple Mount, one can only conclude that these are pilgrimage *mikvaot*. They were built for the purpose of purifying a large number of people quickly on their journey to Jerusalem.[89]

Several *mikvaot* of the type found near Alon Shevut have been found in the Hebron Hills, from Hebron north to Jerusalem.[90] That these ritual baths were used by pilgrims on their way to Jerusalem is substantiated by early rabbinic literature, which alludes to the maintenance of the *mikvaot* prior to the Passover festival: "On the fifteenth day [of Adar] agents of the court go forth and dig cisterns, wells and caves, and repair immersion-pools and water channels" (*t. Sheqalim* 1:2).[91] Just as roads and bridges were repaired, so too were ritual baths prepared for the use of the pilgrims (*m. Sheqalim* 1:1).

Corpse Impurity

The textual evidence indicates that the laws concerning corpse impurity were observed in the Second Temple period. According to an early rabbinic tradition, the demand for purification from corpse impurity was so great during this period that the purificatory waters were made available in twenty-four districts in the

---

87. See David Amit, "A Miqveh Complex near Alon Shevut," *'Atiqot* 38 (1999): 75–84; Yuval Peleg and David Amit, "Another Miqveh near Alon Shevut," *'Atiqot* 48 (2004): 95–98.

88. Amit attests to the uniqueness of this particular partition ("Miqveh Complex," 78).

89. Amit, "Miqveh Complex," 82–83; Peleg, "Another Miqveh," 97–98.

90. David Amit, "Ritual Baths (Miqva'ot) from the Second Temple Period in the Hebron Mountains" (in Hebrew), in *Judea and Samaria Research Studies: Proceedings of the Third Annual Meeting, 1993* (ed. Z. H. Erlich and V. Eshel; Kedumim-Ariel, Israel: College of Judea and Samaria, 1994), 157–89.

91. The cisterns and wells provided water for drinking and washing during the long journey, while the *mikvaot* were used for ritual immersion.

land of Israel (*t. Parah* 3:14).⁹² Whether these waters were used on a regular basis throughout the year cannot be corroborated.⁹³ Nevertheless, the sources indicate a particular concern for corpse impurity prior to Passover. This is substantiated by Josephus, who indicates that the pilgrims had already congregated in Jerusalem a week before Passover (*B.J.* 6.290). The most explicit testimony, however, comes from Philo, who indicates that prior to offering a sacrifice an individual must undergo a purification procedure that lasts seven days (*Spec.* 1.261). The weeklong period implies that in these cases the reference is to purification from corpse impurity (cf. Num 19:14–20).

While these sources point to the observance of the biblical rites concerning corpse impurity, there is other evidence indicating alternative practices. In the Diaspora, we have the example of Tobit, who purified himself with water immediately after burying a corpse (Tob 2:5 [codex S]). Moreover, Philo indicates that only those who wished to enter the temple were required to undergo the seven-day purification process. All others purified themselves immediately after contact with a corpse using "aspersions and ablutions" (*Spec.* 3.205). This apparent laxity in the interpretation of the law was probably a matter of practicality, since those who lived outside the land of Israel would not have had access to the appropriate waters of purification. In contrast, there is evidence for added stringencies among those living in Judea. Most interesting are the legal texts from Qumran, which add to the biblical requirements by mandating first- and third-day ablutions for anyone who has contracted corpse impurity (11QTᵃ XLIX, 17–20; cf. 4Q414):

וכול אשר בא אל הבית ירחץ במים ויכבס בגדיו ביום הראישון
וביום השלישי יזו עליהמה מי נדה וירחצו ויכבסו סלמותמה
ואת הכלים אשר בבית   וביום השביעי
יזו שנית וירחצו ויכבסו בגדיהמה וכליהמה ויטהרו לערב

> As for the people, whoever has been in the house or has entered the house shall bathe in water and shall wash his clothes on the first day. On the third day they shall sprinkle purifying water on them and shall bathe. They shall wash their garments and the utensils in the house. On the seventh day they shall sprinkle [them] a second time. They shall bathe, wash their clothes and utensils and shall be clean by the evening of [the impurity contracted] from the dead . . .⁹⁴

According to Jacob Milgrom, the required immersions on the first and third days removed successive layers of impurity, thereby providing for a gradual purification process.⁹⁵ While not permitted to enter the temple until the seven days were

---

92. So Milgrom, *Numbers*, 161.

93. It is possible that this rabbinic tradition represents an idealized version of what actually happened.

94. As translated by Esther Eshel, "4Q414 Fragment 2: Purification of a Corpse-Contaminated Person," in *Legal Texts and Legal Issues* (ed. M. Bernstein, F. García Martínez, and J. Kampen; Leiden: Brill, 1997), 8.

95. See Jacob Milgrom, "Studies in the Temple Scroll," *JBL* 97 (1978): 501–23, esp. 512–18; idem, "First Day Ablutions in Qumran," in *The Madrid Qumran Congress: Proceedings of the International Congress on the Dead Seas Scrolls, Madrid, 18–21 March 1991* (ed. J. T. Bar-

completed, the individual could still participate in other activities such as eating and drinking without causing major defilement to ordinary food.[96]

The discovery of *mikvaot* in association with first-century tombs suggests that practice of gradual removal of corpse contamination was practiced outside of Qumran as well. In Jerusalem, *mikvaot* have been found in the Tomb of Helene of Adiabene ("Tomb of the Kings") and next to several tombs on Mount Scopus.[97] Most pertinent is the "Goliath Family Tomb" in the Jericho cemetery, which also has a *mikveh* associated with it.[98] According to Rachel Hachlili, several factors point to the possibility that the Goliath family belonged to the large community of priests that resided in Jericho and served the temple in Jerusalem.[99] These include the unusual monumental tomb, the use of names that were common among priests, and the recurrent use of a single name over three consecutive generations, as was the custom among prominent families.[100] If the Goliaths were a priestly family, they most certainly would have practiced the seven-day rite for corpse purification. That they maintained a *mikveh* at their family tomb indicates that they may also have performed first-day ablutions as part of a gradual purification process.[101]

In summary, the evidence indicates that in the late Second Temple period there were several interpretations of the law pertaining to purification from corpse contamination. Some would have practiced the rites prescribed in Num 19:14-20 every time they contracted corpse contamination. Those who did not have access to the purificatory waters, however, would have only performed the prescribed rituals prior to entering the temple or partaking of the paschal meal. Finally, there was a stricter interpretation of the law that required additional ablutions but allowed for a gradual purification process in which successive layers of impurity were removed. The material and textual evidence therefore indicates that the biblical purity laws in the land of Israel were observed quite strictly during the final decades of the Second Temple period.[102]

---

rera and L. V. Montaner; 2 vols.; Leiden: Brill, 1992) 2:561-70; idem, *Leviticus 1-16* (AB 3; New York: Doubleday, 1991), 968-76; cf. Joseph M. Baumgarten, "The Purification Rituals in DJD 7," in *The Dead Sea Scrolls: Forty Years of Research* (ed. Devorah Dimant and Uriel Rappaport; Leiden: Brill, 1992), 199-209; Eshel, "4Q414 Fragment 2," 3-10.

96. Regev, "Non-Priestly Purity," 227-28.

97. Reich, "Miqwa'ot," 243-46.

98. Rachel Hachlili, *Jewish Funerary Customs, Practices, and Rites in the Second Temple Period* (Leiden: Brill, 2005), 8-9, 59-61.

99. Ibid., 295-96.

100. Hachlili positively identifies the use of the name Yeho'ezer once in the first generation, once in the second generation, and three times in the third generation (*Jewish Funerary Customs*, 294 fig. VI-40).

101. Regev contends that the presence of *mikvaot* in tomb complexes dating to the late Second Temple period indicates that Jews were immersing themselves immediately after contact with corpse impurity rather than waiting until the seventh day ("Non-Priestly Purity," 235).

102. Sanders (*Judaism*, 229) suggests that most Jews living in the land of Israel in the first century observed the biblical purity laws.

Jesus the Jewish Pilgrim

Direct evidence for Jesus' travels to Jerusalem can be placed within the context of our analyses of Jewish pilgrimage and purity practices in the first century. The Gospel of John states that there were Jews from the rural areas who went up to Jerusalem prior to Passover to purify themselves (John 11:55). We are also certain that Jesus and his followers came from a rural context.[103] If the rural population took part in pilgrimages to the temple, it is likely that Jesus did so as well. Indeed, it would be noteworthy had he not followed general custom, and the Gospels might have been expected to mention his uniqueness in this regard. As we have seen, the Synoptic traditions record that Jesus made one journey to Jerusalem prior to Passover (Mark 11:1-11 [Matt 21:1-11 || Luke 19:28-40]), and the Johannine tradition recounts at least four pilgrimages: twice for Passover (John 2:13; 11:55), once for Tabernacles (7:10), and once for an unspecified feast (5:1). While it is possible that Jesus made the pilgrimage for every feast, it is more likely that his pilgrimage practices resembled those of other Galilean Jews, who placed particular emphasis on attending the Passover feast.

Jesus on the Road to Jerusalem

The Gospels show little interest in the route Jesus may have taken to Jerusalem. They do not describe the roads upon which Jesus traveled, nor are they necessarily familiar with the geography of the land.[104] Nevertheless, there are traditions about the places Jesus visited on his way from Galilee to Jerusalem, and these can be used to reconstruct the most likely routes taken by Jesus.

In the Synoptic tradition, Jesus travels from Capernaum (Mark 9:33) to the region of Judea (Mark 10:1 [Matt 19:1 || Luke 9:51]).[105] On the road "going up to Jerusalem" (Mark 10:32-33 [Matt 20:17-18 || Luke 18:31]), Jesus passes through Jericho (Mark 10:46 [Matt 20:29 || Luke 18:35]), eventually drawing near Bethphage and Bethany at the Mount of Olives (Mark 11:1 [Matt 21:1 || Luke 19:29]). Two vital details can be discerned from this account. First, Jesus is said to have started his pilgrimage on the northwest shores of the Galilee. Second, the final leg of his journey was on the road ascending from Jericho through the Judean hills to Jerusalem. Given this information, Jesus would probably have traveled to Jerusalem via the rift valley alongside the Jordan River.

The two Passover pilgrimages depicted in John also offer a small amount of information about Jesus' travels. The first Passover pilgrimage recounted in the Gospel begins in Capernaum (2:12). Jesus then makes his way to Jerusalem (2:13), either traveling through Samaria or along the rift valley by the Jordan River. The second Passover pilgrimage begins in the wilderness near the town of Ephraim

---

103. Cf. Acts 21:26-27, which also mentions the seven days of purification prior to making a sacrificial offering.

104. Luke's interpolation of the story of the cleansing of the ten lepers is introduced with an erroneous depiction of Jesus passing between Samaria and Galilee on the way to Jerusalem (Luke 17:11).

105. Capernaum is mentioned only in the Markan tradition.

(11:54). From this location Jesus likely made his way through the foothills of Mount Ephraim, passing by Kefar Othnai to Antipatris and then to Jerusalem. Both of these itineraries are plausible. Although they did not prove the historicity of the Johannine account, they do testify to the Gospel's knowledge of the geography of Israel and travel routes between Galilee and Judea.

Prior to the festivals, the roads were undoubtedly crowded with pilgrims on their way to Jerusalem. Jesus' travelling companions on the road from Jericho to Jerusalem included "his disciples and a great multitude (ὄχλου)" (Mark 10:46 [Matt 20:29 || Luke 18:35-36]). The reference to this large crowd is informative, for it indicates that it was Jesus' followers who were traveling with him on the road to Jerusalem.[106] The Synoptic tradition thus makes it clear that the crowd, together with Jesus' disciples, constituted the pilgrimage caravan in which Jesus was traveling.[107] When the caravan finally reached its destination several days before Passover was to begin, the pilgrims celebrated their arrival as they ushered Jesus into Jerusalem (Mark 11:7-10 [Matt 21:7-9 || Luke 19:35-38]; cf. John 12: 13-19).[108]

Jesus in Jerusalem

While visiting Jerusalem, the Gospels tell us, Jesus and his disciples found lodgings in nearby Bethany (Mark 11:11 [Matt 21:17 || Luke 21:37]).[109] During the days leading up to the festival, Jesus went to Jerusalem where he taught in the temple, probably in one of the porticos surrounding the Court of the Gentiles. His audience, no doubt, consisted of other pilgrims who were in Jerusalem to celebrate Passover. On the day when the festival was about to begin, one of the disciples went into town to make arrangements for them to eat the paschal meal within the city of Jerusalem (Mark 14:12-16 [Matt 26:17-20 || Luke 22:7-14]).[110] Without

---

106. The political significance of Jesus and his followers traveling from Galilee to Roman-ruled Judea should not go unnoticed. Safrai ("Temple," 899) correctly contends that the very gathering of Jews in Jerusalem heightened the religious and national fervor, as well as the resentment against foreign rule. A feast—especially Passover, with its nationalistic overtones—would have afforded an opportune time for anyone who had a message for the people to find an audience. In this instance, Jesus took advantage of the nationalistic fervor associated with pilgrimage to declare himself as the messiah. His gathering of followers on the road to Jerusalem thus climaxes in his triumphant entrance into Jerusalem on a donkey, a staged prophetic enactment of this role.

107. Jeremias (*Jerusalem in the Time of Jesus*, 59) also cites Mark 10:46 when he suggests that Jesus traveled in a pilgrimage caravan. Contrast this pilgrimage with the one depicted in John 7. Here Jesus goes up to Jerusalem for the festival of Tabernacles "not publicly, but in private (ἐν κρυπτῷ)." The implication is that Jesus was not part of a pilgrimage caravan, but traveled alone.

108. At the core of the story of Jesus' triumphal entry into Jerusalem is the arrival of a pilgrimage caravan at their final destination. This is recognized by Fredriksen (*Jesus of Nazareth*, 206), who contends that the "pilgrims account for the celebrating crowds who usher Jesus into Jerusalem."

109. Luke refers to the Mount of Olives.

110. Tsafrir ("Jewish Pilgrimage," 370) highlights the fact that Jesus celebrated Passover eve within the city, according to the law.

giving specific details, the text clearly assumes that one of their number went to the temple to make the required Passover sacrifice.[111] In the evening Jesus and his disciples sat together around a table in the upper room of a Jerusalem householder eating the paschal meal. Again, these details are plausible, even if their historical accuracy cannot be demonstrated with certainty.

Jesus, Purity, and Pilgrimage

As demonstrated, there was a fundamental concern for issues of impurity within the socio-historical context in which Jesus lived. It is likely that the administration of the purificatory waters was a public rite requiring the ministry of a priest. Any abstention on the part of Jesus would certainly been noticed by his followers, as well as by other members of the Jewish community.[112] At the very least, his departure from the norm would have been viewed as strange; more likely, it would have been considered a sacrilege. Indeed, we would expect that a deviation from the law of this magnitude would have been reported in the Gospels.

Given the evidence, it is probable that Jesus, like his fellow pilgrims, arrived in Jerusalem several days before Passover in order to undergo the purification rites for corpse contamination. Yet if Jesus was impure during this period, how could he have been teaching in the temple? An important clue to resolving this conundrum comes from Josephus, who indicates that persons afflicted with gonorrhoea or leprosy were excluded from the city altogether; the temple was closed to women during their menstruation. Men not thoroughly clean were debarred from admission to the inner court, from which even priests were excluded when undergoing purification (*B.J.* 5.227).

While men were required to be pure according to levitical standards in order to gain access to the sacred precincts (Court of the Israelites), they could still enter the outer court (Court of the Gentiles) even if they were not thoroughly pure, provided that they were free from two major classes of impurity: genital discharge and scale disease. Seemingly, the criteria for purification were not as strict in the outer court.[113] What is curious is that Josephus makes no reference to the most serious of the impurities, corpse contamination. Logic dictates that if those afflicted

---

111. So Fredriksen, *Jesus of Nazareth*, 206.

112. This may be the situation described in the Gospel of John (John 12:1, 12). The evangelist emphasizes Jesus' arrival in Jerusalem five days before Passover, indicating that the other pilgrims had been looking for him and speculating as to whether or not he would come to the festival (John 11:55–56). Jesus' tardiness meant that he did not have time to complete the full week of purificatory rituals. This point may hint at a Johannine motif accordance to which Jesus did not need to prepare for the paschal sacrifice because he *is* the paschal sacrifice. Kazen (*Jesus and Purity*, 249 and esp. n. 219), however, offers a different perspective, suggesting that Jesus' late arrival for the seven-day purification period can be seen as part of a Johannine tendency to portray Jesus as opposing the purity laws.

113. It would have been impractical to impose stringent purity standards in the outer court of the temple, since this was an area in which economic transactions took place, assemblies were held, and judicial bodies met. On the temple and its courts, see Levine, *Jerusalem*, 243.

with other major forms of impurity were prohibited from entering the temple or even the city, then the corpse-impure would also be excluded. But that is not what Josephus states.

I would argue that Josephus offers an accurate description of the purity requirements in the temple. Those who were "thoroughly clean" (οἱ... καθάπαν ἡγνευκότες) from all impurities, including corpse contamination, were permitted to enter the inner court. This implies that individuals who were partially clean— that is, those who had performed their first-day ablutions—had access only to the outer court. Josephus's omission of any reference to corpse impurity in connection with the temple implies that he understood that immediate immersion in the *mikveh* removed a layer of impurity, enabling the afflicted to gain access to its outer court.

In positing the use of first-day ablutions at the temple, we not only gain a better understanding of our text from Josephus, we also resolve the apparent discrepancy in Jesus' purity practices. In accordance with the Synoptic traditions, Jesus arrived in Jerusalem about a week prior to Passover, presumably to undergo the purification rite for corpse contamination. After he entered the city, he probably would have immersed in one of the numerous *mikvaot* in the area of the Temple Mount, thereby initiating his gradual purification. Upon completion of this first-day ablution, Jesus would have had access to the outer court of the temple where he taught during the days leading up to the festival.

Conclusion

The historical Jesus was a Galilean Jew living in the first-century land of Israel. The Judaism of his time was characterized by its diversity in its interpretation of the laws of Israel. Yet underlying the disputes between the various factions were basic tenets of practice and belief that were agreed upon by the populace as a whole. The temple figured prominently in the lives of all Jews, even those who lived far afield. In spite of the hardship, Jewish peasants from the rural communities in Galilee made pilgrimages to the temple as often as their circumstances allowed, especially for the feast of Passover. Purity practices were also a prominent feature of Jewish existence, as evidence by the archaeological remains from the cities, towns, and villages in which there was a Jewish presence. The existence of *mikvaot* combined with the pervasive use of stone vessels indicates a substantial concern with ritual purity. It is within this socio-religious milieu that Jesus made his pilgrimages to the temple in Jerusalem to celebrate the festivals. We can trace his path from Galilee to Jerusalem, traveling with his disciples and followers in a pilgrimage caravan and taking refuge in towns and villages along the way. Arriving with the other pilgrims several days before the festival, he stayed in Bethany and spent his days teaching at the temple. As was the custom, he also arranged for a place within the city of Jerusalem where he and his disciples could partake of the paschal meal.

An essential component of the pilgrimage was the purification rites that were associated with it. Jews could not enter the temple, nor could they partake of the paschal meal unless they were in a state of ritual purity. Thus pilgrims arrived in

Jerusalem at least a week before the festival so that they could undergo the seven-day purification rites for corpse contamination. While there is no direct evidence to indicate that Jesus participated in this rite, there is significant support for this assumption. First, it is evident that Jesus made the pilgrimage with other members of the rural Galilean community and arrived well before the onset of the festival. Second, both the archaeological and textual evidence point to a direct connection between pilgrimage and purity practices at the temple. Given that Jesus counted himself among the Jewish pilgrims from rural Galilee and that he participated in all the other rites of pilgrimage, it is probable that he also participated in this rite of purification, which included ritual immersion as well as sprinkling with purificatory waters. The first-day ablutions removed a layer of his impurity, giving him access to the outer court of the temple where he taught, while his immersion on the final day completed the purification process, enabling him to enter the sacred precincts and participate in the paschal meal.

As with most historical questions pertaining to Jesus, we cannot be certain that Jesus kept the purity laws as suggested above. It is highly likely, however, that he did observe them in the same ways and to the same degree as did other Galilean Jews. The burden of proof must remain on those who would argue that Jesus departed from the common practice of his fellow Jews in the way in which he approached the most central Jewish institution of his time, the temple in Jerusalem.

Bibliography

Ancient Texts and Translations

Aland, Barbara, et al. *Greek-English New Testament: Novum Testamententum Graece in the Tradition of Eberhard Nestle and Erwin Nestle.* 8th rev. ed. Stuttgart: Deutsche Bibelgesellschaft, 1994.
Charlesworth, J. H., ed. *The Dead Sea Scrolls: Hebrew, Aramaic, and Greek texts with English Translations.* 6 vols. Louisville: Westminster John Knox, 1994.
Daily Prayer Book: Ha-Siddur Ha-Shalem. Translated by Philip Birnbaum. New York: Hebrew Publishing Company, 1949.
Epstein, Rabbi Isidore, ed. *The Soncino Talmud on CD-ROM.* Davka Corporation Version 3.0.6. 1991–2003.
García Martínez, Florentino, and Eibert J. C. Tigchelaar. *The Dead Sea Scrolls Study Edition.* 2 vols. Leiden: Brill, 1997.
Horbury, William, and David Noy, eds. *Jewish Inscriptions of Graeco-Roman Egypt.* Cambridge: Cambridge University Press, 1992.
Jewish Publication Society. *JPS Hebrew-English Tanakh: The Traditional Hebrew Text and the New JPS Translation.* First pocket ed. Philadelphia: Jewish Publication Society, 2003.
Josephus. Translated by H. St. J. Thackery et al. 10 vols. Loeb Classical Library. Cambridge: Harvard University Press, 1926–65.
Mason, Steve. *Life of Josephus: Translation and Commentary.* Vol. 9 of *Flavius Josephus: Translation and Commentary.* Edited by Steve Mason. Leiden: Brill, 2001.
Newsom, Carol. *Songs of the Sabbath Sacrifice: A Critical Edition.* Harvard Semitic Studies 27. Atlanta: Scholars Press, 1985.
Philo. Translated by F. H. Colson and G. H. Whitaker. 10 vols. Loeb Classical Library. Cambridge: Harvard University Press, 1929–62.
Robinson, James M., Paul Hoffmann, and John S. Kloppenborg, eds. *The Critical Edition of Q: Synopsis Including the Gospels of Matthew and Luke, Mark and Thomas with English, German, and French Translations of Q and Thomas.* Minneapolis: Fortress, 2000.
Tcherikover, V., A. Fuks, and M. Stern, eds. *Corpus papyrorum judaicarum.* 3 vols. Cambridge: Harvard University Press, 1957–64.
Tosefta. Translated by Jacob Neusner. 2 vols. Peabody, MA: Hendrickson, 2002.

Secondary Literature

Aaron, David H. *Biblical Ambiguities: Metaphor, Semantics, and Divine Imagery.* Leiden: Brill, 2001.
Alon, Gedalyahu. "The Bounds of the Laws of Levitical Cleanness." Pages 190–234 in *Jews, Judaism, and the Classical World: Studies in Jewish History in the Times of the Second Temple and Talmud.* Jerusalem: Magnes Press, 1977.
———. *Jews, Judaism, and the Classical World: Studies in Jewish History in the Times of the Second Temple and Talmud.* Jerusalem: Magnes Press, 1977.

Amit, David. "A Miqveh Complex near Alon Shevut." *'Atiqot* 38 (1999): 75–84.
———. "Ritual Baths (Miqva'ot) from the Second Temple Period in the Hebron Mountains." M.A. thesis, Hebrew University, 1996. In Hebrew.
———. "Ritual Baths (Miqva'ot) from the Second Temple Period in the Hebron Mountains." Pages 157–89 in *Judea and Samaria Research Studies: Proceedings of the 3rd Annual Meeting, 1993*. Edited by Z. H. Erlich and V. Eshel. Kedumim-Ariel, Israel: The College of Judea and Samaria, 1994. In Hebrew.
Anderson, Janice Capel, and Stephen Moore, eds. *Mark and Method: New Approaches in Biblical Studies*. Minneapolis: Fortress, 1992.
Archer, Léonie J. *Her Price Is beyond Rubies: The Jewish Woman in Graeco-Roman Palestine*. JSOTSup 60. Sheffield: JSOT Press, 1990.
Aschim, Anders. "Melchizedek and Jesus: 11QMelchizedek and the Epistle to the Hebrews." Pages 129–47 in *The Jewish Roots of Christological Monotheism*. Edited by Carey C. Newman et al. Leiden: Brill, 1999.
Attridge, Harold W. *The Epistle to the Hebrews*. Philadelphia: Fortress, 1989.
Baardia, T., et al. *Text and Testimony: Essays on New Testament and Apocryphal Literature in Honour of A. F. J. Klijn*. Kampen, Netherlands: J. H. Kok, 1988.
Banks, Robert. *Jesus and the Law in the Synoptic Tradition*. Cambridge: Cambridge University Press, 1975.
Bar-Ilan, Meir. *Some Jewish Women in Antiquity*. BJS 317. Atlanta: Scholars Press, 1998.
Barta, Karen A. "Paying the Price of Paternalism." Pages 24–36 in *Where Can We Find Her?* Edited by Marie-Eloise Rosenblatt. New York: Paulist Press, 1991.
Bauer, David R., and Mark Allen Powell, eds. *Treasures New and Old: Recent Contributions to Matthean Studies*. SBLSymS. Atlanta: Scholars Press, 1996.
Baumgarten, Joseph M. "The Purification Rituals in DJD 7." Pages 199–209 in *The Dead Sea Scrolls: Forty Years of Research*. Edited by Devorah Dimant and Uriel Rappaport. Leiden: Brill, 1992.
———. "Sacrifice and Worship among the Jewish Sectarians of the Dead Sea (Qumran) Scrolls." *HTR* 46, no. 3 (1953): 141–59.
———. *Studies in Qumran Law*. Leiden: Brill, 1977.
Ben-Dov, Meir. *In the Shadow of the Temple: The Discovery of Ancient Jerusalem*. Translated by Ina Friedman. Jerusalem: Keter, 1985.
Biderman, Shlomo, and Ben-Ami Scharfstein, eds. *Interpretation in Religion*. Leiden: Brill, 1992.
Bilde, Per. *Flavius Josephus between Jerusalem and Rome: His Life, His Works, and Their Importance*. JSPSup 2. Sheffield: JSOT, 1988.
Binder, Donald D. *Into the Temple Courts: The Place of the Synagogues in the Second Temple Period*. SBLDS 169. Atlanta: Society of Biblical Literature, 1999.
———. "The Origins of the Synagogue: An Evaluation." Pages 118–31 in *The Ancient Synagogue from Its Origins until 200 C.E.: Papers Presented at an International Conference at Lund University, October 14–17, 2001*. Edited by Birger Olsson and Magnus Zetterholm. ConBNT 39. Stockholm: Almqvist & Wiksell, 2003.
Black, Max. *Models and Metaphors: Studies in Language and Philosophy*. Ithaca, NY: Cornell University Press, 1962.
Blumell, Lincoln H. "'Beware of the Bandits!' The Perils of Land Travel in the Roman Empire." Paper presented at the Canadian Society of Biblical Studies, London, Ontario, May 31, 2005.
Booth, Roger P. *Jesus and the Laws of Purity: Tradition History and Legal History in Mark 7*. JSNTSup 13. Sheffield: JSOT Press, 1986.

Botterweck, G. Johannes, et al., eds. *Theological Dictionary of the Old Testament.* Translated by John T. Willis, David E. Green, and Douglas W. Stott. 15 vols. Grand Rapids: Eerdmans, 1974.
Bow, Beverly, and George W. E. Nickelsburg. "Patriarchy with a Twist: Men and Women in Tobit." Pages 127–43 in *"Women Like This": New Perspectives on Jewish Women in the Greco-Roman World.* Edited by Amy-Jill Levine. Atlanta: Scholars Press, 1991.
Brettler, M., and M. Fishbane, eds. *Minhah le-Nahum: Biblical and Other Studies Presented to Nahum M. Sarna in Honour of His Seventieth Birthday.* JSOTSup 154. Sheffield: JSOT Press, 1993.
Brooke, George J., ed. *Temple Scroll Studies.* Sheffield: JSOT Press, 1989.
Broshi, M., ed. *The Damascus Document Reconsidered.* Jerusalem: Israel Exploration Society, 1992.
Brown, F., S. R. Driver, and C. A. Briggs. *A Hebrew and English Lexicon of the Old Testament.* Oxford: Clarendon Press, 1907.
Brown, William P. *Seeing the Psalms: A Theology of Metaphor.* Louisville: Westminster John Knox, 2002.
Brownlee, William H. *The Dead Sea Manual of Discipline: Translation and Notes.* BASORSup 10–12. New Haven, CT: ASOR, 1951.
———. *The Midrash Pesher of Habakkuk.* Missoula, MT: Scholars Press, 1979.
Büchler, Adolph. *Studies in Sin and Atonement in the Rabbinic Literature of the First Century.* London: Oxford University Press, 1928. Repr., New York: Ktav, 1967.
Burkert, Walter. *Greek Religion.* Translated by J. Raffan. Cambridge: Harvard University Press, 1985.
Campbell, J. *The Use of Scripture in the Damascus Document 1–8, 19–20.* Beihefte zur Zeitschrift für die alttestamentliche Wissenshaft 228. Berlin: de Gruyter, 1995.
Carleton Paget, James. "Quests for the Historical Jesus." Pages 138–55 in *The Cambridge Companion to Jesus.* Edited by M. Bockmuehl. Cambridge: Cambridge University Press, 2001.
Casson, Lionel. *Travel in the Ancient World.* London: George Allen & Unwin, 1974.
Cavadini, John C., ed. *Miracles In Jewish and Christian Antiquity.* Notre Dame, IN: University of Notre Dame Press, 1999.
Chazon, Esther. "The Function of the Qumran Prayer Texts: An Analysis of the Daily Prayers (4Q503)." Pages 217–25 in *The Dead Sea Scrolls Fifty Years after Their Discovery.* Edited by L. H. Schiffman, E. Tov, and J. C. VanderKam. Jerusalem: Israel Exploration Society, 2000.
———. "Prayers from Qumran and their Historical Implications." *DSD* 1 (1994): 265–84.
Chester, A. N. "Hebrews: The Final Sacrifice." Pages 57–72 in *Sacrifice and Redemption.* Edited by S. W. Sykes. Cambridge: Cambridge University Press, 1991.
Choy, Agnes. "The Travelling Peasant and Urban-Rural Relations in Roman Galilee." Paper presented at the Canadian Society of Biblical Studies, London, Ontario, May 31, 2005.
Christiansen, E. J. *The Covenant in Judaism and Paul.* Leiden: Brill, 1995.
Clermont-Ganneau, C. "Une stele du temple de Jérusalem." *Revue d'Assyriologie et d'archéologie orientale nouvelle série* 23 (1872): 214–34, 290–96, and Pl. X.
Cohen, Shaye J. D. *The Jewish Family in Antiquity.* Atlanta: Scholars Press, 1993.
———. "Menstruants and the Sacred in Judaism and Christianity." Pages 273–99 in *Women's History and Ancient History.* Edited by Sarah B. Pomeroy. Chapel Hill: University of North Carolina Press, 1991.
Collins, John J., et al., eds. *Methods of Investigation of the Dead Sea Scrolls and the Khirbet Qumran Site: Present Realities and Future Prospects.* Annals of the New York Academy of Sciences 722. New York: New York Academy of Sciences, 1994.

Collins, John J., and Robert A. Kugler, eds. *Religion in the Dead Sea Scrolls*. SDSSRL. Grand Rapids: Eerdmans, 2000.

Coppens, Joseph C. "The Spiritual Temple in the Pauline Letters and its Background." Pages 53–66 in *Studia Evangelica 6: Papers Presented to the Fourth International Congress on New Testament Studies Held at Oxford*. Edited by E. A. Livingstone. Berlin: Akademie Verlag, 1973.

Corrington, Gail Paterson. "The Milk of Salvation: Redemption by the Mother in Late Antiquity and Early Christianity." *HTR* 82, no. 4 (1989): 393–420.

Coser, Lewis. *The Functions of Social Conflict*. New York: Free Press, 1956.

Cotter, Wendy. *Miracles in Greco-Roman Antiquity: A Sourcebook*. London: Routledge, 1999.

Crenshaw, James L. *Education in Ancient Israel: Across the Deadening Silence*. New York: Doubleday, 1998.

Crossan, John Dominic, and Jonathan L. Reed. *Excavating Jesus: Beneath the Stones, behind the Texts*. Rev. ed. San Francisco: HarperCollins, 2001.

D'Angelo, Mary Rose. "Gender and Power in the Gospel of Mark: The Daughter of Jairus and the Woman with the Flow of Blood." Pages 83–109 in *Miracles in Jewish and Christian Antiquity*. Edited by John C. Cavadini. Notre Dame, IN: University of Notre Dame Press, 1999.

———. *Moses in the Letter to the Hebrews*. SBLDS 42. Missoula, MT: Scholars Press, 1979.

Davies, P. R. *The Damascus Covenant: An Interpretation of the "Damascus Document."* JSOTSup 25. Sheffield: JSOT Press, 1983.

Dawes, Gregory W., ed. *The Historical Jesus Quest: Landmarks in the Search for the Jesus of History*. Louisville: Westminster John Knox, 1999.

Denton, Donald L. *Historiography and Hermeneutics in Jesus Studies: An Examination of the Work of John Dominic Crossan and Ben F. Meyer*. London: T & T Clark, 2004.

Dimant, Devorah, and Uriel Rappaport, eds. *The Dead Sea Scrolls: Forty Years of Research*. Leiden: Brill, 1992.

Doran, Robert. *Temple Propaganda: The Purpose and Character of 2 Maccabees*. CBQMS 12. Washington, DC: Catholic Biblical Association of America, 1981.

Douglas, Mary. "Critique and Commentary." Pages 137–42 in *The Idea of Purity in Ancient Judaism*, by Jacob Neusner. Leiden: Brill, 1973.

———. *In the Wilderness: The Doctrine of Defilement in the Book of Numbers*. Oxford: Oxford University Press, 1993.

———. *Purity and Danger: An Analysis of the Concepts of Pollution and Taboo*. London: Routledge & Kegan Paul, 1970. Repr., London: Routledge Classics, 2002.

Drazin, Nathan. *History of Jewish Education from 515 BCE to 220 CE*. Baltimore: John Hopkins University Press, 1940.

Dunn, James D. G. "Jesus and Purity: An Ongoing Debate." *NTS* 48 (2002): 449–67.

———. *Jesus, Paul, and the Law: Studies in Mark and Galatians*. Louisville: Westminster John Knox, 1990.

Dupont-Sommer, André. *The Essene Writings from Qumran*. Translated by G. Vermès. Cleveland: Meridian, 1957.

Edwards, Douglas R., ed. *Religion and Society in Roman Palestine: Old Questions, New Approaches*. London: Routledge, 2004.

Edwards, M. J., and Simon Swain, eds. *Portraits: Biographical Representation in the Greek and Latin Literature of the Roman Empire*. Oxford: Clarendon Press, 1997.

Eilberg-Schwartz, Howard. *The Savage in Judaism: An Anthropology of Israelite Religion and Ancient Judaism*. Bloomington: Indiana University Press: 1990.

Elbogen, Ismar. *Jewish Liturgy: A Comprehensive History*. Translated by R. P. Scheindlin. Philadelphia: Jewish Publication Society, 1993.
Eshel, Esther. "4Q414 Fragment 2: Purification of a Corpse-Contaminated Person." Pages 3–10 in *Legal Texts and Legal Issues*. Edited by M. Bernstein, F. García Martínez, and J. Kampen. Leiden: Brill, 1997.
Eshel, Hanan. "The Pools of Sepphoris: Ritual Baths or Bathtubs? They're Not Ritual Baths." *BAR* 26, no. 4 (July/August 2000): 42–45.
———. "We Need More Data." *BAR* 26, no. 4 (July/August 2000): 49.
Evans, Craig A., and Donald A. Hagner, eds. *Anti-Semitism and Early Christianity: Issues of Polemic and Faith*. Minneapolis: Fortress, 1993.
Evans, Craig A., and James A. Sanders. *Early Christian Interpretation of the Scriptures of Israel*. JSNTSup 148. Sheffield: Sheffield Academic Press, 1997.
Fardon, Richard. *Mary Douglas: An Intellectual Biography*. London: Routledge, 1999.
Fine, Steven. "From Meeting House to Sacred Realm: Holiness and the Ancient Synagogue." Pages 27–49 in *Sacred Realm: The Emergence of the Synagogue in the Ancient World*. Edited by S. Fine. New York: Oxford University Press, 1996.
———. *This Holy Place: On the Sanctity of the Synagogue during the Greco-Roman Period*. Notre Dame, IN: University of Notre Dame Press, 1997.
———, ed. *Sacred Realm: The Emergence of the Synagogue in the Ancient World*. New York: Oxford University Press, 1996.
Fischer, Moshe, Benjamin Isaac, and Israel Roll. *Roman Roads in Judaea II: The Jaffa-Jerusalem Roads*. BAR International Series 628. Oxford: B.A.R., 1996.
Flint, P. W., and J. C VanderKam, eds. *The Dead Sea Scrolls after Fifty Years*. 2 vols. Leiden: Brill, 1998–99.
Foerster, Gideon. "The Synagogues at Masada and Herodium." Pages 24–29 in *Ancient Synagogues Revealed*. Edited by Lee I. Levine. Jerusalem: Israel Exploration Society, 1981.
Fonrobert, Charlotte. "The Woman with a Blood-Flow (Mark 5.24–34) Revisited: Menstrual Laws and Jewish Culture in Christian Feminist Hermeneutics." Pages 121–40 in *Early Christian Interpretation of the Scriptures of Israel*. Edited by Craig A. Evans and James A. Sanders. JSNTSup 148. Sheffield: Sheffield Academic Press, 1997.
Fontaine, Carole. *Smooth Words: Women, Proverbs, and Performance in Biblical Wisdom*. JSOTSup 356. New York: Sheffield, 2002.
Fredriksen, Paula, "Did Jesus Oppose the Purity Laws?" *Bible Review* 11, no. 3 (1995): 20–25, 42–47.
———. *Jesus of Nazareth, King of the Jews*. New York: Random House, 1999.
Freyne, Sean. *Jesus, a Jewish Galilean: A New Reading of the Jesus-Story*. London: T & T Clark, 2004.
Friedman, Shamma. "The Holy Scriptures Defile the Hands—The Transformation of a Biblical Concept in Rabbinic Theology." Pages 117–32 in *Minhah le-Nahum: Biblical and Other Studies Presented to Nahum M. Sarna in Honour of His Seventieth Birthday*. Edited by M. Brettler and M. Fishbane. JSOTSup 154. Sheffield: JSOT Press, 1993.
Frymer-Kensky, Tikva Simone. "Pollution, Purification, and Purgation in Biblical Israel." Pages 399–410 in *The Word of the Lord Shall Go Forth: Essays in Honor of David Noel Freedman in Celebration of his Sixtieth Birthday*. Edited by C. L. Meyers and M. O'Connor. Winona Lake, IN: Eisenbrauns, 1983.
Gager, John G. "Jews, Christians, and the Dangerous Ones in Between." Pages 249–57 in *Interpretation in Religion*. Edited by Shlomo Biderman and Ben-Ami Scharfstein. Leiden: Brill, 1992.

---. *Kingdom and Community: The Social World of Early Christianity*. Englewood Cliffs, NJ: Prentice-Hall, 1975.
Garnet, P. "Atonement Constructions in the Old Testament and the Qumran Scrolls." *EvQ* 46 (1974): 131-63.
---. *Salvation and Atonement in the Qumran Scrolls*. WUNT 2. Tübingen: J. C. B. Mohr (Paul Siebeck), 1977.
García Martínez, Florentino. "Les limites de la communauté: Pureté et impureté à Qumrân et dans le Nouveau Testament." Pages 111-22 in *Text and Testimony: Essays on New Testament and Apocryphal Literature in Honour of A. F. J. Klijn*. Edited by T. Baardia et al. Kampen, Netherlands: J. H. Kok, 1988.
---. "Priestly Functions in a Community without Temple." Pages 303-19 in *Gemeinde ohne Tempel: Community without Temple*. Edited by B. Ego et al. WUNT 118. Tübingen: Mohr Siebeck, 1999.
---. "The Problem of Purity: The Qumran Solution." Pages 139-57 in *The People of the Dead Sea Scrolls: Their Writings, Beliefs, and Practices*. Edited by Florentino García Martínez and Julio Trebolle Barrera. Leiden: Brill, 1995.
García Martínez, Florentino, and Julio Trebolle Barrera, eds. *The People of the Dead Sea Scrolls: Their Writings, Beliefs, and Practices*. Leiden: Brill, 1995.
Gärtner, Bertil. *The Temple and the Community in Qumran and the New Testament*. SNTSMS 1. Cambridge: Cambridge University Press, 1965.
Gaston, L. *No Stone on Another: Studies in the Significance of the Fall of Jerusalem in the Synoptic Gospels*. NovTSup 23. Leiden: Brill, 1970.
Goldstein, Jonathan A. *I Maccabees*. AB 41. Garden City, NY: Doubleday, 1976.
---. *II Maccabees*. AB 41A. Garden City, NY: Doubleday, 1983.
---. *Semites, Iranians, Greeks, and Romans: Studies in Their Interactions*. Atlanta: Scholars Press, 1990.
Goodman, Martin. "The Pilgrimage Economy of Jerusalem in the Second Temple Period." Pages 69-76 in *Jerusalem: Its Sanctity and Centrality to Judaism, Christianity, and Islam*. Edited by Lee. I. Levine. New York: Continuum, 1999.
---. "Sacred Scripture and 'Defiling the Hands.'" *JTS* 41 (1990): 98-107.
Grenfell, B. P., A. S. Hunt, and J. G. Smyly, eds. *The Tebtunis Papyri*. 4 vols. London: Oxford University Press, 1902.
Gutman, Shmaryahu. "Gamala." Pages 459-63 in vol. 2 of *The New Encyclopedia of Archaeological Excavations in the Holy Land*. Edited by Ephraim Stern. 4 vols. Jerusalem: Israel Exploration Society, 1993.
Haber, Susan. Review of Thomas Kazen, *Jesus and Purity Halakhah: Was Jesus Indifferent to Impurity? Bryn Mawr Classical Review,* March 28, 2006. Online: http://ccat.sas.upenn.edu/bmcr/2006/2006-03-28.html.
Habermann, A. M. *Megilot midbar Yehudah*. Tel-Aviv: Machbaroth Lesifrut, 1959.
Hachlili, Rachel. *Jewish Funerary Customs, Practices, and Rites in the Second Temple Period*. Leiden: Brill, 2005.
Hall, Robert G. "Epispasm: Circumcision in Reverse." *BR* (August 1992): 52-57.
Hanson, K. C. *Ritual and Ceremony in the Graeco-Roman World: A Select Classified Bibliography (1970-1996)*. Minneapolis: Fortress, 1998.
Har-El, Menashe. "Jerusalem and Judea: Roads and Fortifications." *BA* 44 (winter 1981): 8-19.
Harrington, Hannah K. "Did the Pharisees Eat Ordinary Food in a State of Ritual Purity?" *JSJ* 26 (1995): 42-54.

———. *The Impurity Systems of Qumran and the Rabbis: Biblical Foundations*. SBLDS 143. Atlanta: Scholars Press, 1993.

———. "The Nature of Impurity at Qumran." Pages 610-16 in *The Dead Sea Scrolls: Fifty Years after Their Discovery, 1947-1997*. Edited by L. H. Schiffman, E. Tov, and J. C. VanderKam. Jerusalem: Israel Exploration Society, 2000.

———. *The Purity Texts*. New York: Continuum, 2004.

Hayes, Christine E. *Gentile Impurities and Jewish Identities: Intermarriage and Conversion from the Bible to the Talmud*. New York: Oxford University Press, 2002.

Henten, Jan Willem van. "The Ancestral Language of the Jews." Pages 532-68 in *Hebrew Study from Ezra to Ben-Yehuda*. Edited by William Horbury. Edinburgh: T & T Clark, 1999.

———. *The Maccabean Martyrs as Saviours of the Jewish People: A Study of 2 and 4 Maccabees*. Leiden: Brill, 1997.

Henten, Jan Willem van, and Friedrich Avemarie. *Martyrdom and Noble Death: Selected Texts from Graeco-Roman, Jewish, and Christian Antiquity*. London: Routledge, 2002.

Himmelfarb, Martha. "Impurity and Sin in 4QD, 1QS, and 4Q512." *DSD* 8, no. 1 (2001): 9-37.

———. "Jonathan Klawans on Purity." Paper presented at the annual meeting of the Association for Jewish Studies, Boston, 21 December 2003.

———. "Sexual Relations and Purity in the Temple Scroll and the Book of Jubilees." *DSD* 6, no. 1 (1999): 11-36.

Hoffman, Lawrence A. *Covenant of Blood: Circumcision and Gender in Rabbinic Judaism*. Chicago: University of Chicago Press, 1996.

Hoffmann, David Zvi. *Das Buch Leviticus*. 2 vols. Berlin: M. Poppelauer, 1913-22.

———. *Sefer va-Yikra Meforash*. Translated by Z. Har Shefer and A. Liberman. 2 vols. Jerusalem: Mossad HaRav Kook, 1952-53. Translation of *Das Buch Leviticus*. 2 vols. Berlin: M. Poppelauer, 1913-22.

Holm-Nielsen, Svend. *Hodayot: Psalms from Qumran*. Acta Theologica Danica 2. Århus, Denmark: Universitetsforlaget, 1960.

Hopkins, Ian W. J. "The City Region in Roman Palestine." *PEQ* 112 (1980): 19-32.

Horbury, William. "Aaronic Priesthood in Hebrews." *JSNT* 19 (1983): 52-59.

———, ed. *Hebrew Study from Ezra to Ben-Yehuda*. Edinburgh: T & T Clark, 1999.

Horsley, Richard. *Hearing the Whole Story: The Politics of Plot in Mark's Gospel*. Louisville: Westminster John Knox, 2001.

Hull, John M. *Hellenistic Magic and the Synoptic Tradition*. SBT, 2d ser., 28. London: SCM Press, 1974.

Iersel, Bas M. F. van. *Mark: A Reader-Response Commentary*. JSNTSup 164. Sheffield: Sheffield Academic Press, 1998.

Ilan, Tal. *Jewish Women in Greco-Roman Palestine: An Inquiry into Image and Status*. Peabody, MA: Hendrickson, 1996.

Iliffe, J. H. "The *Thanatos* Inscription from Herod's Temple: Fragment of a Second Copy." *QDAP* 6, no. 1 (1936): 1-3, and 2 plates.

Israel Ministry of Foreign Affairs. "Kiryat Sefer: A Synagogue in a Jewish Village of the Second Temple Period." *Archaeological Sites in Israel* 8. http://www.israel-mfa.gov.il/MFA/History/Early+History+-+Archaeology/

Janin, Hunt. *Four Paths to Jerusalem: Jewish, Christian, Muslim, and Secular Pilgrimages, 1000 BCE to 2001 CE*. Jefferson, NC: McFarland, 2002.

Jeremias, Joachim. *Jerusalem in the Time of Jesus: An Investigation into Economic and Social Conditions during the New Testament Period*. London: SCM Press, 1969.

Joosten, J. *People and Land in the Holiness Code.* Leiden: Brill, 1996.
Kampen, J. "The Significance of the Temple in the Manuscripts of the Damascus Document." Pages 185–97 in *The Dead Sea Scrolls at Fifty.* Edited by R. A. Kugler and E. M. Schuller. Atlanta: Scholars Press, 1999.
Käsemann, Ernst. "The Problem of the Historical Jesus." Pages 15–47 in *Essays on New Testament Themes.* Translated by W. J. Montague. SBT 41. London: SCM Press, 1964.
Kazen, Thomas. *Jesus and Purity Halakhah: Was Jesus Indifferent to Impurity?* ConBNT 38. Stockholm: Almqvist & Wiksell, 2002.
Kee, Howard Clark. *Medicine, Miracle, and Magic in New Testament Times.* SNTSMS 55. Cambridge: Cambridge University Press, 1986.
———. *Miracle in the Early Christian World: A Study in Sociohistorical Method.* New Haven: Yale University Press, 1983.
Kerkeslager, Allen. "Jewish Pilgrimage and Jewish Identity." Pages 99–225 in *Pilgrimage and Holy Space in Late Antique Egypt.* Edited by David Frankfurter. Leiden: Brill, 1998.
Kittay, Eva Feder. *Metaphor: Its Cognitive Force and Linguistic Structure.* Oxford: Clarendon Press, 1987.
Kittel, Bonnie. *The Hymns of Qumran: Translation and Commentary.* SBLDS 50. Chico, CA: Scholars Press, 1981.
Klassen, William. "To the Hebrews or Against the Hebrews? Anti-Judaism and the Epistle to the Hebrews." Pages 1–16 in *Separation and Polemic.* Edited by Stephen G. Wilson. Vol. 2 of *Anti-Judaism in Early Christianity.* Edited by Peter Richardson, Steven G. Wilson, and David M. Granskou. Waterloo, ON: Wilfrid Laurier Press, 1986.
Klawans, Jonathan. *Impurity and Sin in Ancient Judaism.* New York: Oxford University Press, 2000.
———. "The Impurity of Immorality in Ancient Judaism." *JJS* 48 (1997): 1–16.
———. "Notions of Gentile Impurity in Ancient Judaism." *Association for Jewish Studies Review* 20 (1995): 285–312.
———. *Purity, Sacrifice, and the Temple: Symbolism and Supersessionism in the Study of Ancient Judaism.* New York: Oxford, 2006.
———. "Ritual Purity, Moral Purity, and Sacrifice in Jacob Milgrom's Leviticus." *RelSRev* 29, no. 1 (2003): 19–28.
Klinghardt, Matthias. "The Manual of Discipline in the Light of Statutes of Hellenistic Associations." Pages 251–70 in *Methods of Investigation of the Dead Sea Scrolls and the Khirbet Qumran Site: Present Realities and Future Prospects.* Edited by J. J. Collins et al. Annals of the New York Academy of Sciences 722. New York: New York Academy of Sciences, 1994.
Klinzing, Georg. *Die Umdeutung des Kultus in der Qumrangemeinde und im Neuen Testament.* Göttingen: Vandenhoeck und Ruprecht, 1971.
Kloppenborg, John S. "Dating Theodotus (CIJ II 1404)." *JJS* 51 (2000): 243–80.
Knibb, Michael A. *The Qumran Community.* Cambridge: Cambridge University Press, 1987.
Knohl, Israel. *The Sanctuary of Silence: The Priestly Torah and the Holiness School.* Minneapolis: Fortress, 1995.
Koester, Craig R. *Hebrews.* AB 36. New York: Doubleday, 2001.
Kraemer, Ross S. "Jewish Women and Christian Origins: Some Caveats." Pages 50–79 in *Women and Christian Origins.* Edited by Ross S. Kraemer and Mary Rose D'Angelo. Oxford: Oxford University Press, 1999.
Kraemer, Ross S., and Mary Rose D'Angelo, eds. *Women and Christian Origins.* Oxford: Oxford University Press, 1999.

Kugler, Robert A. "Priesthood at Qumran." Pages 93–116 in vol. 2 of *The Dead Sea Scrolls after Fifty Years*. Edited by P. W. Flint and J. C. VanderKam. Leiden: Brill, 1999.

———. "Rewriting Rubrics: Sacrifice and the Religion of Qumran." Pages 90–112 in *Religion in the Dead Sea Scrolls*. Edited by John J. Collins and Robert A. Kugler. SDSSRL. Grand Rapids: Eerdmans, 2000.

Lane, William W. *Hebrews 1–8*. WBC 47A. Dallas: Word Books, 1991.

Leaney, A. R. C. *The Rule of Qumran and Its Meaning*. NTL. Philadelphia: Westminister Press, 1966.

Lefkowitz, Mary R., and Maureen B. Fant, eds. *Women's Life in Greece and Rome*. Baltimore: John Hopkins University Press, 1982.

Lehne, Susanne. *The New Covenant in Hebrews*. JSNTSup 44. Sheffield: JSOT Press, 1990.

Levine, Amy-Jill. "Discharging Responsibility: Matthean Jesus, Biblical Law, and Hemorrhaging Woman." Pages 379–97 in *Treasures New and Old: Recent Contributions to Matthean Studies*. Edited by David R. Bauer and Mark Allen Powell. SBLSymS. Atlanta: Scholars Press, 1996.

———, ed. *"Women Like This": New Perspectives on Jewish Women in the Greco-Roman World*. Atlanta: Scholars Press, 1991.

Levine, Baruch A. *In the Presence of the Lord: A Study of Cult and Some Cultic Terms in Ancient Israel*. SJLA 5. Leiden: Brill, 1974.

———. *The JPS Torah Commentary: Leviticus*. Philadelphia: Jewish Publication Society, 1989.

Levine, Lee I. *The Ancient Synagogue: The First Thousand Years*. New Haven: Yale University Press, 2000.

———. "The First Century C.E. Synagogue in Historical Perspective." Pages 613–41 in *The Ancient Synagogue from Its Origins until 200 C.E.: Papers Presented at an International Conference at Lund University, October 14–17, 2001*. Edited by B. Olsson and M. Zetterholm. ConBNT 39. Stockholm: Almqvist & Wiksell, 2003.

———. "The First-Century Synagogue: Critical Reassessments and Assessment of the Critical." Pages 613–41 in *Religion and Society in Roman Palestine: Old Questions, New Approaches*. Edited by Douglas R. Edwards. London: Routledge, 2004.

———. *Jerusalem: Portrait of the City in the Second Temple Period (538 B.C.E.–70 C.E.)*. Philadelphia: Jewish Publication Society, 2002.

———. *Judaism and Hellenism in Antiquity: Conflict or Confluence?* Seattle: University of Washington Press, 1998.

———. "The Nature and Origin of the Palestinian Synagogue Reconsidered." *JBL* 115, no. 3 (1996): 425–48.

———, ed. *Ancient Synagogues Revealed*. Jerusalem: Israel Exploration Society, 1981.

Lichtenberger, Hermann. "Atonement and Sacrifice in the Qumran Community." Pages 159–71 in vol. 2 of *Approaches to Ancient Judaism*. Edited by W. S. Green. Chico, CA: Scholars Press, 1980.

Loader, William R. G. *Jesus' Attitude towards the Law: A Study of the Gospels*. WUNT 97. Tübingen: Mohr Siebeck, 1997.

Loos, Hendrik van der. *The Miracles of Jesus*. NovTSup 9. Leiden: Brill, 1965.

Magen, Yitzhak. "Ancient Israel's Stone Age: Purity in Second Temple Time." *BAR* 24, no. 5 (September/October 1998): 46–52.

———. "Jerusalem as a Center of the Stone Vessel Industry during the Second Temple Period." Pages 244–56 in *Ancient Judaism Revealed*. Edited by Hillel Geva. Jerusalem: Israel Exploration Society, 1994.

———. *The Stone Vessel Industry in the Second Temple Period: Excavations at Hizma and the Jerusalem Temple Mount*. Edited by Levana Tsfania. Jerusalem: Israel Exploration Society, 2002.

Magness, Jodi. *The Archaeology of Qumran and the Dead Sea Scrolls*. Grand Rapids: Eerdmans, 2002.

Malbon, Elizabeth Struthers. "Narrative Criticism: How Does the Story Mean?" Pages 23–49 in *Mark and Method: New Approaches in Biblical Studies*. Edited by Janice Capel Anderson and Stephen Moore. Minneapolis: Fortress, 1992.

Mansoor, M. *The Thanksgiving Hymns*. Leiden: Brill, 1961.

Marcus, Joel. *Mark 1–8: A New Translation with Introduction and Commentary*. AB 27. New York: Doubleday, 1999.

Marshall, I. Howard. *The Gospel of Luke: A Commentary on the Greek Text*. Grand Rapids: Eerdmans, 1978.

Mason, Steve. "Josephus and His Roman Audience: Reading between the Lines." Paper presented at "Flavius Josephus in Flavian Rome," Toronto, May 7, 2001.

Mazar, Eilat. *The Complete Guide to the Temple Mount Excavations*. Translated by D. Glick and N. Panitz-Cohen. Jerusalem: Old City Press, 2002.

McCready, W., and A. Reinhartz. *Common Judaism Explored: Second Temple Judaism in Context*. Minneapolis: Fortress, 2008.

Meeks, Wayne. *The First Urban Christians: The Social World of the Apostle Paul*. New Haven: Yale University Press, 1983.

Meier, John P. *A Marginal Jew: Rethinking the Historical Jesus*. 3 vols. New York: Doubleday, 1991–2001.

Meigs, Anna S. "A Papuan Perspective on Pollution." *Man* 13 (1978): 304–18.

Mendelson, Alan. *Philo's Jewish Identity*. Atlanta: Scholars Press, 1988.

Metso, S. *The Textual Development of the Qumran Community Rule*. STDJ 21. Leiden: Brill, 1997.

Meyers, C. L., and M. O'Connor, eds. *The Word of the Lord Shall Go Forth: Essays in Honor of David Noel Freedman in Celebration of His Sixtieth Birthday*. Winona Lake, IN: Eisenbrauns, 1983.

Meyers, Eric M. "Yes, They Are." *BAR* 26, no. 4 (July/August 2000): 46–48.

Milgrom, Jacob. *Cult and Conscience: The Asham and the Priestly Doctrine of Repentance*. SJLA 18. Leiden: Brill, 1976.

———. "First Day Ablutions in Qumran." Pages 561–70 in vol. 2 of *The Madrid Qumran Congress: Proceedings of the International Congress on the Dead Seas Scrolls, Madrid 18–21 March 1991*. Edited by J. T. Barrera and L. V. Montaner. 2 vols. Leiden: Brill, 1992.

———. "Israel's Sanctuary: The Priestly 'Picture of Dorian Gray.'" *Revue Biblique* 83 (1976): 390–99.

———. *JPS Torah Commentary: Numbers*. Philadelphia: Jewish Publication Society, 1990.

———. *Leviticus 1–16: A New Translation with Introduction and Commentary*. AB 3A. New York: Doubleday, 1991.

———. *Leviticus 17–22: A New Translation with Introduction and Commentary*. AB 3B. New York: Doubleday, 2000.

———. "The Qumran Cult: Its Exegetical Principles" Pages 165–80 in *Temple Scroll Studies*. Edited by George J. Brooke. Sheffield: JSOT Press, 1989.

———. "Rationale for Cultic Law: The Case of Impurity." *Semeia* 45 (1989): 103–9.

———. "Sin-Offering, or Purification-Offering?" *VT* 21 (1971): 237–39.

———. "Studies in the Temple Scroll." *JBL* 97 (1978): 501–23.

Milikowsky, Chaim. "Reflections on Hand-Washing, Hand Purity, and Holy Scripture in

Rabbinic Literature." Pages 149-62 in *Purity and Holiness: The Heritage of Leviticus*. Edited by M. Porthuis and J. Schwartz. Leiden: Brill, 2000.

Naude, J. "Holiness in the Dead Sea Scrolls." Pages 171-99 in vol. 2 of *The Dead Sea Scrolls after Fifty Years*. Edited by P. W. Flint and J. C Vanderkam. 2 vols. Leiden: Brill, 1998-99.

Netzer, Ehud. *Masada: The Yigael Yadin Excavations, 1963-1965. Final Reports*. 6 vols. Jerusalem: Israel Exploration Society, 1989.

———. "A Synagogue from the Hasmonean Period Exposed at Jericho." *Bible and Interpretation*. http://www.bibleinterp.com/articles/Synagogue.htm.

———. "A Synagogue from the Hasmonean Period Recently Exposed in the Western Plain of Jericho." *IEJ* 49 (1999): 203-21.

Neusner, Jacob. *Approaches to Ancient Judaism: New Series*. Edited by Jacob Neusner. 16 vols. Chico, CA: Scholars Press, 1990-99.

———. *From Politics to Piety: The Emergence of Pharisaic Judaism*. Englewood Cliffs, NJ: Prentice-Hall, 1973.

———. *The Idea of Purity in Ancient Judaism*. Leiden: Brill, 1973.

———. *Judaic Law from Jesus to the Mishnah: A Systematic Reply to Professor E. P. Sanders*. Atlanta: Scholars Press, 1993.

———. *The Rabbinic Traditions about the Pharisees before 70*. 3 vols. Leiden: Brill, 1971.

Newman, Carey C., et al. *The Jewish Roots of Christological Monotheism*. Leiden: Brill, 1999.

Newton, Michael. *The Concept of Purity at Qumran and in the Letters of Paul*. Cambridge: Cambridge University Press, 1985.

Nickelsburg, George W. E. *Resurrection, Immortality, and Eternal Life in Intertestamental Judaism*. Harvard Theological Studies 26. Cambridge: Harvard University Press, 1972.

Nitzan, B. "Repentance in the Dead Sea Scrolls." Pages 145-70 in vol. 2 of *The Dead Sea Scrolls after Fifty Years*. Edited by P. W. Flint and J. C. VanderKam. 2 vols. Leiden: Brill, 1998-99.

Olsson, B., O. Brandt, and D. Mitternacht, eds. *The Synagogue of Ancient Ostia and the Jews of Rome: Interdisciplinary Studies*. ActaRom-4o 57. Stockholm: Paul Åströms, 2001.

Olsson, B., and M. Zetterholm, eds. *The Ancient Synagogue from Its Origins until 200 C.E.: Papers Presented at an International Conference at Lund University, October 14-17, 2001*. ConBNT 39. Stockholm: Almqvist & Wiksell, 2003.

Peleg, Yuval, and David Amit. "Another Miqveh near Alon Shevut." *'Atiqot* 48 (2004): 95-98.

Peters, F. E. "The Holy Places." Pages 37-59 in *City of the Great King: Jerusalem from David to the Present*. Edited by Nitza Rosovsky. Cambridge: Harvard University Press, 1996.

Peterson, Sigrid. "Maccabean Martyrdoms: Versions and Varieties." Paper presented at the Annual Meeting of the Society of Biblical Literature, Toronto, November 24, 2002.

Plaskow, Judith. "Anti-Judaism in Christian Feminist Interpretation." Pages 117-29 in vol. 1 of *Searching the Scriptures: A Feminist Introduction*. Edited by Elisabeth Schüssler Fiorenza. 2 vols. New York: Crossroad, 1993.

Poirier, John C. "Purity beyond the Temple in the Second Temple Era." *JBL* 122 (2003): 247-65.

Pomeroy, Sarah B., ed. *Women's History and Ancient History*. Chapel Hill: University of North Carolina Press, 1991.

Porthuis, M. J. H. M., and J. Schwartz, eds. *Purity and Holiness: The Heritage of Leviticus*. Leiden: Brill, 2000.

Rabin, Chaim, ed. *The Zadokite Documents*. Oxford: Clarendon Press, 1958.

Rajak, Tessa. "Dying for the Law: The Martyr's Portrait in Jewish-Greek Literature." Pages 39–67 in *Portraits: Biographical Representation in the Greek and Latin Literature of the Roman Empire*. Edited by M. J. Edwards and Simon Swain. Oxford: Clarendon Press, 1997.

Reed, Jonathan L. *Archaeology and the Galilean Jesus: A Re-examination of the Evidence*. Harrisburg, PA: Trinity Press International, 2000.

Regev, Eyal. "Non-Priestly Purity and Its Religious Aspects according to Historical Sources and Archaeological Findings." Pages 223–44 in *Purity and Holiness: The Heritage of Leviticus*. Edited by M. J. H. M. Poorthuis and J. Schwartz. Leiden: Brill, 2000.

———. "Pure Individualism: The Idea of Non-Priestly Purity in Ancient Judaism." *Journal for the Study of Judaism* 31 (2000): 176–202.

Reich, Ronny. "Miqwa'ot (Jewish Ritual Immersion Baths) in Eretz-Israel in the Second Temple and the Mishna and Talmud Periods." Ph.D. diss., Hebrew University, 1990. In Hebrew.

———. "The Synagogue and the Miqweh in Eretz-Israel in the Second-Temple, Mishnaic, and Talmudic Periods." Pages 289–97 in vol. 1 of *Ancient Synagogues: Historical Analysis and Archaeological Discovery*. Edited by Dan Urman and Paul V. M. Flesher. 2 vols. Leiden: Brill, 1995.

———. "They Are Ritual Baths: Immerse Yourself in the Ongoing Sepphoris Mikveh Debate." *BAR* 28, no. 2 (March/April 2002): 50–55.

Reich, Ronny, Gideon Avni, and Tamar Winter. *The Jerusalem Archaeological Park*. Jerusalem: Israel Antiquities Authority, 1999.

Reinhartz, Adele. "Parents and Children: A Philonic Perspective." Pages 61–88 in *The Jewish Family in Antiquity*. Edited by Shaye J. D. Cohen. Atlanta: Scholars Press, 1993.

———. *"Why Ask My Name?" Anonymity and Identity in Biblical Narrative*. Oxford: Oxford University Press, 1998.

Richards, I. A. *The Philosophy of Rhetoric*. Oxford: Oxford University Press, 1936.

Richardson, Peter. "An Architectural Case for Synagogues and Associations." Pages 90–117 in *The Ancient Synagogue from Its Origins until 200 C.E.: Papers Presented at an International Conference at Lund University, October 14–17, 2001*. Edited by Birger Olsson and Magnus Zetterholm. ConBNT 39. Stockholm: Almqvist & Wiksell, 2003.

———. *Building Jewish in the Roman East*. Waco, TX: Baylor University Press, 2004.

Richardson, Peter, Steven G. Wilson, and David M. Granskou, eds. *Anti-Judaism in Early Christianity*. Waterloo, ON: Wilfrid Laurier Press, 1986.

Ricoeur, Paul. "The Metaphorical Process as Cognition, Imagination, and Feeling." Pages 141–58 in *On Metaphor*. Edited by S. Sacks. Chicago: University of Chicago Press, 1979.

———. *The Rule of Metaphor: The Creation of Meaning in Language*. Translated by Robert Czerny, Kathleen McLaughlin, and John Costello. London: Routledge, 2003.

Rosenblatt, Marie-Eloise, ed. *Where Can We Find Her?* New York: Paulist Press, 1991.

Runesson, Anders. "A Monumental Synagogue from the First Century: The Case of Ostia." *Journal for the Study of Judaism* 33 (2002): 171–220.

———. "The Oldest Synagogue Building in the Diaspora: A Response to L. Michael White." *HTR* 92 (1999): 409–33.

———. *The Origins of the Synagogue: A Socio-Historical Study*. ConBNT 37. Stockholm: Almqvist & Wiksell, 2001.

———. "Re-thinking the Parting(s) of the Ways." Paper presented at the Annual Meeting of the Society of Biblical Literature, Philadelphia, November 19, 2005.

———. "The Synagogue at Ancient Ostia: The Building and Its History." Pages 29–99 in *The

Synagogue of Ancient Ostia and the Jews of Rome: Interdisciplinary Studies. Edited by B. Olsson, O. Brandt, and D. Mitternacht. ActaRom-4o 57. Stockholm: Paul Åströms, 2001.

———. "Water and Worship: Ostia and the Ritual Bath in the Diaspora Synagogue." Pages 115–29 in *The Synagogue of Ancient Ostia and the Jews of Rome: Interdisciplinary Studies.* Edited by B. Olsson, O. Brandt, and D. Mitternacht. ActaRom-4o 57. Stockholm: Paul Åströms, 2001.

Rutgers, Leonard Victor. "Diaspora Synagogues: Synagogue Archaeology in the Greco-Roman World." Pages 67–95 in *Sacred Realm: The Emergence of the Synagogue in the Ancient World.* Edited by Steven Fine. New York: Oxford University Press, 1996.

Ryken, Leland. "Metaphor in the Psalms." *Christianity and Literature* 31, no. 3 (1982): 9–29.

Sacks. S., ed. *On Metaphor.* Chicago: University of Chicago Press, 1979.

Safrai, Shemuel. *Pilgrimage at the Time of the Second Temple Period.* Tel Aviv: Am Hassefer, 1965. In Hebrew.

———. "Pilgrimage to Jerusalem at the End of the Second Temple Period." Pages 12–21 in *Studies on the Jewish Background of the New Testament.* Edited by O. Michel et al. Assen, Netherlands: Van Gorcum, 1969.

———. "Temple." Pages 865–907 in *The Jewish People in the First Century.* Edited by S. Safrai and M. Stern. 2 vols. Assen, Netherlands: Van Gorcum, 1974–76.

Saldarini, Anthony J. *Matthew's Christian-Jewish Community.* Chicago: University of Chicago Press, 1994.

Salevao, Iutisone. *Legitimation in the Letter to the Hebrews: The Construction and Maintenance of a Symbolic Universe.* JSNTSup 219. Sheffield: Sheffield Academic Press, 2002.

Sama, Nahum. *The JPS Torah Commentary: Exodus.* Philadelphia: Jewish Publication Society, 1991.

Sanders, E. P. "Did the Pharisees Eat Ordinary Food in Purity?" Pages 248–50 in *Jewish Law from Jesus to the Law from Jesus to the Mishnah: Five Studies.* London: SCM Press, 1990.

———. *Jewish Law from Jesus to the Law from Jesus to the Mishnah: Five Studies.* London: SCM Press, 1990.

———. *Judaism: Practice and Belief, 63 BCE–66 CE.* London: SCM Press, 1992.

———. *Paul and Palestinian Judaism.* Philadelphia: Fortress, 1977.

Schäfer, Peter. *Judeophobia: Attitudes toward the Jews in the Ancient World.* Cambridge: Harvard University Press, 1997.

Schiffman, Lawrence H. *Archaeology and History in the Dead Sea Scrolls: The New York University Conference in Memory of Yigael Yadin.* Journal for the Study of Pseudepigrapha: Supplement Series 8. Journal for the Study of the Old Testament and American Schools of Oriental Research Monographs 2. Sheffield: JSOT Press, 1990.

Schiffman, L. H., E. Tov, and J. C. VanderKam, eds. *The Dead Sea Scrolls: Fifty Years after Their Discovery, 1947–1997.* Jerusalem: Israel Exploration Society, 2000.

Scholer, John M. *Proleptic Priests: Priesthood in the Epistle to the Hebrews.* JSNTSup 49. Sheffield: JSOT Press, 1991.

Schüssler Fiorenza, Elisabeth. "Cultic Language in Qumran and in the New Testament." *CBQ* 38, no. 2 (1976): 159–77.

———, ed. *Searching the Scriptures: A Feminist Introduction.* 2 vols. New York: Crossroad, 1993.

Schwartz, D. R. "On Two Aspects of a Priestly View of Descent at Qumran." Pages 157–79 in *Archaeology and History in the Dead Sea Scrolls: The New York University Conference in Memory of Yigael Yadin*. Edited by Lawrence H. Schiffman. Journal for the Study of Pseudepigrapha: Supplement Series 8. Journal for the Study of the Old Testament and American Schools of Oriental Research Monographs 2. Sheffield: JSOT Press, 1990.

———. "The Three Temples of 4Q Florilegium." *RevQ* 10 (1979–81): 83–92.

———. "To Join Oneself to the House of Judah [Damascus Document IV, 11]." *Revue Qumran* 10 (1981): 435–46.

Segal, Alan. "Matthew's Jewish Voice." Pages 3–37 in *Social History of the Matthean Community: Cross-Disciplinary Approaches*. Edited by David Balch. Minneapolis: Fortress, 1991.

Selvidge, Marla J. *Woman, Cult, and Miracle Recital: A Redactional Critical Investigation on Mark 5.24–34*. London: Associated University Press, 1990.

Stacey, David. "Was There a Synagogue in Hasmonean Jericho?" *Bible and Interpretation*. http://www.bibleinterp.com/articles/Hasmonean_Jericho.htm.

Stambaugh, John E. "The Functions of Roman Temples." *ANRW* 16.1:579. Part 2, *Principat*, 16.1. Edited by H. Temporini and W. Haase. New York: de Gruyter, 1978.

Stern, Ephraim, ed. *The New Encyclopedia of Archaeological Excavations in the Holy Land*. 4 vols. Jerusalem: Israel Exploration Society, 1993.

Strange, James F. "First-Century Galilee from Archaeology and from the Texts." Pages 81–90 in *SBL Seminar Papers, 1994*. Society of Biblical Literature Seminar Papers 33. Chico, CA: Scholars Press, 1994

Swidler, Leonard. "Jesus Was a Feminist." *The Catholic World* (January 1971): 177–83.

Swift, Fletcher Harper. *Education in Ancient Israel: From Earliest Times to 70 AD*. Chicago: Open Court, 1919.

Sykes, S. W., ed. *Sacrifice and Redemption*. Cambridge: Cambridge University Press, 1991.

Syon, Danny. "Gamla: Portrait of a Rebellion." *BAR* 18, no. 1 (1992): 21–37.

Taylor, Vincent. *The Gospel according to St Mark*. London: Macmillan, 1952.

Telford, William R. "Major Trends and Interpretive Issues in the Study of Jesus." Pages 33–74 in *Studying the Historical Jesus: Evaluations of Current Research*. Edited by B. Chilton and C. A. Evans. Leiden: Brill, 1997.

Temporini H., and W. Haase, eds. *Aufstieg und Niedergang der römischen Welt: Geschichte und Kultur Roms im Spiegel der neueren Forschung*. Part 2, *Principat*: Vols. 9–37. Berlin: de Gruyter, 1975–94.

Theissen, Gerd. *The Miracle Stories of the Early Christian Tradition*. Translated by Francis McDonagh. Philadelphia: Fortress, 1983.

Theissen, Gerd, and Annette Merz. *The Historical Jesus: A Comprehensive Guide*. Translated by J. Bowden. London: SCM Press, 1998.

Tigay, Jeffrey H. *The JPS Torah Commentary: Deuteronomy*. Philadelphia: Jewish Publication Society, 1996.

Trenchard, Warren C. *Ben Sira's View of Women: A Literary Analysis*. BJS 38. Chico, CA: Scholars Press, 1982.

Trümper, Monika. "The Oldest Original Synagogue Building in the Diaspora: The Delos Synagogue Reconsidered." *Hesperia: Journal for the American School of Classical Studies at Athens* 73 (2004): 513–98.

Tsafrir, Yoram. "Jewish Pilgrimage in the Roman and Byzantine Periods." Pages 369–76 in vol. 1 of *Akten des XII internationalen Kongresses für christliche Archäologie*. 2 vols. Munster, Germany: Aschendorff, 1995.

Van Voorst, Robert E. *Jesus outside the New Testament: An Introduction to the Ancient Evidence*. Grand Rapids: Eerdmans, 2000.

Vermès, Géza, ed. *The Dead Sea Scrolls in English*. Harmondsworth, England: Penguin, 1970.

Wall, Robert W., and William L. Lane. "Polemic in Hebrews and the Catholic Epistles." Pages 166-98 in *Anti-Semitism and Early Christianity: Issues of Polemic and Faith*. Edited by Craig A. Evans and Donald A. Hagner. Minneapolis: Fortress, 1993.

Waltke, B. R., and M. O'Connor. *An Introduction to Biblical Hebrew Syntax*. Winona Lake, IN: Eisenbrauns, 1990.

Wassen, Cecilia. "Common Demonology and Rules of Exclusion in the Dead Sea Scrolls." In *Common Judaism Explored: Second Temple Judaism in Context*. Edited by W. McCready and A. Reinhartz. Minneapolis: Fortress, 2008.

———. *Women in the Damascus Document*. Leiden: Brill, 2005.

Watts, James W., ed. *Persia and Torah: The Theory of Imperial Authorization of the Pentateuch*. Atlanta: Society of Biblical Literature, 2001.

Weinfeld, Moshe. *Deuteronomy 1-11*. AB 5. New York: Doubleday, 1991.

———. *The Organizational Pattern and the Penal Code of the Qumran Sect*. Göttingen: Vandenhoeck & Ruprecht, 1986.

Wenham, Gordon. "Purity." Pages 378-94 in vol. 2 of *The Biblical World*. Edited by John Barton. 2 vols. London: Routledge, 2002.

Wernberg-Møller, P. *The Manual of Discipline: Translated and Annotated with an Introduction*. STDJ 1. Leiden: Brill, 1957.

White, L. Michael. "The Delos Synagogue Revisited: Recent Fieldwork in the Graeco-Roman Diaspora." *HTR* 80 (1987): 133-60.

———. "Reading the Ostia Synagogue: A Reply to A. Runesson." *HTR* 92 (1999): 435-64.

———. "Synagogue and Society in Imperial Ostia: Archaeological and Epigraphic Evidence." *HTR* 90 (1997): 23-58.

Wild, Robert A. *Water in the Cultic Worship of Isis and Sarapis*. Leiden: Brill, 1981.

Wilkinson, John. "The Way from Jerusalem to Jericho." *BA* 38 (March 1975): 10-24.

Wilson, Stephen G. *Related Strangers: Jews and Christians, 70-170 C.E.* Minneapolis: Fortress, 1995.

———, ed. *Separation and Polemic*. Vol. 2 of *Anti-Judaism in Early Christianity*. Edited by Peter Richardson, Steven G. Wilson, and David M. Granskou. Waterloo, Ontario: Wilfrid Laurier Press, 1986.

Wright, Benjamin G., III. "Jewish Ritual Baths—Interpreting the Digs and the Texts: Some Issues in the Social History of Second Temple Judaism." Pages 190-214 in *The Archaeology of Israel: Constructing the Past, Interpreting the Present*. Edited by N. A. Silberman and D. Small. JSOTSup 237. Sheffield: Sheffield Academic Press, 1997.

Wright, David P. *The Disposal of Impurity: Elimination Rites in the Bible and in Hittite and Mesopotamian Literature*. Atlanta: Scholars Press, 1987.

———. "Jacob Milgrom on Purity." Paper presented at the Annual Meeting of the Association for Jewish Studies, Boston, December 21, 2003.

———. "The Spectrum of Priestly Impurity." Pages 150-81 in *Priesthood and Cult in Ancient Israel*. Edited by Gary A. Anderson and Saul M. Olyan. Sheffield: JSOT Press, 1991.

———. "Two Types of Impurity in the Priestly Writings of the Bible." *Koroth* 9 (1988): 180-93.

———. "Unclean and Clean (OT)." *ABD* 6:729-41.

Yadin, Yigael. *The Temple Scroll*. 3 vols. Jerusalem: Israel Exploration Society, 1983.

Young, Robin Darling. "The 'Woman with the Soul of Abraham': Traditions about the Mother of the Maccabean Martyrs." Pages 67-81 in *"Women Like This": New Perspectives on Jewish Women in the Greco-Roman World*. Edited by Amy-Jill Levine. Atlanta: Scholars Press, 1991.

Zimmerman, Frank. *The Book of Tobit: An English Translation with Introduction and Commentary.* New York: Harper & Brothers, 1958.

Zissu, Boaz. "Rural Settlement in the Judaean Hills and Foothills from the Late Second Temple Period to the Bar-Kokhba Revolt." Ph.D. diss., Hebrew University, 2001. In Hebrew.

Index of Ancient Sources

Hebrew Bible

Genesis
1:27	60
1:28	56
4:10–12	20
6:1–4	43
7:7–9	60
14:17–20	151, 152
17:20	151

Exodus
4:24–26	79
5:3	150
7:23	150
7:27–28	150
12:49	143
20:12	85
24:1–8	145, 147
29:29	150
40:9–11	147
40:12–15	150

Leviticus
1	25
1–16	9
1:3	115, 116
3:1–9	116
4–5	154
4:1–5	25
4:5–7	18
4:16–18	18
4:20	149
4:25	18
4:26	19, 149
4:27–35	21
4:30	18
4:31	149
5:1–4	25
5:1–13	130
5:2–3	25
5:10	149
5:20–26	101
6:2	143
6:7	143
6:18	143
7:1–11	143
7:19–21	25
7:20–21	23, 184, 194
8:10–11	147
8:15	97
9:1	42
9:9	18
9:12	42
10:1–20	36
10:10	117
11–15	24
11:1–47	27, 95, 163, 193
11:4–8	24
11:10–12	25
11:13–20	25
11:23	25
11:24–40	10
11:39	55
11:40	56
11:41–45	25
11:43	11
12	10, 22, 67
12–15	17
12:1–5	65
12:1–8	27, 95, 163, 193
12:2	104
12:3	78
13–14	22
13:1–14:32	27, 95, 163, 193
13:3	104
13:8	104
13:15	104
14	10
14:4–6	147
14:5–7	143
14:9	97

Leviticus (cont'd)
14:19 19
14:34 57
14:49–52 97, 147
15 10, 22, 125, 127–29, 133, 136
15:1–33 27, 95, 163, 193
15:4 104
15:5–11 97
15:8 104
15:11 128
15:18 97
15:19–24 65
15:25 104
15:25–30 127
15:28 135
15:31 22, 169, 184, 194
16:1 36
16:5 154
16:6 154
16:11 154
16:11–22 163
16:14–16 155
16:15 154
16:16 149, 154
16:16–19 18
16:19–21 19
16:21 25
16:26 10
16:27–28 10
16:28 27, 95, 163
16:33–34 149
17–27 9
18 23, 42, 60–61
18:1–28 12
18:6–23 25
18:13 60
18:19 60
18:20 104
18:23 104
18:24 28, 95, 163
18:24–25 11
18:24–30 12, 19, 28, 95, 163
18:25 20, 28
18:26 43
18:27 45
18:28 20
19:5 115
19:11 101
19:15 59
19:31 11, 28, 95, 104, 163

19:35 59
20:1–3 28, 43, 95, 163
20:1–5 23
20:2–5 25
20:3 28, 95, 163
20:18 25
20:21 42
20:27 23
21:17–20 53
22:3–7 25, 184, 194
22:3–9 23
22:5 10
22:8 25
22:17–25 116
22:19–29 115
22:20 115
23:11 115
26:14–38 20
26:14–45 115
26:21 57
26:40 25
26:43 114

Numbers
5:1–4 128–29
5:2 65
5:6–7 25
6:6–7 25
6:22–27 117
7:1 146–47
7:10 146
9:10–12 194
10:14–20 154
12:10 57
12:10–15 23
15:22–29 25
15:27–31 18
15:29 143
15:37–41 133
18:2–4 121
18:21–24 151, 152
18:28 152
19 10, 24
19:1–10 154
19:2 143
19:6 147
19:7–10 10
19:8 27, 95, 163
19:10–22 27, 95, 163, 193
19:11–21 22, 137

Index of Ancient Sources

19:13	130	26:23	57
19:13, 20	25	36:14	32
19:14	143		
19:14–20	194, 200, 201	**Ezra**	
19:19	97	6:21	41
19:21	103	9	42
20:22–29	151	9:1	42
27:21	117	9:1–3	41
34:35–37	20	9:10–12	42
35:15	43	9:11	12, 57
35:25	150	9:11–14	41
35:33	12	10:2	43
35:33–34	20, 26, 28, 95, 163		
35:34	113	**Nehemiah**	
		8:1–12	17
Deuteronomy		13:1	42
1:31 (LXX)	85	13:26	42
7:1–4	42	13:30	41
13:7–12	23		
14:26	192	**Job**	
16:16	184–88	4:17	96
17:2–7	23		
17:17	60	**Psalms**	
19:13	23	51	97
21:1–9	20	51:4–9	98–99
21:8	23, 112	51:13	99
21:23	12	63:2	94
23:2–9	42	110[109]:4	151
23:10–15	65		
24:4	12	**Proverbs**	
25:15–16	59, 62	8:35	86
28:27	57	16:5	61–62
		20:9	96
1 Samuel		31:1–9	87
1:17	135		
2:35	121–22	**Isaiah**	
24:5–12	133	1:15–17	96
		22:14	112
2 Samuel		24:5	60
7:16	120–21	24:17	59, 60
		64:4–5	96
2 Kings			
5:27	23, 57	**Jeremiah**	
		2:4–28	12
3 Kingdoms		16:18	12
8:63	146	31:31–34	145
		33:8	96
2 Chronicles			
7:5	146	**Lamentations**	
26:19–21	23	1:8	57

Lamentations (*cont'd*)
1:17	57, 96
2:22	85

Hosea
6:6	116

Ezekiel
5:11	28, 95, 163
7:19–20	57
16:49–50	61
36:17	28, 95, 96, 163
36:17–18	12
43:20–23	97
44:10–14	120
44:15	120, 122
44:23–24	117
45:18	97

Zechariah
13:1	57

NEW TESTAMENT

Matthew
14:33	137
19:1	202
20:17–18	202
20:29	202, 203
21:1–11	183, 202
21:7–9	203
21:17	203
23:23	182
26:17–20	203

Mark
1:40	137
1:44	136
2:1–12	139
2:3–12	133
3:1–6	133, 133
3:10	133
5:6	137
5:24–34	125–41
5:28	135
5:29	134–35
5:34–36	138
5:41	138
6:56	133
7:1–23	136
7:15	183
7:26	137
7:31–37	133
8:22–26	133
9:20	133
9:21	133
9:33	202
10:1	202
10:32–33	202
10:46	202, 203
10:46–52	133
11:1–11	183, 202
11:7–10	203
11:11	192, 203
14:12–16	203

Luke
2:41–42	186
2:44	191
5:8	137
8:44	133
9:51	202
9:53	189
11:42	182
13:11	133
17:11	202
17:16	137
18:31	202
18:35	202
18:35–36	203
19:28–40	183, 202
19:35–38	203
21:37	192, 203
22:7–14	203
23:56	182

John
2:12–13	202
2:13	183, 202
4:5	189
5:1	184, 202
5:5	133
6:1–4	184
7:10	184, 202
9:1	133
10:22	184
11:54	203
11:55	183, 202

11:55–56	204	6:4–6	156
12:1	204	7:3	151
12:12	204	7:4–10	152
12:13–19	203	7:5	152
		7:5–28	144

Acts

2:9–11	186	7:11–12	152
3:1–10	183	7:16	152
3:2	133	7:18	152
4:22	133	7:19	144
6:9	192	7:20–21	152
9:33	133	7:22	143
14:8	133	7:24	151, 152
16:13	171	7:25	149, 153
21:26–27	202	7:26	143
22:3	87	7:27	149, 154
		8:2	149, 153
		8:3	150

Galatians

3:15–17	148	8:4	144, 152
4:21–31	148	8:7	145
		8:8–13	148
		8:9	145

Ephesians

2:22	148	8:10	144
		8:13	145, 148
		9:1	145

Hebrews

1:1–2	144	9:6–7	153
1:3	149–52	9:9	154
2:2	144	9:9–12	153
2:3	144	9:11–12	149
2:11	157	9:12	143, 154
2:17	149, 152	9:13	150, 154
2:17–3:1	149	9:13–14	152
2:18	149, 150	9:15	145, 148, 157
3:1	157	9:18–22	145–46
3:1–2	149	9:19	144, 154
3:12–15	149	9:21–25	153
3:19	149	9:22	144
4:3	149, 157	9:23	152
4:9	157	9:24	149, 153
4:14–16	149, 153	9:26	149
4:14–5:10	149	9:27–28	149
4:15	150, 151	10:1	144
5:1	150	10:1–3	153
5:1–4	150	10:2–4	154
5:2	150	10:4	154
5:4	150	10:8	144
5:6	151	10:10	149
5:7–8	150	10:11	154
5:13	150	10:16	144
		10:20	146

Hebrews (cont'd)
10:22	147
10:25	156, 157
10:26–31	152
10:28	144
10:28–29	148
10:32–34	156
12:1–13	157
12:24	147
12:29	152
13:1	157
13:3	156, 157
13:24	157

Romans
9:4	148
11:27	148

1 Corinthians
3:16	148

2 Corinthians
3	148
6:16	148

Apocrypha

Tobit
1:6	187
1:8	87
2:5 (codex S)	200
2:9	40
3:15	33
4:3–4	85
4:5–12	87
35:5	85
35:9–13	85

Judith
12:6–10	40

Ben Sira
3:2	85

1 Maccabees
1:15	79
1:60–61	79, 80

2 Maccabees
2:19–15:39	75
2:23	75
4:14	89
4:15	90
4:18–20	89
4:32–34	89
5:16	32
6:4	32
6:6	77
6:7–7:42	75–91
6:8–9	77
6:10–11	75–78, 80
6:18–27	90
6:18–31	76
6:20	82
6:25	78
7	76
7:8	83
7:9–19	88
7:20–21	82
7:21–29	83
7:25–27	83–84
12:37	83
15:29	83

1 Esdras
1:49	32

4 Maccabees
4:11–16:25	89
4:24–25	79–80
6:13	150
15:30	82
16:14	82
17:4	82

Old Testament Pseudepigrapha

Psalms of Solomon
2:3	33
8:26	33

1 Enoch
7:1–6	43
9–10	43
9:8	43
10:7	44
10:11	43
12:4	43
14:4–5	43
15:3	43

Jubilees
1:9	58
3:8–14	49, 58
4:22	58
7:20–21	49
7:21–22	58
7:33	49, 58
12:2	58
15:1–4	79
15:11–14	79
15:26	79
15:33	79
16:18	66
20:3	49
20:3–6	58
20:3–7	58
20:6–7	49
20:7	58
21:15	58
21:19	58
21:21	58
22:16	49
22:16–22	58
22:17–18	58
22:19–20	49
22:22	58
23:18–21	58
26:9	88
30:3	58
30:7	58
30:8–9	58
30:13–14	49, 58
30:15–16	66
32:13	58
33:1–20	66
33:7	58
33:18–20	58
33:19	66
33:20	66
35:1	88
35:25	88

Letter of Aristeas
304–6	40, 131, 164

Psalms of Solomon
1:7–8	45
4:5	45
8:9	45

Sibylline Oracles
3:591–93	41, 131, 164, 174
4:162–66	40

Testament of Asher
4:3–5	44
7:1–2	44

Testament of Benjamin
6:7	44
8:2–3	44

Testament of Issachar
4:4	44

Testament of Joseph
4:6	33, 44

Testament of Judah
14:3–5	44

Testament of Levi
7:4	33
9:9	44
9:10	33
14:5–15:1	44
14:6–7	33
16:1–5	33

Testament of Reuben
1:6	44
4:8	44
6:1	44

Testament of Simeon
2:13	44
5:3–5	44

Wisdom
8:3	86

JOSEPHUS

Against Apion (C. Ap.)
1.279–86	34
2.103–4	34

Antiquities of the Jews (A.J.)
1.109	186
2.55	35

Antiquities of the Jews (A.J.) (cont'd)
3.275	35
3.261	129
4.80	34
4.81	138, 154
5.42	35
7.168	35
8.245	35
9.262	35
9.263	35
9.273	35
10.81	35
12.106	174
12.241	79
12.286	35
14.258	171
15.417	193
17.26	190
17.213–17	191
18.18–22	34
18.19	35
18.38	34
18.271	35
18.313	190
20.113–117	190
20.118	189
20.227	151

The Jewish War (B.J.)
1.148–53	35, 36
2.44	192
2.120–61	34
2.123	34
2.125	190
2.129–31	34
2.132	35
2.138	34
2.139	34
2.149	35
2.228–30	190
2.232	189
2.233	190
2.280	185
2.289	35
2.513–2.555	189
2.515	190
3.39	187
4.205	35
5.50–51	189
5.194	34, 169, 193
5.227	34, 129, 169, 204
6.124–28	36
6.290	200
6.423	193
6.425	185
6.426–27	34, 169
7.44–45	175

Life of Josephus (Vita)
126–27	190
269	187

Philo

De cherubim (Cher.)
94–95	37, 169

De migratione Abrahami (De migr. Abr.)
24.13	86

De vita Mosis
2.138	37

Quod deterius potiori insidiari soleat (Det.)
20	37, 46, 169

Against Flaccus (Flacc.)
12–123	171
48	175

Quis rerum divinarum heres sit (Her.)
276	46

Legum allegoriae (Leg.)
3.11	82
3.49–50	82

Legatio ad Gaium (Legat.)
137	175
320	82

De mutatione nominum (Mut.)
240	46

De praemiis et poenis (Praem.)
68	45

Quod omnis probus liber sit (Prob.)
81–82	176

De Providentia (Prov.)
2.64   186, 187

De somniis (Somn.)
1.202   38
1.209-12   154

De specialibus legibus (Spec.)
1.69   186
1.117-19   46
1.118   46
1.256-61   45
1.259-60   37
1.261   174, 200
1.269   46
2.29   87
2.115   150
2.228   87
2.234-35   88
3.32   37
3.63   174
3.171   175
3.199-200   86
3.205   37, 174, 200
3.205-6   40, 131, 138, 164
3.205-8   46
3.209   46
4.68   87
4.202   150

De virtutibus (Virt.)
130   86

DEAD SEA SCROLLS

1QH
IV, 37   112
XIV [VI], 8-9   48
XVI, 10-11   48
XIX[XI], 10-11   63
XLV, 11-12   66

1QH^a
IV, 19   101
VIII, 19-20   99
IX, 22   102
IX, 32   99
XI, 21-22   100
XII, 37   99
XIII, 15-16   101

XIV, 20-21   102
XIV, 8   100
XV, 29-30   100
XIX, 10-11   100
XIX, 30-31   99
XX, 24-25   102
XXI bottom, 16   101

1QM
XIV, 2-3   138
XLV, 11-12   169

1QpHab
VIII, 8-13   61, 62
VIII, 10   61
X, 9-10   61
XI, 4-6   61
XII, 3-4   107
XII, 6-9   61, 62

1QS
II, 1-2   117
II, 8   111
II, 19-23   109
II, 25   109
III, 3-6   48
III, 4-9   68, 104, 105
III, 4, 5, 7, 9 68
III, 5   68
III, 5-6   63
III, 6-7   112
III, 6, 8   111
III, 6-9   64
III, 6-11   56
III, 8-9   48
III, 9   68
III, 9-12   112
III, 19, 21   63
IV, 9   63
IV, 10-11   63
IV, 20-22   103
IV, 21-22   63
V, 1   111
V, 4   67
V, 5-7   107, 110
V, 6   111, 114
V, 7-8   113
V, 8-9   117
V, 13   103
V, 13-14   56, 68, 63, 96, 105

1QS (cont'd)

V, 18–20	63
V, 19–20	96, 105
V, 20	109
V, 22	111
VI, 2–5	168
VI, 16	48
VI, 16–21	117
VI, 20–21	54
VI, 24–VII, 21	48
VI, 24–VII, 25	54
VI, 25	56, 103
VII, 2–3	63
VII, 15–16	63
VII, 16	56
VII, 19	56
VII, 23	56
VIII, 1	117
VIII, 1–IX, 11	112, 114, 117
VIII, 4–11	107–8
VIII, 5	109
VIII, 6	110, 111, 115
VIII, 6–7	113
VIII, 8–9	109
VIII, 9	117
VIII, 9–17	113
VIII, 10	110, 111, 113
VIII, 15	114
VIII, 16–18	52, 63
VIII, 16–24	68
VIII, 17	103
VIII, 21	109
VIII, 21–24	52
VIII, 24	52, 63
VIII, 26	52
IX, 2	109
IX, 3–6	107, 115
IX, 4	111, 114
IX, 4–5	116
IX, 6	109
IX, 7–11	113
XI, 14	111
XI, 14–15	103

4Q266

6 i 1–13	67
6 i 14–16	67
6 ii 10–11	67

4Q272

1 ii 3–7	67
1 ii 7	67
1 i 1–20	67

4Q276

1	155

4Q277

1	155

4Q394

3–7, i, 16–20	155

4Q428

10, 4	101

4Q429

IV, I, 9	102

4Q512

III, 17	69
IV	57
V, 15–17	69
V, 17	69
VII, 8–9	64
VII, 9	69
VIII	57
IX–X	57
XII, 3	57
XII, 14	57
XII, 16	69

4QFlor

I, 1–7	107

4QMMT[b]

13–17	62
49–54	62

4QOrd[c]

4–7	56

4QpIsa[d]

107

11Q19

XLVI, 16–18	130
XLVIII, 14–17	130

XLIX, 16–17	138
L, 10–14	138

11QT

XXXIX, 7–9	58
XL, 11–12	53
XLV, 7–LI, 10	58
XLV, 7–10	66
XLV, 12–14	58
XLVI, 16–18	65
XLVIII, 14–17	65
XLIX, 17–19	58
XLIX, 17–20	200
L, 10–11	53
LI, 1–2	56
LI, 11–15	59

CD

I, 1–IV, 12a	118
I–VIII	118
III, 18–IV, 12	107, 119
III, 19	120, 121
III, 21–IV, 1	120
IV, 6	122
IV, 12–21	60
IV, 12–V, 11	59, 60
IV, 12b–VII, 9	118
V, 6–7	49
V, 6–9	60
V, 9–11	60
VI, 14	63
VII, 5–VIII, 19	118
IX–XVI	118
IX, 16–23	54, 63
IX, 33–XX, 34	118
X, 2–3	52
X, 12	48
XI, 19–21	48, 169
XI, 22	48
XII, 1–2	48, 169
XII, 19–20	48
XIV, 7	122–23
XIX–XX	118

Rabbinic Literature

b. ʿAbod. Zar.

27a	79

b. Ket.

60a	86

b. Kidd.

29a–b	81

b. Sanhedrin

32b	190

b. Taan

21b	129

b. Yebam.

64b	80

m. Git.

7:6	86

m. Hullin

4:3	53

m. Kel.

1:8	129

m. Middot

1:3	192

m. Mikwaʾot

1:7	196
2:3	197
2:4	195
6:1	197

m. Ohal.

5:5	40, 194, 195

m. Parah

5:5	194

m. Pesahim

5:5–7	186

m. Sheqalim

1:1	190, 199

m. Yadayim

1:2	194

t. Ma'aser Sheni
1:12   192

t. Mikwa'ot
5:5   197

t. Nid.
2:2–4   86

t. Par.
3:14   138
5:6   138
7:4   138
10:2   138

t. Parah
3:14   200

t. Pesahim
4:15   185

t. Sheqalim
1:1   190
1:2   191, 197

Other Texts

Acts of Thecla
40   82

Euripedes
Iph. taur.
380–384   36

Plutarch
Dem.
29.5   36

Index of Modern Authors

Aaron, David H., 93
Alon, Gedalyahu, 38
Amit, David, 195
André, G., 48, 95
Archer, Léonie J., 81
Aschim, Anders, 151
Attridge, Harold, 148
Avemarie, Friedrich, 84

Bar-Ilan, Meir, 80, 81
Barta, Karen A., 125, 129
Baumgarten, Joseph M., 67, 69, 106, 107, 116
Ben-Dov, Meir, 197
Bilde, Per, 36
Binder, Donald D., 163–68, 173, 175
Black, Max, 93
Blumell, Lincoln H., 190
Booth, Roger P., 183
Bow Beverly, 87
Broshi, Magen, 122
Brownlee, William H., 61, 62, 111, 116
Büchler, Adolph, 10, 11, 28, 22, 24, 26, 28, 45
Burkert, Walter, 174

Campbell, Jonathan G., 121
Casson, Lionel, 188
Charlesworth, James H., 106, 122
Chazon, Esther, 176
Chester, A. N., 143, 156
Choy, Agnes, 191
Christiansen, E. J., 106, 109, 114
Cohen, Shaye, 87, 130, 131
Coppens, Joseph C., 119
Corrington, Gail Paterson, 86, 87
Coser, Lewis, 157, 158
Cotter, Wendy, 138
Cover, Robin C., 100
Crenshaw, James L., 87, 88
Crossan, John Dominic, 181, 185

D'Angelo, Mary Rose, 77, 126, 131, 132, 136, 138, 140, 145–48
Davies, Philip R., 118, 120, 122, 123
Dawes, Gregory W., 181
Denton, Donald L., 181
Doran, Robert, 90
Douglas, Mary, 10–16, 21–23, 27
Drazin, Nathan, 88
Dunn, James D. G., 182, 183

Eilberg-Schwartz, Howard, 13
Elbogen, Ismar, 171
Eshel, Esther, 200, 201
Eshel, Hanan, 196,

Fant, Maureen B., 86
Fardon, Richard, 13, 15
Fine, Steven, 161, 169, 172, 177
Fischer, Moshe, 188–90
Foerster, Gideon, 167, 168
Fonrobert, Charlotte, 125–28, 132, 134
Fontaine, Carole, 87
Fredriksen, Paula, 130, 181, 183, 203
Freyne, Sean, 184
Friedman, Shamma, 169, 197
Frymer-Kensky, Tikvah Simone. 9, 10, 21–29

Gager, John G., 157
Garnet, P., 111, 112
Gärtner, Bertil, 48–49, 55, 107–10, 116, 119, 120–21, 157
Gaston, Lloyd, 119
Goldstein, Jonathan A., 75–76, 78–80, 85
Goodman, Martin 169, 177, 187
Gutman, Shmaryahu, 167

Habermann, A. M., 111
Hachlili, Rachel, 201
Hall, Robert G., 79
Har-El, Menashe, 188–90

Harrington, Hannah K., 12, 38, 47, 55–57, 70–71
Hayes, Christine, 43, 164, 165
Himmelfarb, Martha, 27, 47, 64–70, 104–5
Hoffmann, David Zvi, 9–11, 18, 22, 24, 28
Hoffman, Lawrence, A., 79
Hoffmann, Paul, 182
Holm-Nielsen, Svend, 99
Hopkins, Ian W. J., 91
Horbury, William, 83, 152, 165
Horsley, Richard, 127, 131, 181
Hull, John M., 138,

Ilan, Tal, 85, 86
Iliffe, J. H., 93

Janin, Hunt, 185
Jeremias, Joachim, 185, 186, 203

Kampen, John, 53, 116, 200
Käsemann, Ernst, 181
Kazen, Thomas, 183, 204
Kee, Howard Clark, 138, 139
Kerkeslager, Allen, 187
Kittay, Eva Feder, 93
Kittel, Bonnie, 98–99
Klawans, Jonathan, 9–17, 20–22, 26–31, 40–47, 56–64, 67–70, 94–100, 105, 109, 155, 162–63, 183
Klinghardt, Matthias, 168
Klinzing, Georg, 51, 55, 116, 122
Kloppenborg, John S., 166, 168, 169, 182, 198
Knibb, Michael A., 107, 108
Knohl, Israel, 9, 20, 21, 113, 115,
Koester, Craig, 145, 150, 151, 153
Kraemer, Ross S., 77
Kugler, Robert A., 109, 116, 117, 121

Lane, William L., 144,
Lane, William W., 151
Leaney, A. R. C., 112
Lefkowitz, Mary. R., 86
Lehne, Susanne, 143–44, 148
Levine, Amy-Jill, 75, 87, 126, 132
Levine, Baruch A., 95, 143
Levine, Lee L., 84, 161, 166–68, 172–73, 175, 177, 185–87, 191, 193, 204
Lichtenberger, Hermann, 109, 116

Loader, William R. G., 182

Magen, Yitzhak, 194, 195
Magness, Jodi, 107, 168
Malbon, Elizabeth Struthers, 137
Mansoor, Menahem, 112
Marcus, Joel, 125, 132, 134, 171, 181
Marshall, I. Howard, 186
Mason, Steve, 35, 189
Mazar, Eilat, 197, 198
Meeks, Wayne, 157
Meier, John P., 181
Meigs, Anna S., 14
Merz, Annette, 184
Metso, Sarianna, 111
Meyers, Eric M., 196
Milgrom, Jacob, 9–29, 55–59, 95, 100, 111, 113, 115, 117, 128–29, 135, 137, 139, 146–47, 164, 165, 194, 200
Milikowsky, Chaim, 169

Nanos, Mark, 183
Naude, Jacobus J., 109
Netzer, Ehud, 166, 167
Newsom, Carol, 176
Nickelsburg, George W. E., 83, 86, 89
Nitzan, Bilhah, 112
Noy, David, 175

O'Connor M., 9, 116, 112

Peleg, Yuval, 199
Peters, F. E., 185
Peterson, Sigrid, 90
Plaskow, Judith, 126
Poirier, John C., 40, 164

Rabin, Chaim, 48, 121, 122, 123
Rajak, Tessa, 76, 82
Reed, Jonathan L., 185
Regev, Eyal, 40, 194, 195, 201
Reich, Ronny, 164, 169, 195–98, 201
Reinhartz, Adele, 4, 76, 87, 102, 125, 126, 132, 184
Richards, I. A., 93
Richardson, Peter, 165–66, 170, 173
Ricoeur, Paul, 93–94
Ringgren, H., 95
Robinson, James M., 182, 195

Runesson, Anders, 1, 5, 161–62, 166–68, 170–73, 177, 183
Rutgers, Leonard Victor, 172, 174
Ryken, Leland, 93, 96, 97

Safrai, Shemuel, 186–89, 191, 193, 203
Saldarini, Anthony, 182
Salevao, Iutisone, 156, 157
Sanders, E. P., 4, 38–39, 108, 114, 125, 130–31, 161, 163–64, 178–81, 186–87, 192, 196
Sarna, Nahum, 169
Schäfer, Peter, 76, 79, 144
Scholer, John M., 149
Schuller, Eileen, 1, 5, 91, 116
Schüssler Fiorenza, Elisabeth, 116, 126, 148
Schwartz, Daniel R., 107, 109, 119, 121, 122,
Schwartz, Joshua, 40, 169, 194
Segal, Alan, 182
Selvidge, Marla J., 125–27, 129, 131, 136, 140
Stacey, David, 166
Stambaugh, John E., 174
Strange, James F., 188
Swidler, Leonard, 125, 129

Swift, Fletcher Harper, 87

Taylor, Vincent, 134
Telford, William R., 182
Thiessen, Gerd, 181, 184
Tigay, Jeffrey H., 185
Trenchard, Warren C., 85
Trümper, Monika, 164, 170, 173
Tsafrir, Yoram, 192, 203

Van der Loos, Hendrik, 132, 134
Van Henten, Jan Willem, 75, 77, 82–87, 89, 90
Van Iersel, Bas M. F., 134

Wall, Robert W., 144
Waltke, Bruce R., 116
Wernberg-Moller, P., 116
White, L. Michael, 97, 173
Wild, Robert A., 176
Wilson, Stephen G., 144, 158
Wright, Benjamin G., III, 196
Wright, David P., 10, 20, 21, 24–27

Yadin, Yigal, 59, 109, 167
Young, Robin Darling, 75–76, 82–84

Subject Index

ablutions, 4–5, 17, 37, 45, 48, 56, 58–59, 104, 131, 162–65, 169–76, 178, 193, 199–201, 205–6
abominations, 13, 19, 28, 42, 50, 58–59, 61–63, 68, 95, 100, 103, 163
allegory, 36–37, 45, 187
altar, 17–18, 25, 35, 39, 95, 97, 116, 147, 163, 165
animals, 10, 14, 24–25, 27, 37, 45, 98, 110, 116, 145–46, 150, 154–55, 163, 188, 190, 192
archaeology, 40, 130, 161, 164–73, 184–85, 188, 194, 196, 198, 205–6
atonement, 3, 11, 17, 45, 48, 51, 54–55, 64, 67, 96–119, 123, 130, 143–44, 146–50, 152–56, 163

baptism, 68–69
blood, Christ's, 143, 145, 149–50, 153–54, 156
blood, emission of, 4, 22, 60, 125–40
blood, sacrificial, 18–19, 110, 119–20, 145–49, 153, 155
bloodshed and murder, 3, 12, 20–21, 23–24, 26–28, 35–36, 45, 50, 58, 61–62, 81, 95, 100, 102, 113, 163, 172–73, 190

childbirth, 10, 17, 22, 27, 34, 50, 65, 95, 163, 193
Christianity, 2, 44, 82, 125–26, 140–41, 148, 157–58, 181
Christology, 126, 139–40, 144–45, 147–49, 156
circumcision, 3, 75–82, 89, 91, 110, 144
corpse impurity, 5, 10, 15, 22, 25, 27, 34–37, 49, 56–57, 65, 96–98, 103, 129, 137–38, 147, 154–55, 163, 174, 193–94, 199, 100–101, 204–6
covenant, 1–4, 79–82, 102, 108–24, 143–49, 156, 158

cult, sacrificial, 15–18, 20–21, 24–25, 27, 31–34, 37–38, 49–56, 96, 107, 109–18, 122–23, 130, 143–58, 182

Day of Atonement (Yom Kippur), 18–19, 25, 146, 153–55, 163–64
diaspora, 4, 31, 130–31, 161–64, 168, 170–76, 178–89, 186–87, 192, 200
dietary laws, 1, 13, 25, 76, 144

eschatology, 55, 68, 112–14, 117, 123, 181
Essenes, 34–35, 176, 178–79
expiation, 22, 51–52, 110–17, 123, 128, 146, 149–50, 153, 156

food, 1, 11, 34, 38–39, 44, 50, 54, 63, 68–69, 103, 105, 184, 194, 201

Galilee, 182–85, 188–91, 194, 196–98, 201–6
genital discharges, 10, 17, 22, 27, 65, 67, 95, 127, 129, 155, 163, 193, 204
Gentiles, 32, 41–45, 50, 58, 102–3, 164–65, 172, 176–77, 179, 192, 203–4
Greco-Roman world, 35–36, 76, 78, 82, 86, 144, 162, 174, 176, 179

Hellenism, 36, 75, 79, 84, 90, 129, 138, 154, 168, 181
high priest, 18–19, 25, 35, 61–62, 143–44, 149–56, 165

idolatry, 3, 11–12, 15–16, 21, 24, 27–28, 32–33, 35, 43, 45, 50, 58, 62, 95, 100, 163, 171, 175, 179

Jesus, 4–5, 125–26, 129, 132–41, 149, 151, 155, 181–91, 202–6

land defilement, 24, 42

leprosy, 10, 17, 22–23, 34, 27, 129, 204
liturgy/prayer, 33, 40, 48, 69, 117–18, 124, 160, 162, 168, 170–71, 174, 176–79, 188

Manetho, 34–35
Masada, 165–68, 196
Melchizedek, 151–52
menstruation, 1, 22, 37, 42, 49–50, 56–57, 60, 64–65, 67, 69, 96, 125–28, 130–31, 204
metaphor, 2–4, 12, 15–16, 20, 28, 31–33, 37–38, 49, 53, 69, 86, 93–122, 137, 153

Pharisees, 38–39, 58, 62, 130–31, 182

rabbinic tradition, 10–11, 15, 38, 40, 59, 62, 67, 79–81, 129, 138, 151, 155, 169, 173, 185, 188, 191–92, 194, 196, 197, 199–200
resurrection, 83–84, 89
ritual bath (*mikveh*), 5, 40, 98, 130–31, 161, 166–76, 184–85, 194–99, 201, 205
ritual immersion, 53, 56, 58–59, 67, 128, 130–31, 162–64, 169, 174, 178, 193–201, 205–6

Rome, 1, 35–36, 174, 186, 188, 190–92, 203

Sabbath, 75–76, 90, 139, 144, 161, 164, 170–71, 176, 178–79, 182
sacrifice, 17–25, 31–37, 44–45, 48–49, 51–52, 55, 66, 89, 95, 105, 107, 109–10, 112, 114–18, 122–23, 128, 143–56, 165, 176, 185–86, 192–93, 194, 200, 202, 204
Sadducees, 53, 59, 62, 131
sanctuary, 17–19, 25, 28–29, 32, 34–36, 43–46, 50, 52–53, 58–62, 65–66, 68, 95, 97, 119–20, 122, 143, 149, 153, 163, 172, 174
sexual misconduct, 23, 25, 33, 45, 66
stone vessels, 40, 107, 184–85, 194–95, 205

Theodotus inscription, 166, 168, 192, 198
Torah scrolls, 169–79

women, 10–11, 22, 32–34, 37, 41–44, 49–50, 53, 60, 65, 66–67, 75–91, 96–97, 125–42, 164–65, 171, 182, 204

www.ingramcontent.com/pod-product-compliance
Lightning Source LLC
Chambersburg PA
CBHW030341240426
43661CB00052B/1702